One hot guy + One funny-looking guy

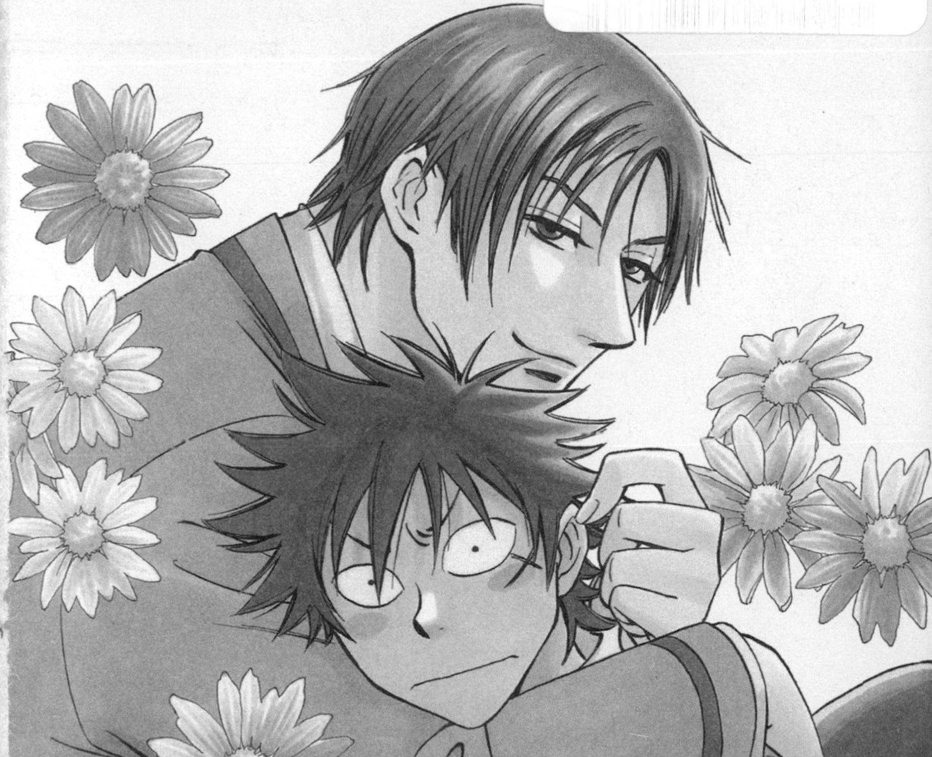

His Favorite

Story & Art by Suzuki **TANAKA**

Awkward Yoshida is hated by all the girls in school for his perceived closeness with hot guy Sato, who uses hanging out with Yoshida as an excuse to turn them all down. If Yoshida is merely an excuse, why does Sato taunt him in private about "his favorite"? Is it possible Sato's feelings run deeper than friendship? And what could he possibly see in the funny-looking Yoshida? Watch Yoshida's life turn upside down with hilarious results!

SUBLIME

Your Toys Love Boys' Love

Own your SuBLime book as a convenient PDF document that is downloadable to the following devices:

- ♥ Computer
- ♥ Kindle™
- ♥ NOOK™
- ♥ iPad™, iPhone™, and iPod Touch™
- ♥ Any device capable of reading a PDF document

SUBLIME
www.SuBLimeManga.com

Downloading is as easy as:

1

Login/Email
Password

LOGIN
REGISTER NOW
Forgot Password

2

PAY with PayPal

— OR —

Pay Now with amazon
The Simple, Trusted Way to Pay

Digital Edition includes **BOTH**
Download-to-own PDF and
online viewing option.

3

View your purchase as:

DOWNLOAD-TO-OWN PDF

Awkward Silence
Volume 4
SuBLime Manga Edition

Story and Art by **Hinako Takanaga**

Translation—**Tetsuichiro Miyaki**
Touch-up Art and Lettering—**NRP Studios**
Cover and Graphic Design—**Fawn Lau**
Editor—**Nancy Thistlethwaite**

Bukiyou na Silent ④ © 2013 Hinako Takanaga
Originally published in Japan in 2013 by Libre Publishing Co.,
Ltd. Tokyo.
English translation rights arranged with Libre Publishing Co.,
Ltd. Tokyo.

Printed in the U.S.A.

Published by SuBLime Manga
P.O. Box 77010
San Francisco, CA 94107

10 9 8 7 6 5 4 3 2 1
First printing, December 2013

www.SuBLimeManga.com

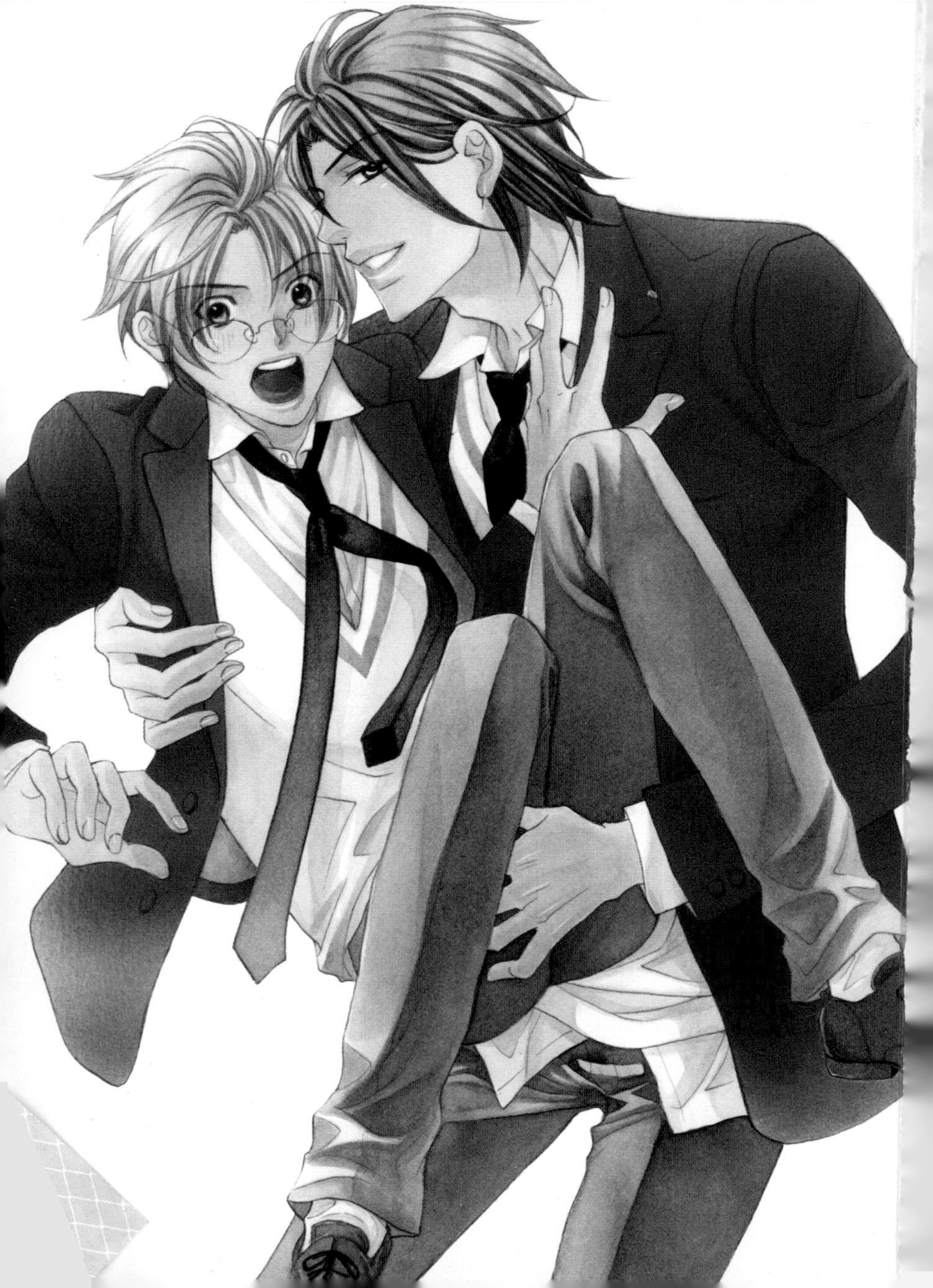

Awkward Silence

Story and Art by **Hinako Takanaga**　　　volume **4**

CONTENTS

SUBLIME

SuBLime Manga Edition

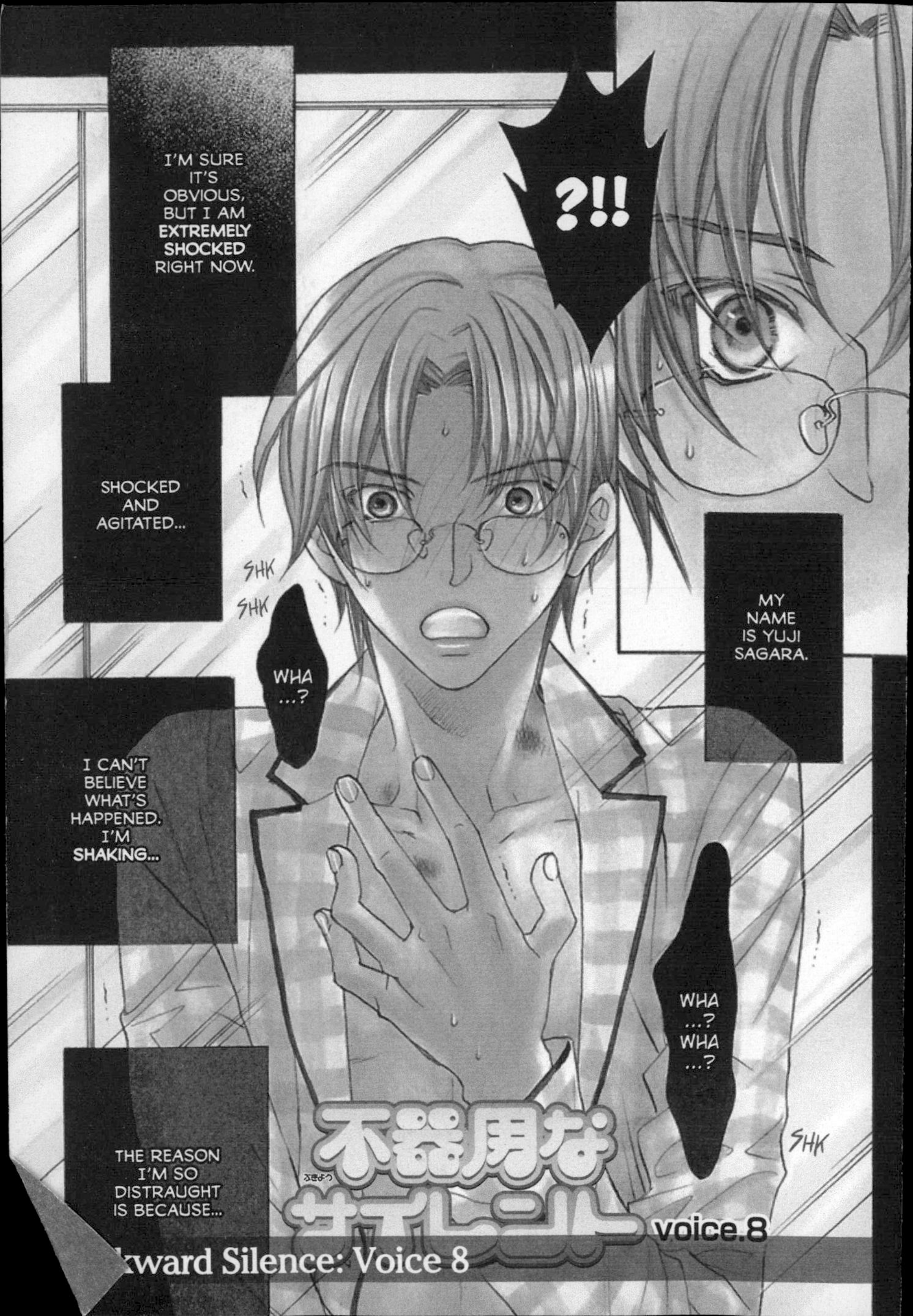
?!!
I'M SURE IT'S OBVIOUS, BUT I AM EXTREMELY SHOCKED RIGHT NOW.
MY NAME IS YUJI SAGARA.
SHOCKED AND AGITATED...
SHK
SHK
WHA ...?
I CAN'T BELIEVE WHAT'S HAPPENED. I'M SHAKING...
WHA ...? WHA ...?
SHK
THE REASON I'M SO DISTRAUGHT IS BECAUSE...
不器用な
ふきよう
voice.8
kward Silence: Voice 8

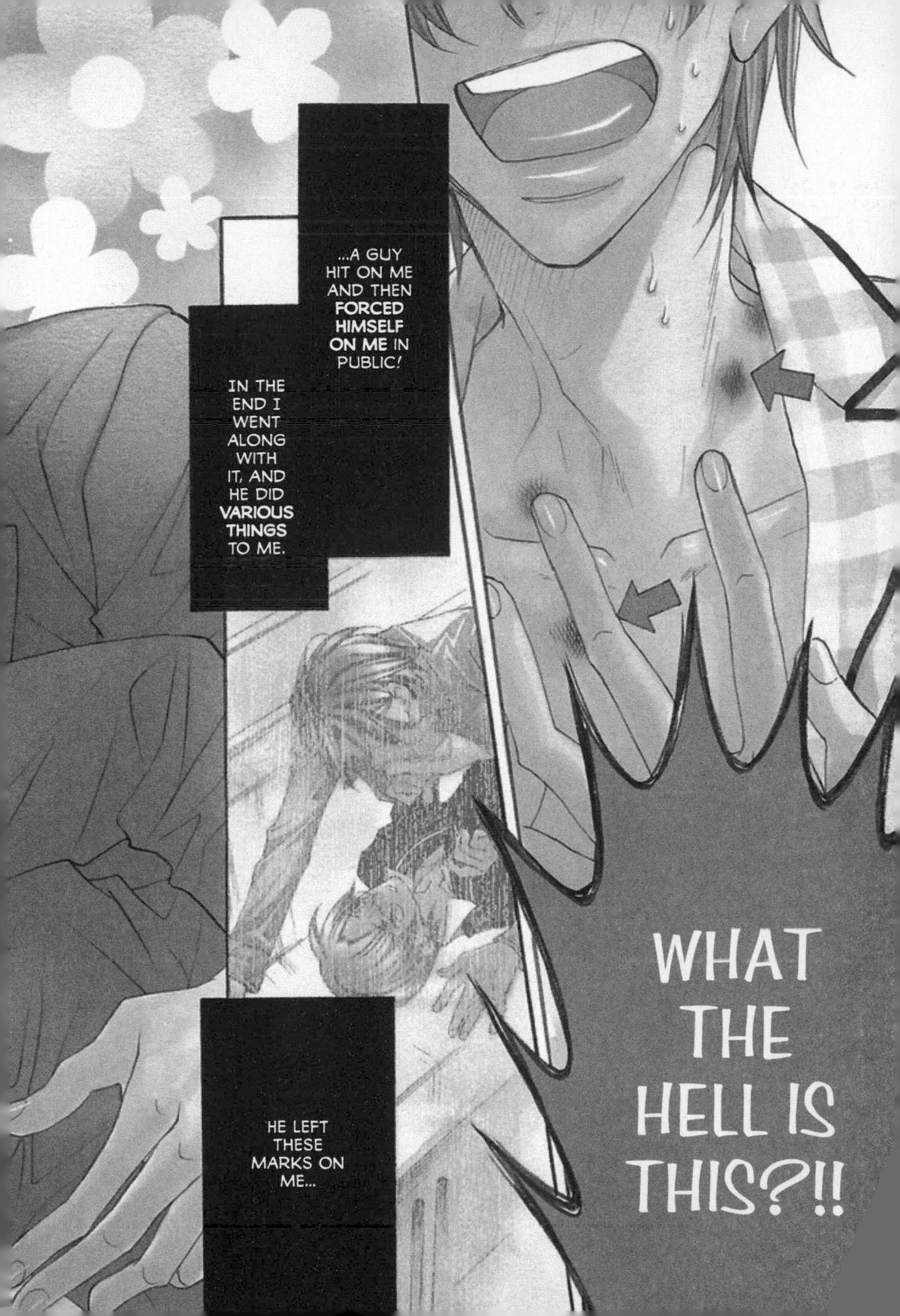
...A GUY HIT ON ME AND THEN FORCED HIMSELF ON ME IN PUBLIC!
IN THE END I WENT ALONG WITH IT, AND HE DID VARIOUS THINGS TO ME.
WHAT THE HELL IS THIS?!!
HE LEFT THESE MARKS ON ME...

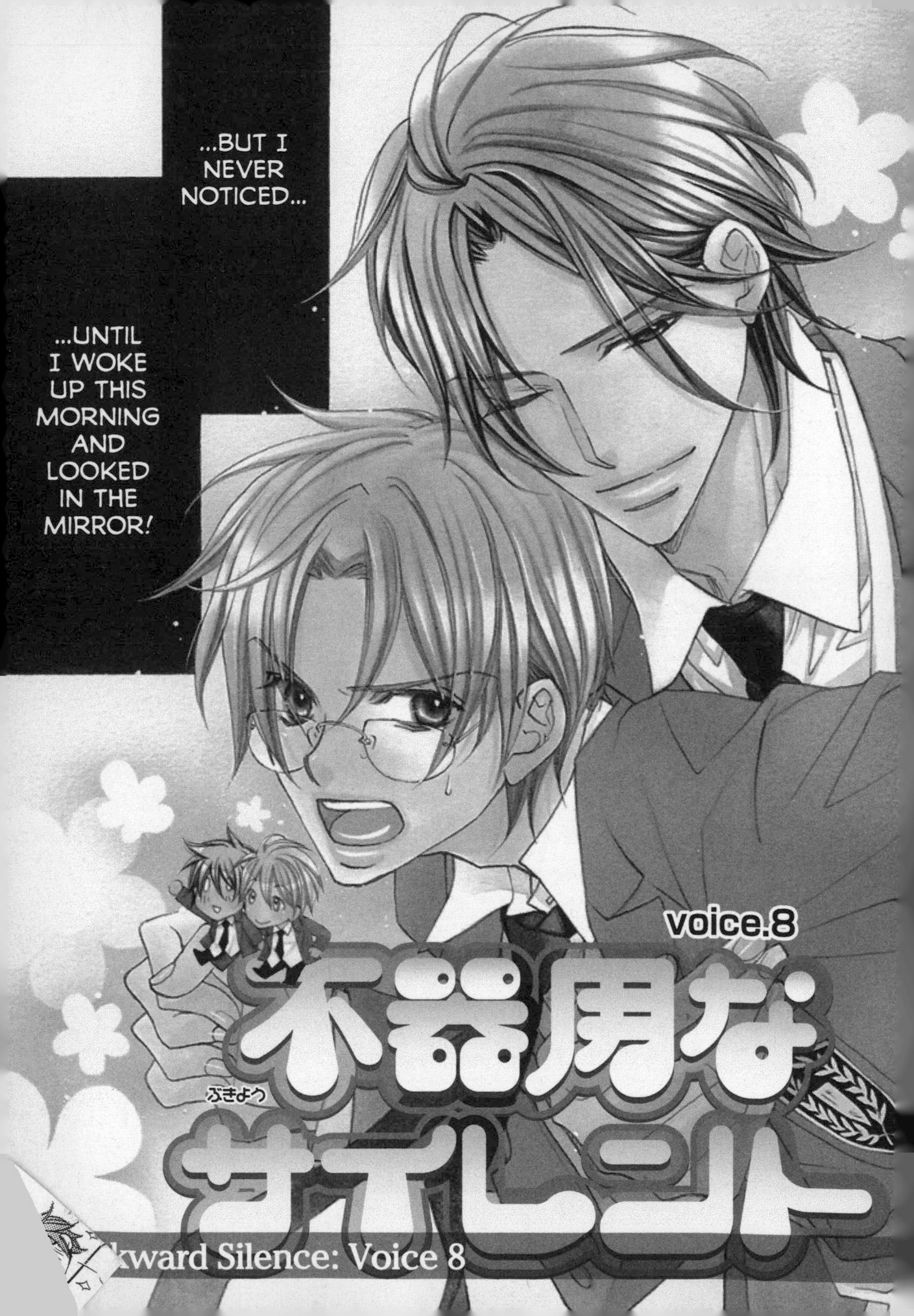
...BUT I NEVER NOTICED...
...UNTIL I WOKE UP THIS MORNING AND LOOKED IN THE MIRROR!
voice.8
不器用なサイレント
ぶきよう
kward Silence: Voice 8

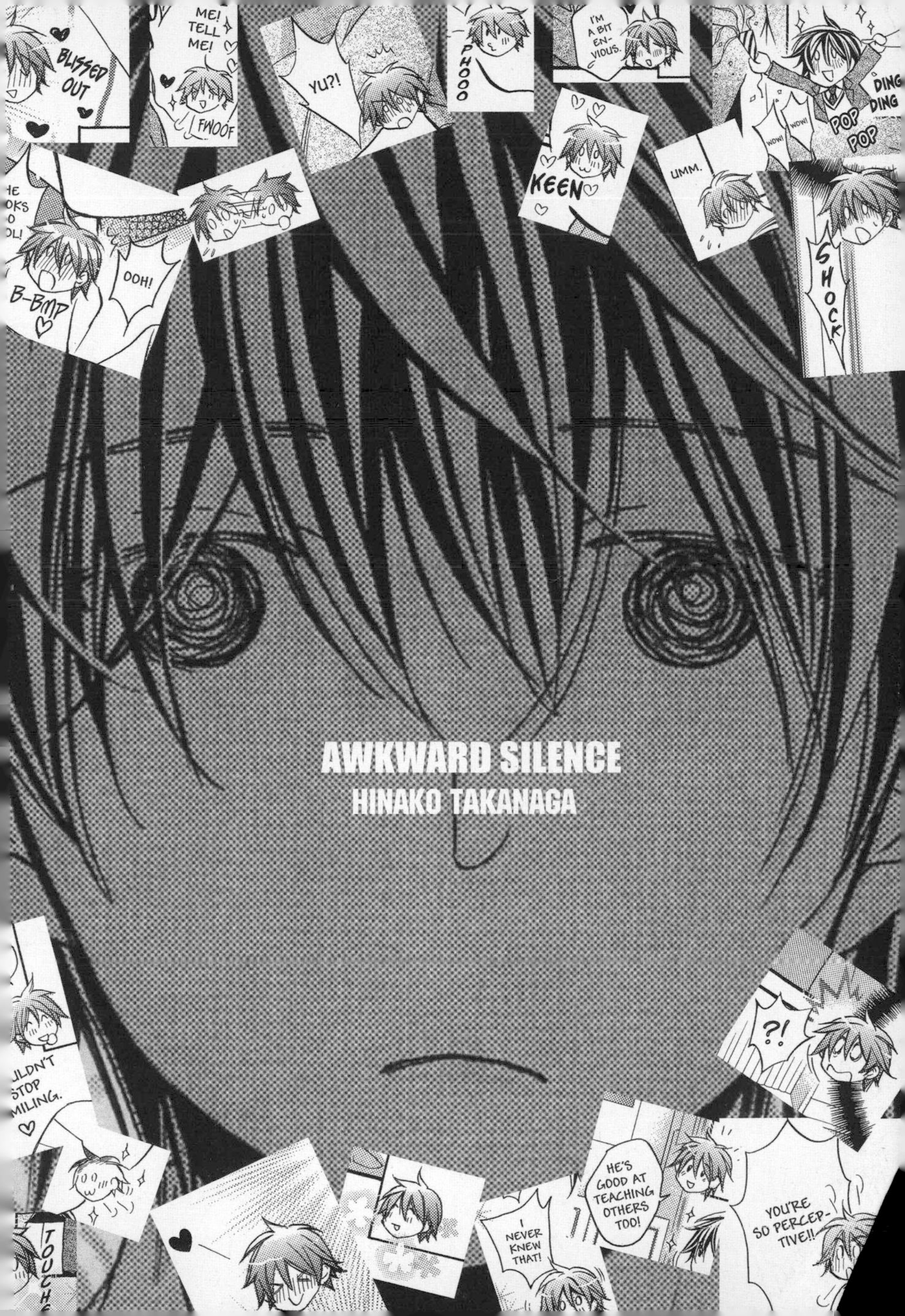
DING DING
POP POP
WOW!
WOW!
I'M A BIT EN-VIOUS.
PHOOO
YU?!
ME! TELL ME!
FWOOF
BLISSED OUT
SHOCK
UMM.
KEEN
OOH!
B-BMP
AWKWARD SILENCE
HINAKO TAKANAGA
?!
YOU'RE SO PERCEP-TIVE!!
HE'S GOOD AT TEACHING OTHERS TOO!
I NEVER KNEW THAT!

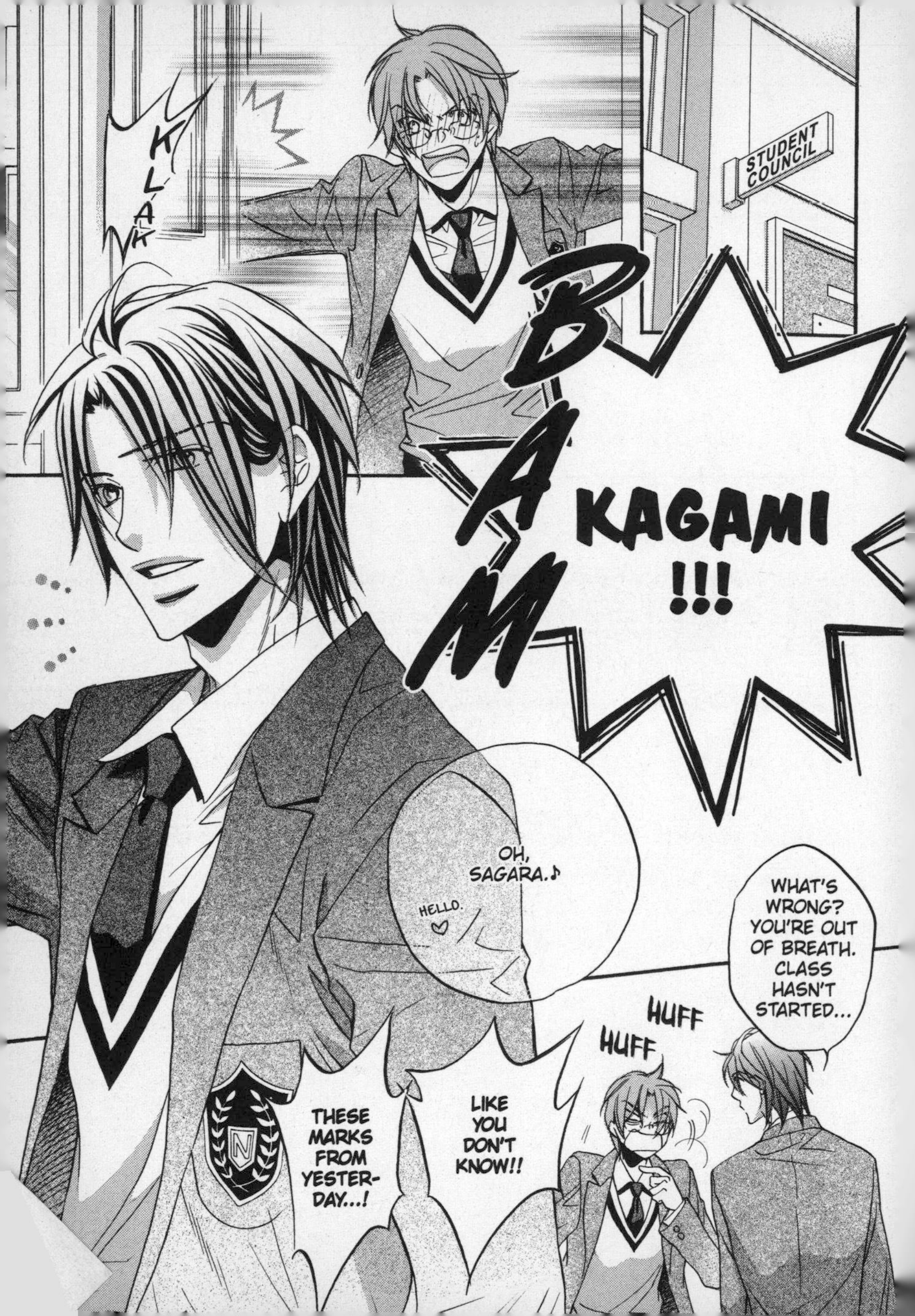
STUDENT COUNCIL
BAM
KLAK
KAGAMI!!!
OH, SAGARA.♪
HELLO. ♡
WHAT'S WRONG? YOU'RE OUT OF BREATH. CLASS HASN'T STARTED...
HUFF HUFF
LIKE YOU DON'T KNOW!!
THESE MARKS FROM YESTER-DAY...!

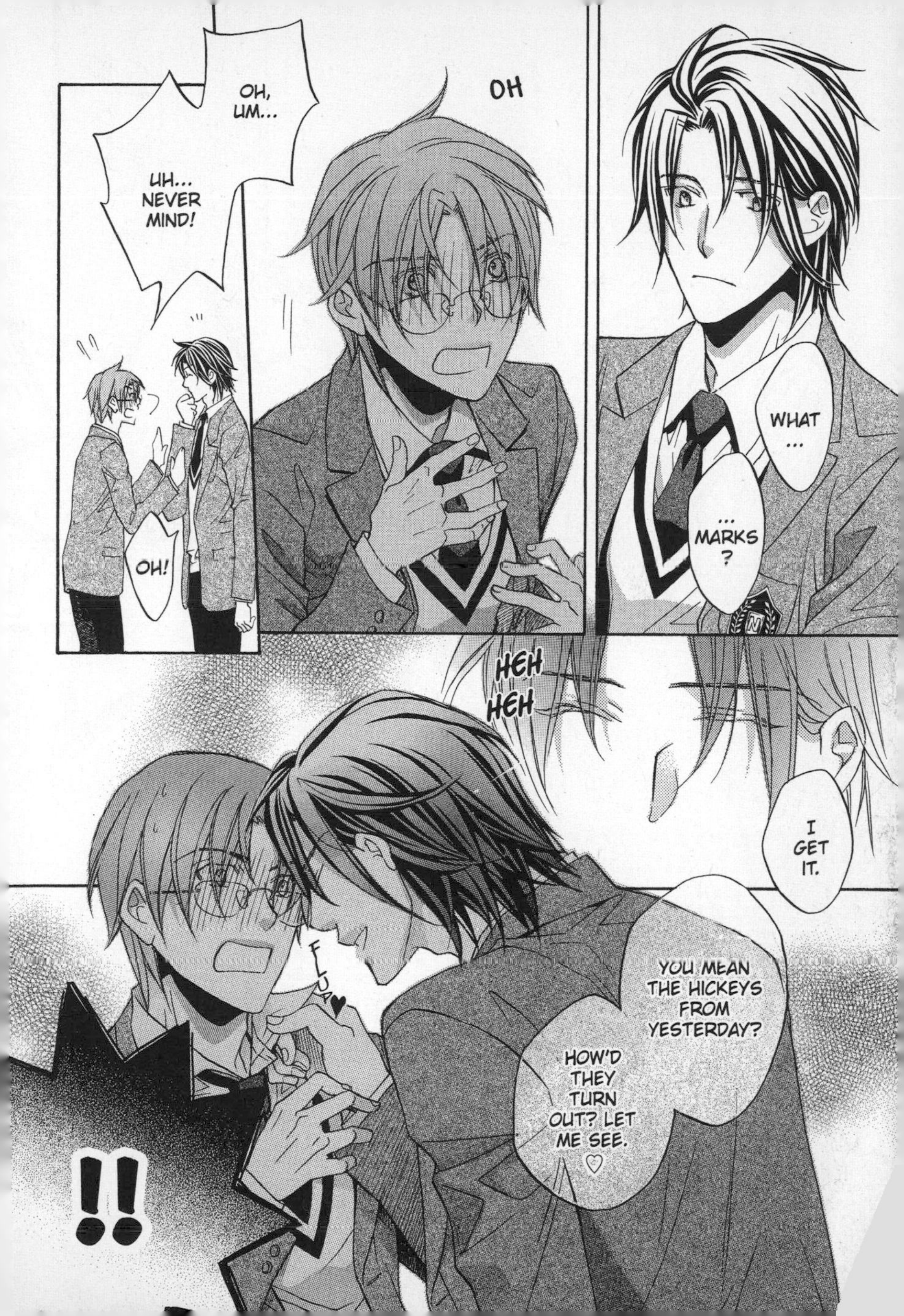
WHAT ...
... MARKS ?
OH
OH, UM...
UH... NEVER MIND!
OH!
HEH HEH
I GET IT.
YOU MEAN THE HICKEYS FROM YESTERDAY?
HOW'D THEY TURN OUT? LET ME SEE. ♡
FLUA♥
!!

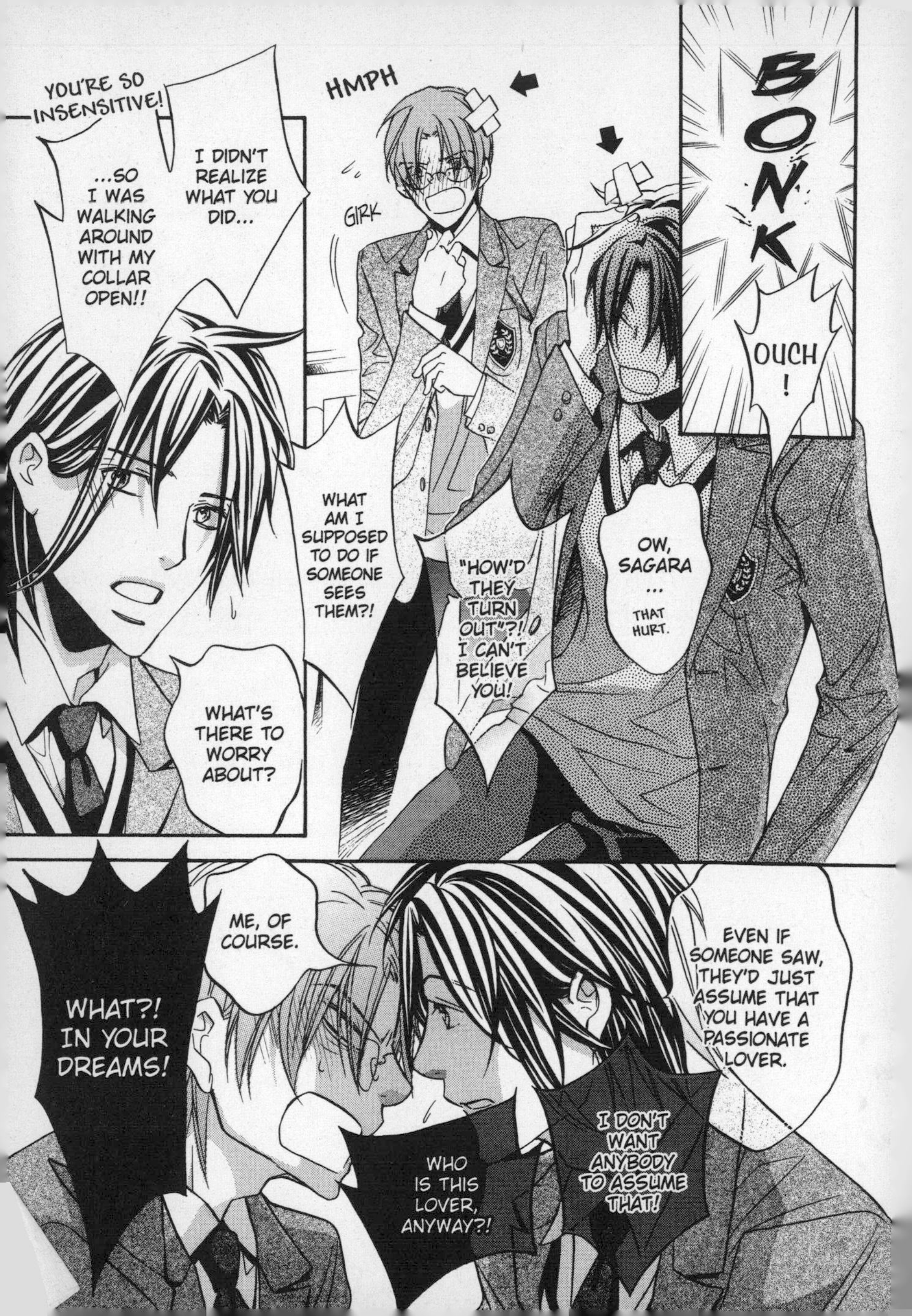
BONK
OUCH!
HMPH
GIRK
OW, SAGARA...
THAT HURT.
"HOW'D THEY TURN OUT"?! I CAN'T BELIEVE YOU!
WHAT AM I SUPPOSED TO DO IF SOMEONE SEES THEM?!
I DIDN'T REALIZE WHAT YOU DID...
...SO I WAS WALKING AROUND WITH MY COLLAR OPEN!!
YOU'RE SO INSENSITIVE!
WHAT'S THERE TO WORRY ABOUT?
EVEN IF SOMEONE SAW, THEY'D JUST ASSUME THAT YOU HAVE A PASSIONATE LOVER.
I DON'T WANT ANYBODY TO ASSUME THAT!
WHO IS THIS LOVER, ANYWAY?!
ME, OF COURSE.
WHAT?! IN YOUR DREAMS!

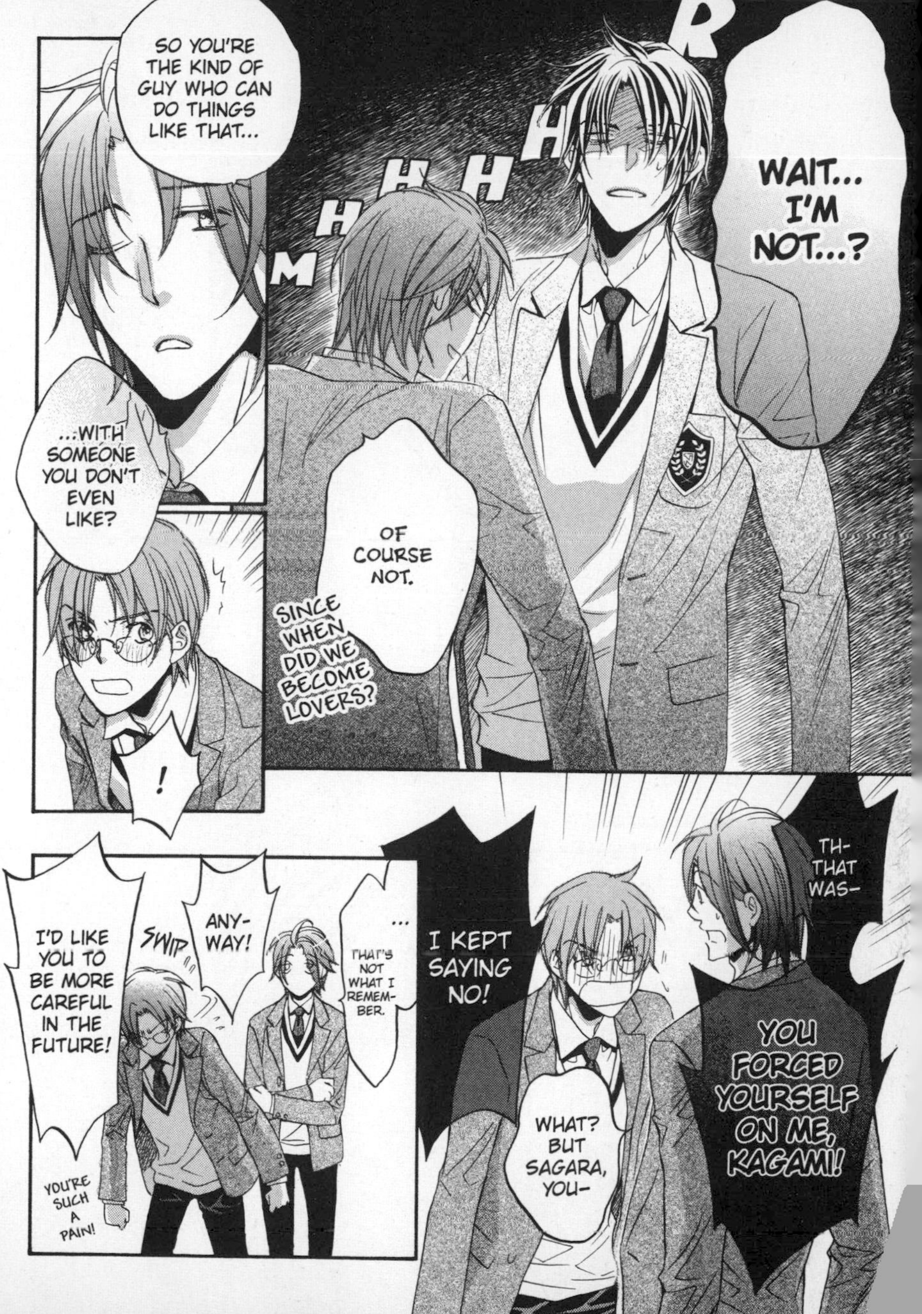
MHHHHR
WAIT... I'M NOT...?
OF COURSE NOT.
SINCE WHEN DID WE BECOME LOVERS?
SO YOU'RE THE KIND OF GUY WHO CAN DO THINGS LIKE THAT...
...WITH SOMEONE YOU DON'T EVEN LIKE?
!
TH- THAT WAS-
YOU FORCED YOURSELF ON ME, KAGAMI!
I KEPT SAYING NO!
WHAT? BUT SAGARA, YOU-
...
THAT'S NOT WHAT I REMEMBER.
ANY-WAY!
SWIP
I'D LIKE YOU TO BE MORE CAREFUL IN THE FUTURE!
YOU'RE SUCH A PAIN!

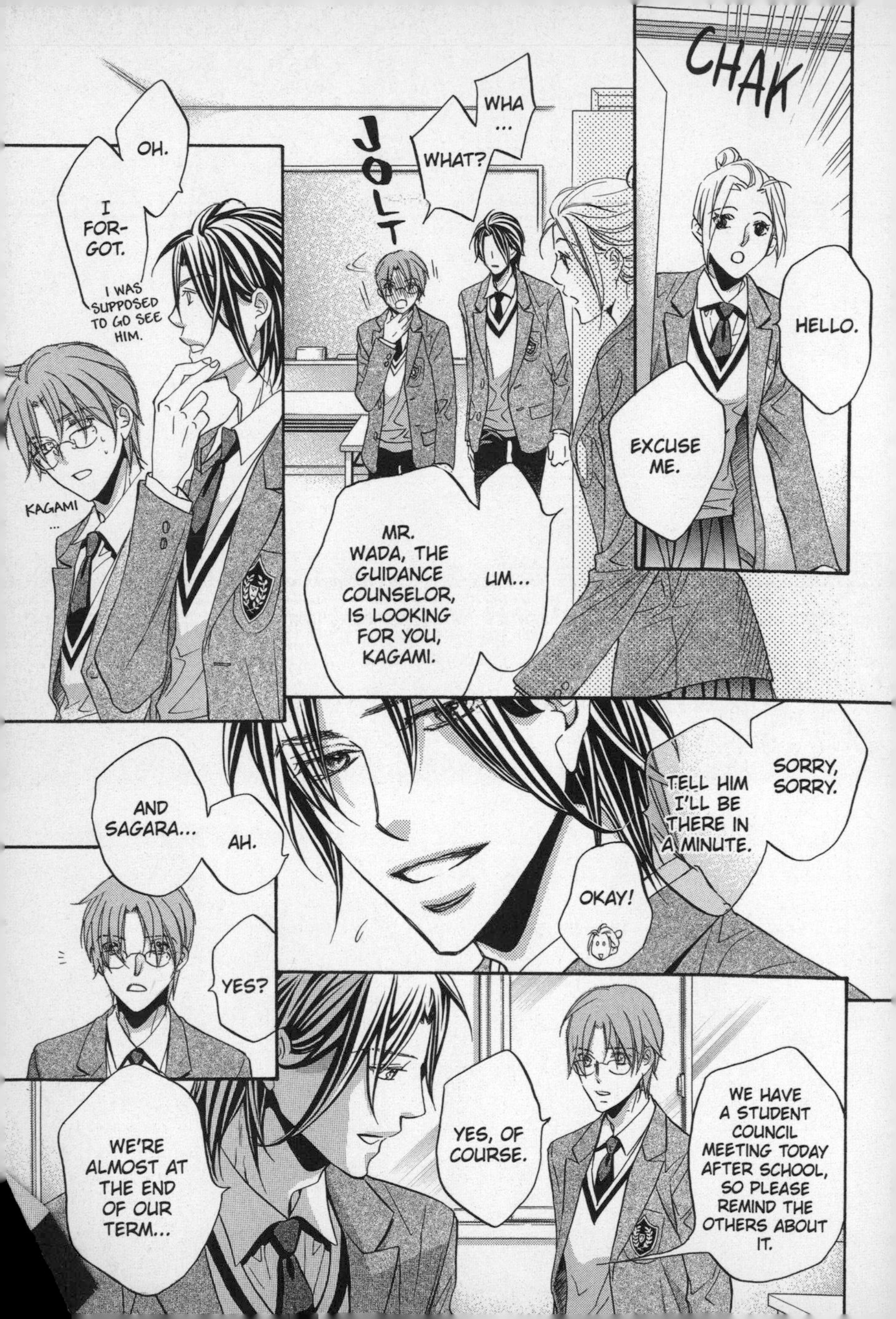
CHAK
HELLO.
EXCUSE ME.
WHA ... WHAT?
JOLT
UM...
MR. WADA, THE GUIDANCE COUNSELOR, IS LOOKING FOR YOU, KAGAMI.
OH.
I FOR-GOT.
I WAS SUPPOSED TO GO SEE HIM.
KAGAMI ...
SORRY, SORRY.
TELL HIM I'LL BE THERE IN A MINUTE.
OKAY!
AND SAGARA...
AH.
YES?
WE HAVE A STUDENT COUNCIL MEETING TODAY AFTER SCHOOL, SO PLEASE REMIND THE OTHERS ABOUT IT.
YES, OF COURSE.
WE'RE ALMOST AT THE END OF OUR TERM...

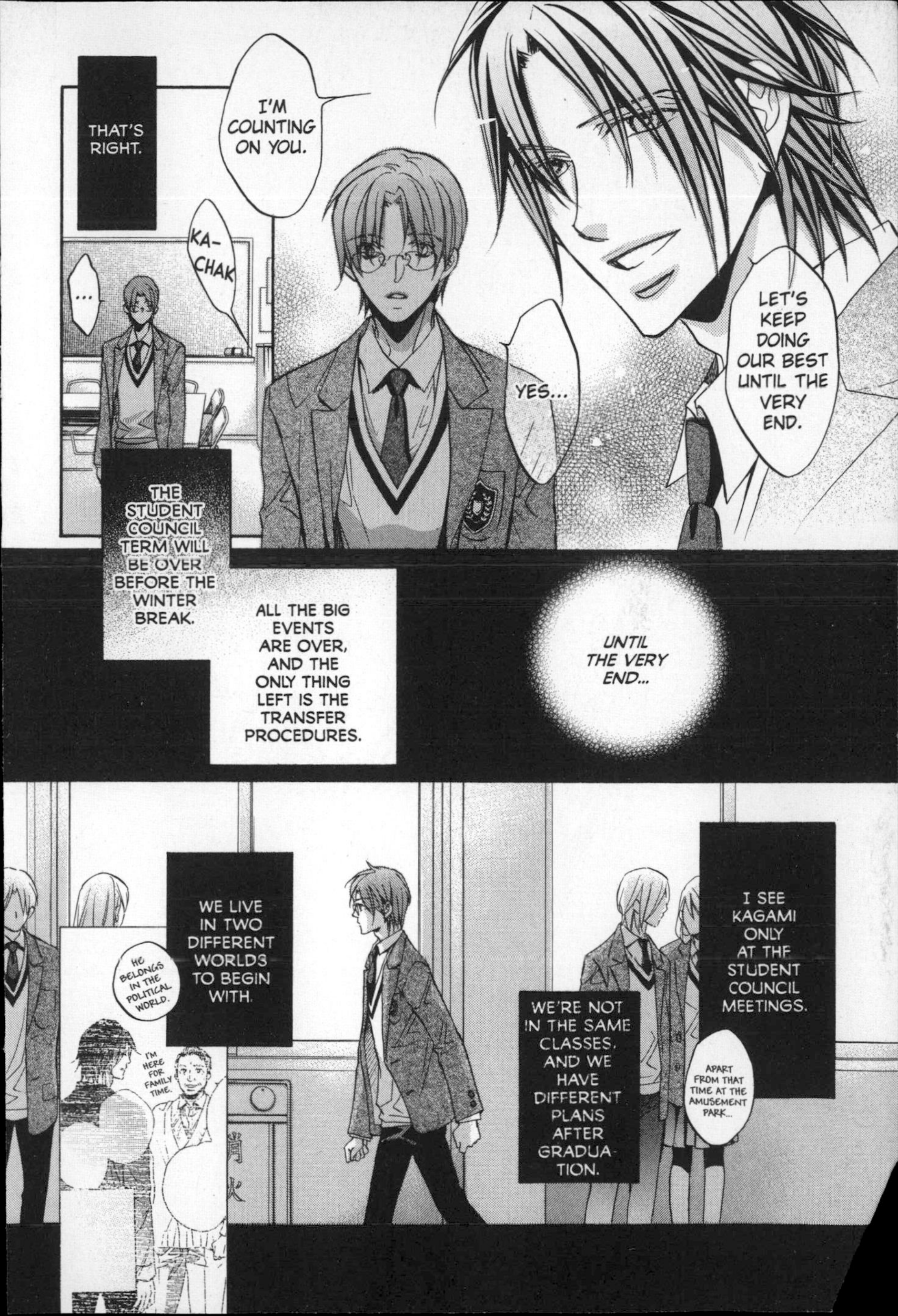
LET'S KEEP DOING OUR BEST UNTIL THE VERY END.
YES...
I'M COUNTING ON YOU.
KA-CHAK
THAT'S RIGHT.
...
THE STUDENT COUNCIL TERM WILL BE OVER BEFORE THE WINTER BREAK.
UNTIL THE VERY END...
ALL THE BIG EVENTS ARE OVER, AND THE ONLY THING LEFT IS THE TRANSFER PROCEDURES.
I SEE KAGAMI ONLY AT THE STUDENT COUNCIL MEETINGS.
APART FROM THAT TIME AT THE AMUSEMENT PARK...
WE'RE NOT IN THE SAME CLASSES, AND WE HAVE DIFFERENT PLANS AFTER GRADUATION.
WE LIVE IN TWO DIFFERENT WORLDS TO BEGIN WITH.
HE BELONGS IN THE POLITICAL WORLD.
I'M HERE FOR FAMILY TIME.

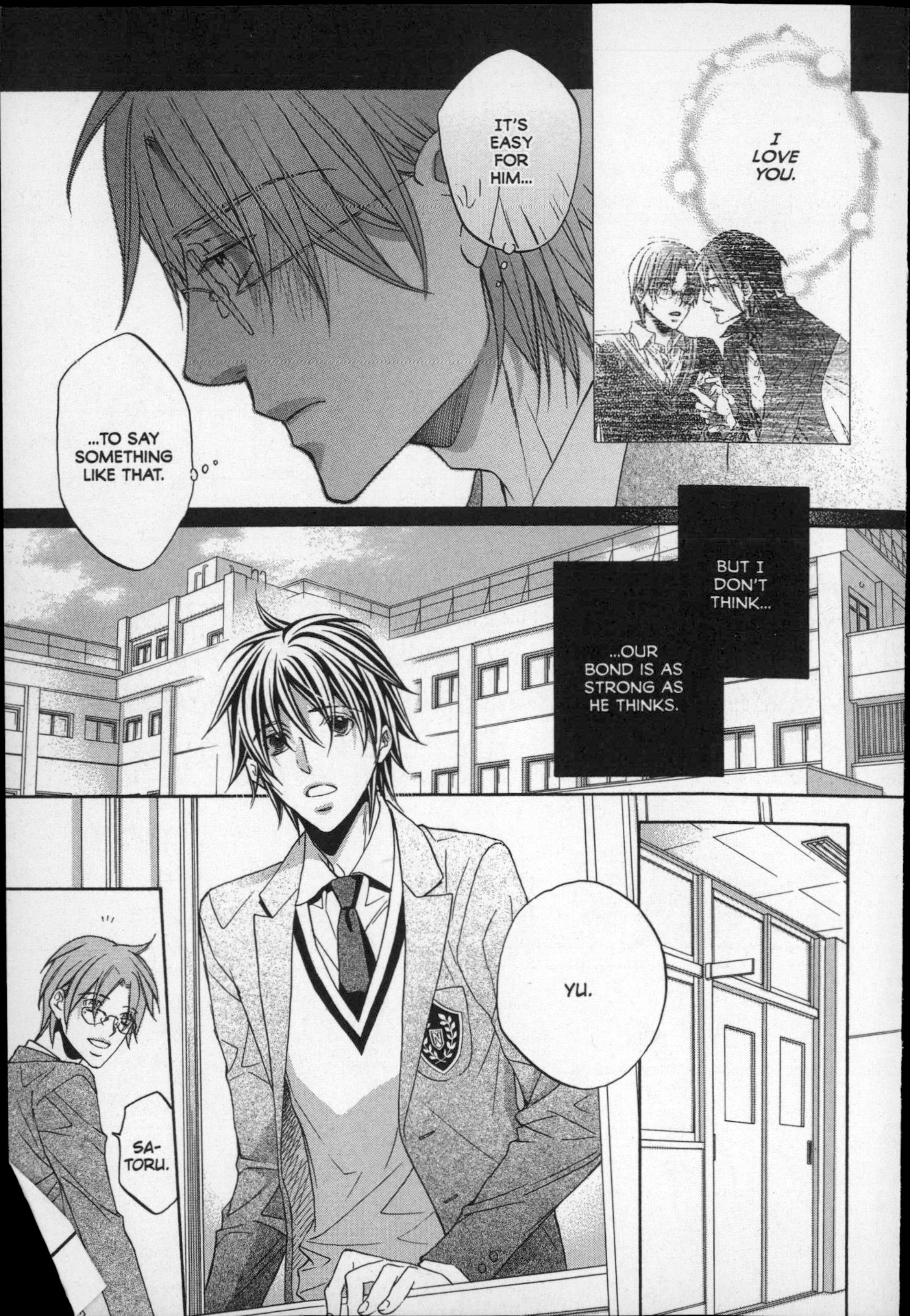
I LOVE YOU.
IT'S EASY FOR HIM...
...TO SAY SOMETHING LIKE THAT.
BUT I DON'T THINK...
...OUR BOND IS AS STRONG AS HE THINKS.
YU.
SA-TORU.

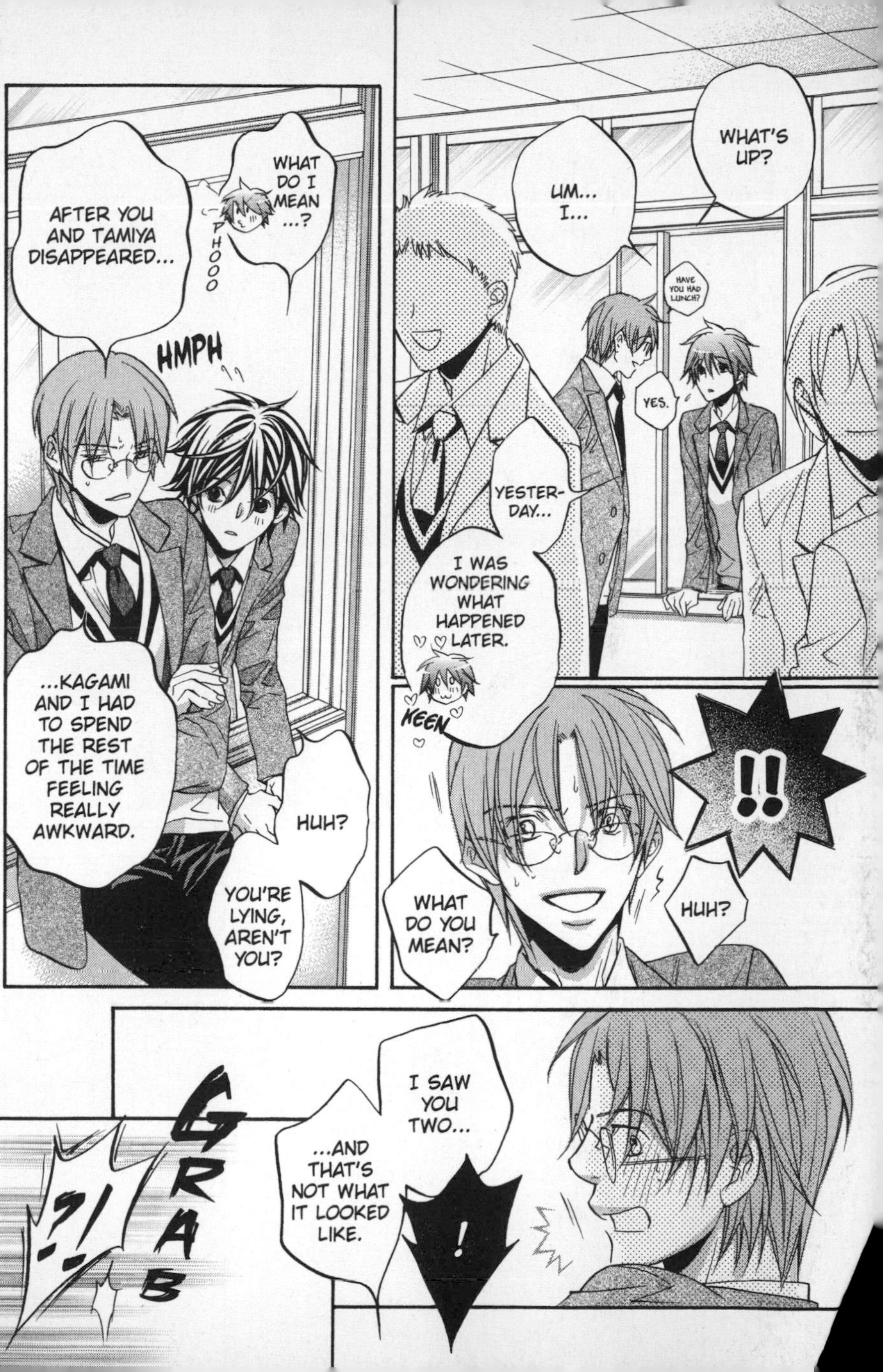
WHAT'S UP?
UM... I...
HAVE YOU HAD LUNCH?
YES.
YESTER-DAY...
I WAS WONDERING WHAT HAPPENED LATER.
KEEN
!!
HUH?
WHAT DO YOU MEAN?
WHAT DO I MEAN ...?
PHOOOO
AFTER YOU AND TAMIYA DISAPPEARED...
HMPH
...KAGAMI AND I HAD TO SPEND THE REST OF THE TIME FEELING REALLY AWKWARD.
HUH?
YOU'RE LYING, AREN'T YOU?
I SAW YOU TWO...
!
...AND THAT'S NOT WHAT IT LOOKED LIKE.
GRAB
?!

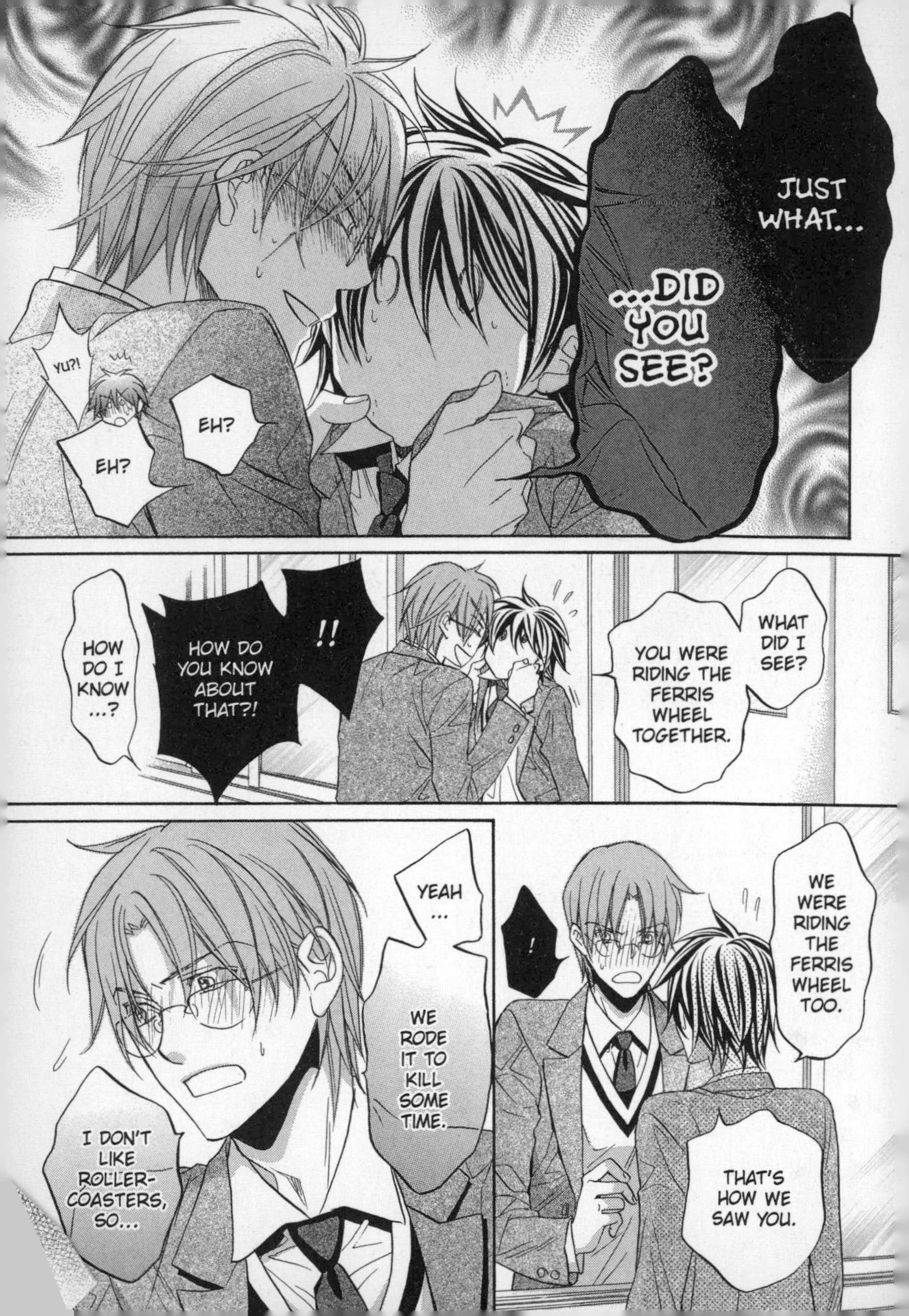
JUST WHAT...
...DID YOU SEE?
EH?
YU?!
EH?
WHAT DID I SEE?
YOU WERE RIDING THE FERRIS WHEEL TOGETHER.
!!
HOW DO YOU KNOW ABOUT THAT?!
HOW DO I KNOW ...?
WE WERE RIDING THE FERRIS WHEEL TOO.
!
THAT'S HOW WE SAW YOU.
YEAH ...
WE RODE IT TO KILL SOME TIME.
I DON'T LIKE ROLLER-COASTERS, SO...

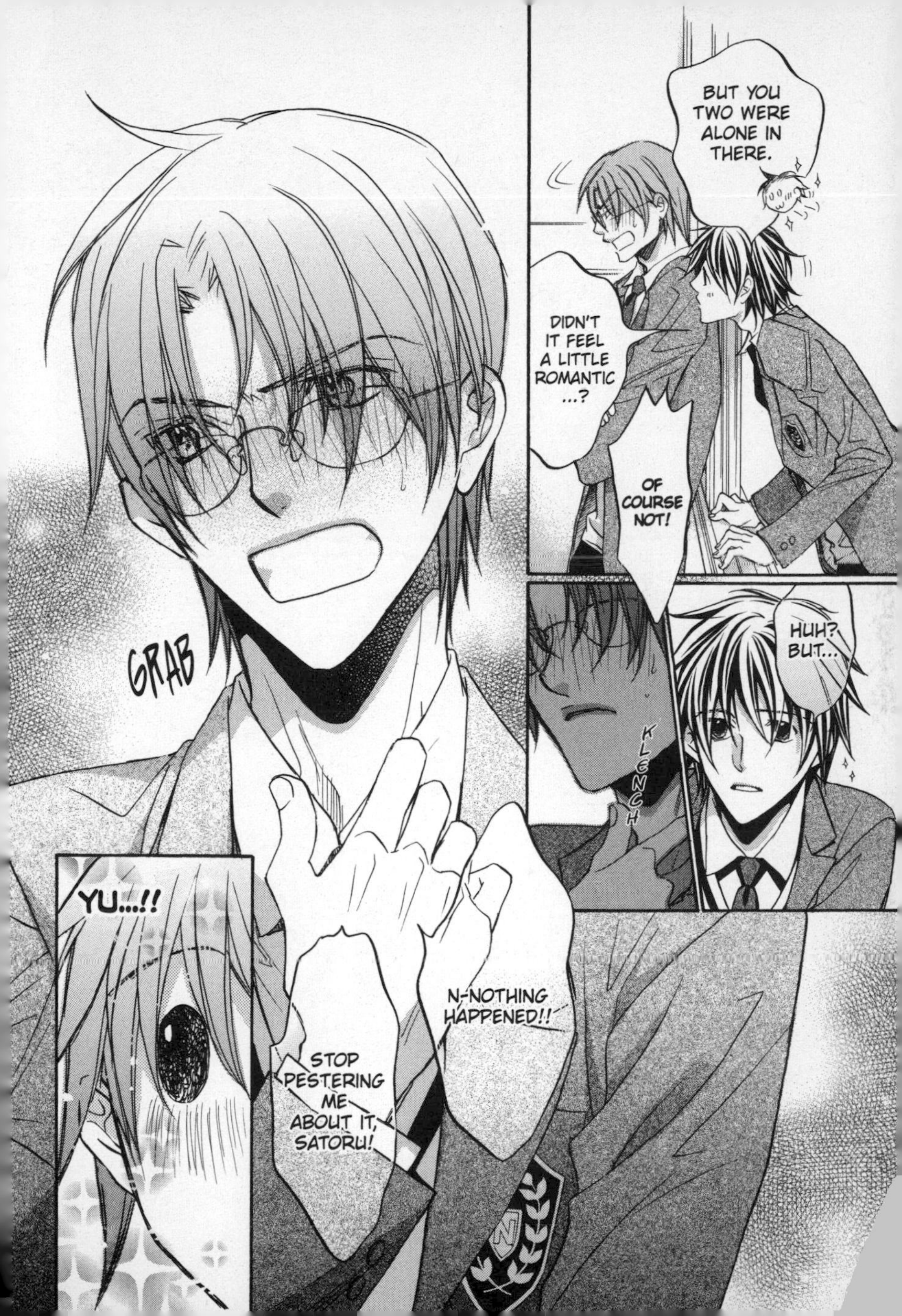
BUT YOU TWO WERE ALONE IN THERE.
DIDN'T IT FEEL A LITTLE ROMANTIC ...?
OF COURSE NOT!
HUH? BUT...
KLENCH
GRAB
N-NOTHING HAPPENED!!
STOP PESTERING ME ABOUT IT, SATORU!
YU...!!

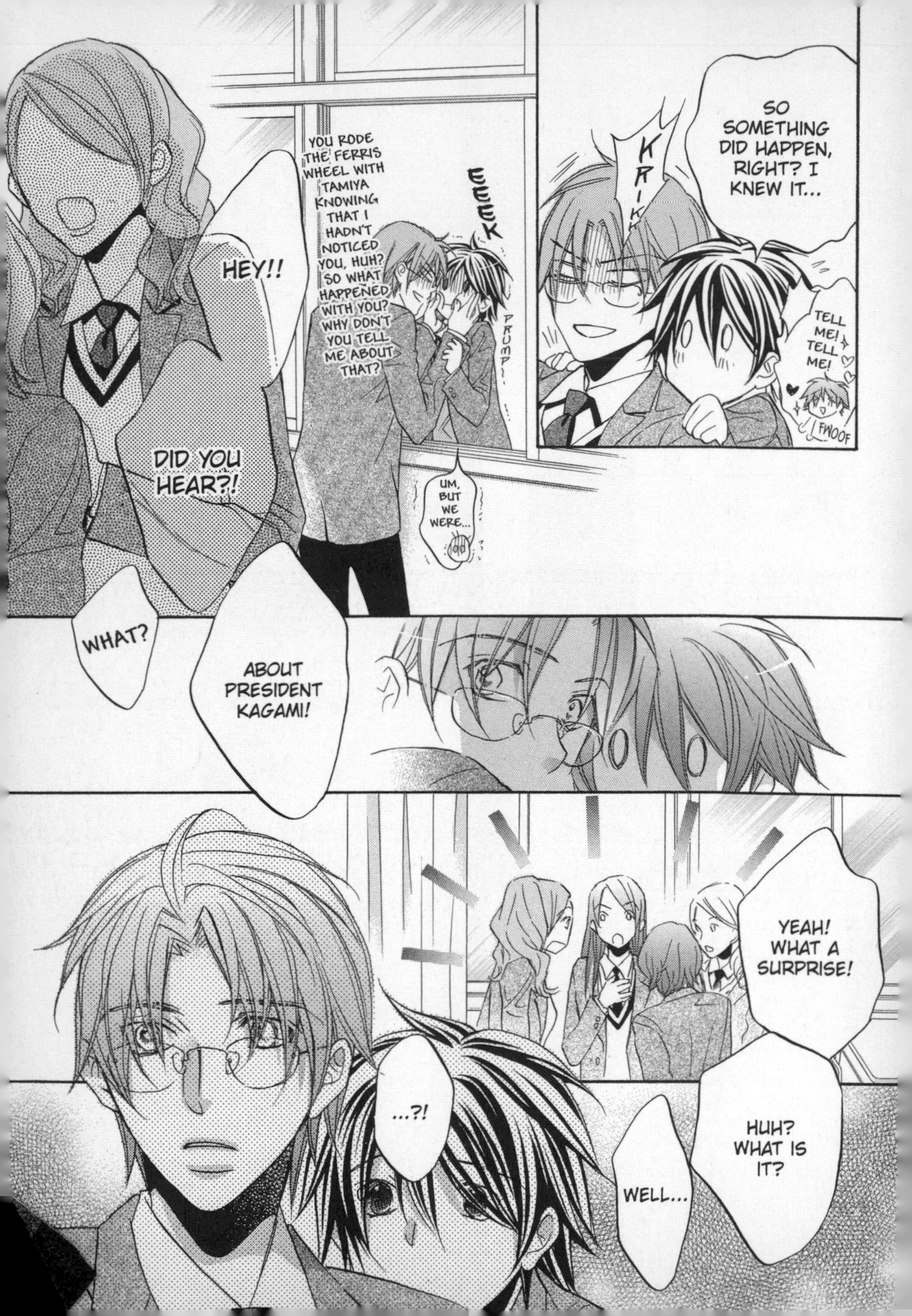
SO SOMETHING DID HAPPEN, RIGHT? I KNEW IT...
KRIK
TELL ME! TELL ME!
FWOOF
YOU RODE THE FERRIS WHEEL WITH TAMIYA KNOWING THAT I HADN'T NOTICED YOU, HUH? SO WHAT HAPPENED WITH YOU? WHY DON'T YOU TELL ME ABOUT THAT?
EEEK
PRUMP
UM, BUT WE WERE...
HEY!!
DID YOU HEAR?!
WHAT?
ABOUT PRESIDENT KAGAMI!
YEAH! WHAT A SURPRISE!
HUH? WHAT IS IT?
WELL...
...?!

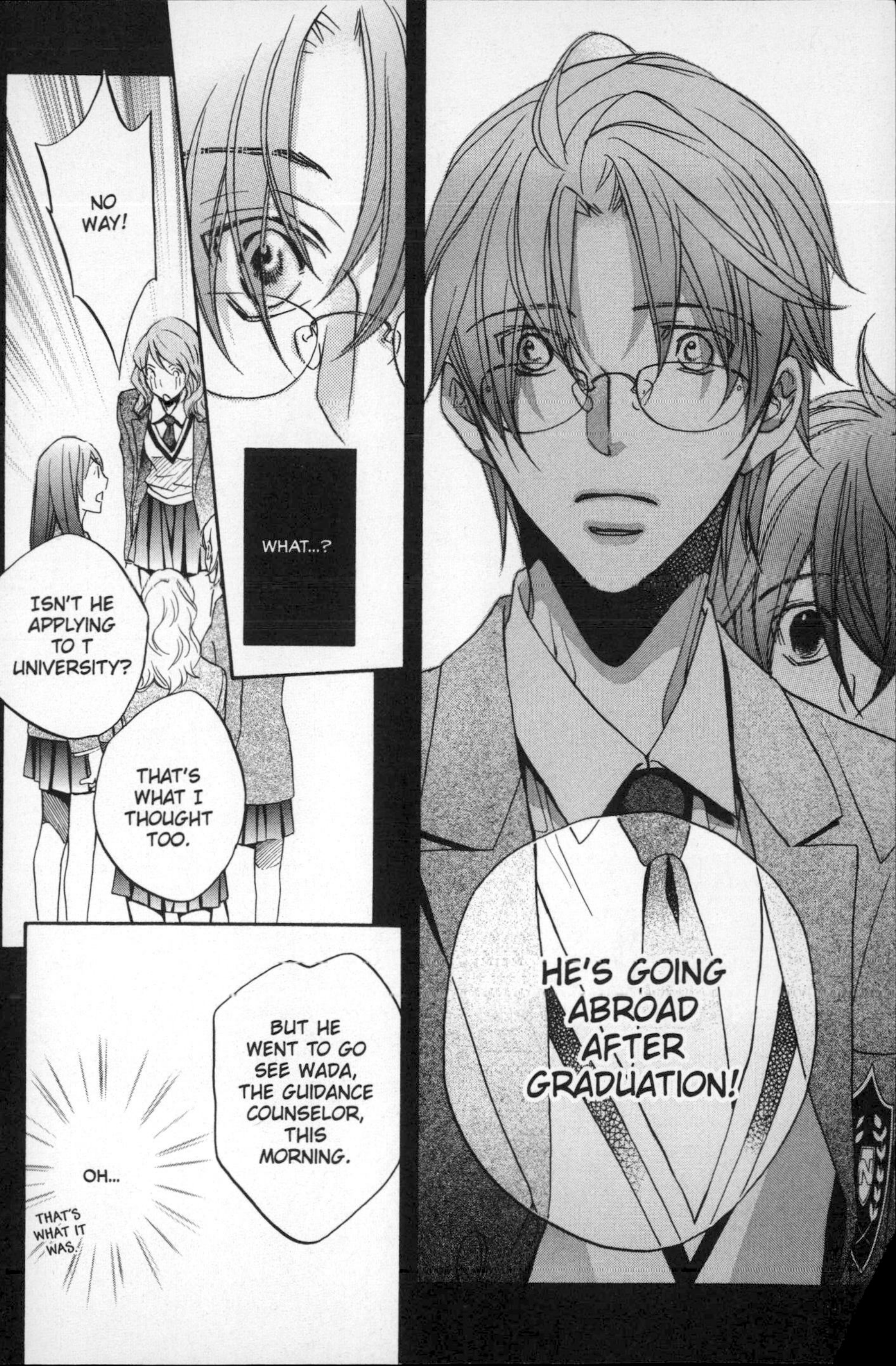
HE'S GOING ABROAD AFTER GRADUATION!
WHAT...?
NO WAY!
ISN'T HE APPLYING TO T UNIVERSITY?
THAT'S WHAT I THOUGHT TOO.
BUT HE WENT TO GO SEE WADA, THE GUIDANCE COUNSELOR, THIS MORNING.
OH...
THAT'S WHAT IT WAS.

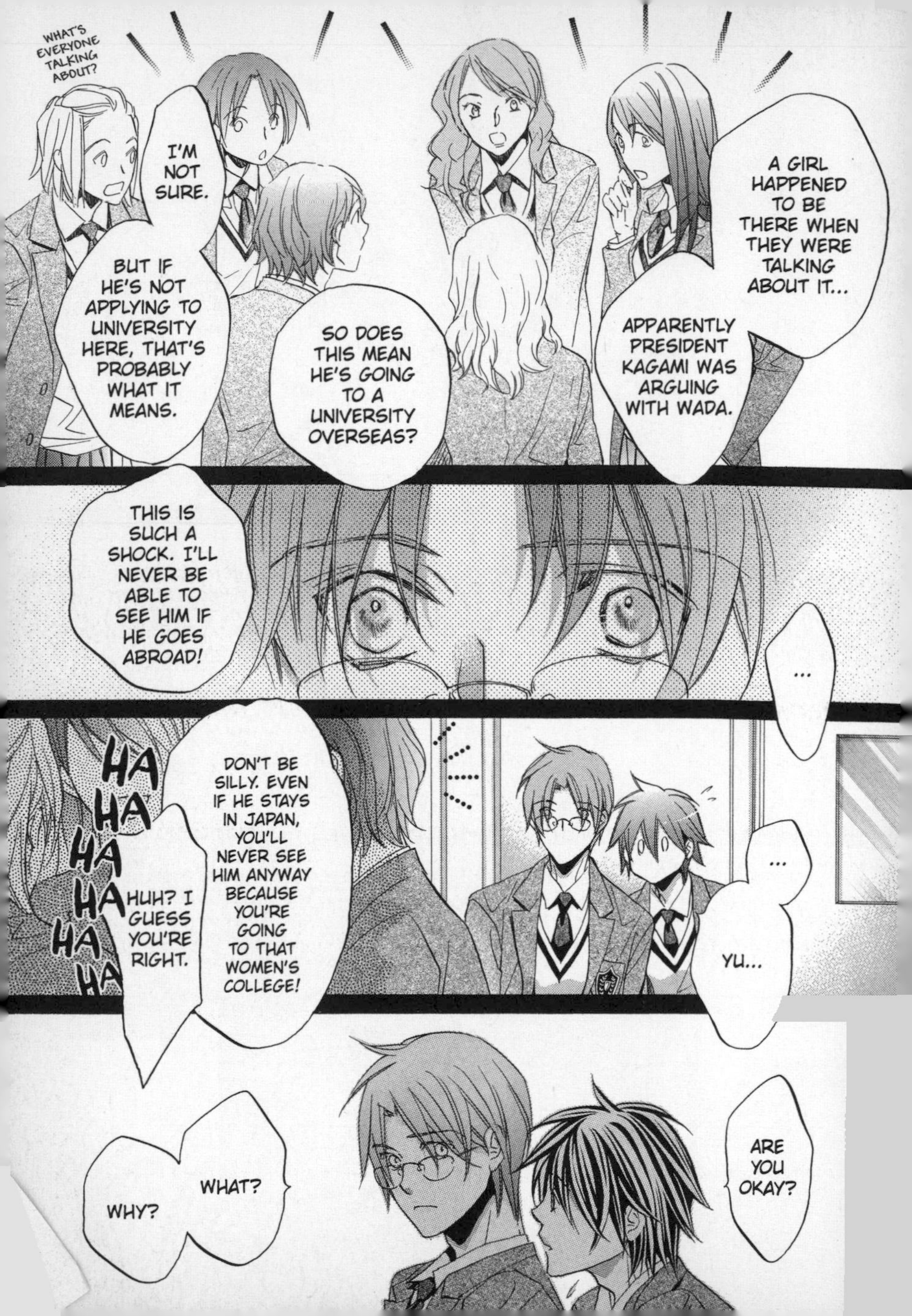
A GIRL HAPPENED TO BE THERE WHEN THEY WERE TALKING ABOUT IT...
APPARENTLY PRESIDENT KAGAMI WAS ARGUING WITH WADA.
SO DOES THIS MEAN HE'S GOING TO A UNIVERSITY OVERSEAS?
WHAT'S EVERYONE TALKING ABOUT?
I'M NOT SURE.
BUT IF HE'S NOT APPLYING TO UNIVERSITY HERE, THAT'S PROBABLY WHAT IT MEANS.
THIS IS SUCH A SHOCK. I'LL NEVER BE ABLE TO SEE HIM IF HE GOES ABROAD!
...
...
DON'T BE SILLY. EVEN IF HE STAYS IN JAPAN, YOU'LL NEVER SEE HIM ANYWAY BECAUSE YOU'RE GOING TO THAT WOMEN'S COLLEGE!
HUH? I GUESS YOU'RE RIGHT.
HA HA HA HA HA HA HA
YU...
ARE YOU OKAY?
WHAT?
WHY?

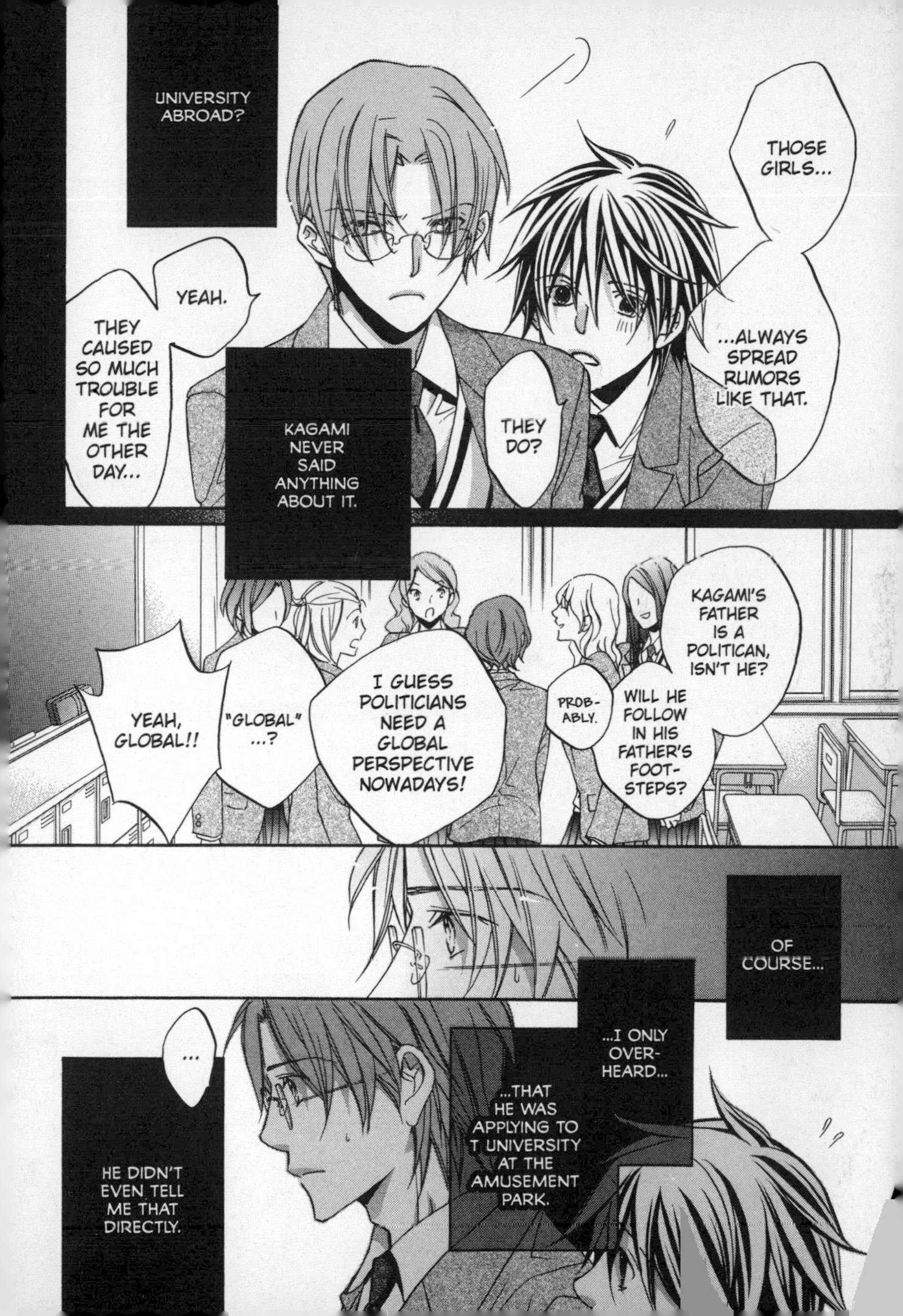
THOSE GIRLS...
...ALWAYS SPREAD RUMORS LIKE THAT.
THEY DO?
UNIVERSITY ABROAD?
YEAH.
THEY CAUSED SO MUCH TROUBLE FOR ME THE OTHER DAY...
KAGAMI NEVER SAID ANYTHING ABOUT IT.
KAGAMI'S FATHER IS A POLITICAN, ISN'T HE?
WILL HE FOLLOW IN HIS FATHER'S FOOT-STEPS?
PROB-ABLY.
I GUESS POLITICIANS NEED A GLOBAL PERSPECTIVE NOWADAYS!
"GLOBAL" ...?
YEAH, GLOBAL!!
OF COURSE...
...I ONLY OVER-HEARD...
...THAT HE WAS APPLYING TO T UNIVERSITY AT THE AMUSEMENT PARK.
...
HE DIDN'T EVEN TELL ME THAT DIRECTLY.

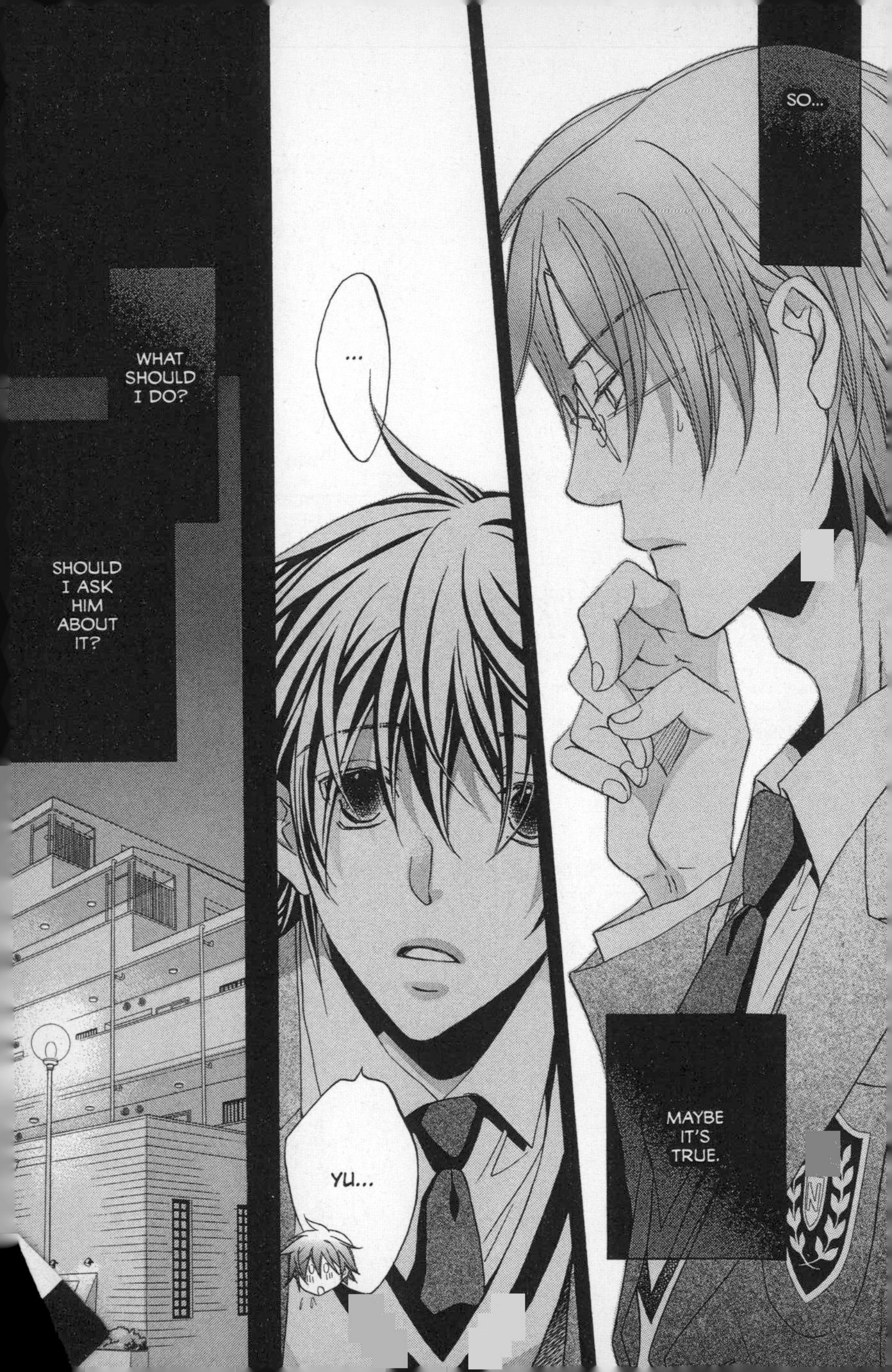
SO...
MAYBE IT'S TRUE.
...
YU...
WHAT SHOULD I DO?
SHOULD I ASK HIM ABOUT IT?

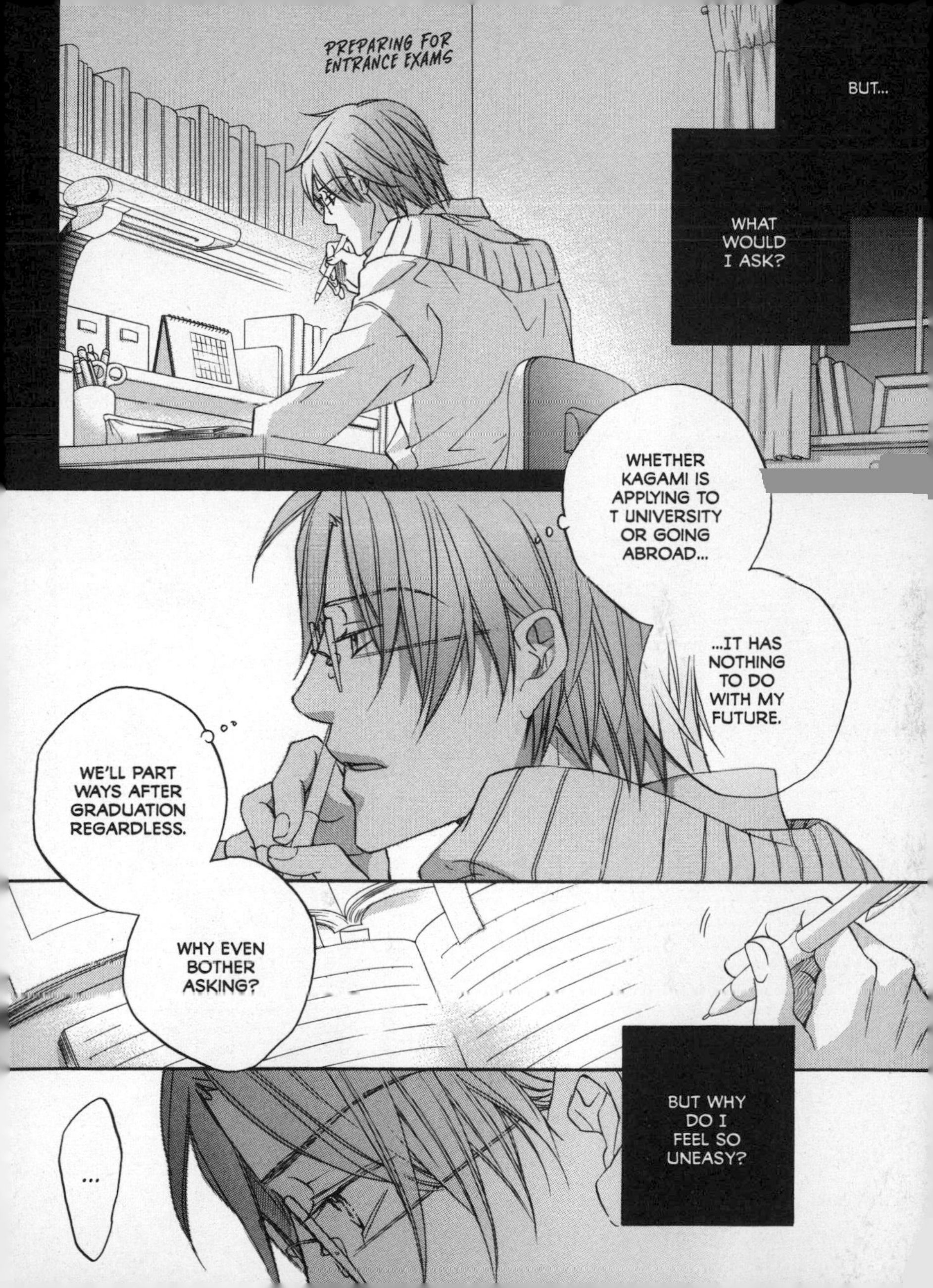
BUT...
WHAT WOULD I ASK?
PREPARING FOR ENTRANCE EXAMS
WHETHER KAGAMI IS APPLYING TO T UNIVERSITY OR GOING ABROAD...
...IT HAS NOTHING TO DO WITH MY FUTURE.
WE'LL PART WAYS AFTER GRADUATION REGARDLESS.
WHY EVEN BOTHER ASKING?
BUT WHY DO I FEEL SO UNEASY?
...

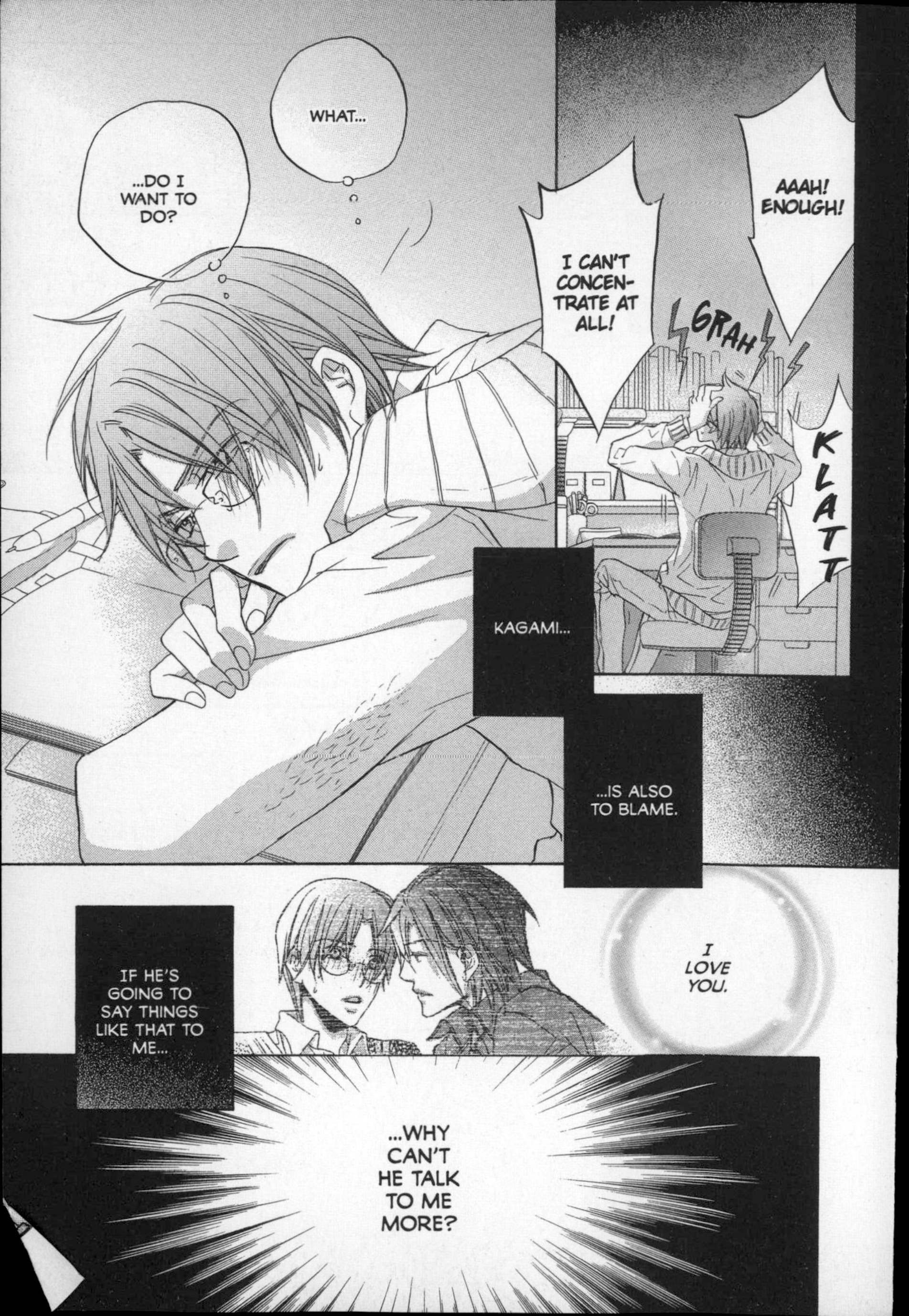
AAAH! ENOUGH!
I CAN'T CONCENTRATE AT ALL!
GRAH
KLATT
WHAT...
...DO I WANT TO DO?
KAGAMI...
...IS ALSO TO BLAME.
I LOVE YOU.
IF HE'S GOING TO SAY THINGS LIKE THAT TO ME...
...WHY CAN'T HE TALK TO ME MORE?

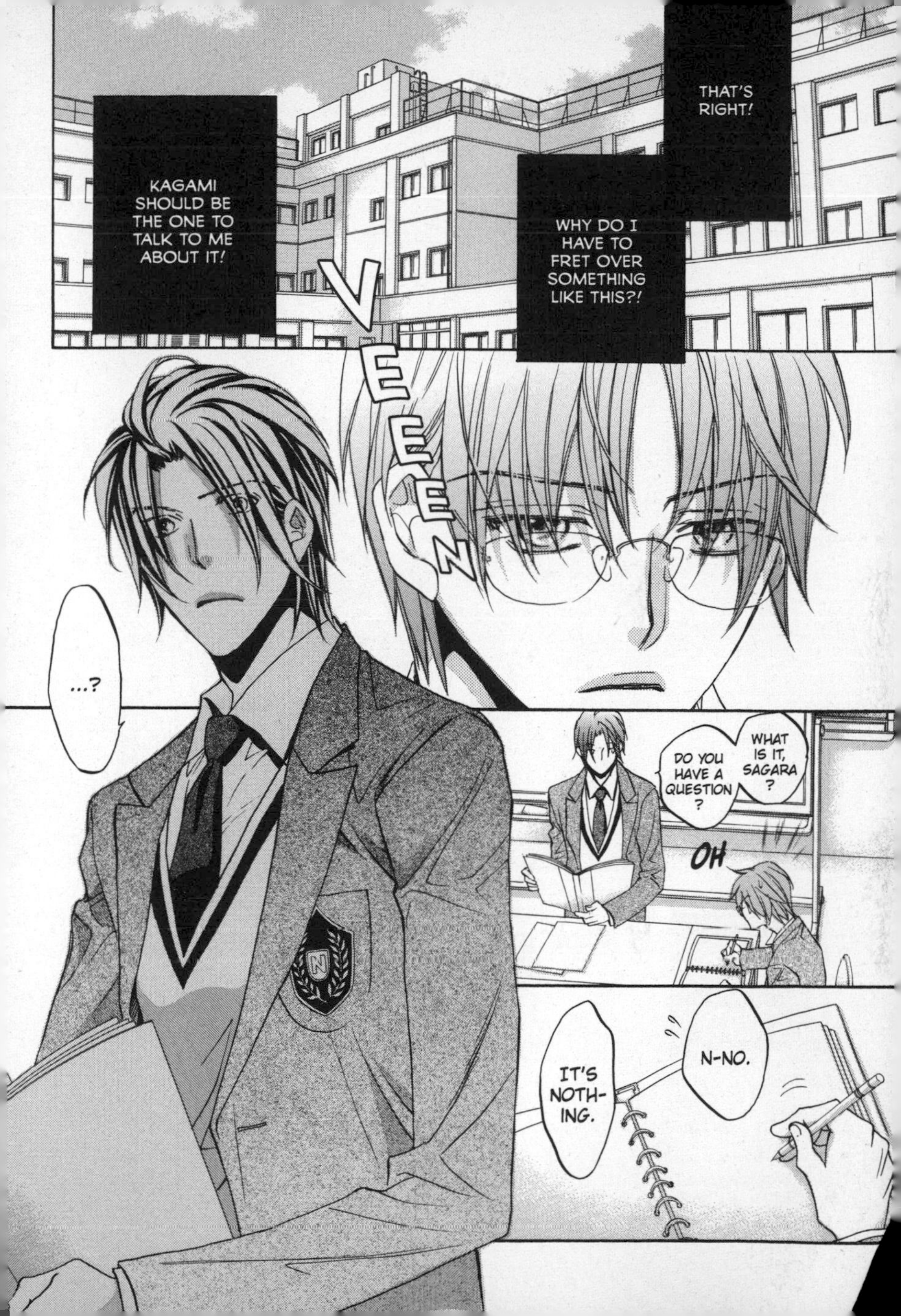
THAT'S RIGHT!
WHY DO I HAVE TO FRET OVER SOMETHING LIKE THIS?!
KAGAMI SHOULD BE THE ONE TO TALK TO ME ABOUT IT!
VEEEEN
WHAT IS IT, SAGARA?
DO YOU HAVE A QUESTION?
OH
N-NO.
IT'S NOTHING.
...?

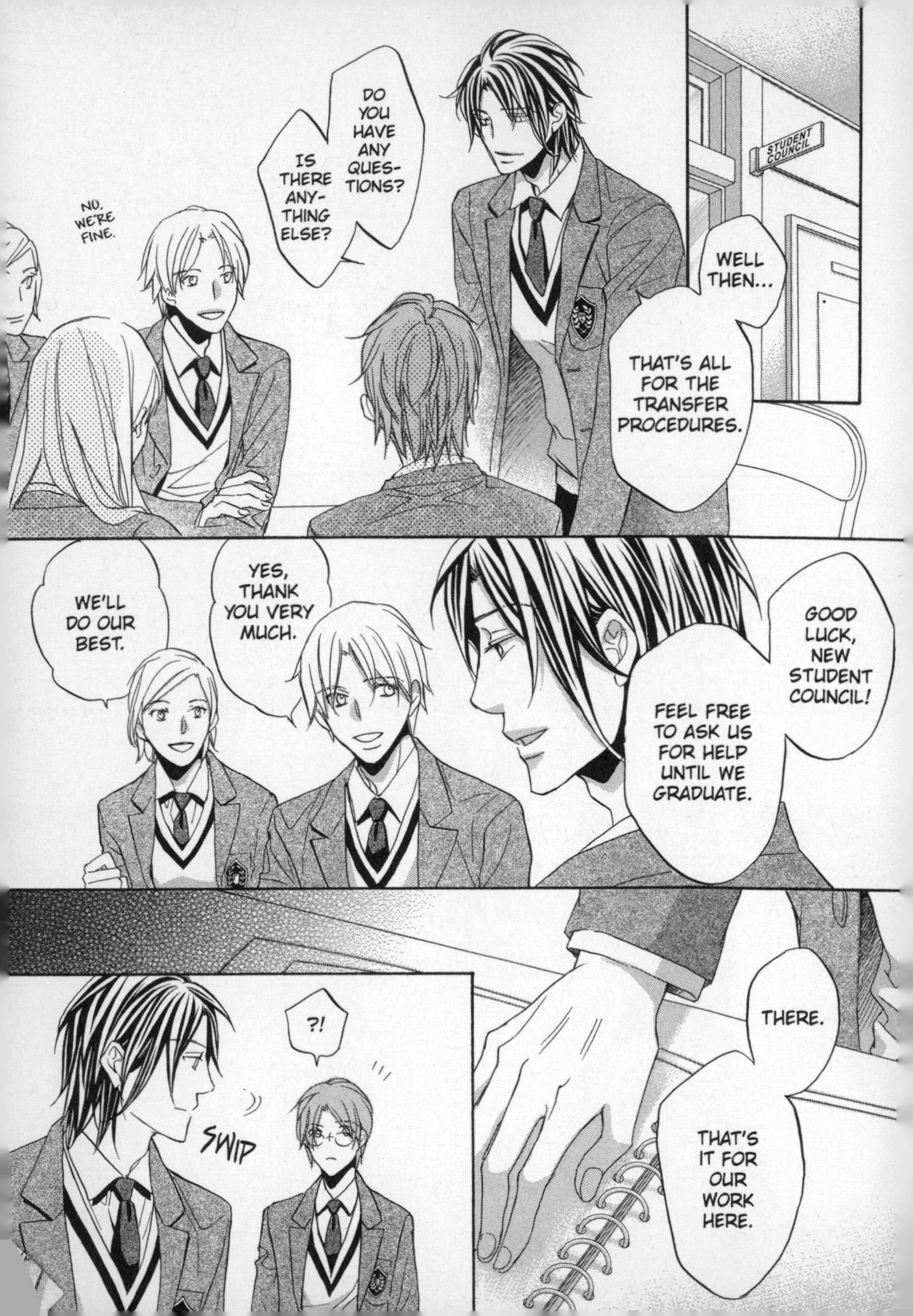
STUDENT COUNCIL
WELL THEN...
THAT'S ALL FOR THE TRANSFER PROCEDURES.
DO YOU HAVE ANY QUES-TIONS?
IS THERE ANY-THING ELSE?
NO, WE'RE FINE.
GOOD LUCK, NEW STUDENT COUNCIL!
FEEL FREE TO ASK US FOR HELP UNTIL WE GRADUATE.
YES, THANK YOU VERY MUCH.
WE'LL DO OUR BEST.
THERE.
THAT'S IT FOR OUR WORK HERE.
?!
SWIP

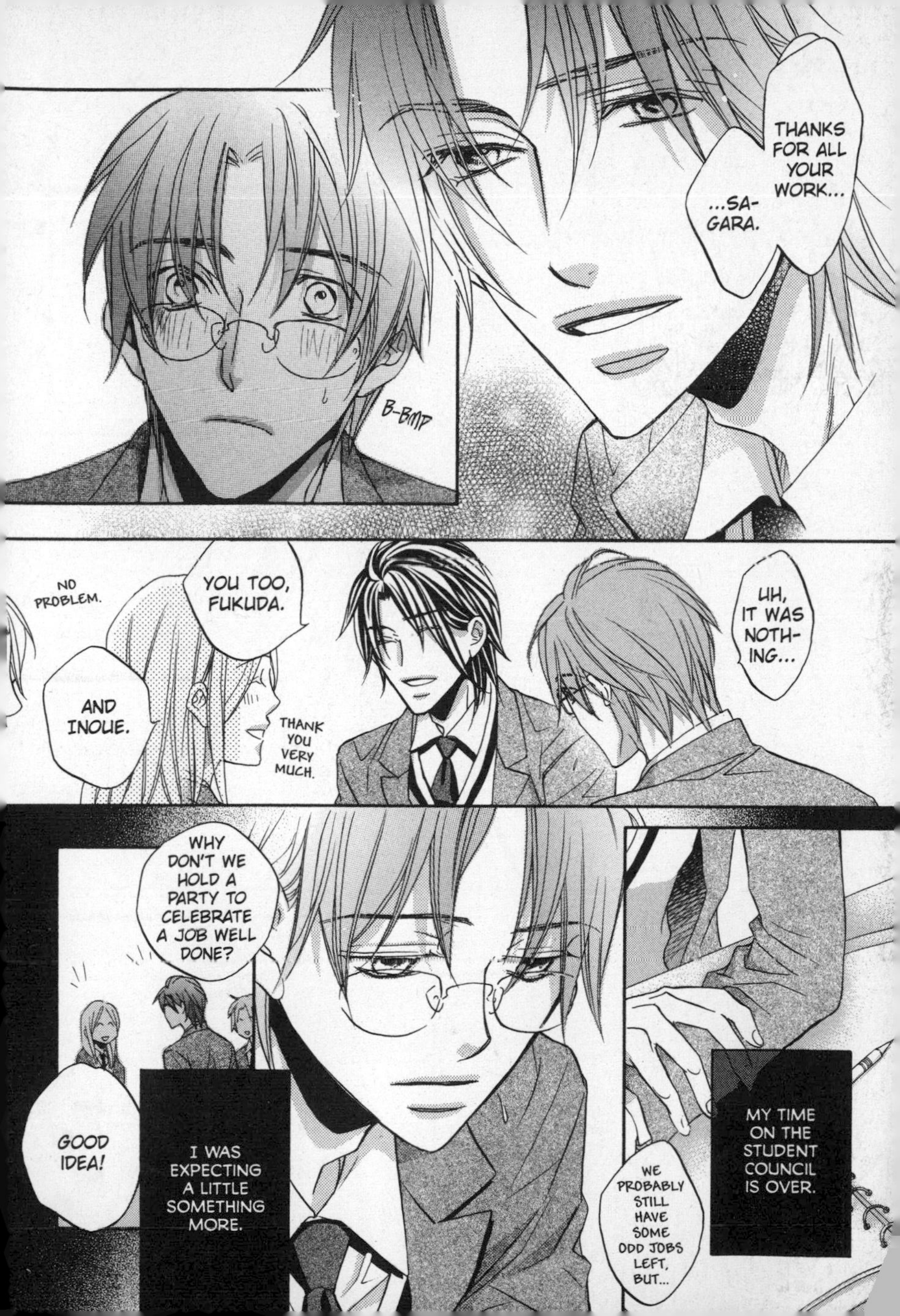
THANKS FOR ALL YOUR WORK...
...SA-GARA.
B-BMP
UH, IT WAS NOTHING...
YOU TOO, FUKUDA.
THANK YOU VERY MUCH.
AND INOUE.
NO PROBLEM.
MY TIME ON THE STUDENT COUNCIL IS OVER.
WE PROBABLY STILL HAVE SOME ODD JOBS LEFT, BUT...
WHY DON'T WE HOLD A PARTY TO CELEBRATE A JOB WELL DONE?
GOOD IDEA!
I WAS EXPECTING A LITTLE SOMETHING MORE.

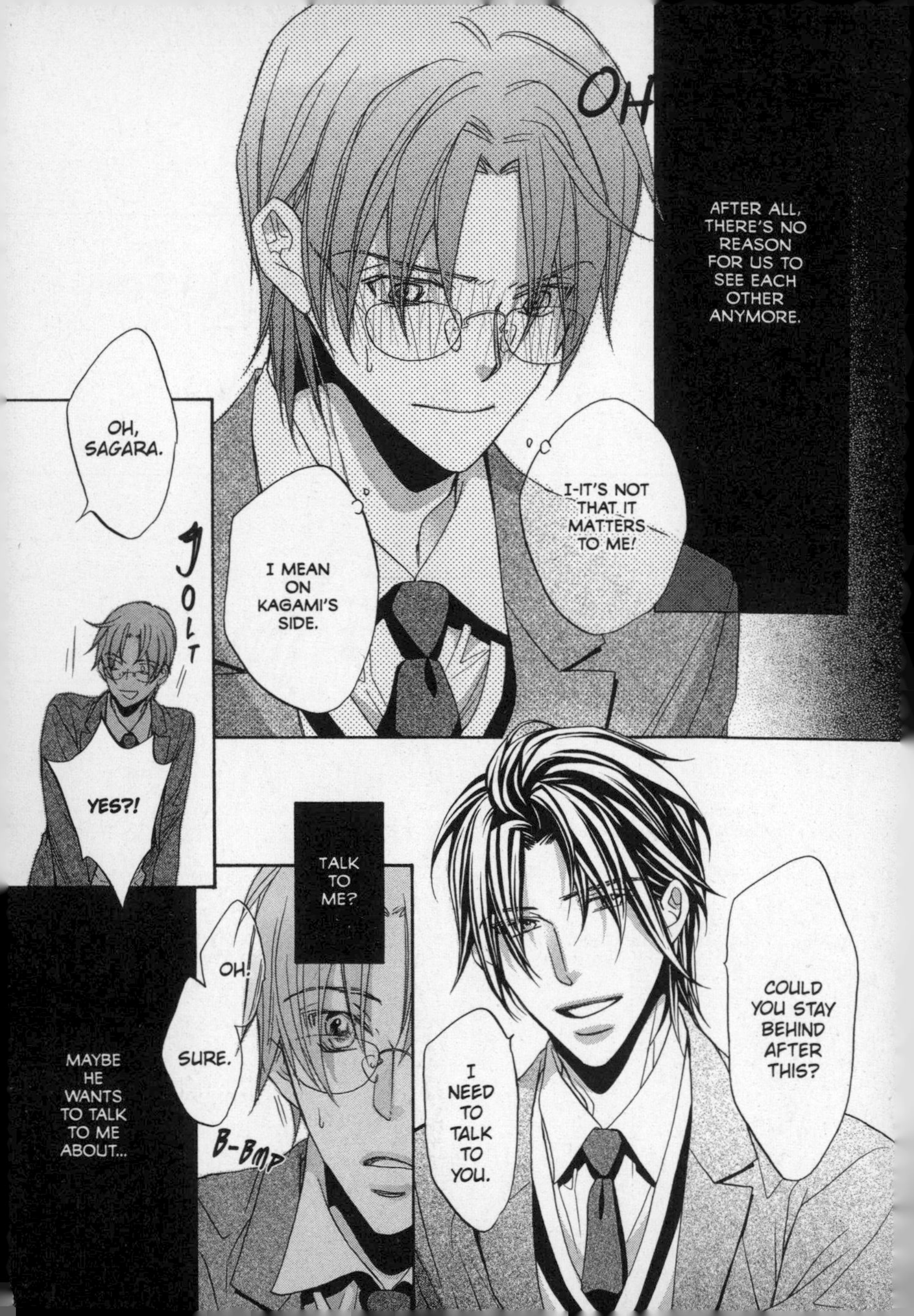
OH
AFTER ALL, THERE'S NO REASON FOR US TO SEE EACH OTHER ANYMORE.
I-IT'S NOT THAT IT MATTERS TO ME!
I MEAN ON KAGAMI'S SIDE.
OH, SAGARA.
JOLT
YES?!
COULD YOU STAY BEHIND AFTER THIS?
I NEED TO TALK TO YOU.
TALK TO ME?
OH!
SURE.
B-BMP
MAYBE HE WANTS TO TALK TO ME ABOUT...

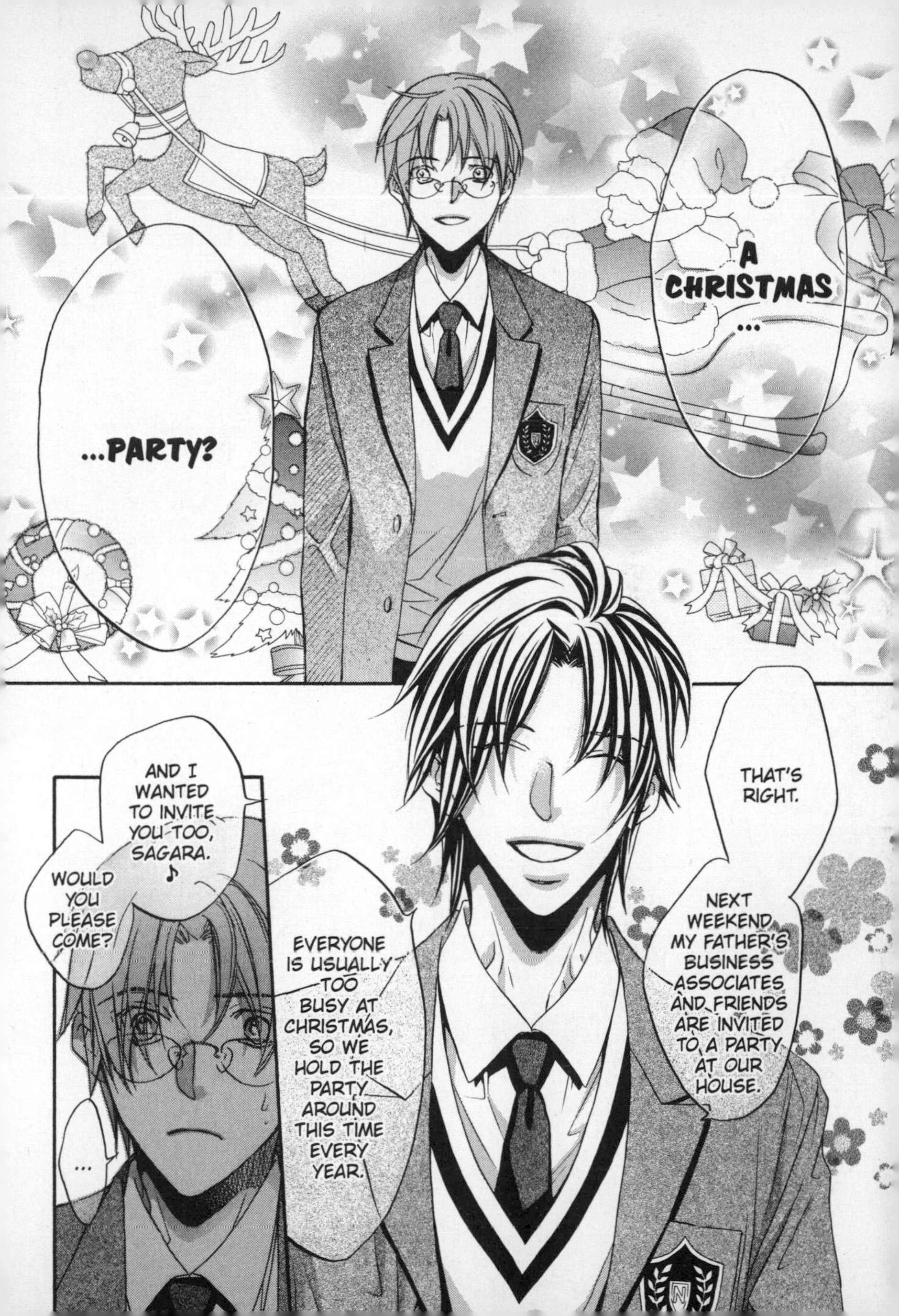
A CHRISTMAS ...
...PARTY?
THAT'S RIGHT.
NEXT WEEKEND MY FATHER'S BUSINESS ASSOCIATES AND FRIENDS ARE INVITED TO A PARTY AT OUR HOUSE.
EVERYONE IS USUALLY TOO BUSY AT CHRISTMAS, SO WE HOLD THE PARTY AROUND THIS TIME EVERY YEAR.
AND I WANTED TO INVITE YOU TOO, SAGARA. ♪
WOULD YOU PLEASE COME?
...

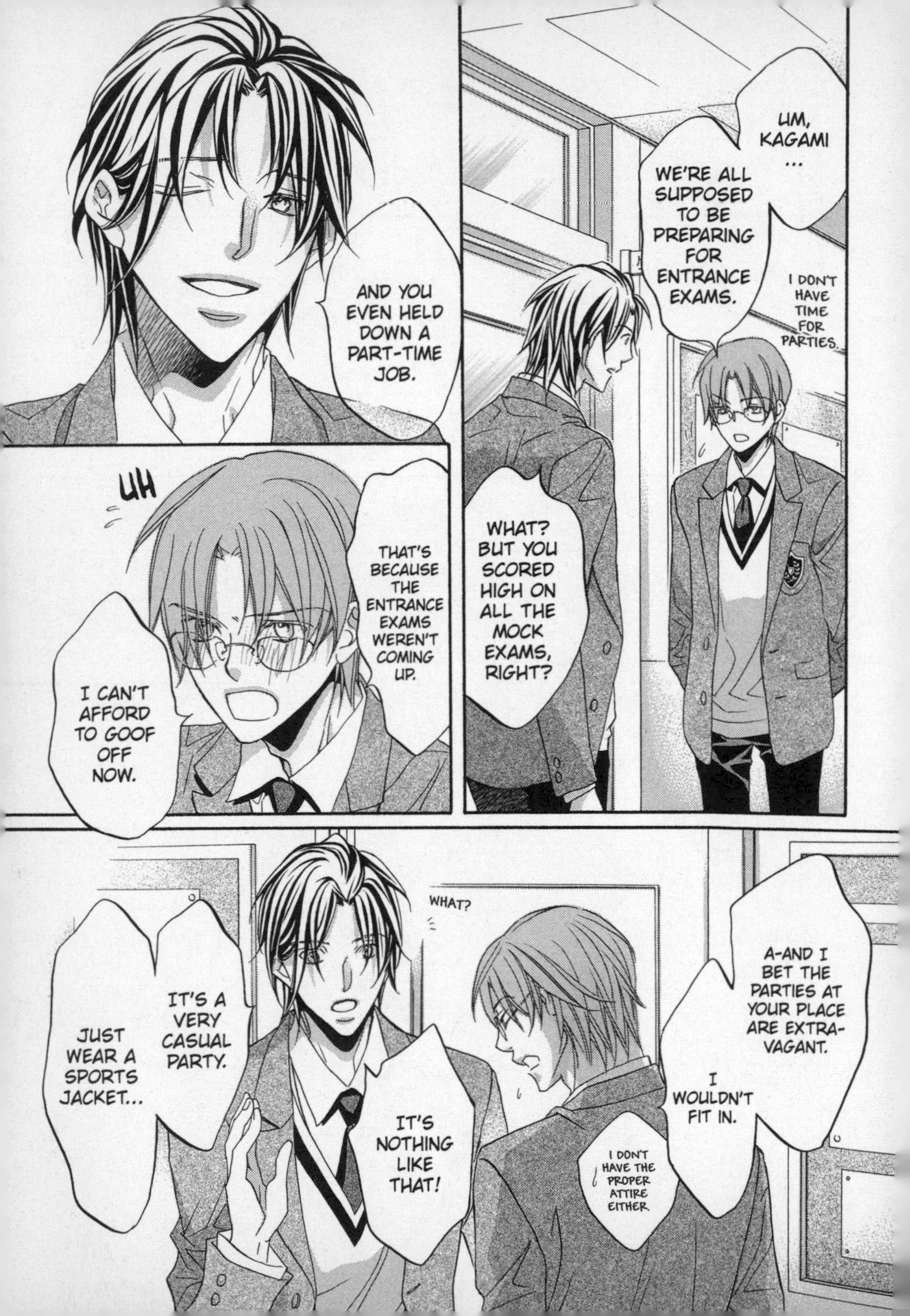
UM, KAGAMI...
WE'RE ALL SUPPOSED TO BE PREPARING FOR ENTRANCE EXAMS.
I DON'T HAVE TIME FOR PARTIES.
WHAT? BUT YOU SCORED HIGH ON ALL THE MOCK EXAMS, RIGHT?
AND YOU EVEN HELD DOWN A PART-TIME JOB.
UH
THAT'S BECAUSE THE ENTRANCE EXAMS WEREN'T COMING UP.
I CAN'T AFFORD TO GOOF OFF NOW.
A-AND I BET THE PARTIES AT YOUR PLACE ARE EXTRA-VAGANT.
I WOULDN'T FIT IN.
I DON'T HAVE THE PROPER ATTIRE EITHER.
WHAT?
IT'S NOTHING LIKE THAT!
IT'S A VERY CASUAL PARTY.
JUST WEAR A SPORTS JACKET...

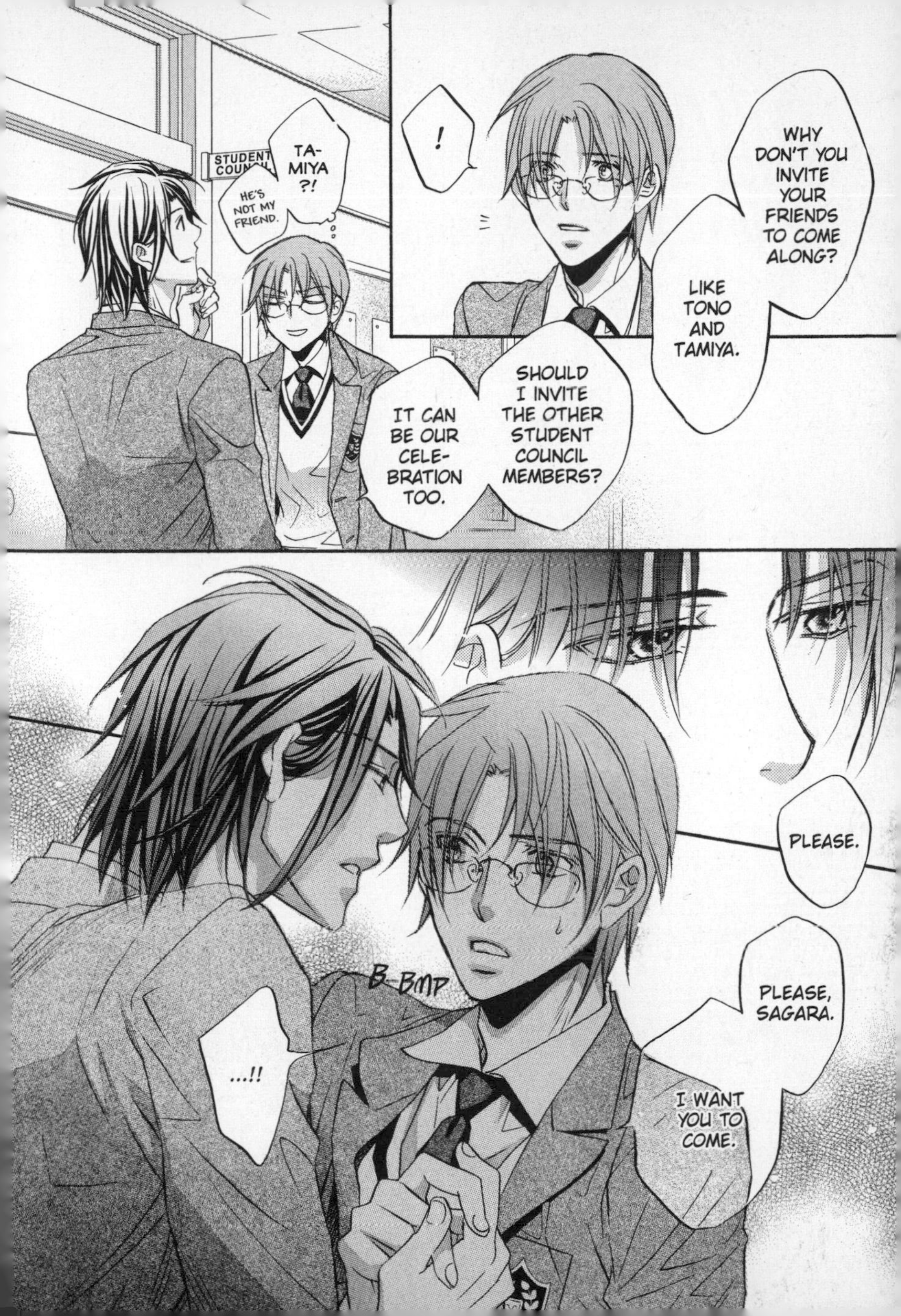
WHY DON'T YOU INVITE YOUR FRIENDS TO COME ALONG?
LIKE TONO AND TAMIYA.
!
STUDENT
TA-MIYA ?!
HE'S NOT MY FRIEND.
SHOULD I INVITE THE OTHER STUDENT COUNCIL MEMBERS?
IT CAN BE OUR CELE-BRATION TOO.
PLEASE.
PLEASE, SAGARA.
I WANT YOU TO COME.
B-BMP
...!!

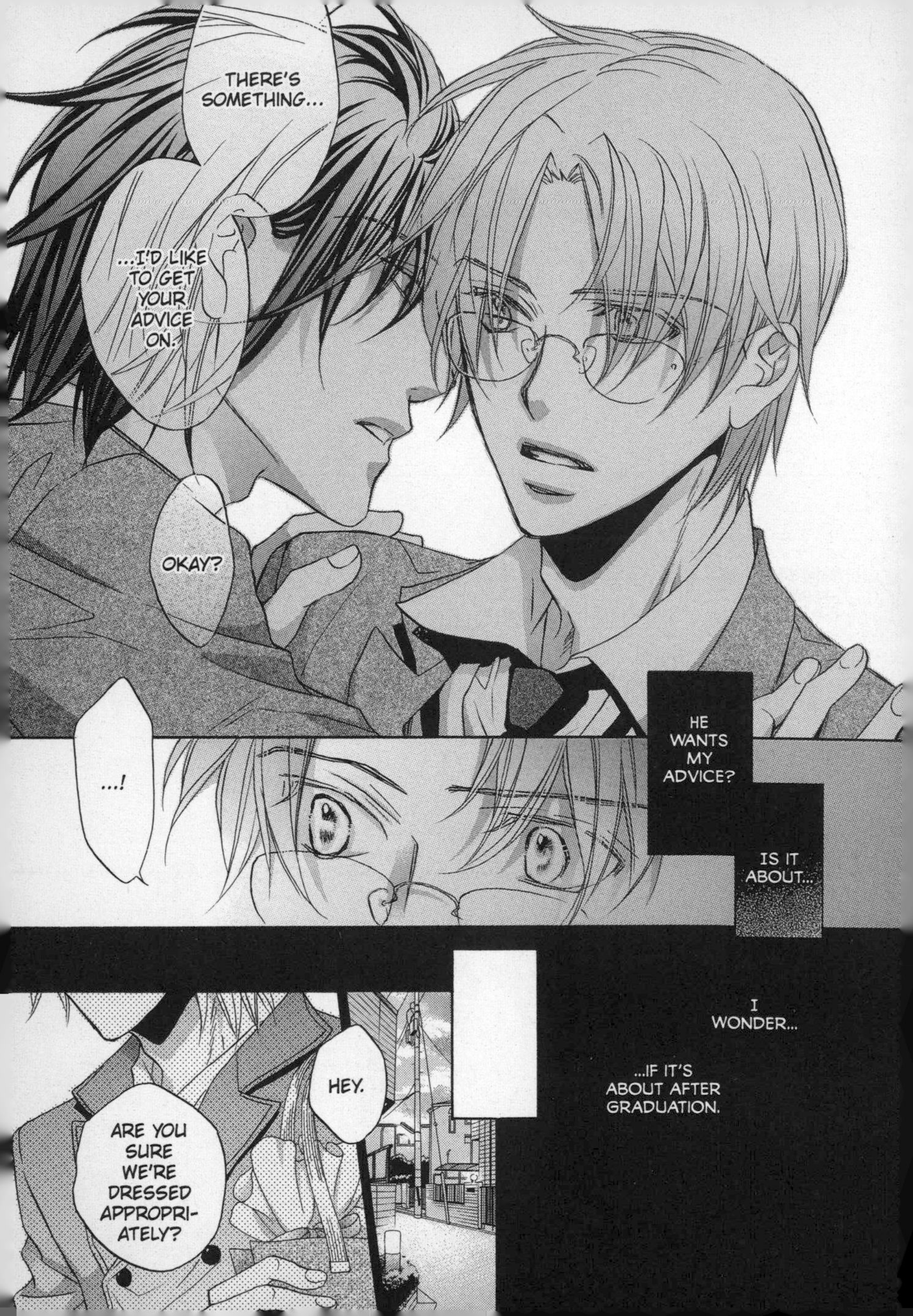
THERE'S SOMETHING...
...I'D LIKE TO GET YOUR ADVICE ON.
OKAY?
HE WANTS MY ADVICE?
IS IT ABOUT...
...!
I WONDER...
...IF IT'S ABOUT AFTER GRADUATION.
HEY.
ARE YOU SURE WE'RE DRESSED APPROPRI-ATELY?

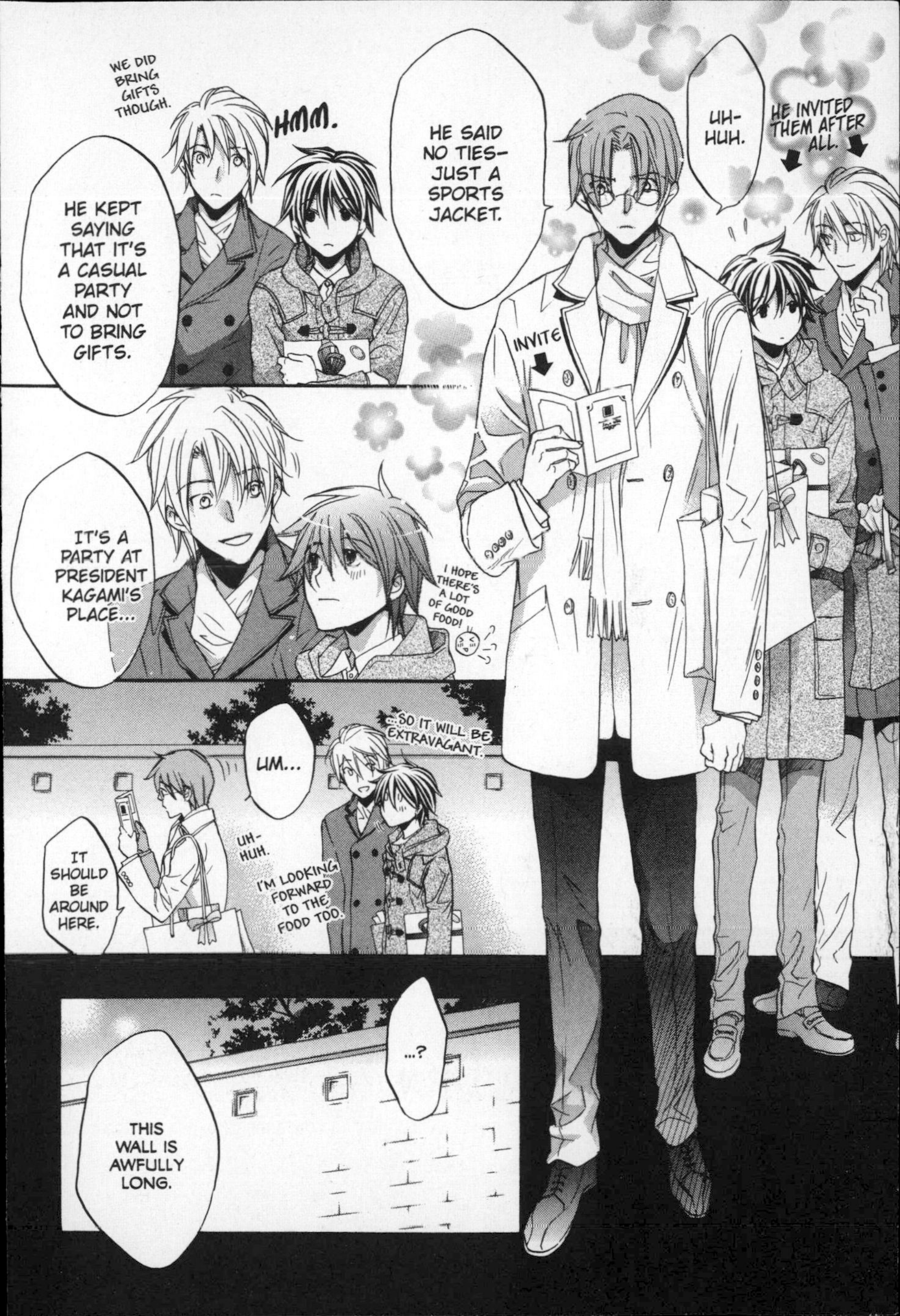
HE INVITED THEM AFTER ALL.
UH-HUH.
HE SAID NO TIES- JUST A SPORTS JACKET.
INVITE
HE KEPT SAYING THAT IT'S A CASUAL PARTY AND NOT TO BRING GIFTS.
HMM.
WE DID BRING GIFTS THOUGH.
I HOPE THERE'S A LOT OF GOOD FOOD!
IT'S A PARTY AT PRESIDENT KAGAMI'S PLACE...
...SO IT WILL BE EXTRAVAGANT.
UM...
UH-HUH.
I'M LOOKING FORWARD TO THE FOOD TOO.
IT SHOULD BE AROUND HERE.
...?
THIS WALL IS AWFULLY LONG.

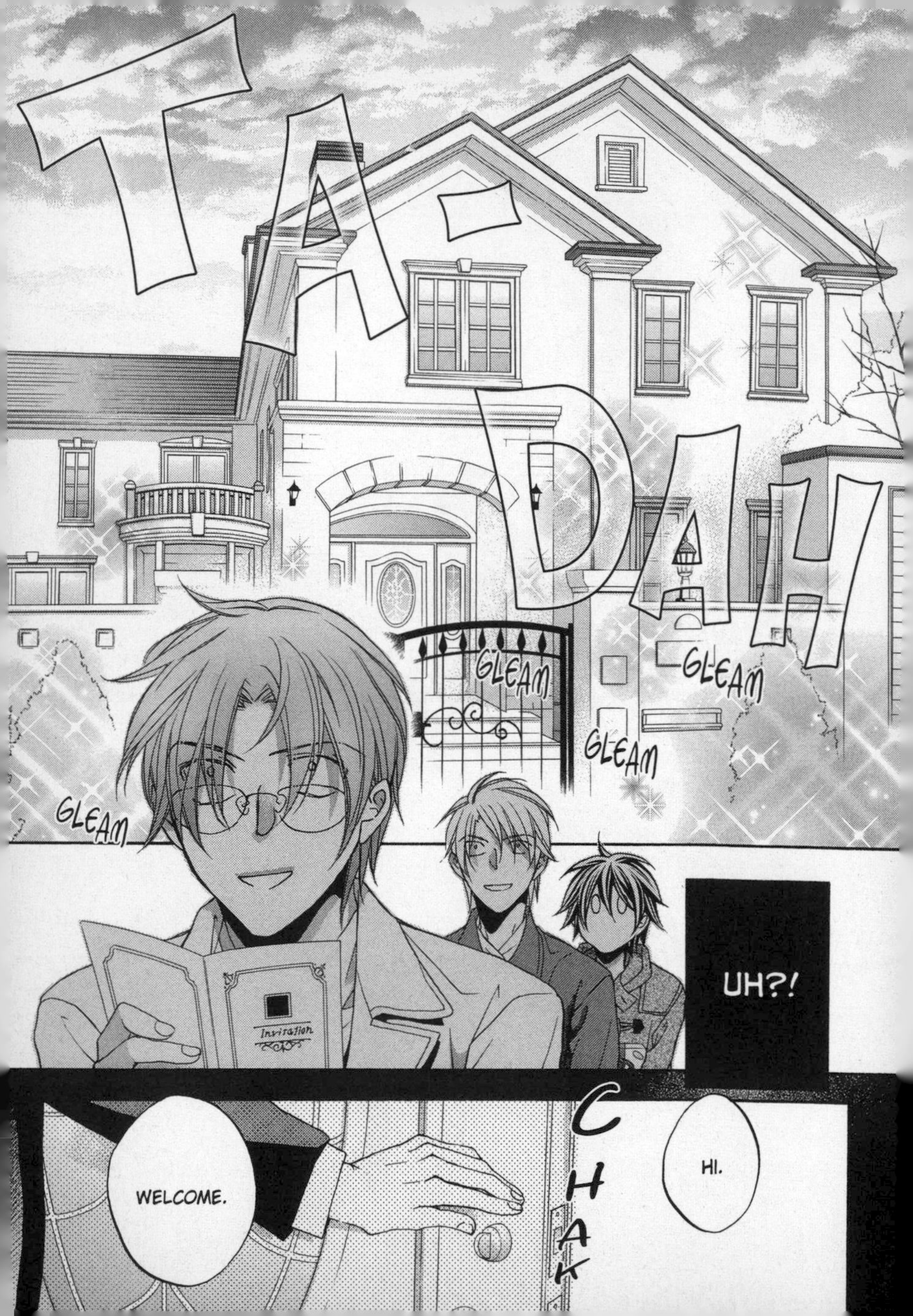
TA-DAH
GLEAM
GLEAM
GLEAM
GLEAM
UH?!
Invitation
HI.
CHAK
WELCOME.

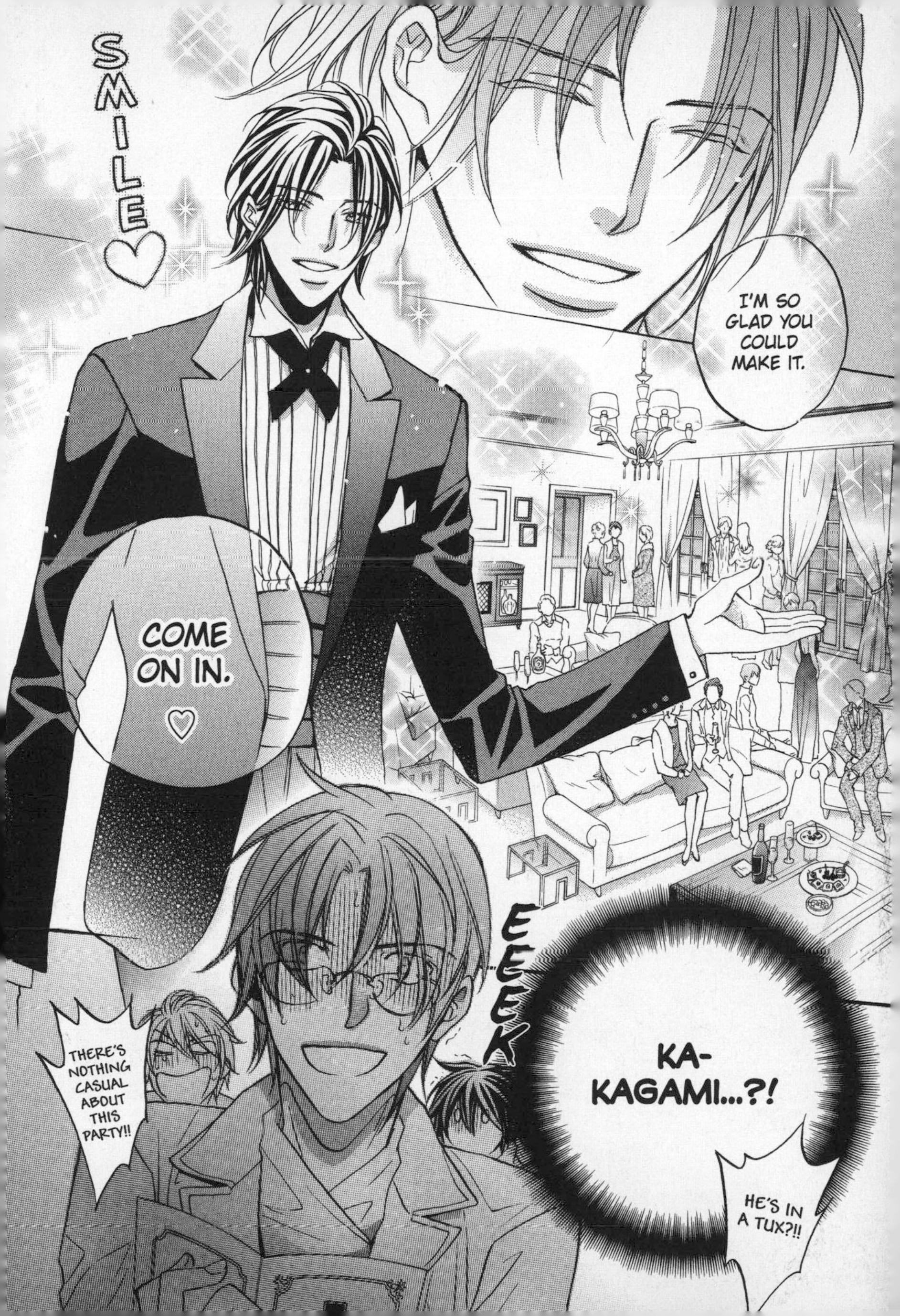
I'M SO GLAD YOU COULD MAKE IT.
SMILE ♥
COME ON IN. ♥
KA-KAGAMI...?!
EEEEK
HE'S IN A TUX?!!
THERE'S NOTHING CASUAL ABOUT THIS PARTY!!

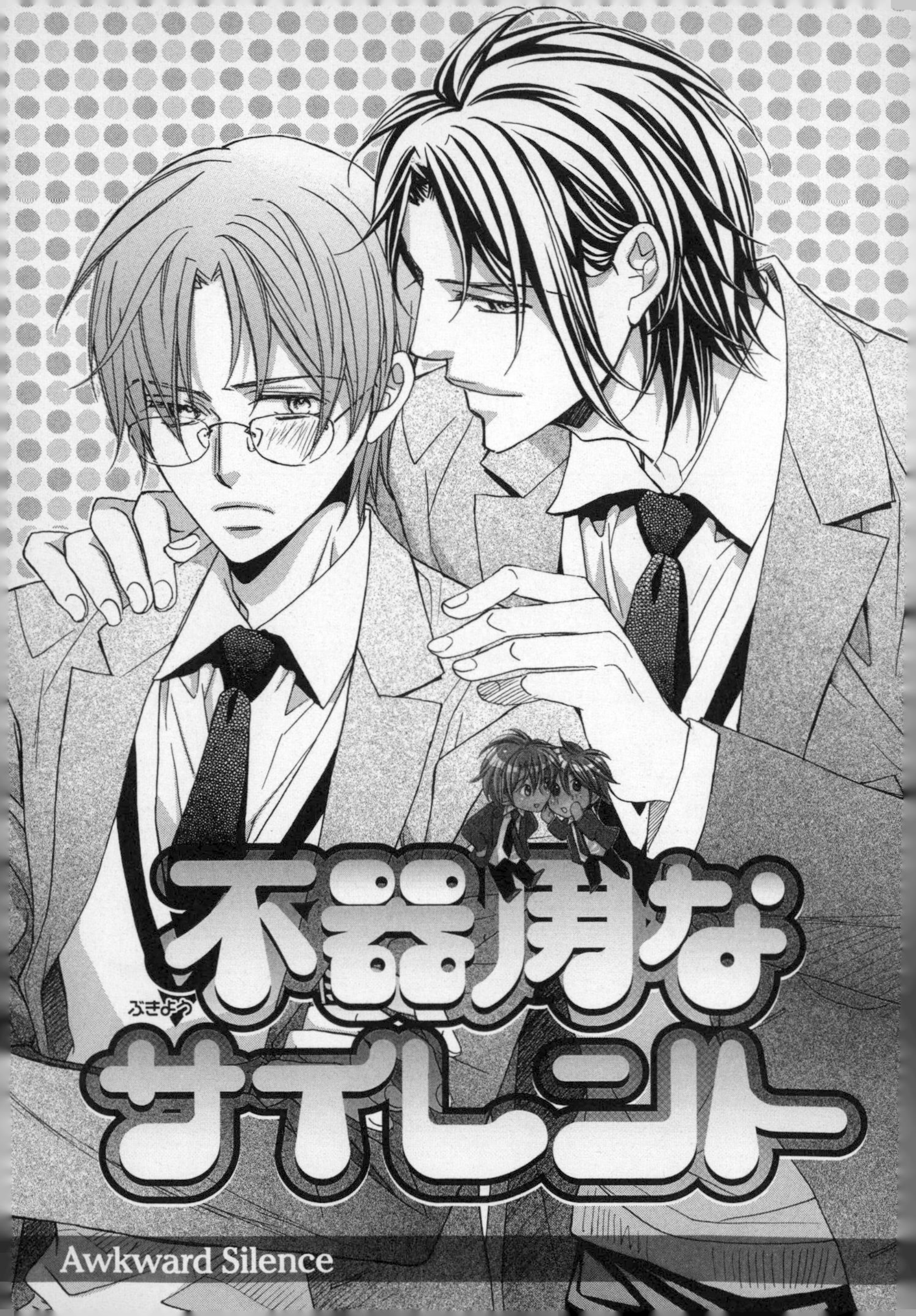
不器用なサイレント
ぶきよう
Awkward Silence

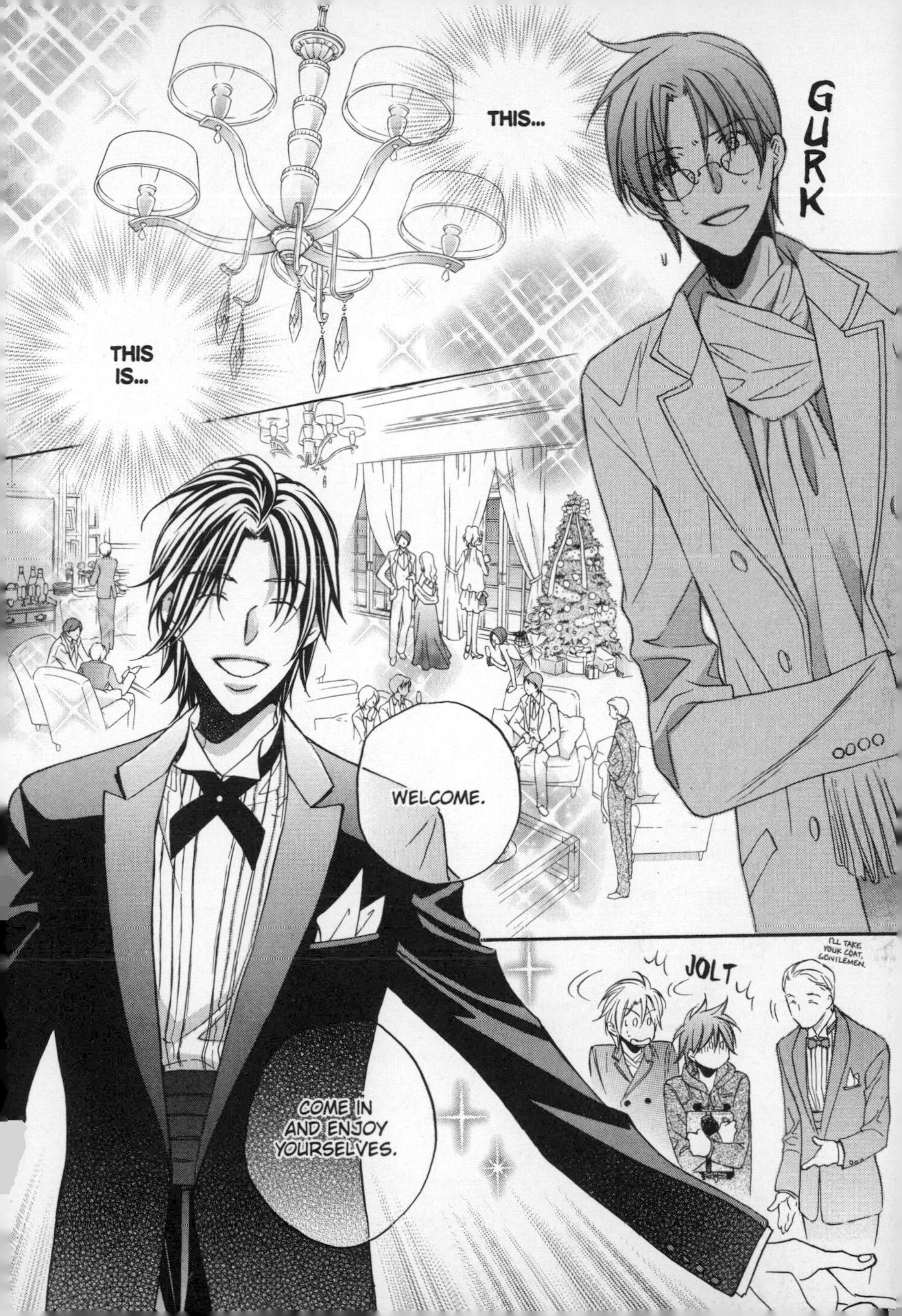
GURK
THIS...
THIS IS...
WELCOME.
COME IN AND ENJOY YOURSELVES.
JOLT
I'LL TAKE YOUR COAT, GENTLEMEN.

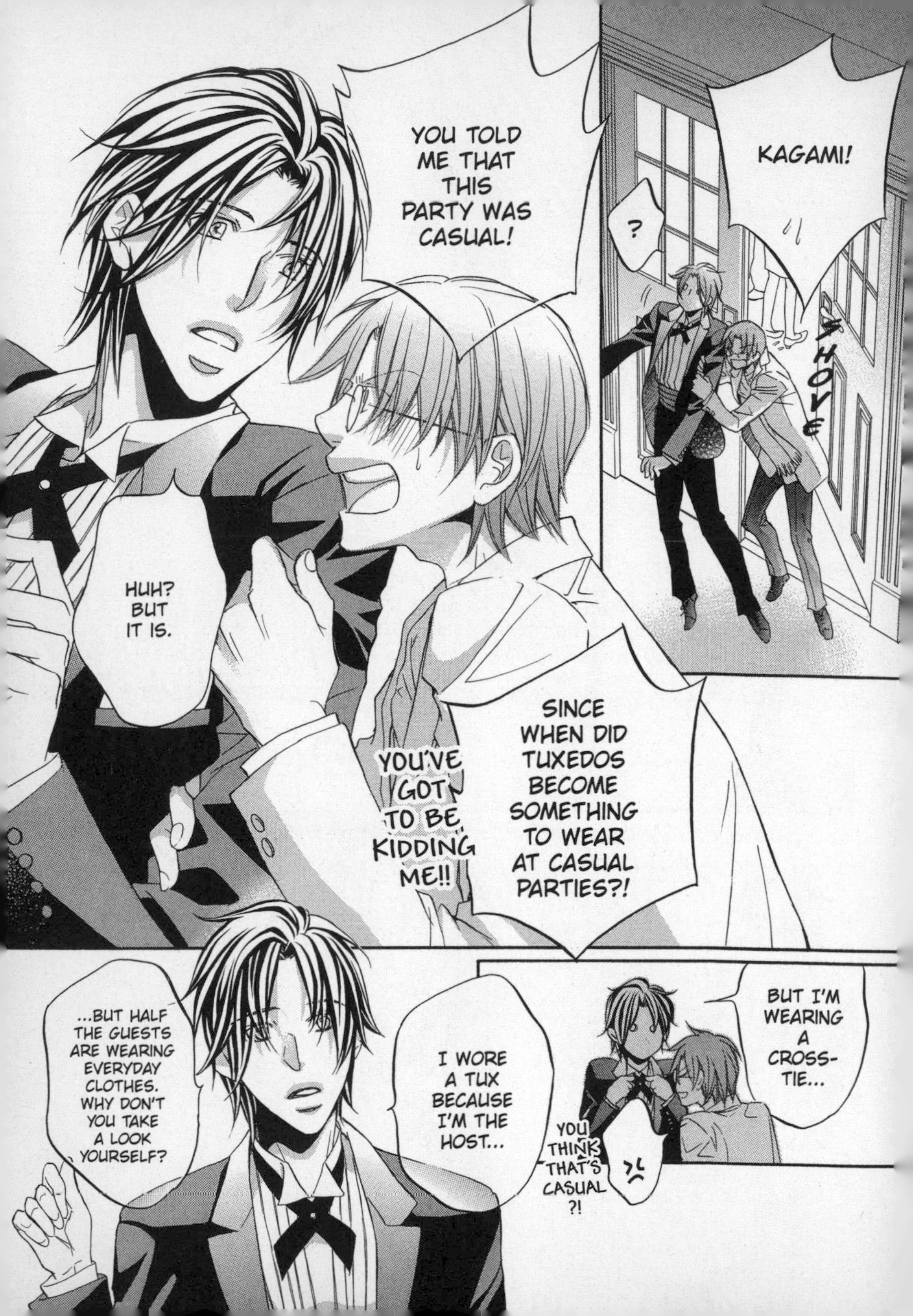
KAGAMI!
?
SHOVE
YOU TOLD ME THAT THIS PARTY WAS CASUAL!
HUH? BUT IT IS.
SINCE WHEN DID TUXEDOS BECOME SOMETHING TO WEAR AT CASUAL PARTIES?!
YOU'VE GOT TO BE KIDDING ME!!
BUT I'M WEARING A CROSS-TIE...
YOU THINK THAT'S CASUAL ?!
I WORE A TUX BECAUSE I'M THE HOST...
...BUT HALF THE GUESTS ARE WEARING EVERYDAY CLOTHES. WHY DON'T YOU TAKE A LOOK YOURSELF?

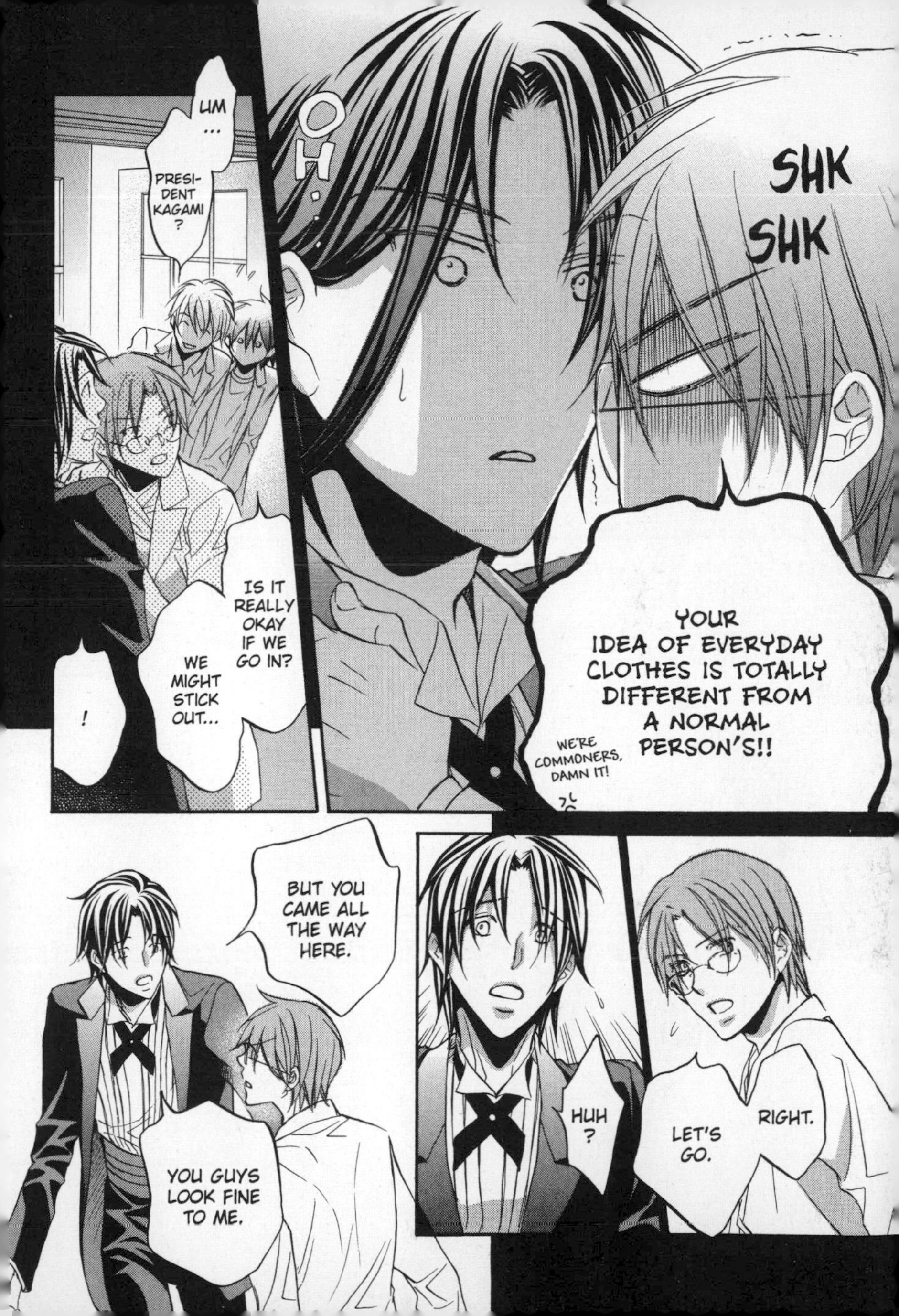
SHK
SHK
OH...
YOUR IDEA OF EVERYDAY CLOTHES IS TOTALLY DIFFERENT FROM A NORMAL PERSON'S!!
WE'RE COMMONERS, DAMN IT!
UM ...
PRESIDENT KAGAMI?
IS IT REALLY OKAY IF WE GO IN?
WE MIGHT STICK OUT...
!
RIGHT.
LET'S GO.
HUH?
BUT YOU CAME ALL THE WAY HERE.
YOU GUYS LOOK FINE TO ME.

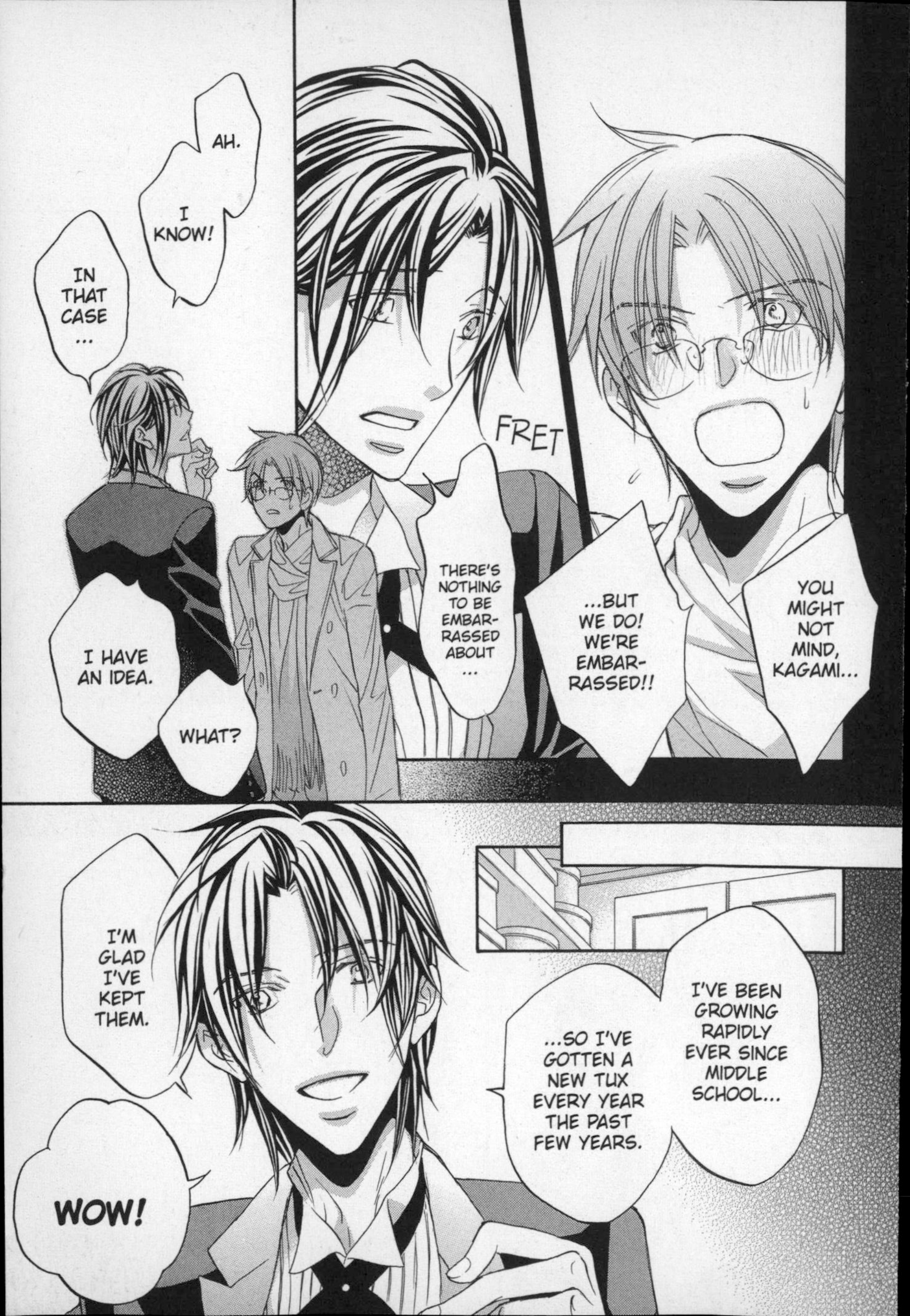
YOU MIGHT NOT MIND, KAGAMI...
...BUT WE DO! WE'RE EMBARRASSED!!
FRET
THERE'S NOTHING TO BE EMBARRASSED ABOUT...
AH.
I KNOW!
IN THAT CASE...
I HAVE AN IDEA.
WHAT?
I'VE BEEN GROWING RAPIDLY EVER SINCE MIDDLE SCHOOL...
...SO I'VE GOTTEN A NEW TUX EVERY YEAR THE PAST FEW YEARS.
I'M GLAD I'VE KEPT THEM.
WOW!

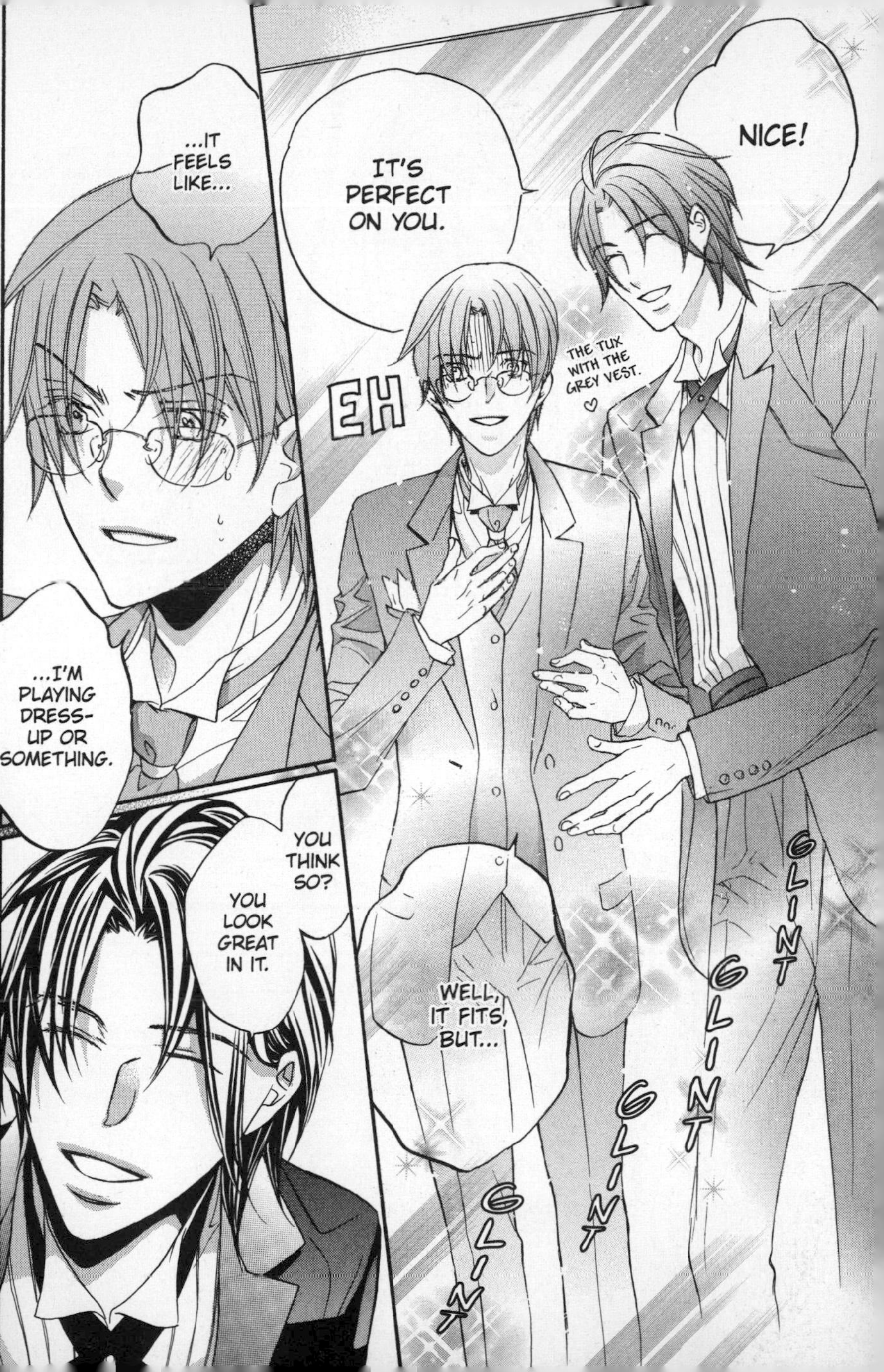
NICE!
IT'S PERFECT ON YOU.
THE TUX WITH THE GREY VEST. ♡
EH
GLINT
GLINT
GLINT
GLINT
WELL, IT FITS, BUT...
...IT FEELS LIKE...
...I'M PLAYING DRESS-UP OR SOMETHING.
YOU THINK SO?
YOU LOOK GREAT IN IT.

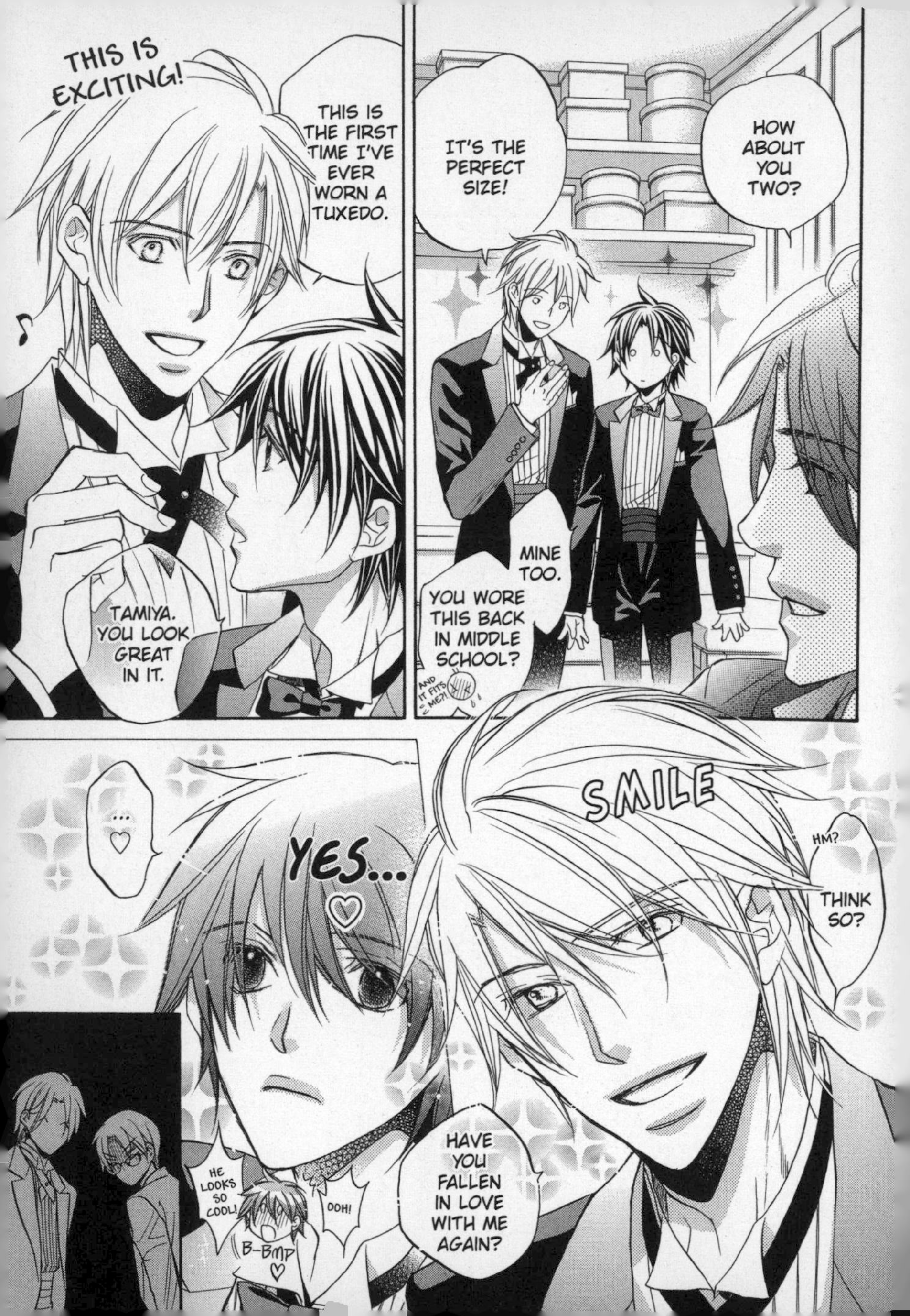
HOW ABOUT YOU TWO?
IT'S THE PERFECT SIZE!
MINE TOO.
YOU WORE THIS BACK IN MIDDLE SCHOOL?
AND IT FITS ME?!
THIS IS THE FIRST TIME I'VE EVER WORN A TUXEDO.
THIS IS EXCITING!
TAMIYA. YOU LOOK GREAT IN IT.
SMILE
HM?
THINK SO?
HAVE YOU FALLEN IN LOVE WITH ME AGAIN?
YES... ♡
... ♡
OOH!
HE LOOKS SO COOL!
B-BMP ♡

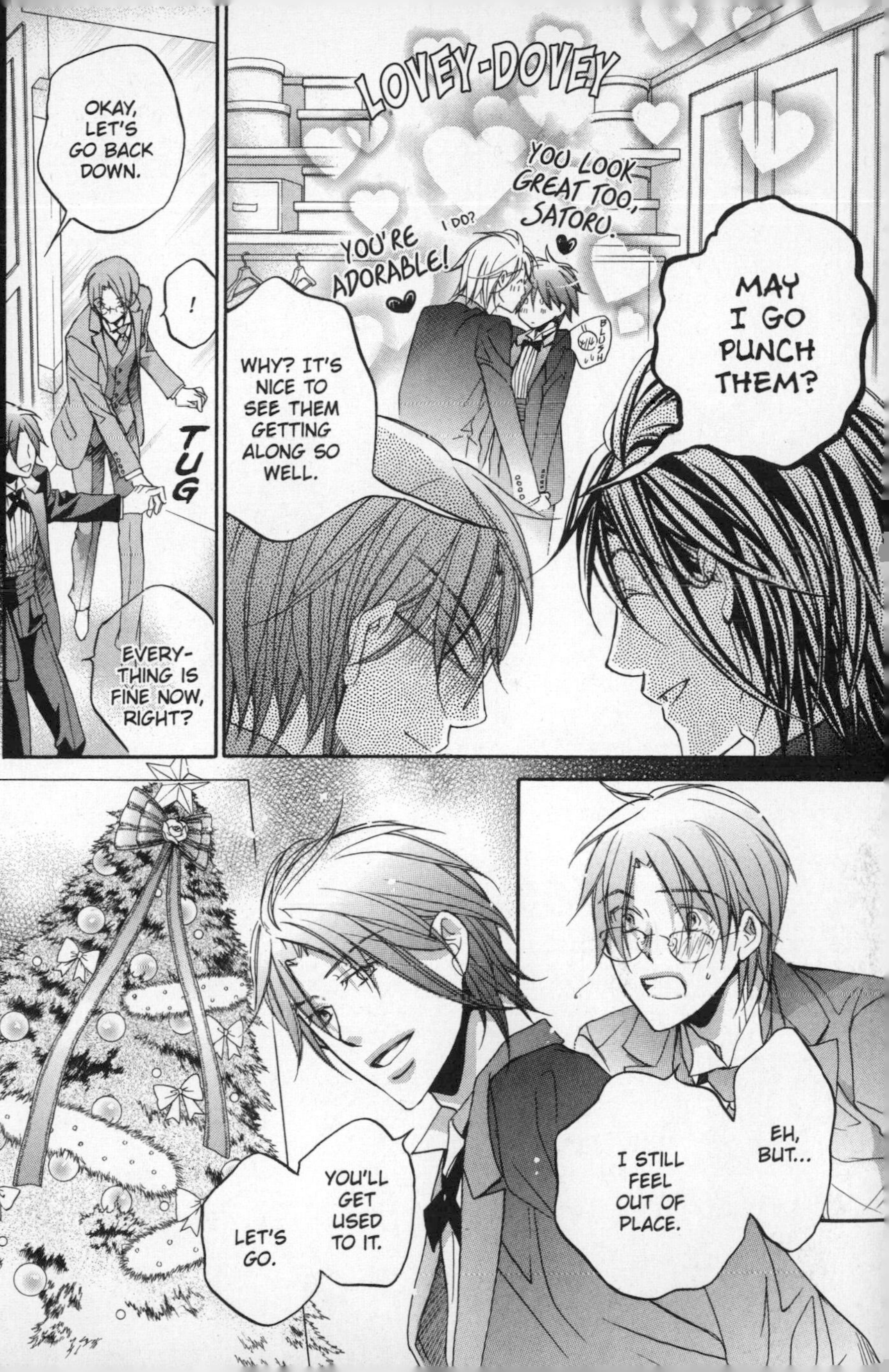
LOVEY-DOVEY
YOU LOOK GREAT TOO, SATORU.
I DO?
YOU'RE ADORABLE!
BLUSH
MAY I GO PUNCH THEM?
WHY? IT'S NICE TO SEE THEM GETTING ALONG SO WELL.
OKAY, LET'S GO BACK DOWN.
!
TUG
EVERY-THING IS FINE NOW, RIGHT?
EH, BUT...
I STILL FEEL OUT OF PLACE.
YOU'LL GET USED TO IT.
LET'S GO.

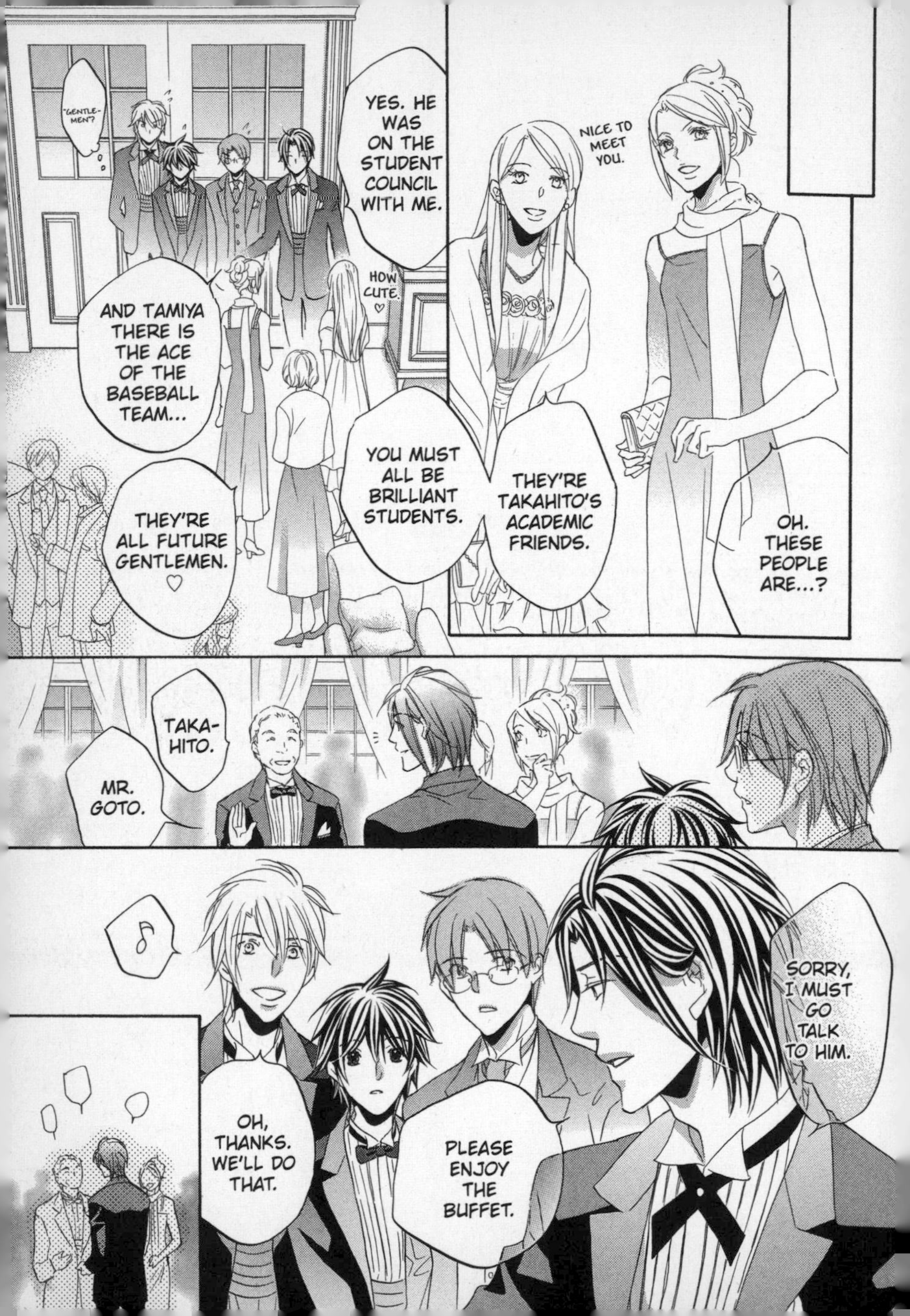

OH. THESE PEOPLE ARE...?
THEY'RE TAKAHITO'S ACADEMIC FRIENDS.
NICE TO MEET YOU.
YES. HE WAS ON THE STUDENT COUNCIL WITH ME.
HOW CUTE. ♡
AND TAMIYA THERE IS THE ACE OF THE BASEBALL TEAM...
YOU MUST ALL BE BRILLIANT STUDENTS.
THEY'RE ALL FUTURE GENTLEMEN. ♡
"GENTLEMEN"?
TAKA-HITO.
MR. GOTO.
SORRY, I MUST GO TALK TO HIM.
PLEASE ENJOY THE BUFFET.
OH, THANKS. WE'LL DO THAT.
♪

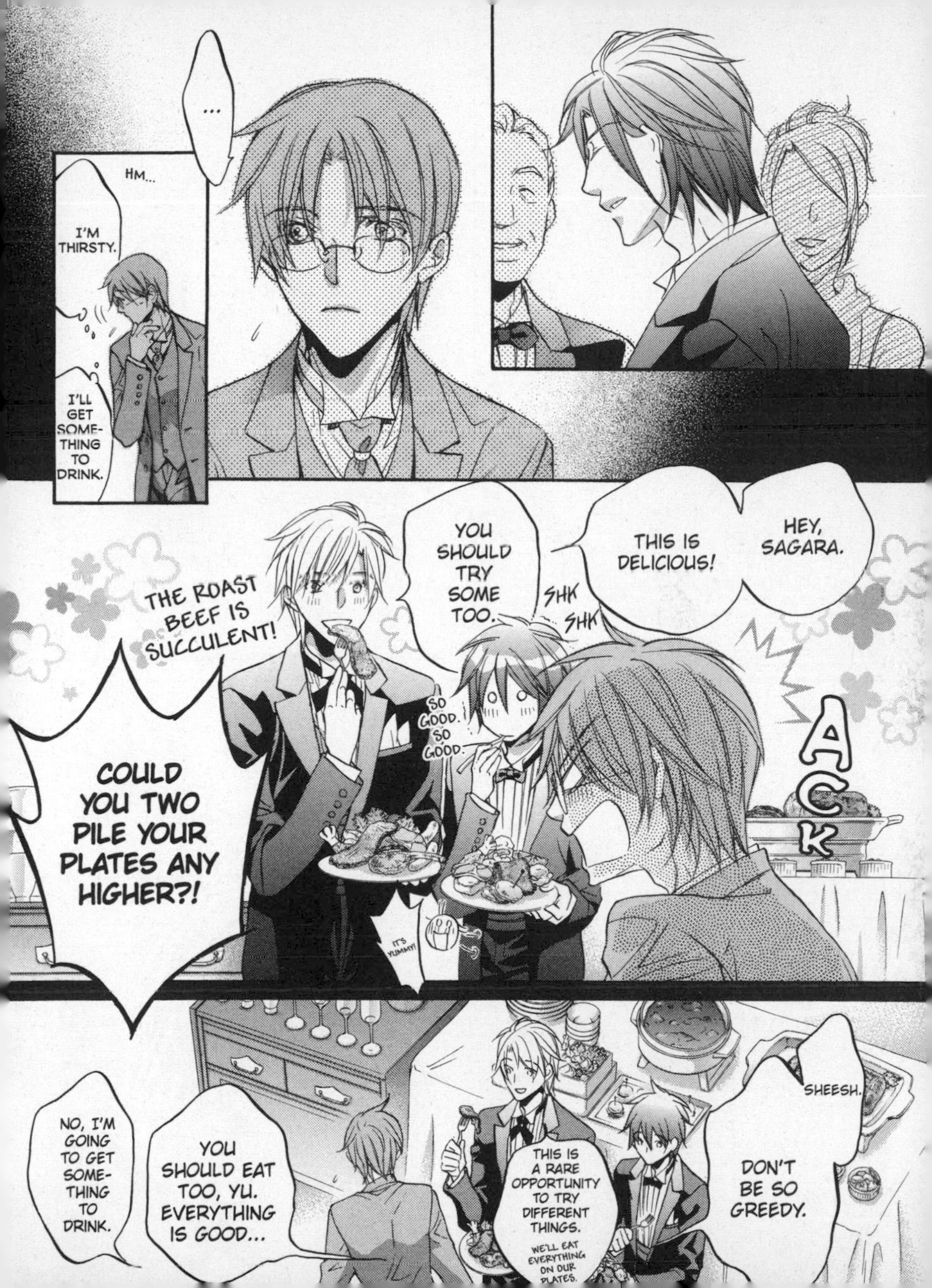
...
HM...
I'M THIRSTY.
I'LL GET SOMETHING TO DRINK.
HEY, SAGARA.
THIS IS DELICIOUS!
SHK SHK
YOU SHOULD TRY SOME TOO.
THE ROAST BEEF IS SUCCULENT!
ACK
SO GOOD. SO GOOD.
COULD YOU TWO PILE YOUR PLATES ANY HIGHER?!
IT'S YUMMY!
SHEESH.
DON'T BE SO GREEDY.
THIS IS A RARE OPPORTUNITY TO TRY DIFFERENT THINGS.
WE'LL EAT EVERYTHING ON OUR PLATES.
YOU SHOULD EAT TOO, YU. EVERYTHING IS GOOD...
NO, I'M GOING TO GET SOMETHING TO DRINK.

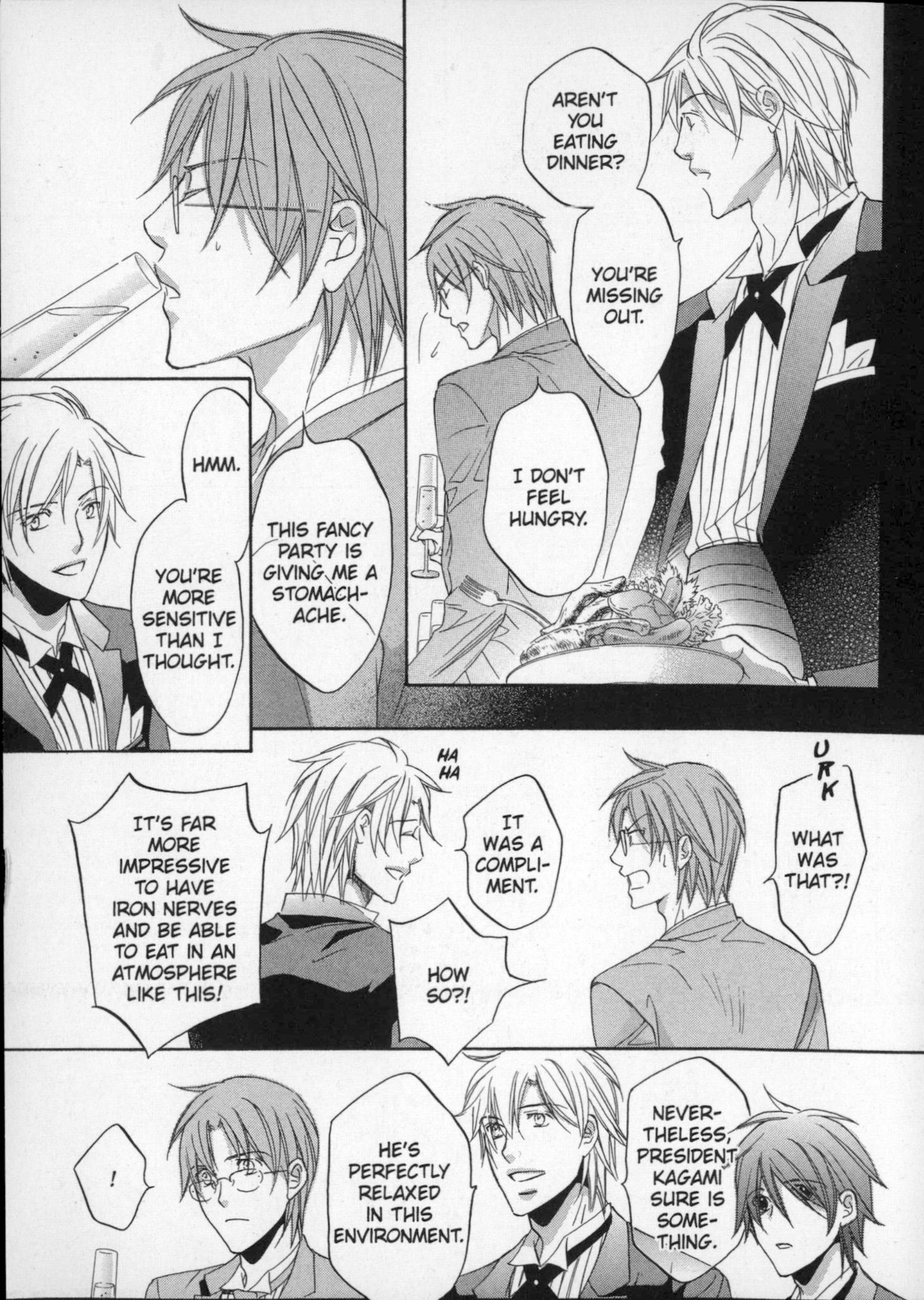
AREN'T YOU EATING DINNER?
YOU'RE MISSING OUT.
I DON'T FEEL HUNGRY.
THIS FANCY PARTY IS GIVING ME A STOMACH-ACHE.
HMM.
YOU'RE MORE SENSITIVE THAN I THOUGHT.
URK
WHAT WAS THAT?!
HA HA
IT WAS A COMPLI-MENT.
HOW SO?!
IT'S FAR MORE IMPRESSIVE TO HAVE IRON NERVES AND BE ABLE TO EAT IN AN ATMOSPHERE LIKE THIS!
NEVER-THELESS, PRESIDENT KAGAMI SURE IS SOME-THING.
HE'S PERFECTLY RELAXED IN THIS ENVIRONMENT.
!

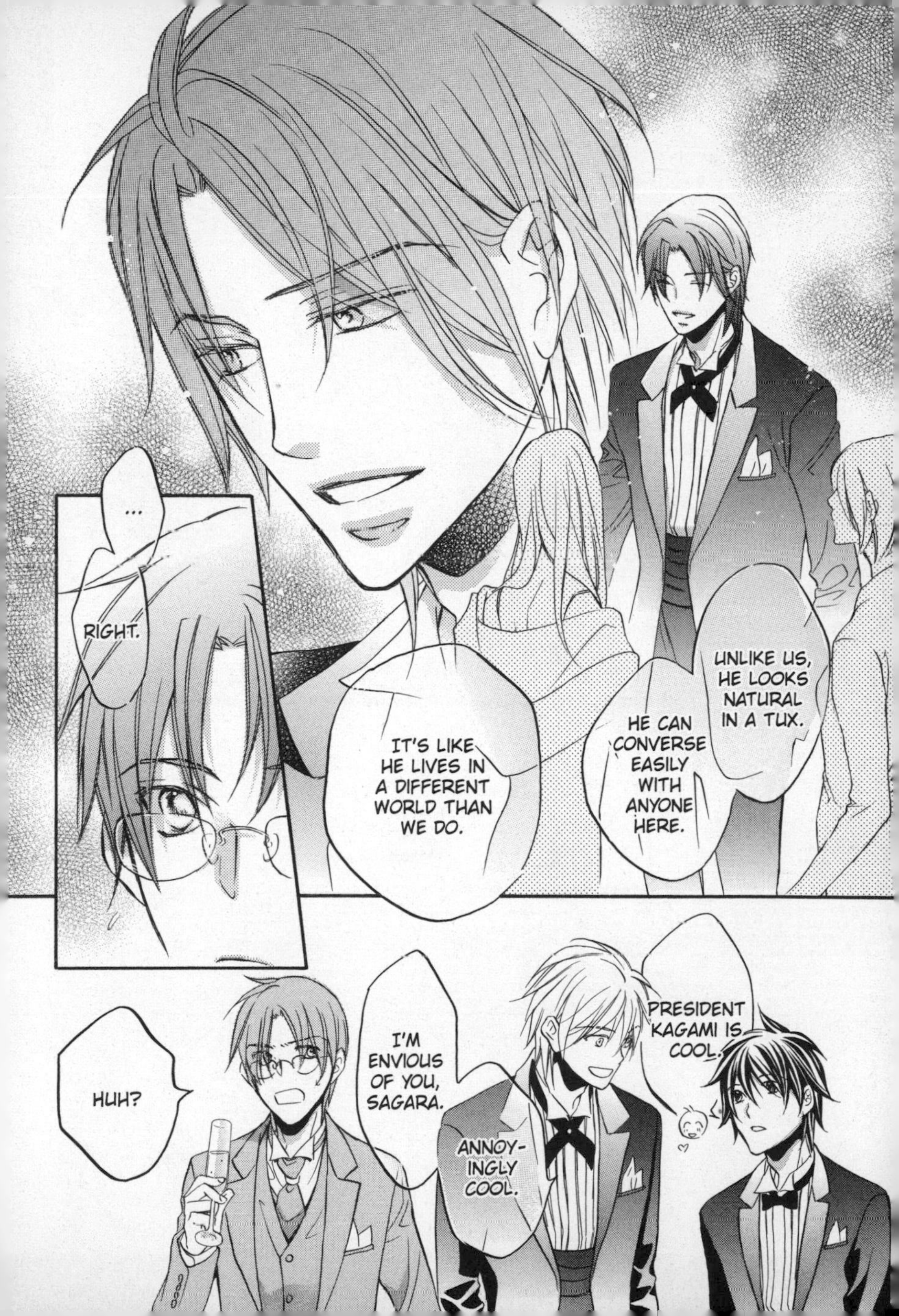
UNLIKE US, HE LOOKS NATURAL IN A TUX.
HE CAN CONVERSE EASILY WITH ANYONE HERE.
IT'S LIKE HE LIVES IN A DIFFERENT WORLD THAN WE DO.
...
RIGHT.
PRESIDENT KAGAMI IS COOL.
I'M ENVIOUS OF YOU, SAGARA.
ANNOY-INGLY COOL.
HUH?

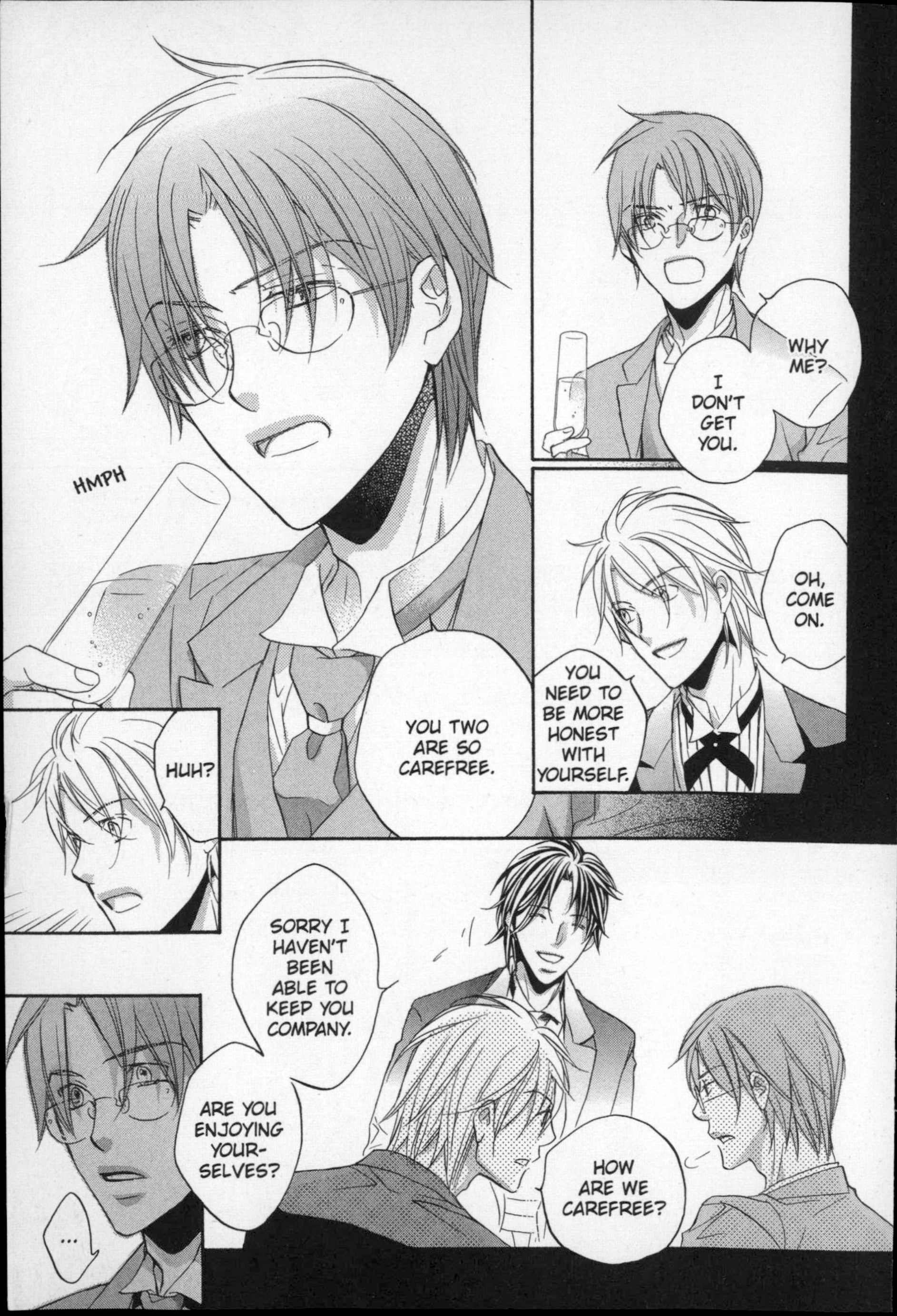
WHY ME?
I DON'T GET YOU.
OH, COME ON.
YOU NEED TO BE MORE HONEST WITH YOURSELF.
HMPH
YOU TWO ARE SO CAREFREE.
HUH?
SORRY I HAVEN'T BEEN ABLE TO KEEP YOU COMPANY.
ARE YOU ENJOYING YOUR-SELVES?
HOW ARE WE CAREFREE?
...

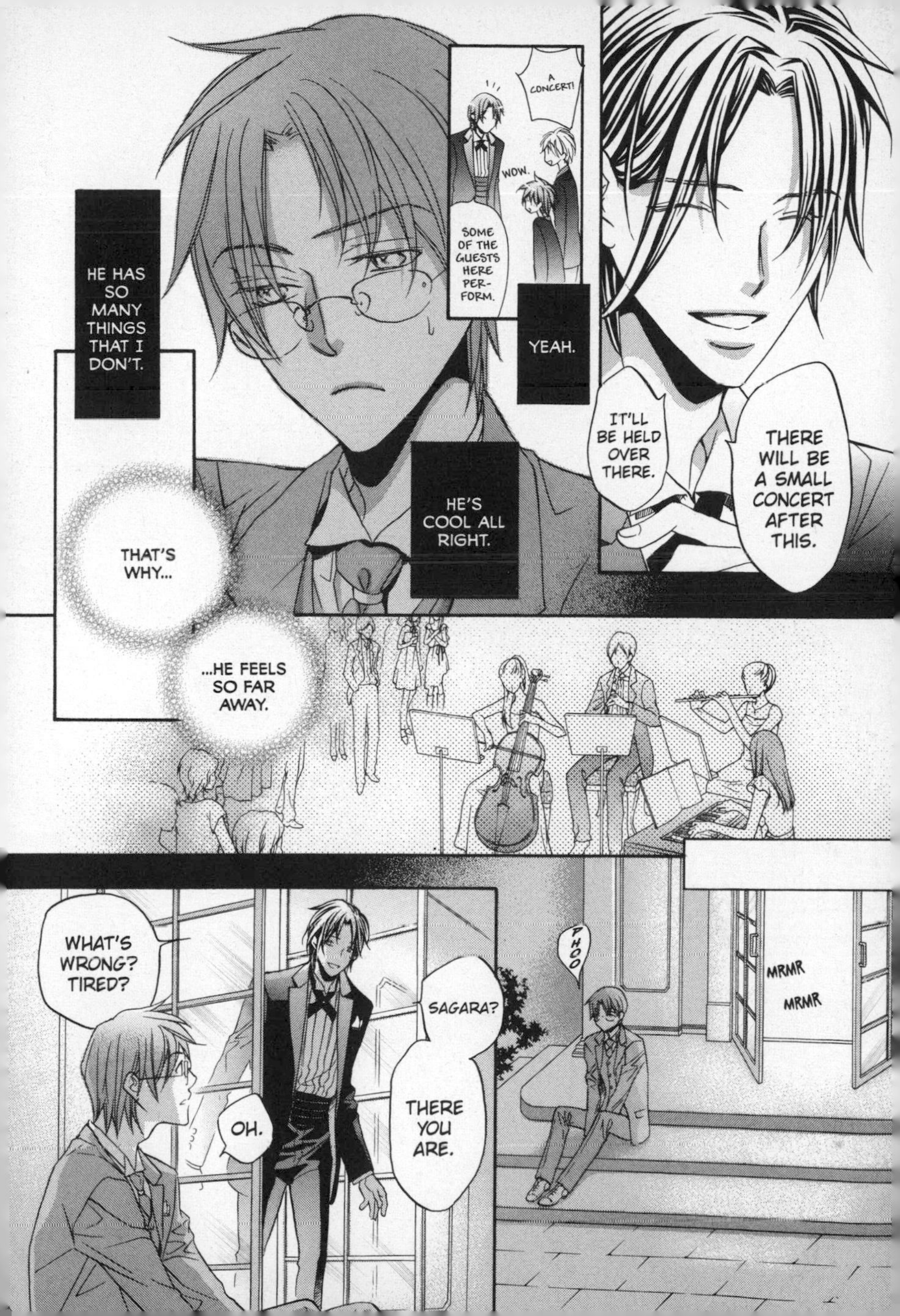
THERE WILL BE A SMALL CONCERT AFTER THIS.
IT'LL BE HELD OVER THERE.
YEAH.
A CONCERT!
WOW.
SOME OF THE GUESTS HERE PER-FORM.
HE'S COOL ALL RIGHT.
HE HAS SO MANY THINGS THAT I DON'T.
THAT'S WHY...
...HE FEELS SO FAR AWAY.
PHOO
MRMR
MRMR
SAGARA?
THERE YOU ARE.
OH.
WHAT'S WRONG? TIRED?

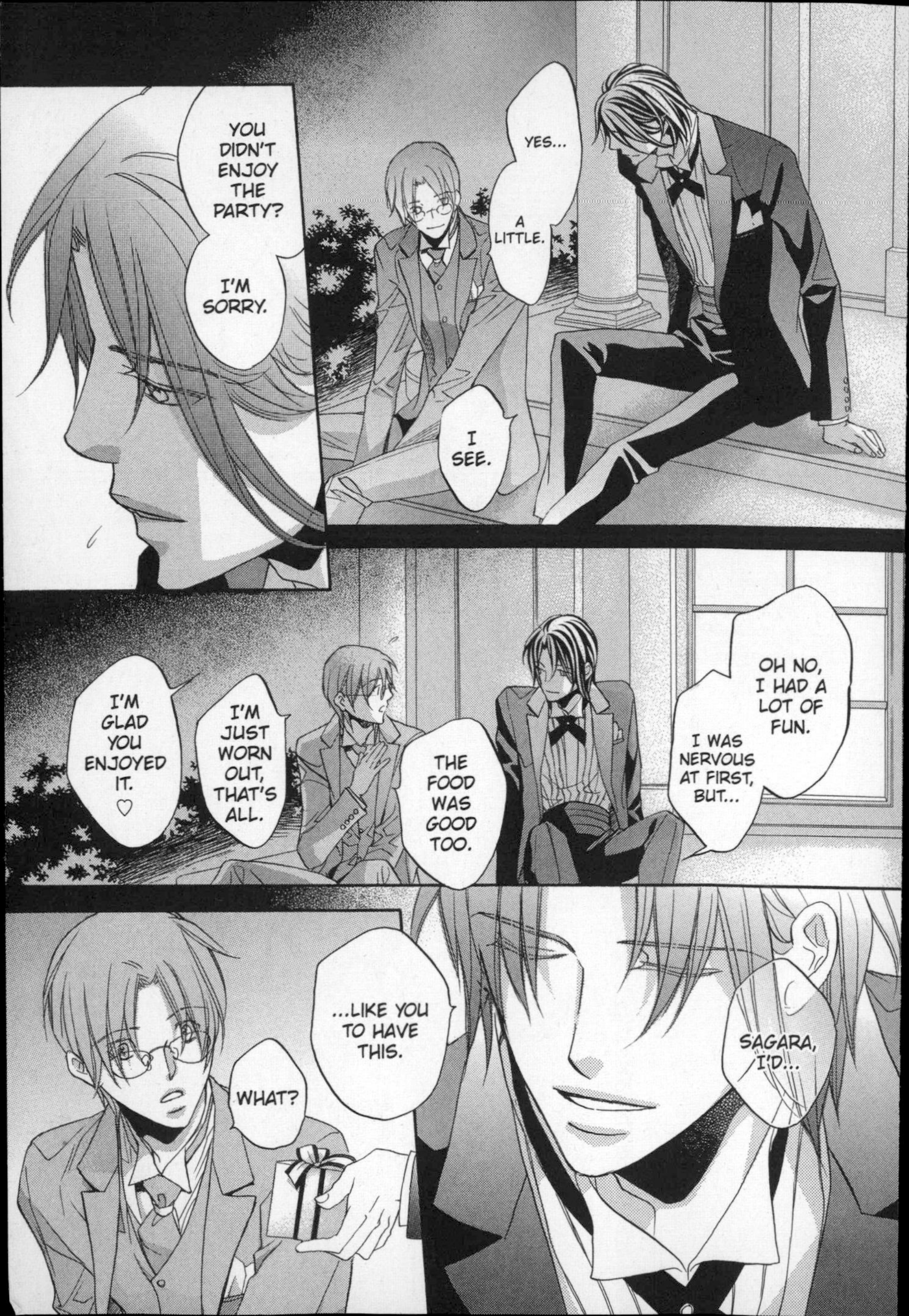
YES...
A LITTLE.
I SEE.
YOU DIDN'T ENJOY THE PARTY?
I'M SORRY.
OH NO, I HAD A LOT OF FUN.
I WAS NERVOUS AT FIRST, BUT...
THE FOOD WAS GOOD TOO.
I'M JUST WORN OUT, THAT'S ALL.
I'M GLAD YOU ENJOYED IT. ♡
SAGARA, I'D...
...LIKE YOU TO HAVE THIS.
WHAT?

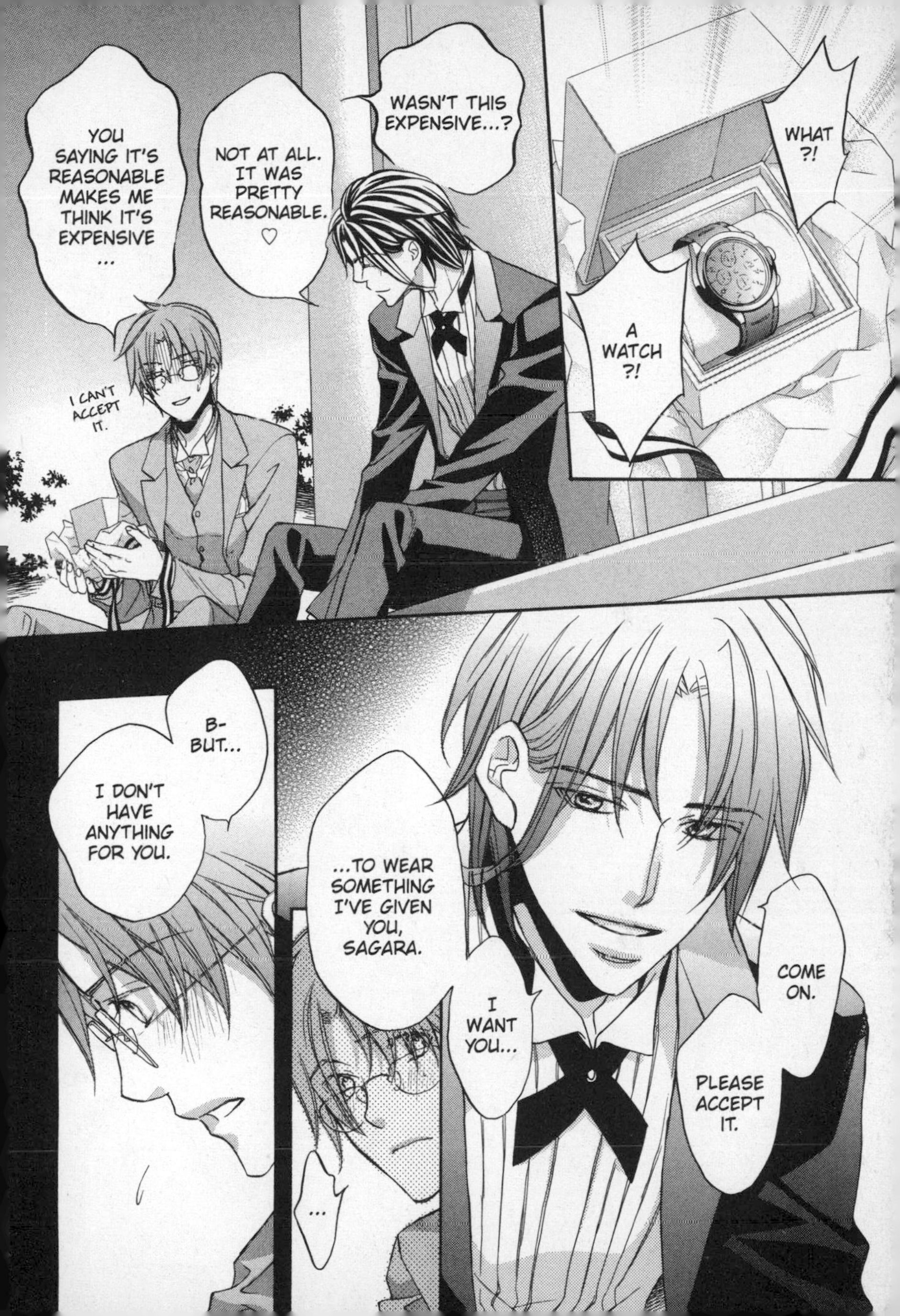
WHAT ?!
A WATCH ?!
WASN'T THIS EXPENSIVE...?
NOT AT ALL. IT WAS PRETTY REASONABLE. ♡
YOU SAYING IT'S REASONABLE MAKES ME THINK IT'S EXPENSIVE ...
I CAN'T ACCEPT IT.
COME ON.
PLEASE ACCEPT IT.
I WANT YOU...
...TO WEAR SOMETHING I'VE GIVEN YOU, SAGARA.
...
B- BUT...
I DON'T HAVE ANYTHING FOR YOU.

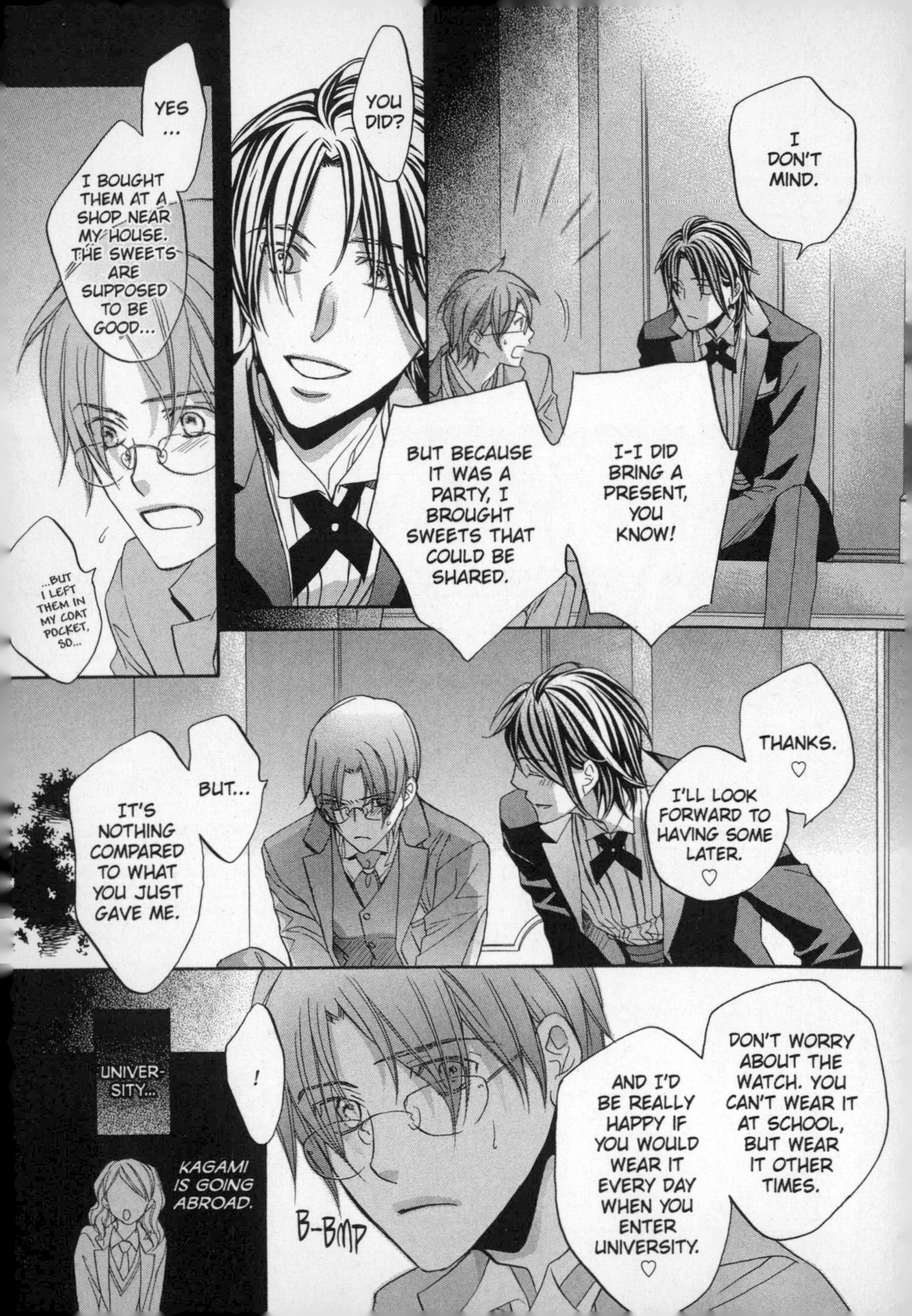
I DON'T MIND.
I-I DID BRING A PRESENT, YOU KNOW!
YOU DID?
BUT BECAUSE IT WAS A PARTY, I BROUGHT SWEETS THAT COULD BE SHARED.
YES ...
I BOUGHT THEM AT A SHOP NEAR MY HOUSE. THE SWEETS ARE SUPPOSED TO BE GOOD...
...BUT I LEFT THEM IN MY COAT POCKET, SO...
THANKS. ♡
I'LL LOOK FORWARD TO HAVING SOME LATER. ♡
BUT...
IT'S NOTHING COMPARED TO WHAT YOU JUST GAVE ME.
DON'T WORRY ABOUT THE WATCH. YOU CAN'T WEAR IT AT SCHOOL, BUT WEAR IT OTHER TIMES.
AND I'D BE REALLY HAPPY IF YOU WOULD WEAR IT EVERY DAY WHEN YOU ENTER UNIVERSITY. ♡
B-BMP
!
UNIVER-SITY...
KAGAMI IS GOING ABROAD.

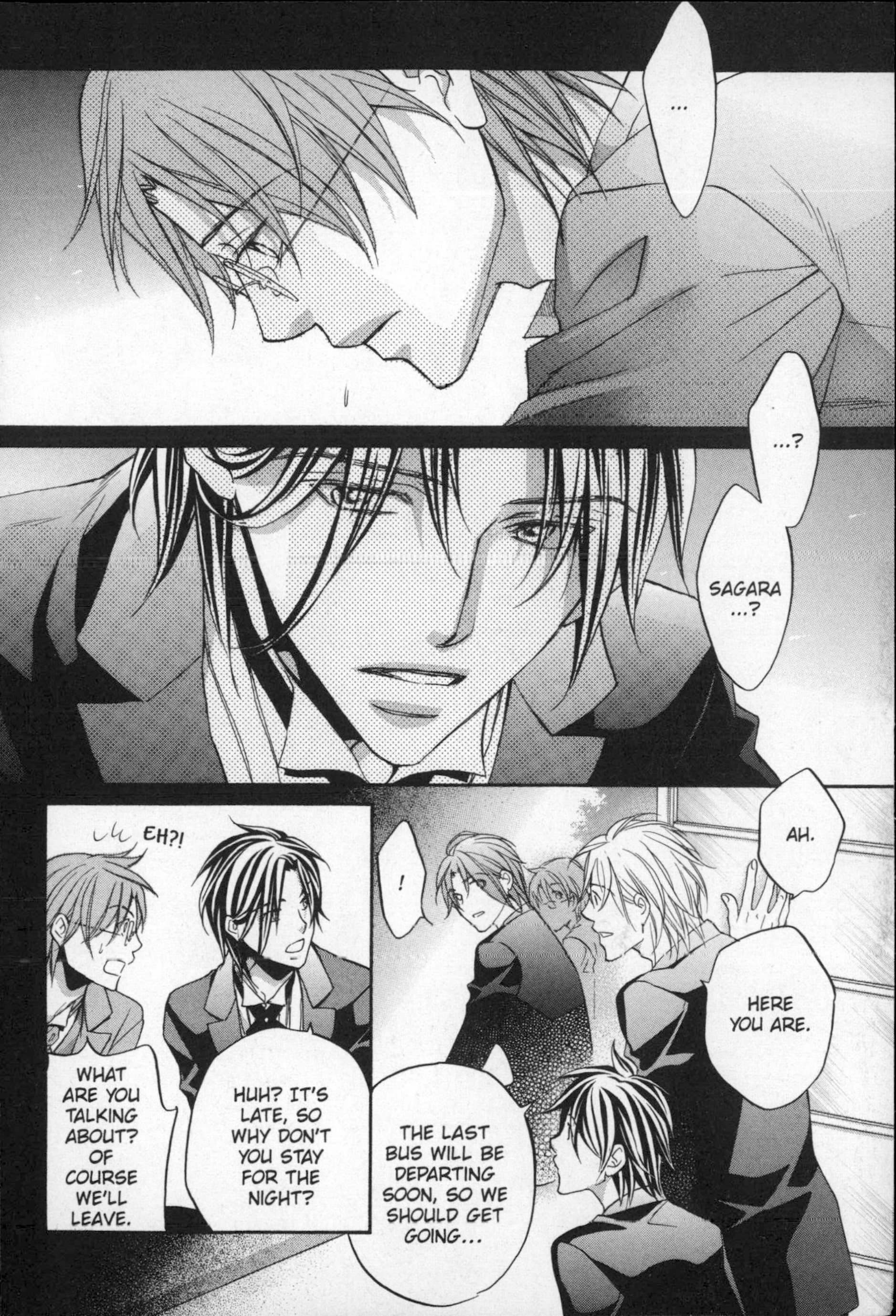
...
...?
SAGARA ...?
AH.
!
HERE YOU ARE.
THE LAST BUS WILL BE DEPARTING SOON, SO WE SHOULD GET GOING...
HUH? IT'S LATE, SO WHY DON'T YOU STAY FOR THE NIGHT?
EH?!
WHAT ARE YOU TALKING ABOUT? OF COURSE WE'LL LEAVE.

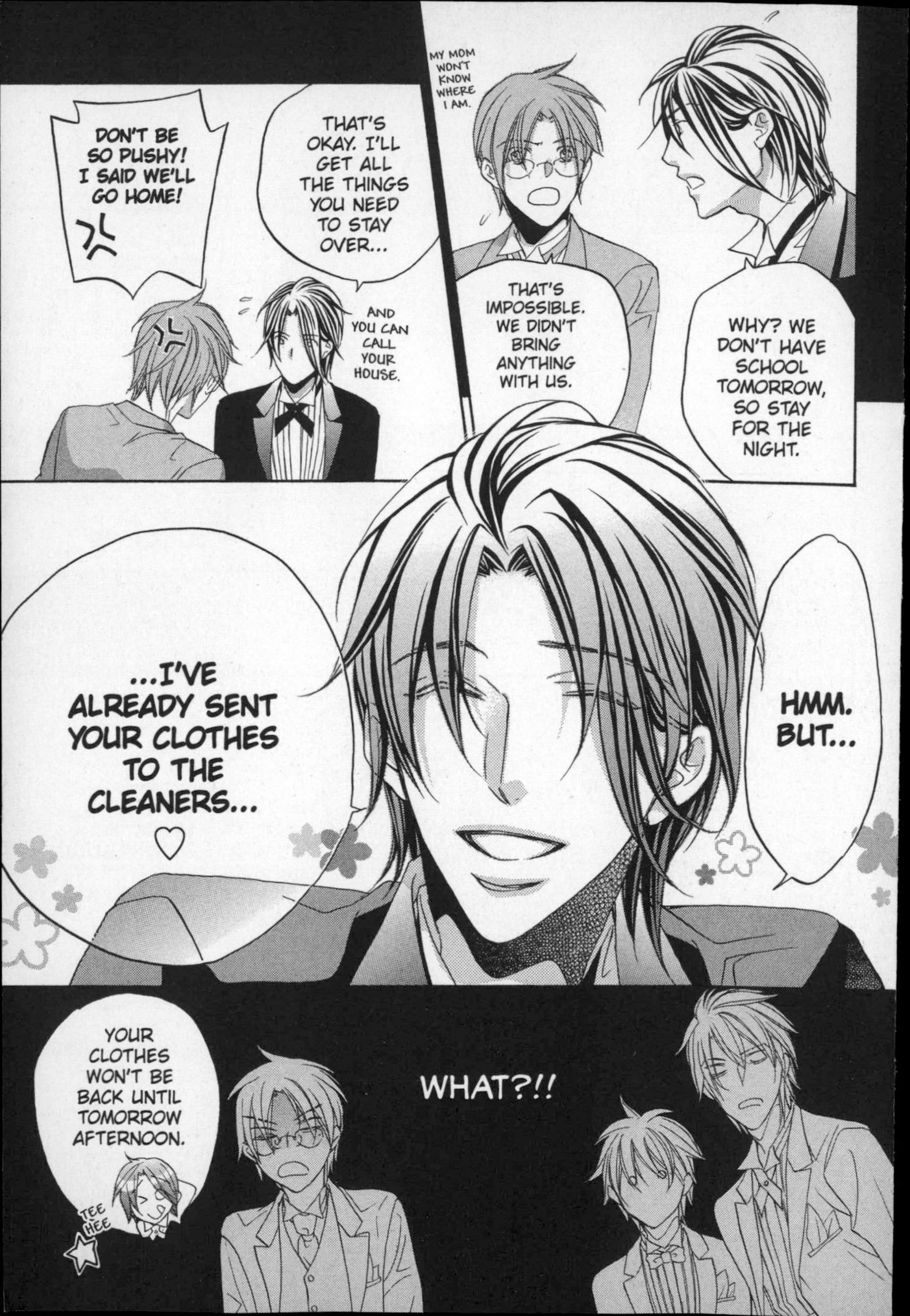
WHY? WE DON'T HAVE SCHOOL TOMORROW, SO STAY FOR THE NIGHT.
THAT'S IMPOSSIBLE. WE DIDN'T BRING ANYTHING WITH US.
MY MOM WON'T KNOW WHERE I AM.
THAT'S OKAY. I'LL GET ALL THE THINGS YOU NEED TO STAY OVER...
AND YOU CAN CALL YOUR HOUSE.
DON'T BE SO PUSHY! I SAID WE'LL GO HOME!
HMM. BUT...
...I'VE ALREADY SENT YOUR CLOTHES TO THE CLEANERS... ♡
WHAT?!!
YOUR CLOTHES WON'T BE BACK UNTIL TOMORROW AFTERNOON.
TEE HEE

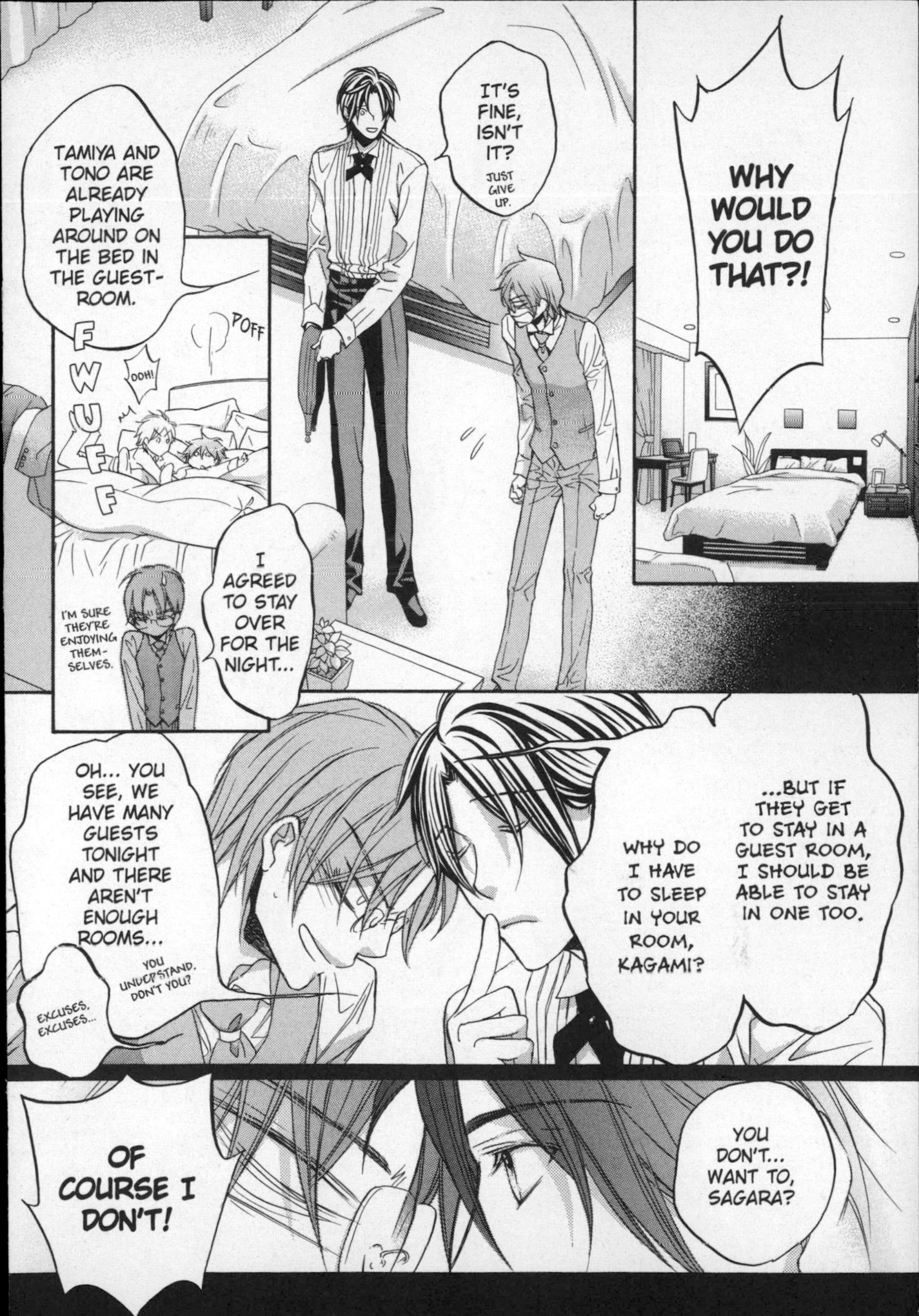
WHY WOULD YOU DO THAT?!
IT'S FINE, ISN'T IT?
JUST GIVE UP.
TAMIYA AND TONO ARE ALREADY PLAYING AROUND ON THE BED IN THE GUEST-ROOM.
POFF
OOH!
FWUFF
I AGREED TO STAY OVER FOR THE NIGHT...
I'M SURE THEY'RE ENJOYING THEM-SELVES.
...BUT IF THEY GET TO STAY IN A GUEST ROOM, I SHOULD BE ABLE TO STAY IN ONE TOO.
WHY DO I HAVE TO SLEEP IN YOUR ROOM, KAGAMI?
OH... YOU SEE, WE HAVE MANY GUESTS TONIGHT AND THERE AREN'T ENOUGH ROOMS...
YOU UNDERSTAND, DON'T YOU?
EXCUSES, EXCUSES...
YOU DON'T... WANT TO, SAGARA?
OF COURSE I DON'T!

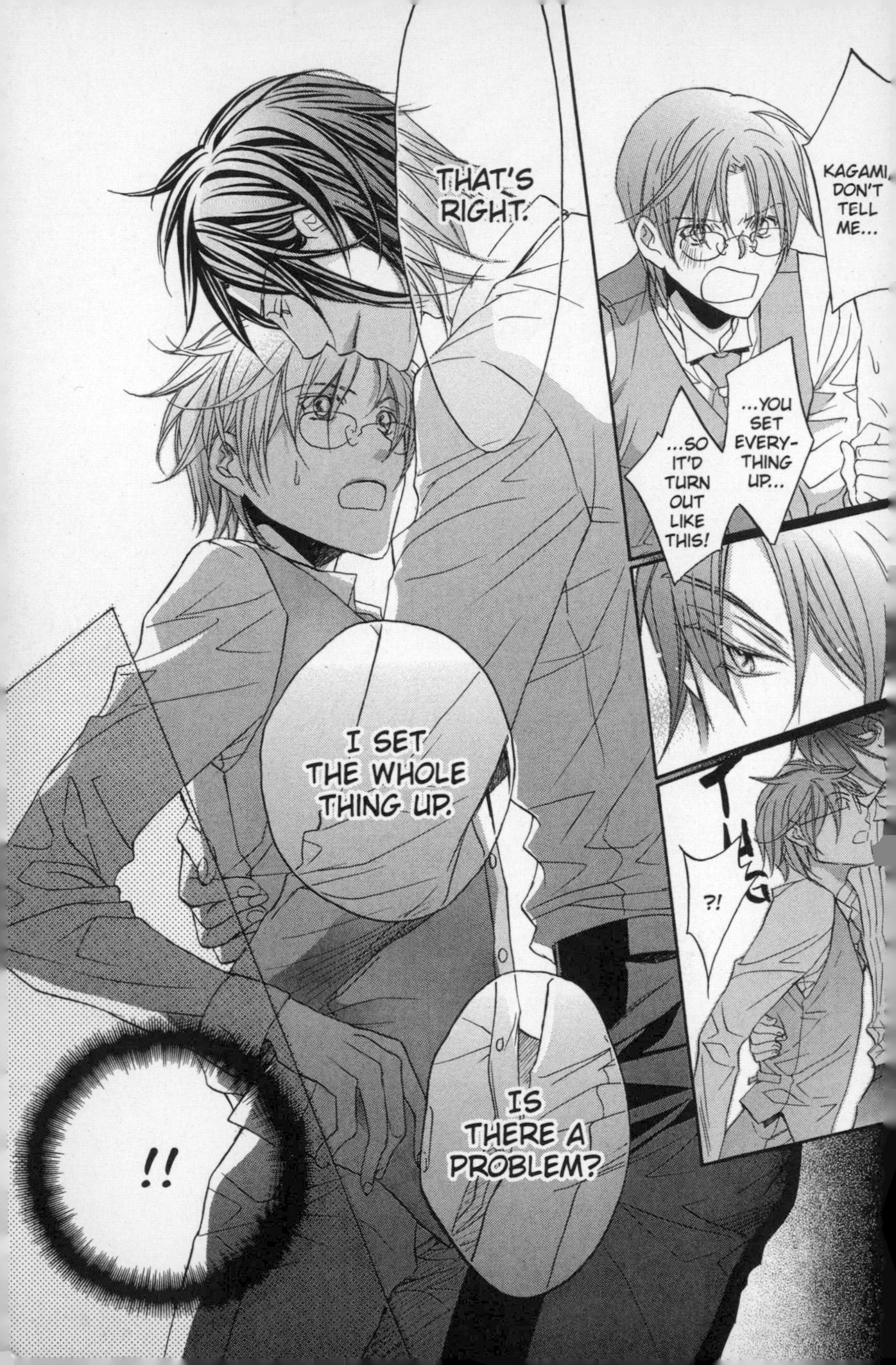
KAGAMI, DON'T TELL ME...
...YOU SET EVERY-THING UP...
...SO IT'D TURN OUT LIKE THIS!
TUG
?!
THAT'S RIGHT.
I SET THE WHOLE THING UP.
IS THERE A PROBLEM?
!!

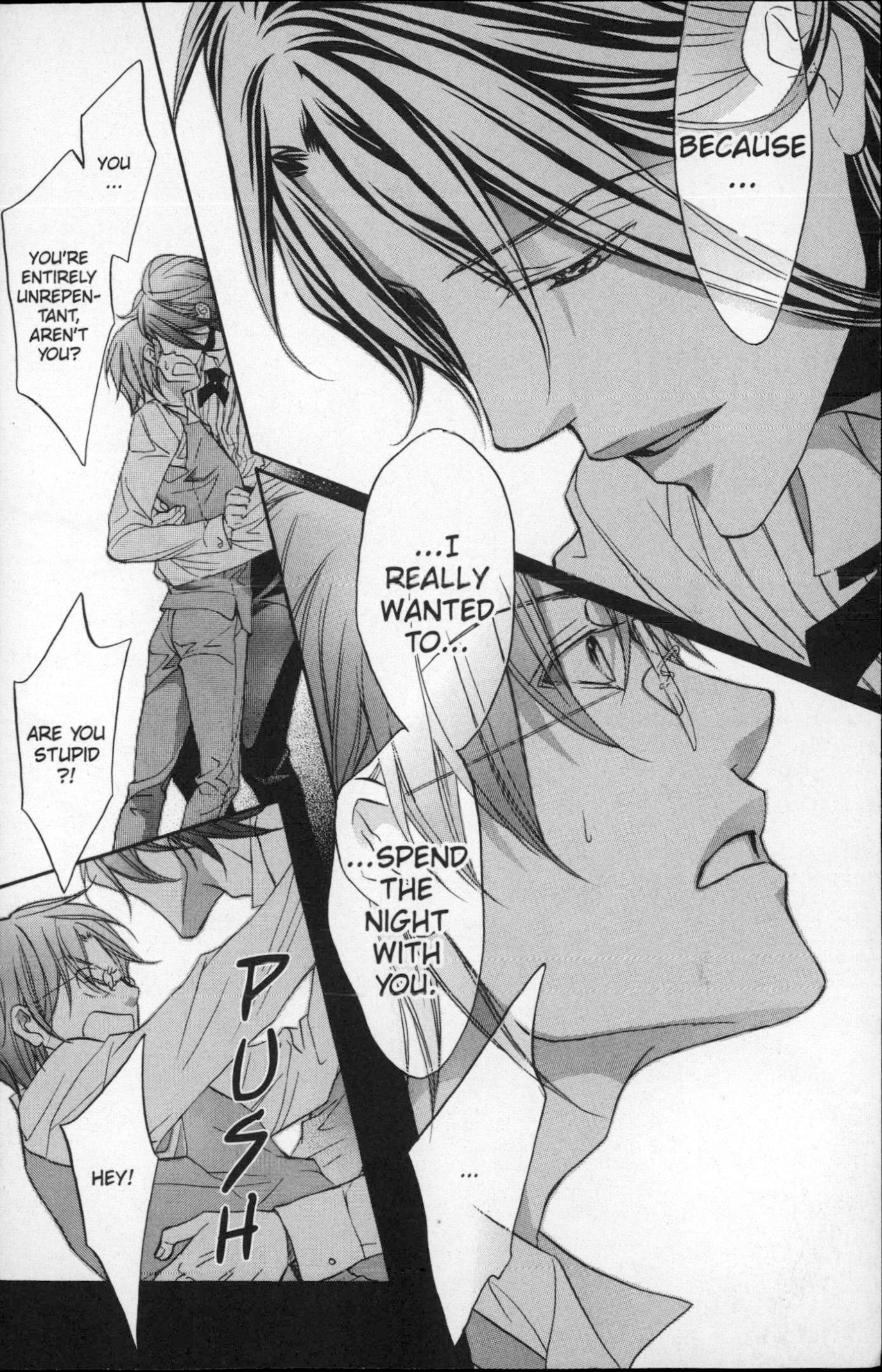
BECAUSE ...
...I REALLY WANTED TO...
...SPEND THE NIGHT WITH YOU.
...
YOU ...
YOU'RE ENTIRELY UNREPENTANT, AREN'T YOU?
ARE YOU STUPID ?!
PUSH
HEY!

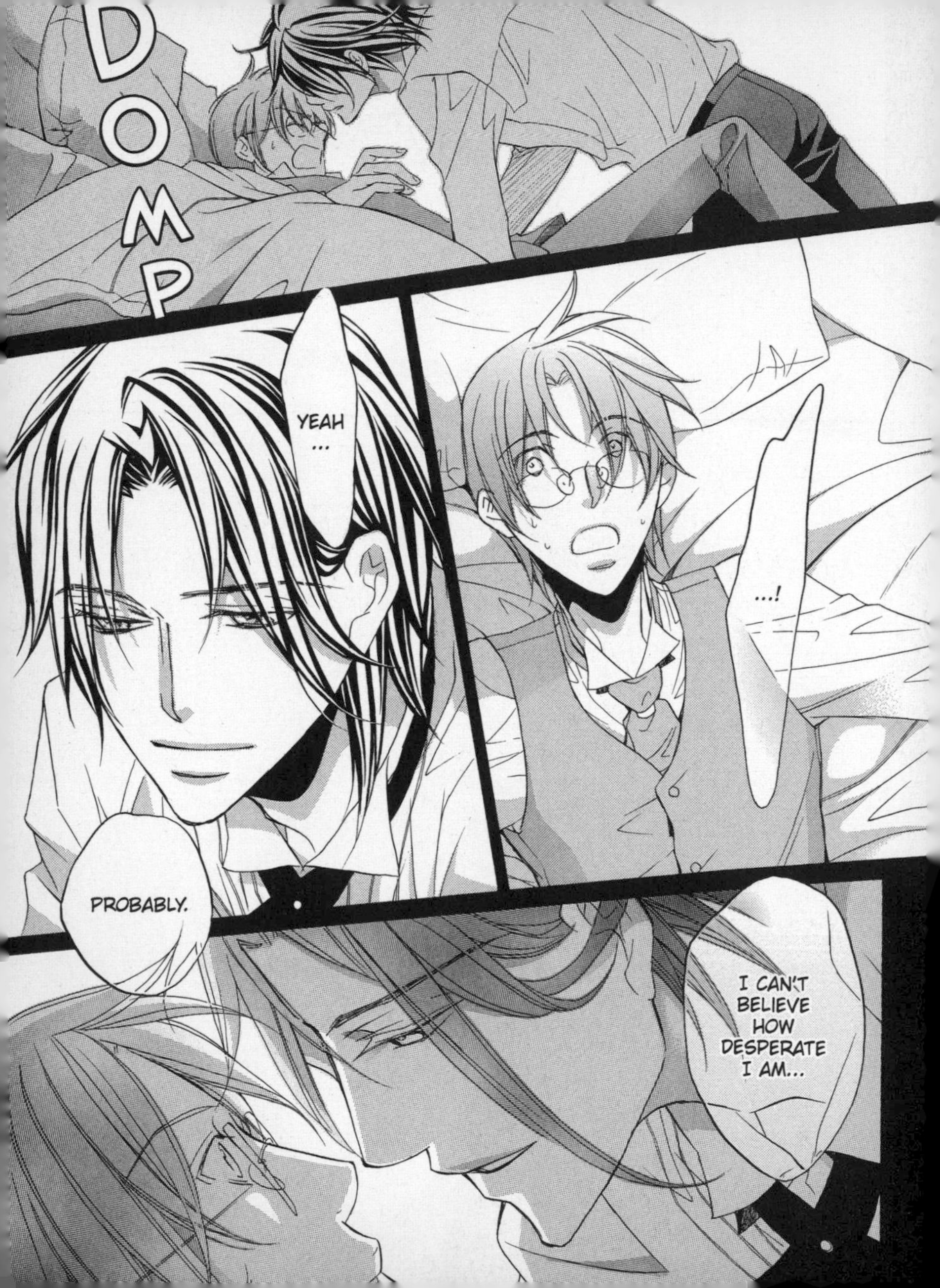
DOMP
...!
YEAH ...
PROBABLY.
I CAN'T BELIEVE HOW DESPERATE I AM...

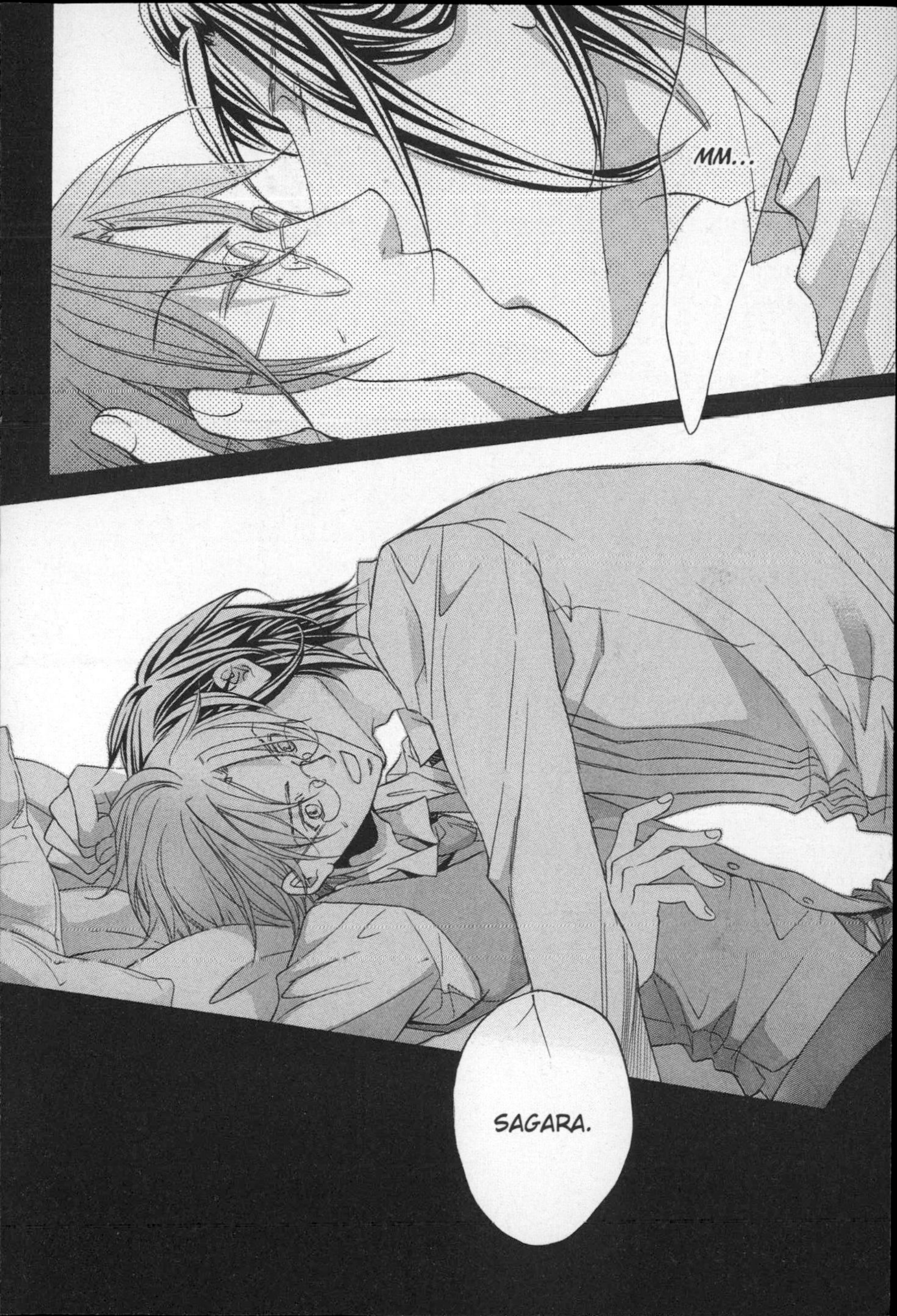
MM...
SAGARA.

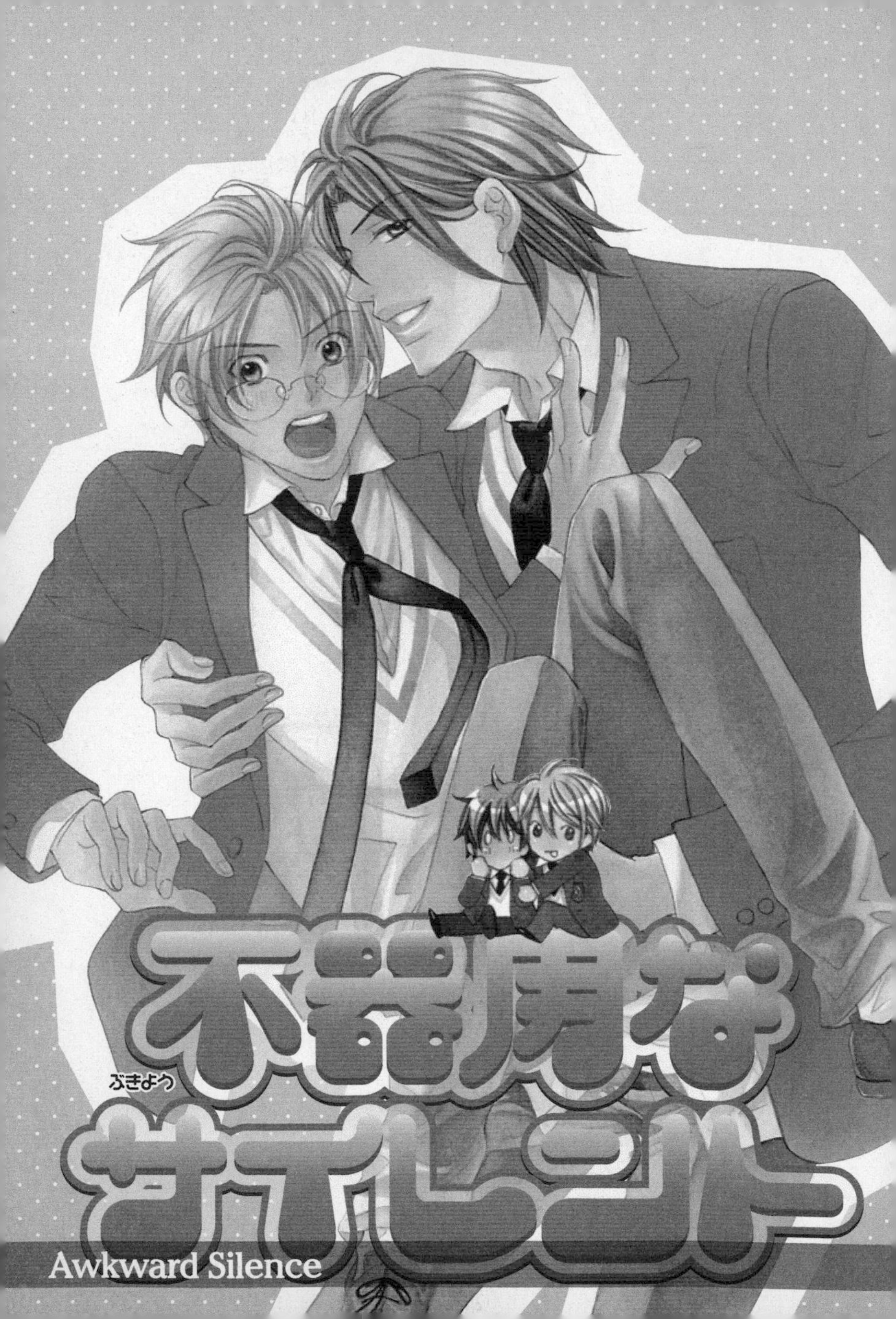

ぶきよう
不器用なサイレント
Awkward Silence

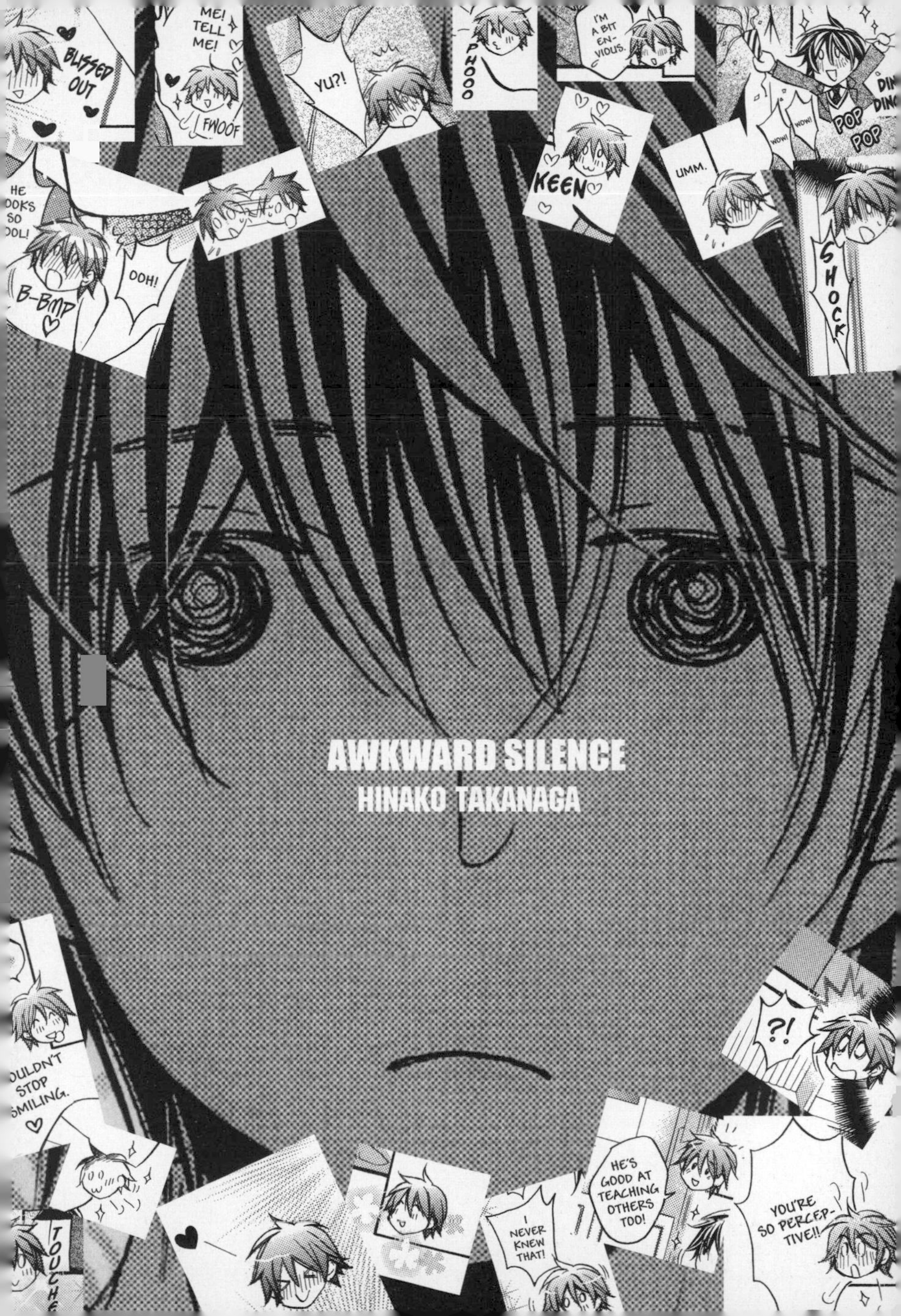
DING DING
POP POP
WOW!
WOW!
I'M A BIT ENVIOUS.
PHOOO
YU?!
ME! TELL ME!
FWOOF
BLISSED OUT
SHOCK
UMM.
KEEN
OOH!
B-BMP
AWKWARD SILENCE
HINAKO TAKANAGA
?!
YOU'RE SO PERCEPTIVE!!
HE'S GOOD AT TEACHING OTHERS TOO!
I NEVER KNEW THAT!

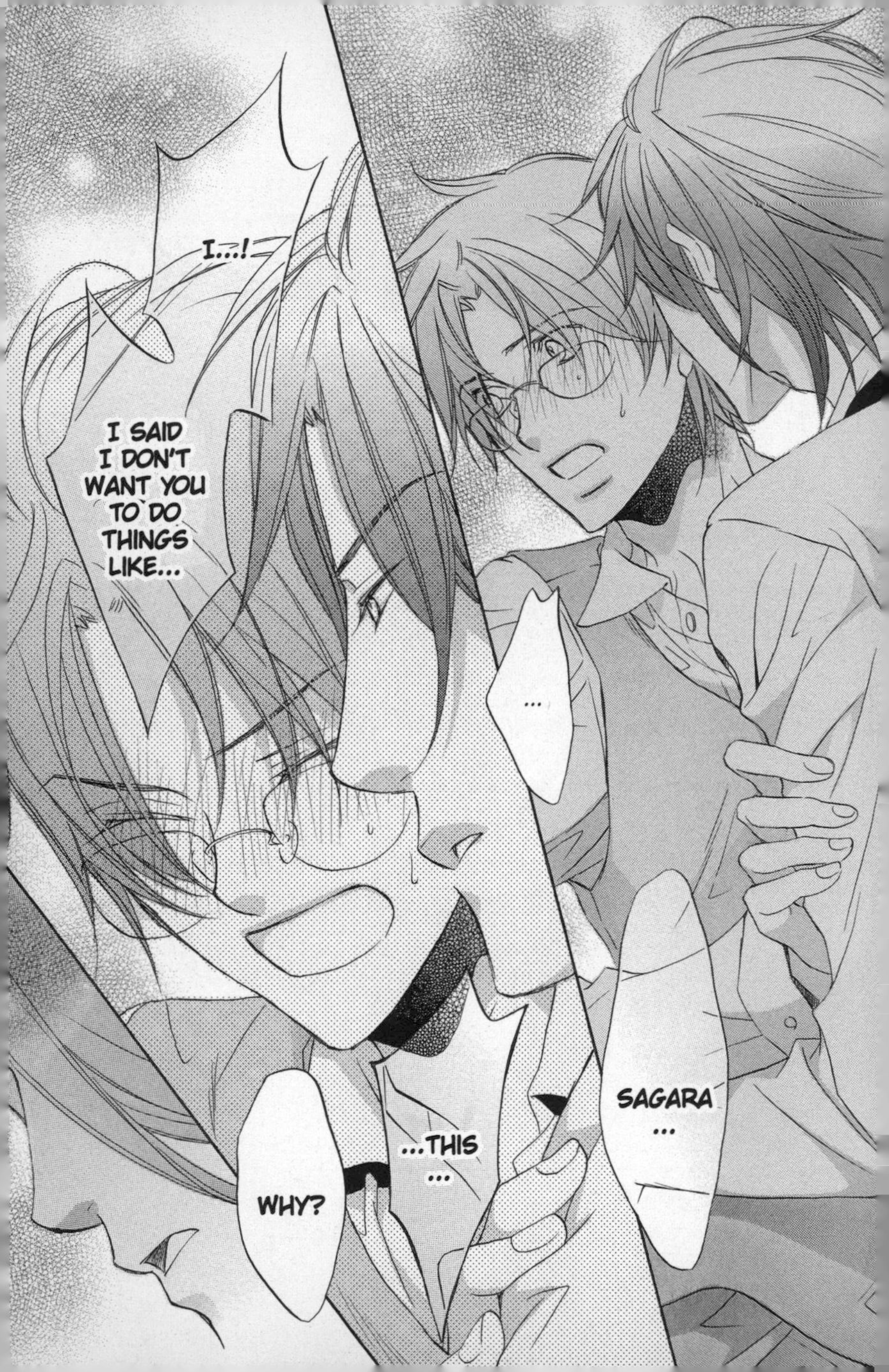
...
SAGARA ...
I...!
I SAID I DON'T WANT YOU TO DO THINGS LIKE...
...THIS ...
WHY?

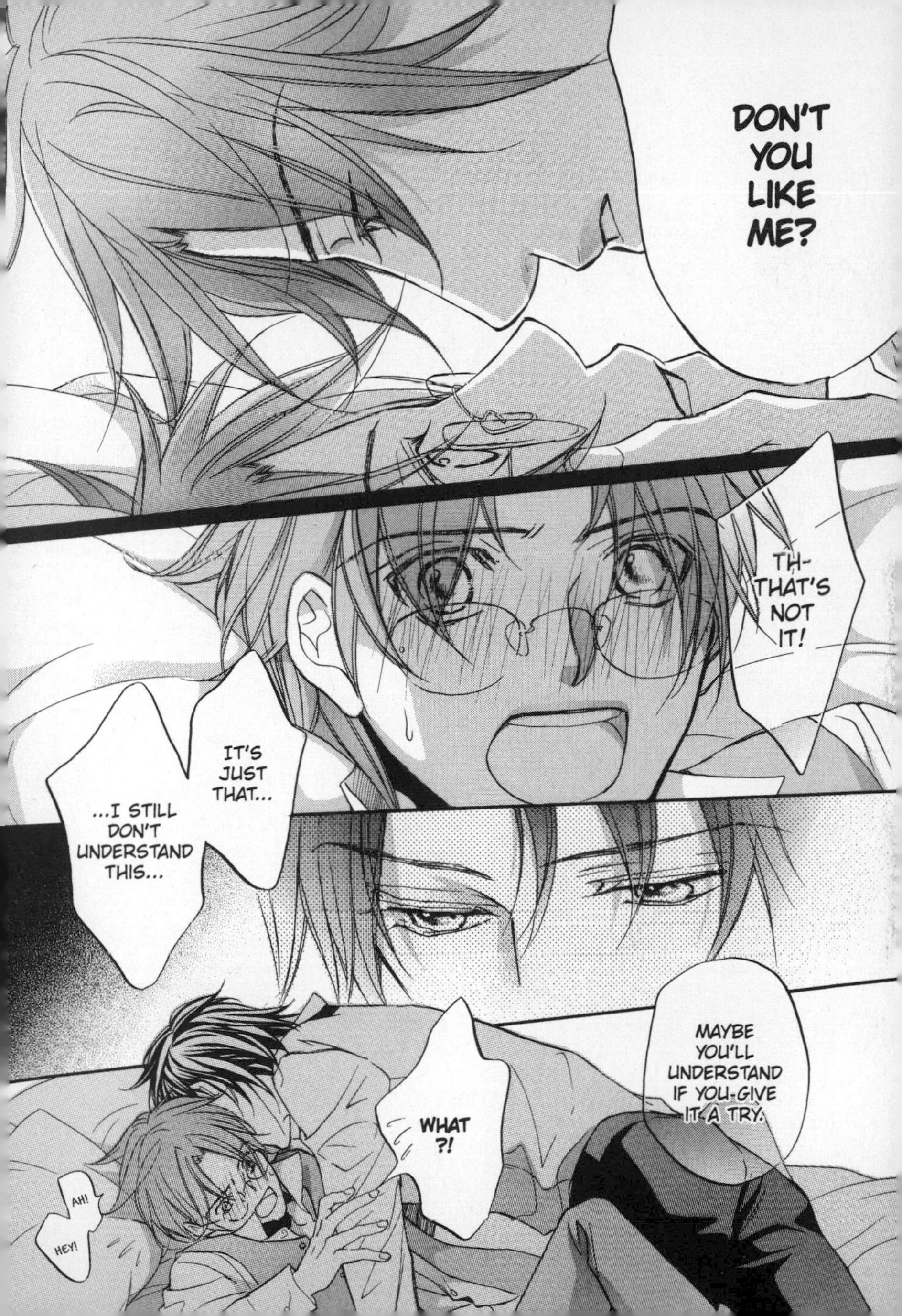
DON'T YOU LIKE ME?
TH-THAT'S NOT IT!
IT'S JUST THAT...
...I STILL DON'T UNDERSTAND THIS...
MAYBE YOU'LL UNDERSTAND IF YOU GIVE IT A TRY.
WHAT?!
AH!
HEY!

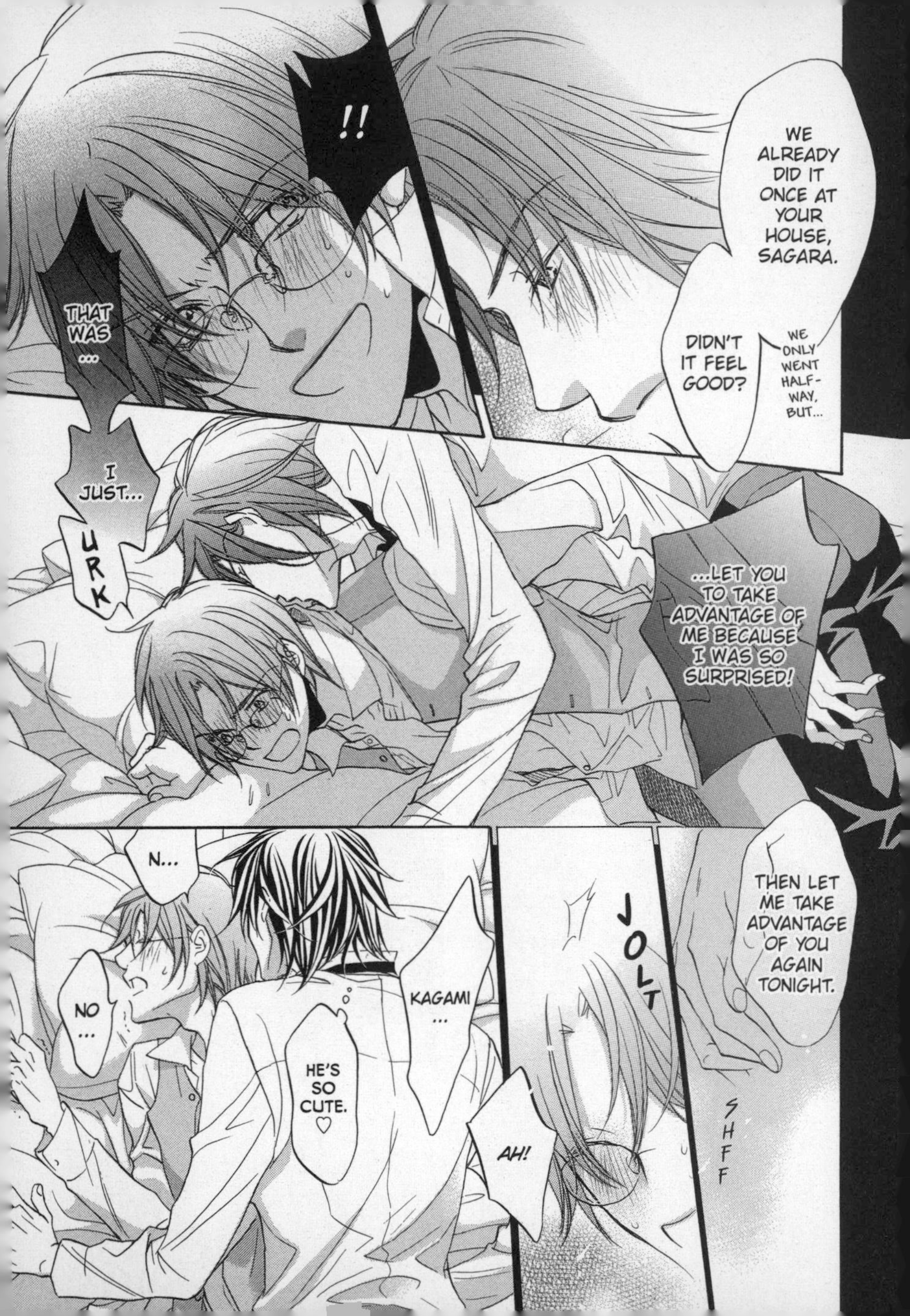
WE ALREADY DID IT ONCE AT YOUR HOUSE, SAGARA.
WE ONLY WENT HALF-WAY, BUT...
DIDN'T IT FEEL GOOD?
!!
THAT WAS...
I JUST...
URK
...LET YOU TO TAKE ADVANTAGE OF ME BECAUSE I WAS SO SURPRISED!
THEN LET ME TAKE ADVANTAGE OF YOU AGAIN TONIGHT.
JOLT
SHFF
AH!
KAGAMI...
HE'S SO CUTE. ♡
N...
NO...

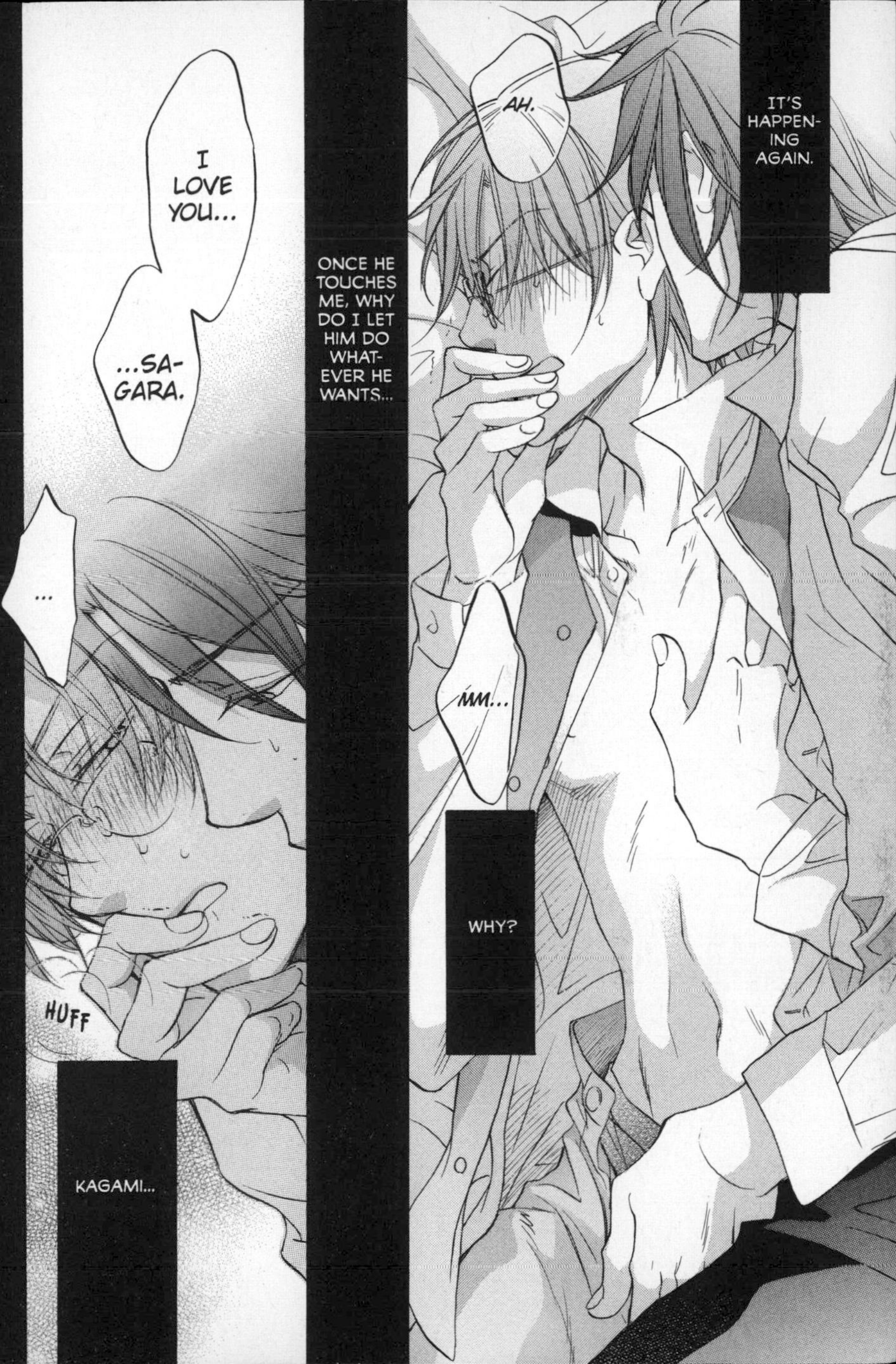
IT'S HAPPEN-ING AGAIN.
AH.
MM...
WHY?
ONCE HE TOUCHES ME, WHY DO I LET HIM DO WHAT-EVER HE WANTS...
I LOVE YOU...
...SA-GARA.
...
HUFF
KAGAMI...

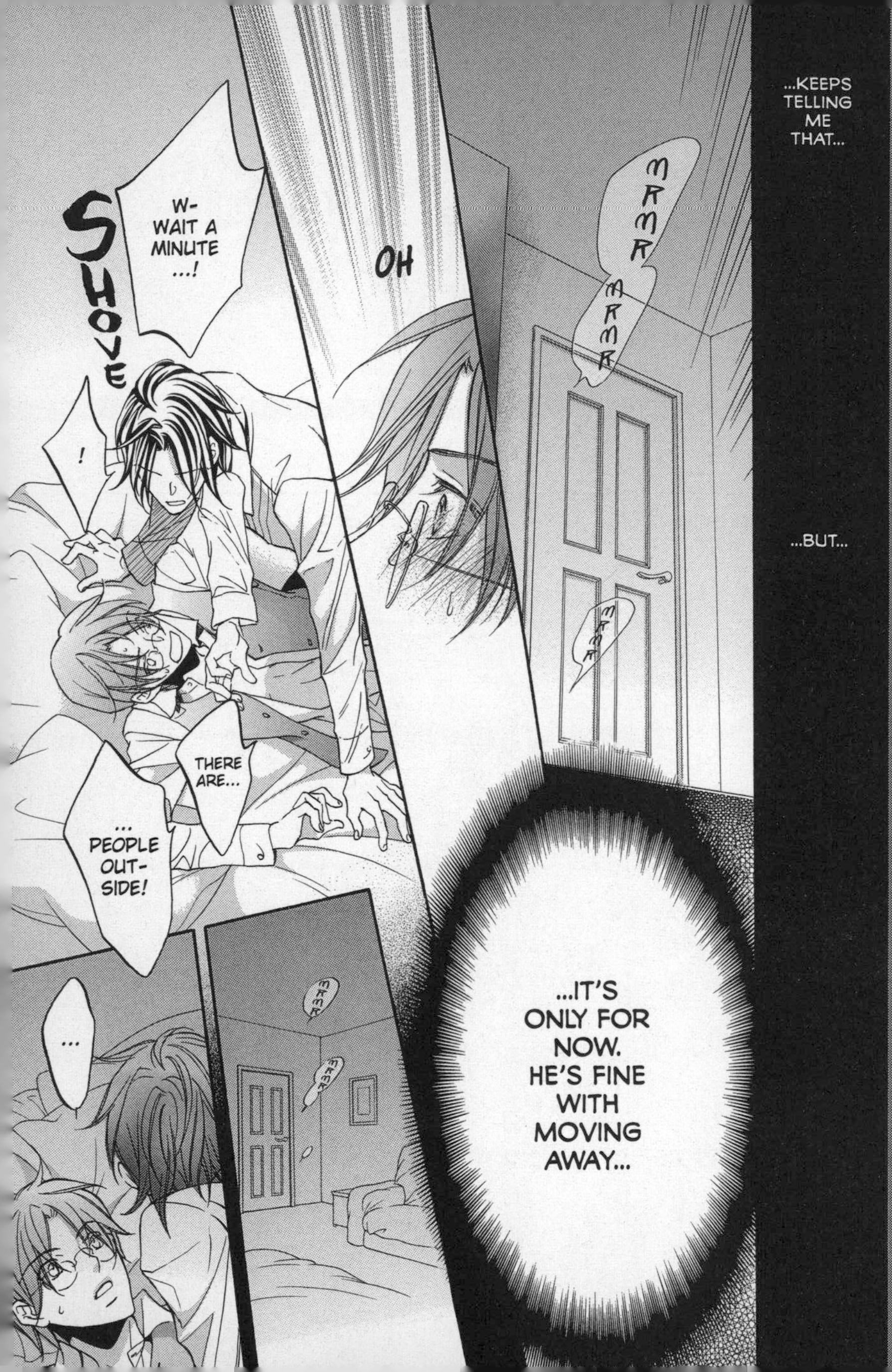
...KEEPS TELLING ME THAT...
...BUT...
MRMR MRMR
MRMR
...IT'S ONLY FOR NOW. HE'S FINE WITH MOVING AWAY...
OH
W- WAIT A MINUTE ...!
SHOVE
!
THERE ARE...
... PEOPLE OUT-SIDE!
MRMR
...

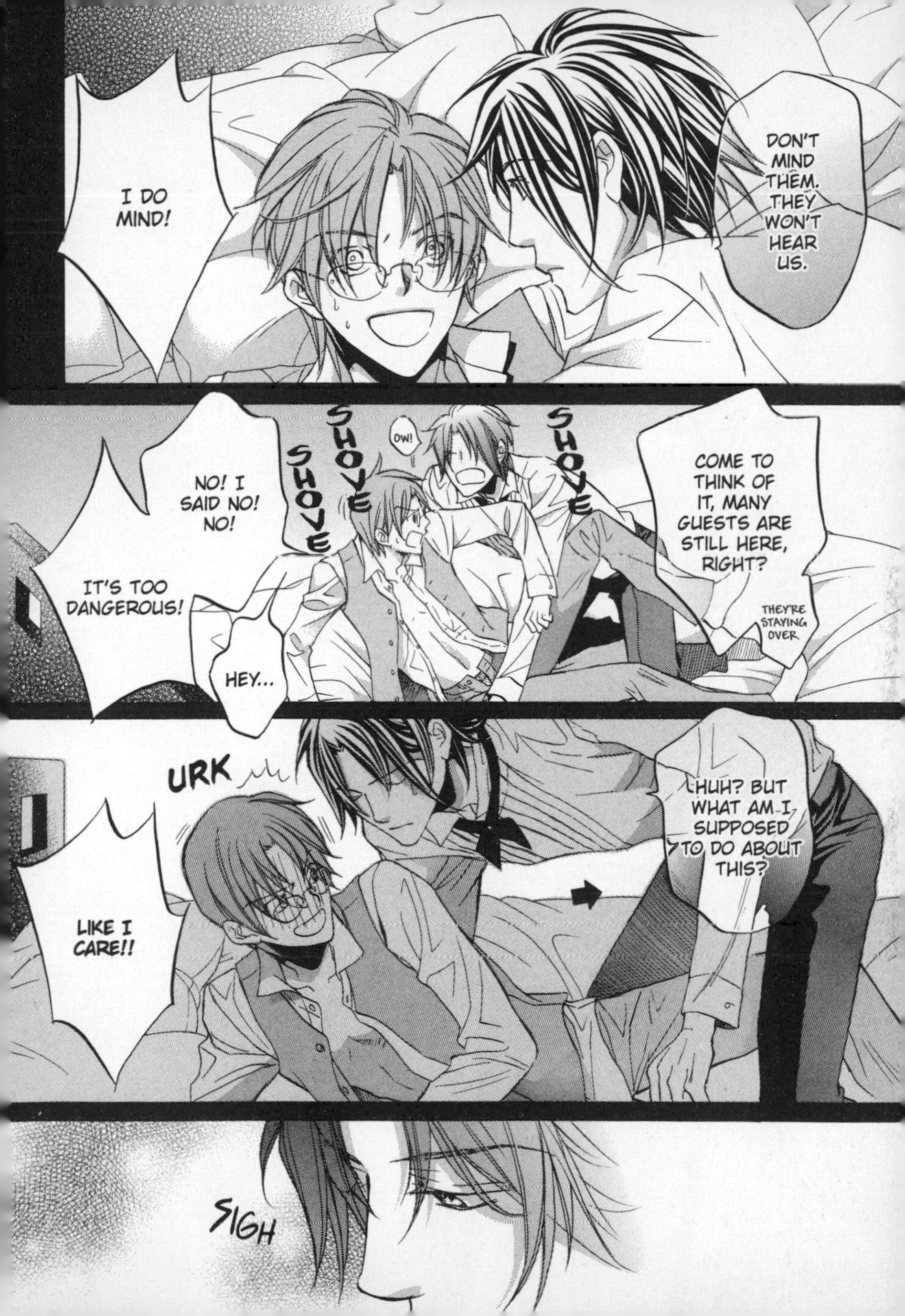
DON'T MIND THEM. THEY WON'T HEAR US.
I DO MIND!
COME TO THINK OF IT, MANY GUESTS ARE STILL HERE, RIGHT?
THEY'RE STAYING OVER.
SHOVE
OW!
SHOVE
SHOVE
NO! I SAID NO! NO!
IT'S TOO DANGEROUS!
HEY...
HUH? BUT WHAT AM I SUPPOSED TO DO ABOUT THIS?
URK
LIKE I CARE!!
SIGH

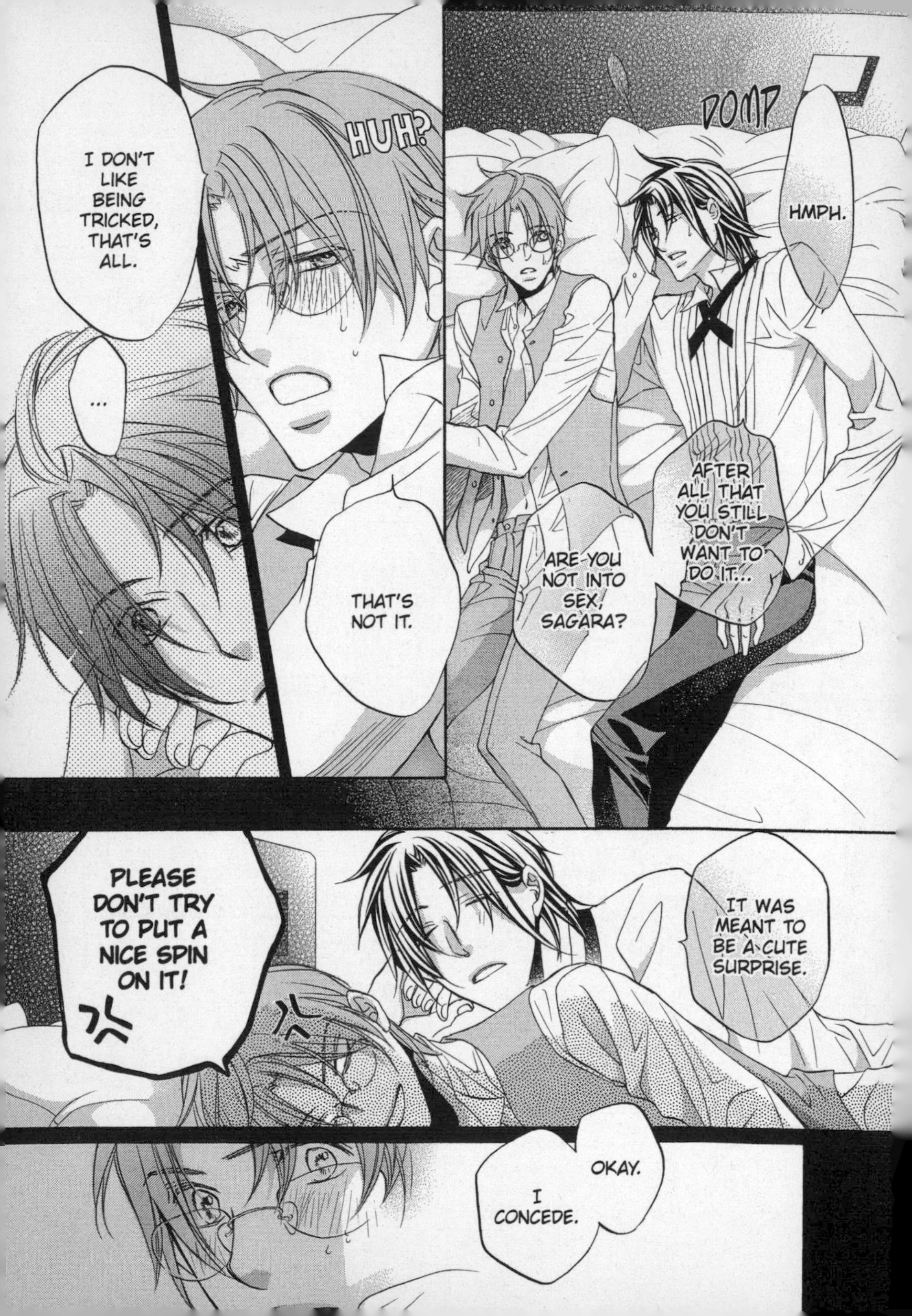
DOMP
HMPH.
AFTER ALL THAT YOU STILL DON'T WANT TO DO IT...
ARE YOU NOT INTO SEX, SAGARA?
HUH?
THAT'S NOT IT.
I DON'T LIKE BEING TRICKED, THAT'S ALL.
...
IT WAS MEANT TO BE A CUTE SURPRISE.
PLEASE DON'T TRY TO PUT A NICE SPIN ON IT!
OKAY. I CONCEDE.

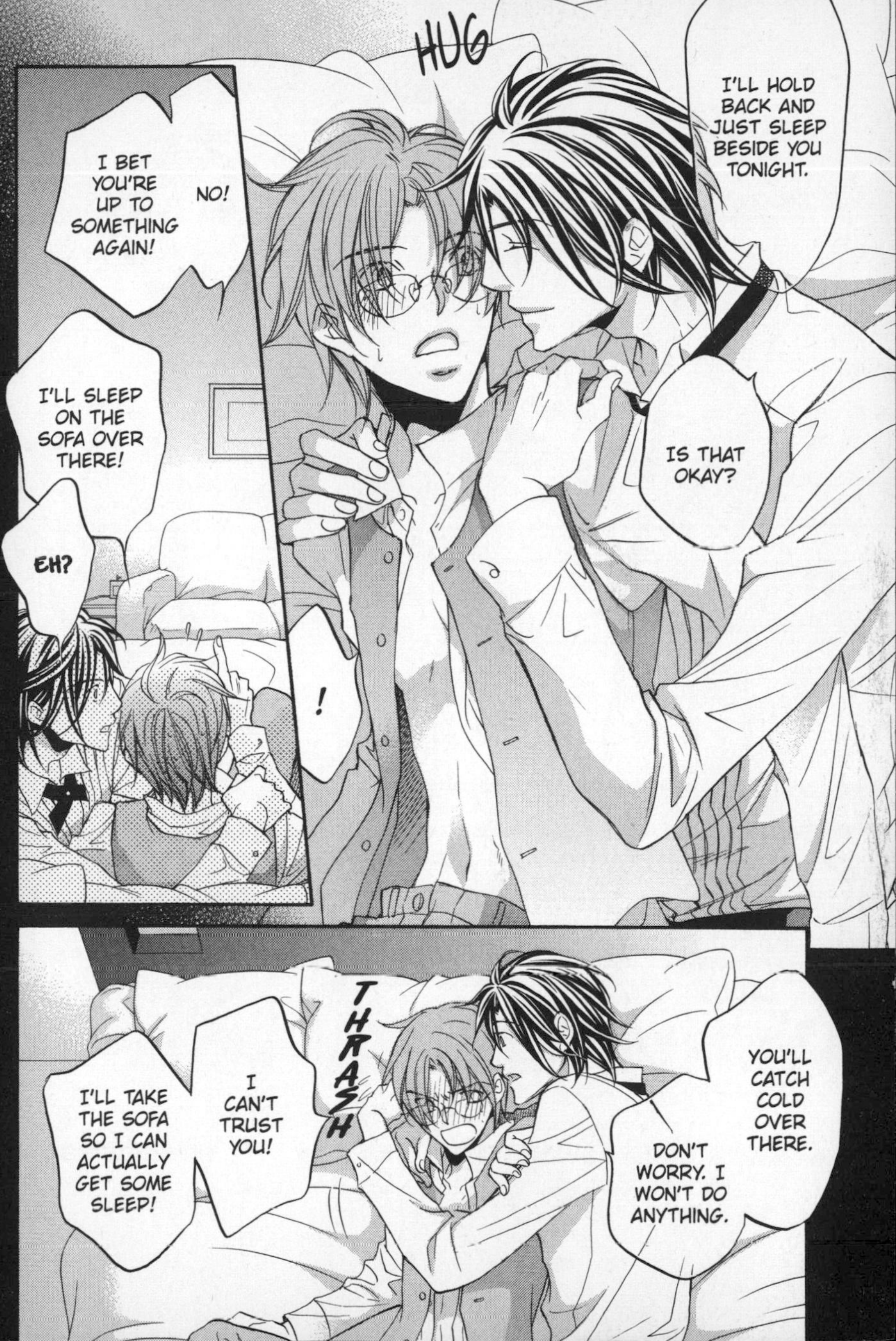
HUG
I'LL HOLD BACK AND JUST SLEEP BESIDE YOU TONIGHT.
IS THAT OKAY?
!
I BET YOU'RE UP TO SOMETHING AGAIN!
NO!
I'LL SLEEP ON THE SOFA OVER THERE!
EH?
YOU'LL CATCH COLD OVER THERE.
DON'T WORRY. I WON'T DO ANYTHING.
THRASH
I CAN'T TRUST YOU!
I'LL TAKE THE SOFA SO I CAN ACTUALLY GET SOME SLEEP!

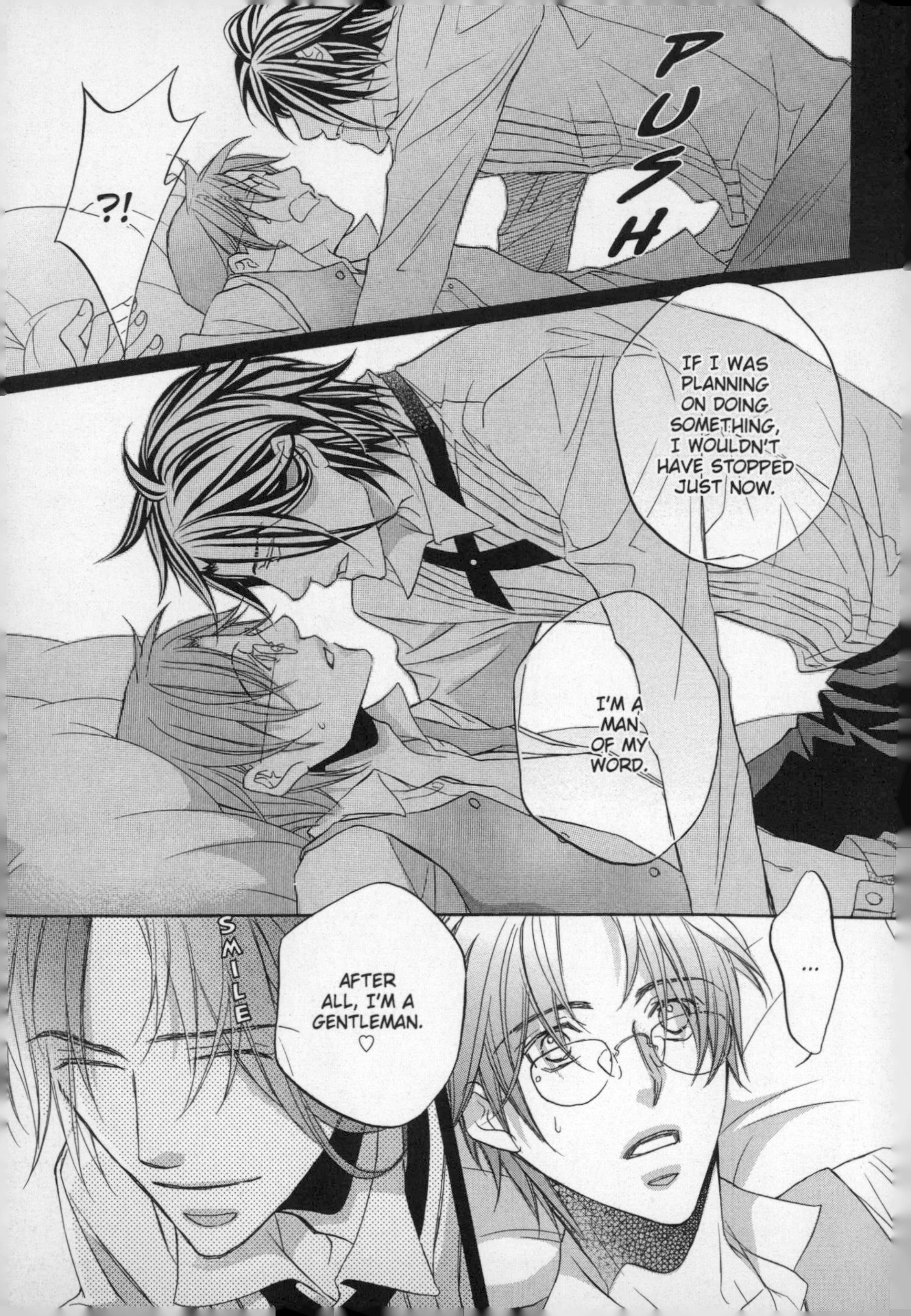
PUSH
?!
IF I WAS PLANNING ON DOING SOMETHING, I WOULDN'T HAVE STOPPED JUST NOW.
I'M A MAN OF MY WORD.
...
AFTER ALL, I'M A GENTLEMAN. ♡
SMILE

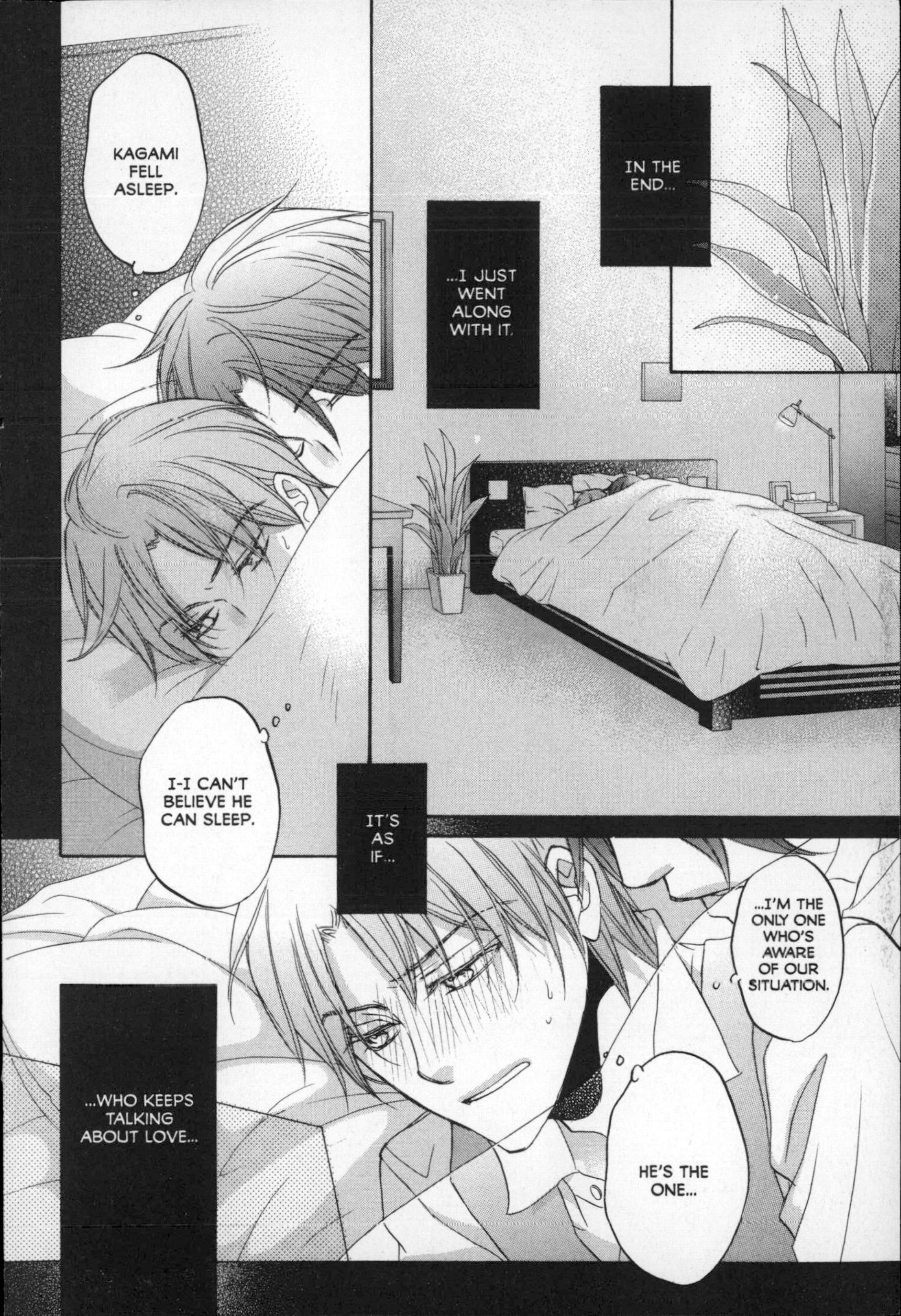
IN THE END...
...I JUST WENT ALONG WITH IT.
KAGAMI FELL ASLEEP.
I-I CAN'T BELIEVE HE CAN SLEEP.
IT'S AS IF...
...I'M THE ONLY ONE WHO'S AWARE OF OUR SITUATION.
HE'S THE ONE...
...WHO KEEPS TALKING ABOUT LOVE...

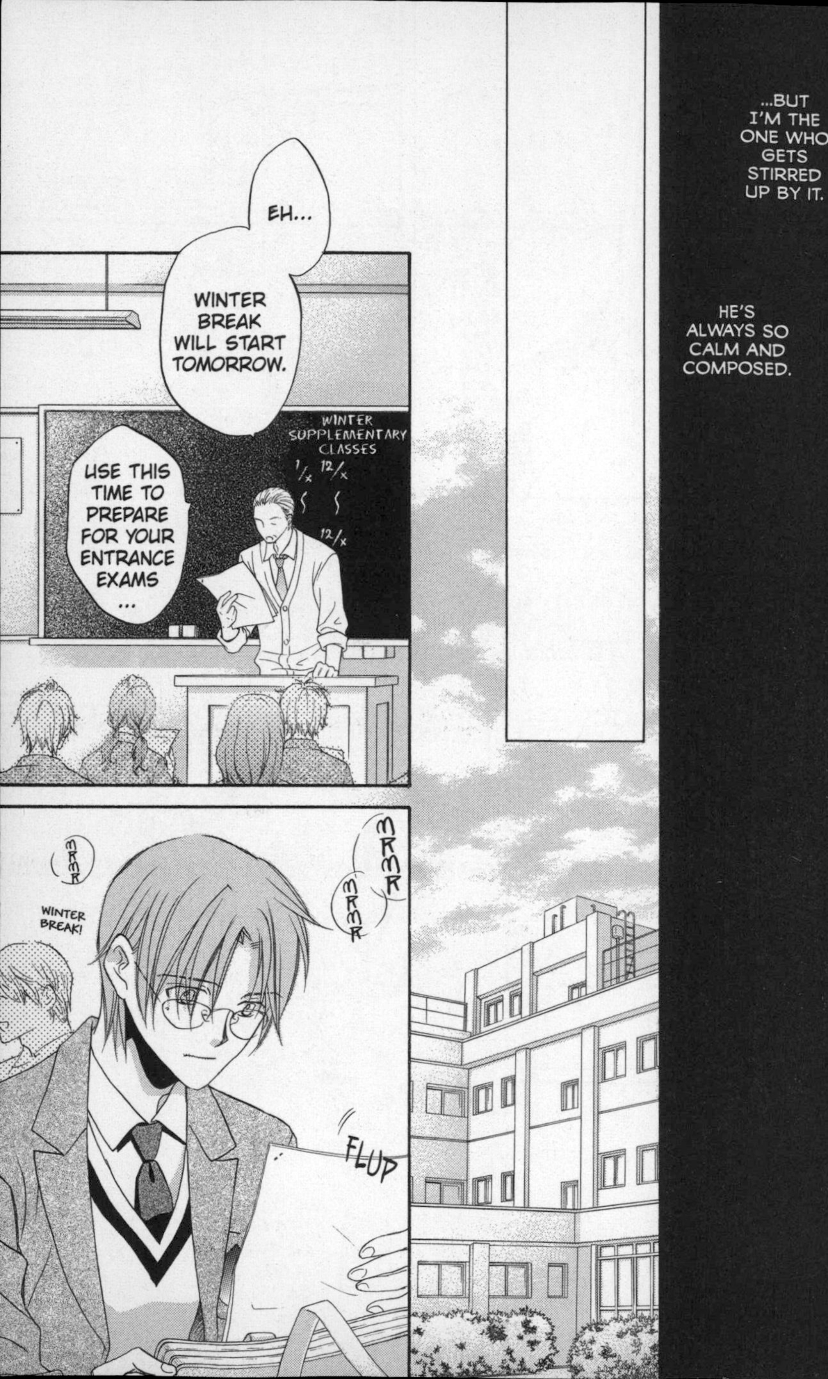

...BUT I'M THE ONE WHO GETS STIRRED UP BY IT.
HE'S ALWAYS SO CALM AND COMPOSED.
EH...
WINTER BREAK WILL START TOMORROW.
WINTER SUPPLEMENTARY CLASSES
USE THIS TIME TO PREPARE FOR YOUR ENTRANCE EXAMS ...
MRMR
MRMR
FLUP
MRMR
WINTER BREAK!

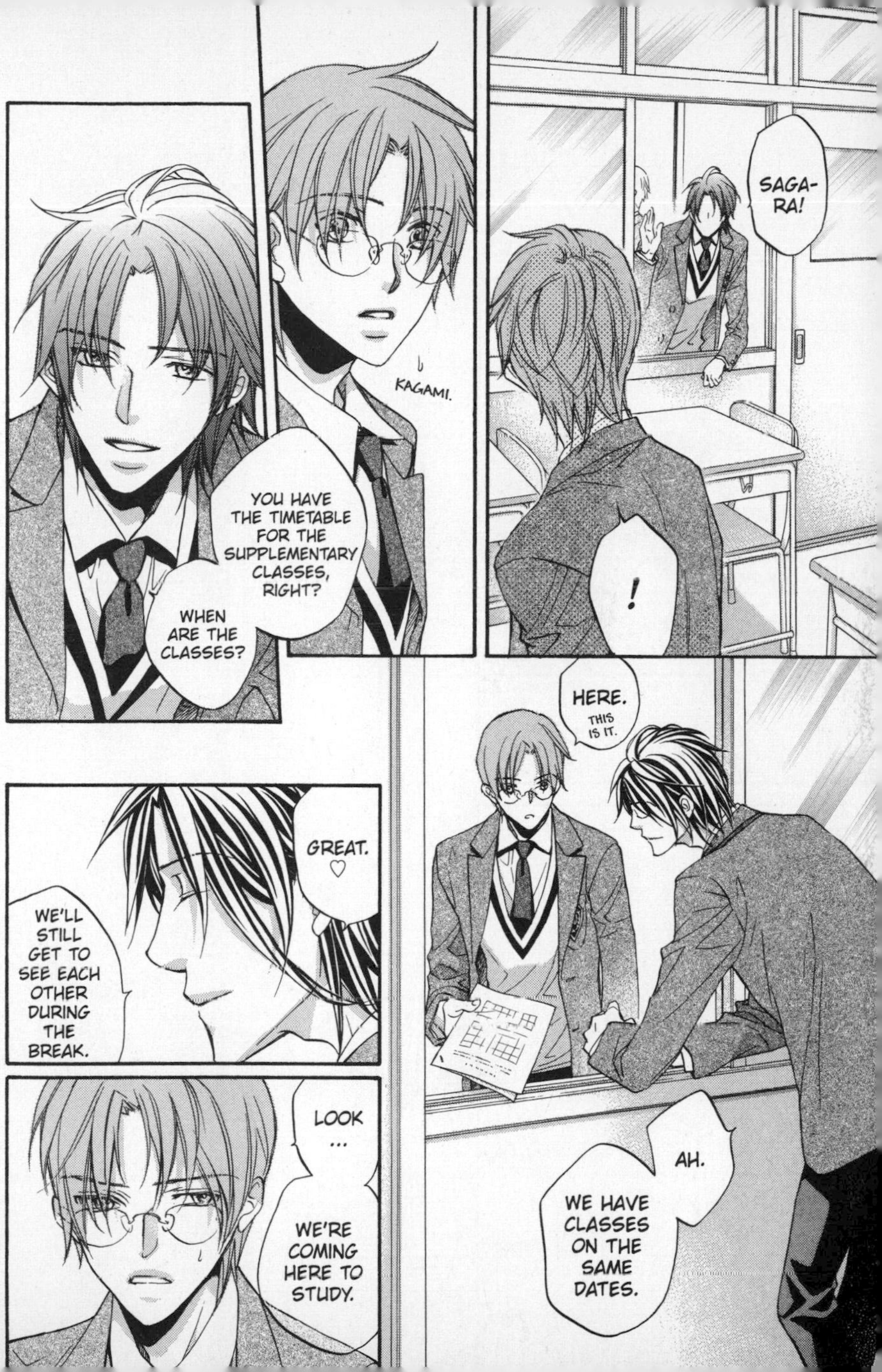
SAGA-RA!
!
KAGAMI.
YOU HAVE THE TIMETABLE FOR THE SUPPLEMENTARY CLASSES, RIGHT?
WHEN ARE THE CLASSES?
HERE.
THIS IS IT.
AH.
WE HAVE CLASSES ON THE SAME DATES.
GREAT. ♡
WE'LL STILL GET TO SEE EACH OTHER DURING THE BREAK.
LOOK ...
WE'RE COMING HERE TO STUDY.

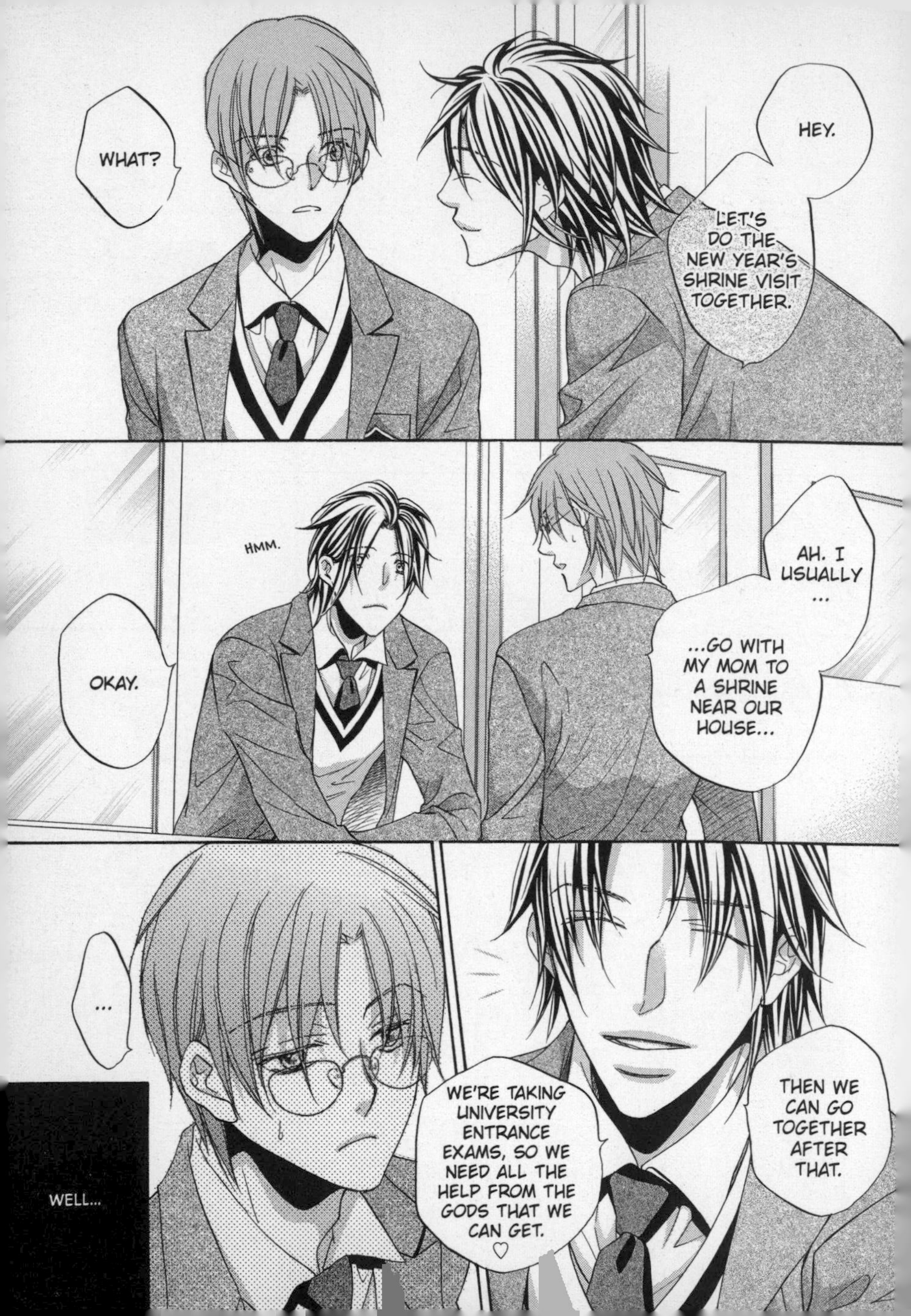
HEY.
LET'S DO THE NEW YEAR'S SHRINE VISIT TOGETHER.
WHAT?
AH. I USUALLY ...
...GO WITH MY MOM TO A SHRINE NEAR OUR HOUSE...
HMM.
OKAY.
THEN WE CAN GO TOGETHER AFTER THAT.
WE'RE TAKING UNIVERSITY ENTRANCE EXAMS, SO WE NEED ALL THE HELP FROM THE GODS THAT WE CAN GET. ♡
...
WELL...

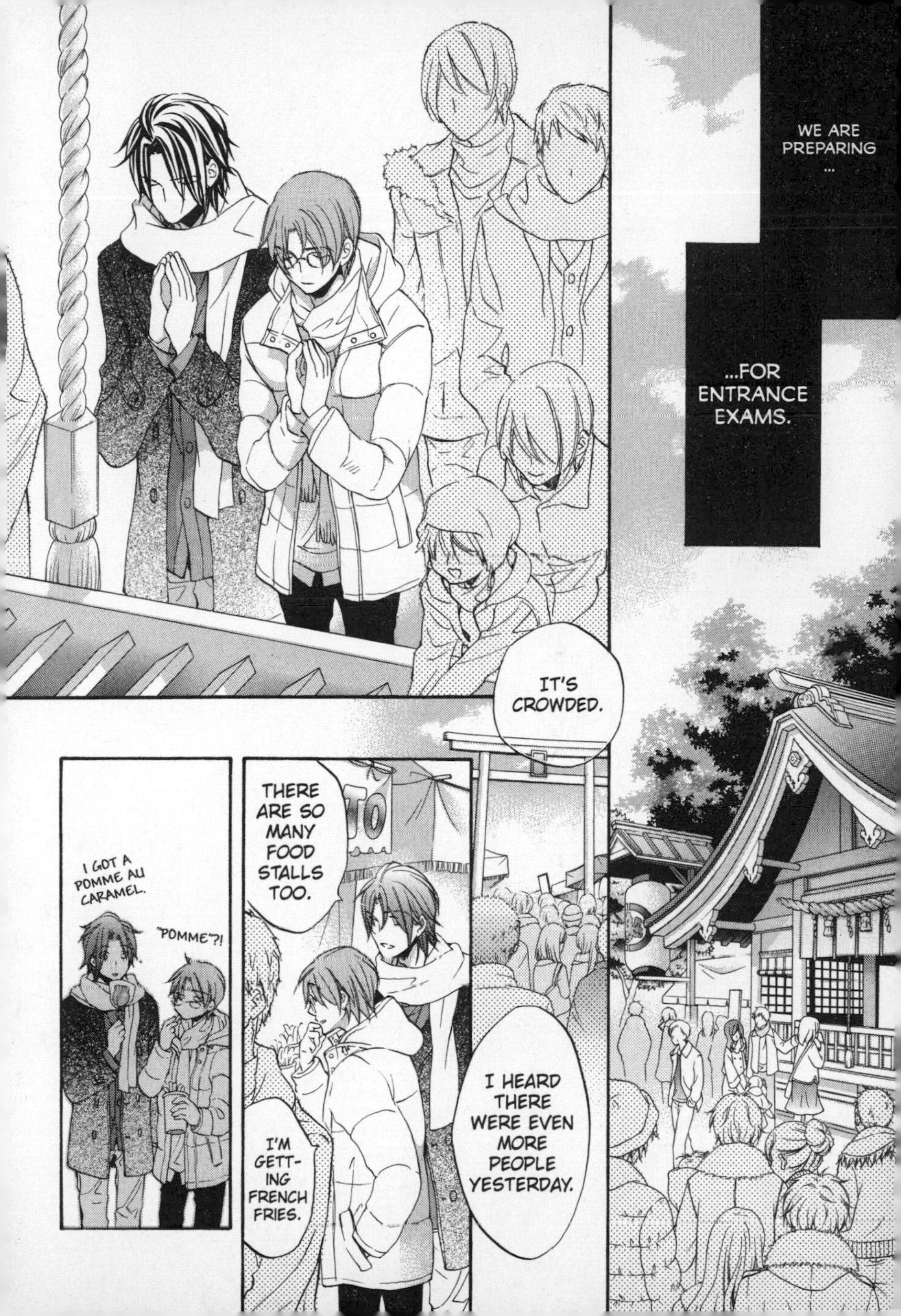
WE ARE PREPARING ...
...FOR ENTRANCE EXAMS.
IT'S CROWDED.
THERE ARE SO MANY FOOD STALLS TOO.
I HEARD THERE WERE EVEN MORE PEOPLE YESTERDAY.
I'M GETT-ING FRENCH FRIES.
I GOT A POMME AU CARAMEL.
"POMME"?!

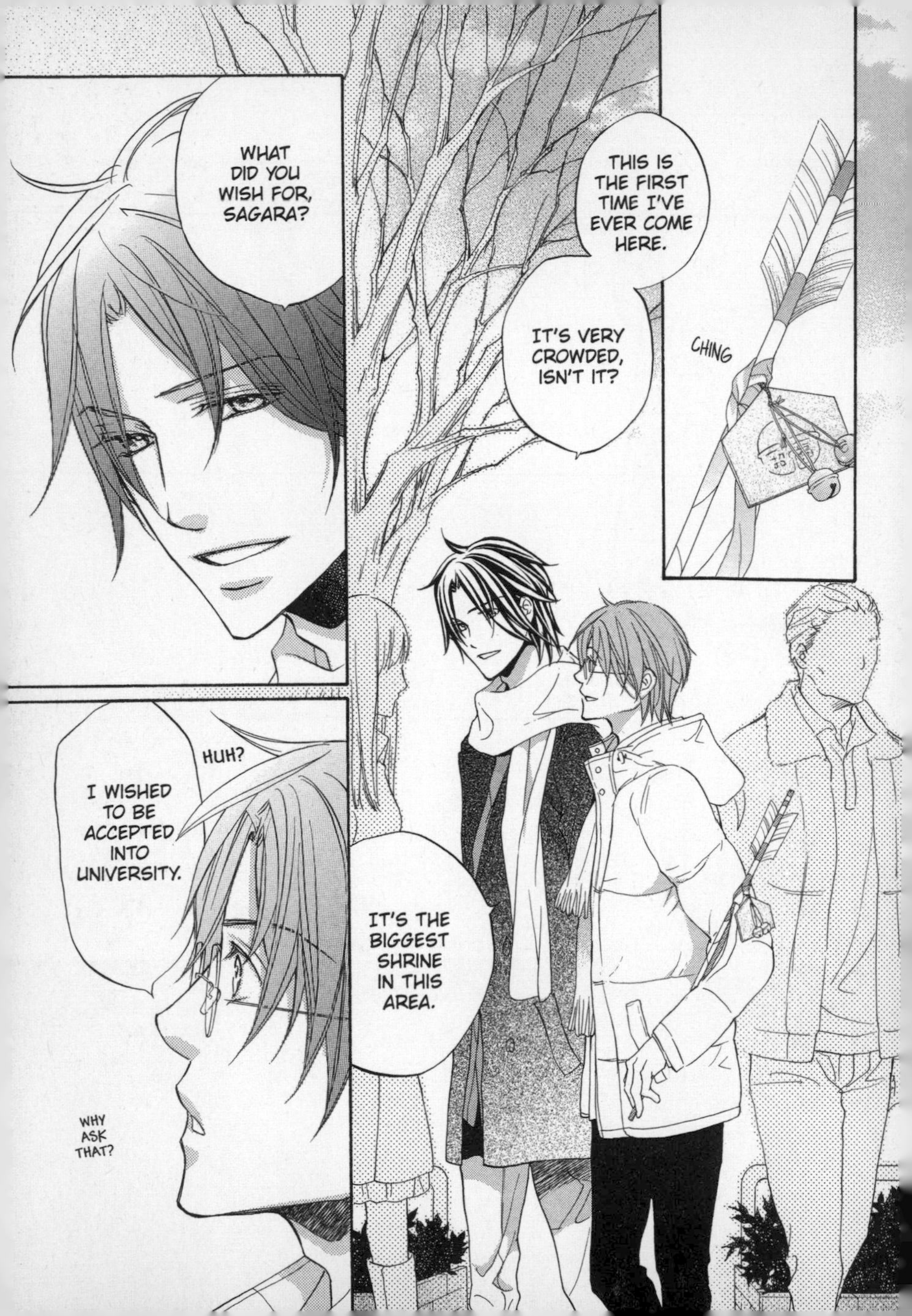
THIS IS THE FIRST TIME I'VE EVER COME HERE.
IT'S VERY CROWDED, ISN'T IT?
CHING
IT'S THE BIGGEST SHRINE IN THIS AREA.
WHAT DID YOU WISH FOR, SAGARA?
HUH?
I WISHED TO BE ACCEPTED INTO UNIVERSITY.
WHY ASK THAT?

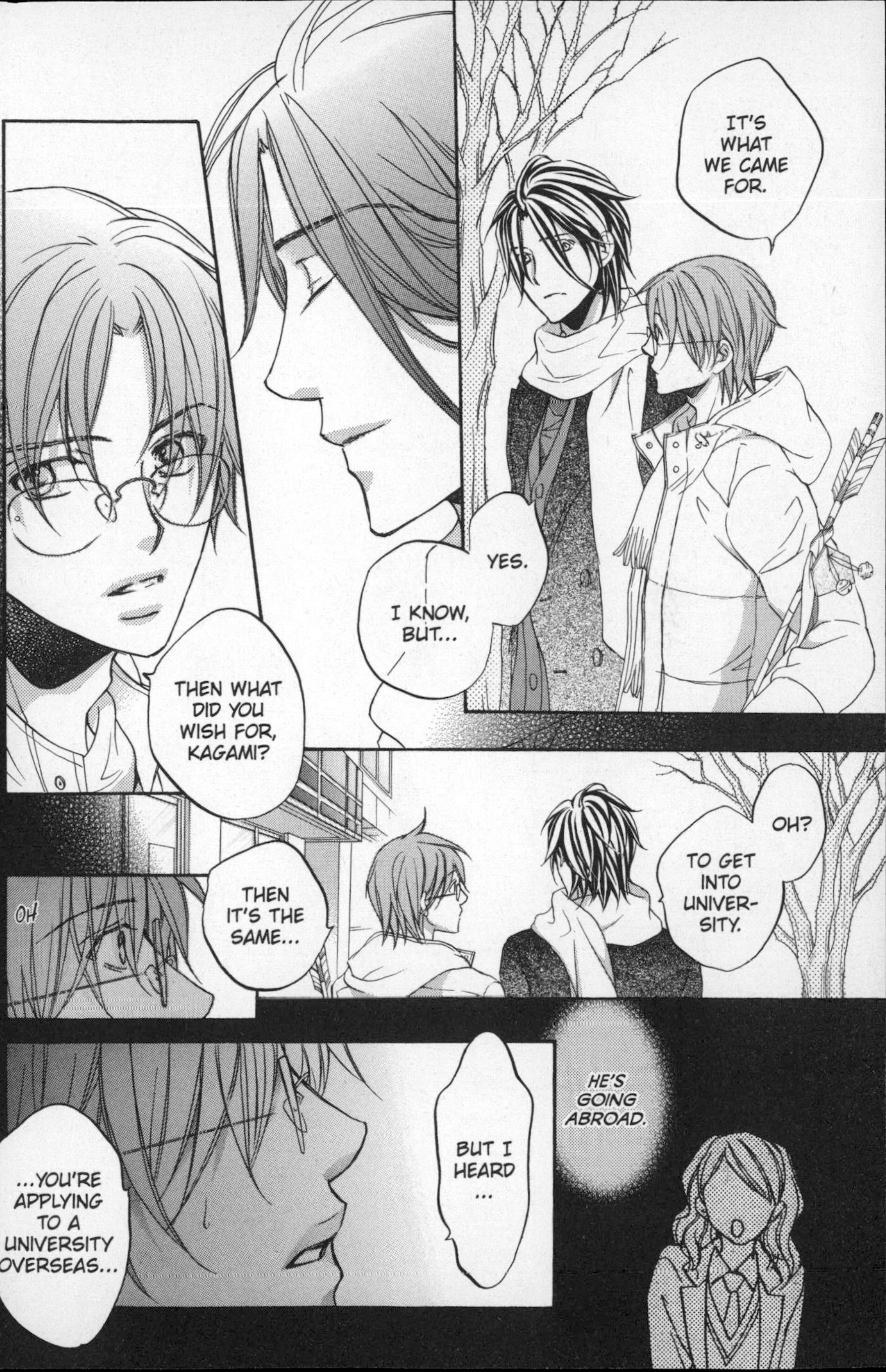
IT'S WHAT WE CAME FOR.
YES.
I KNOW, BUT...
THEN WHAT DID YOU WISH FOR, KAGAMI?
OH? TO GET INTO UNIVER-SITY.
THEN IT'S THE SAME...
OH
HE'S GOING ABROAD.
BUT I HEARD ...
...YOU'RE APPLYING TO A UNIVERSITY OVERSEAS...

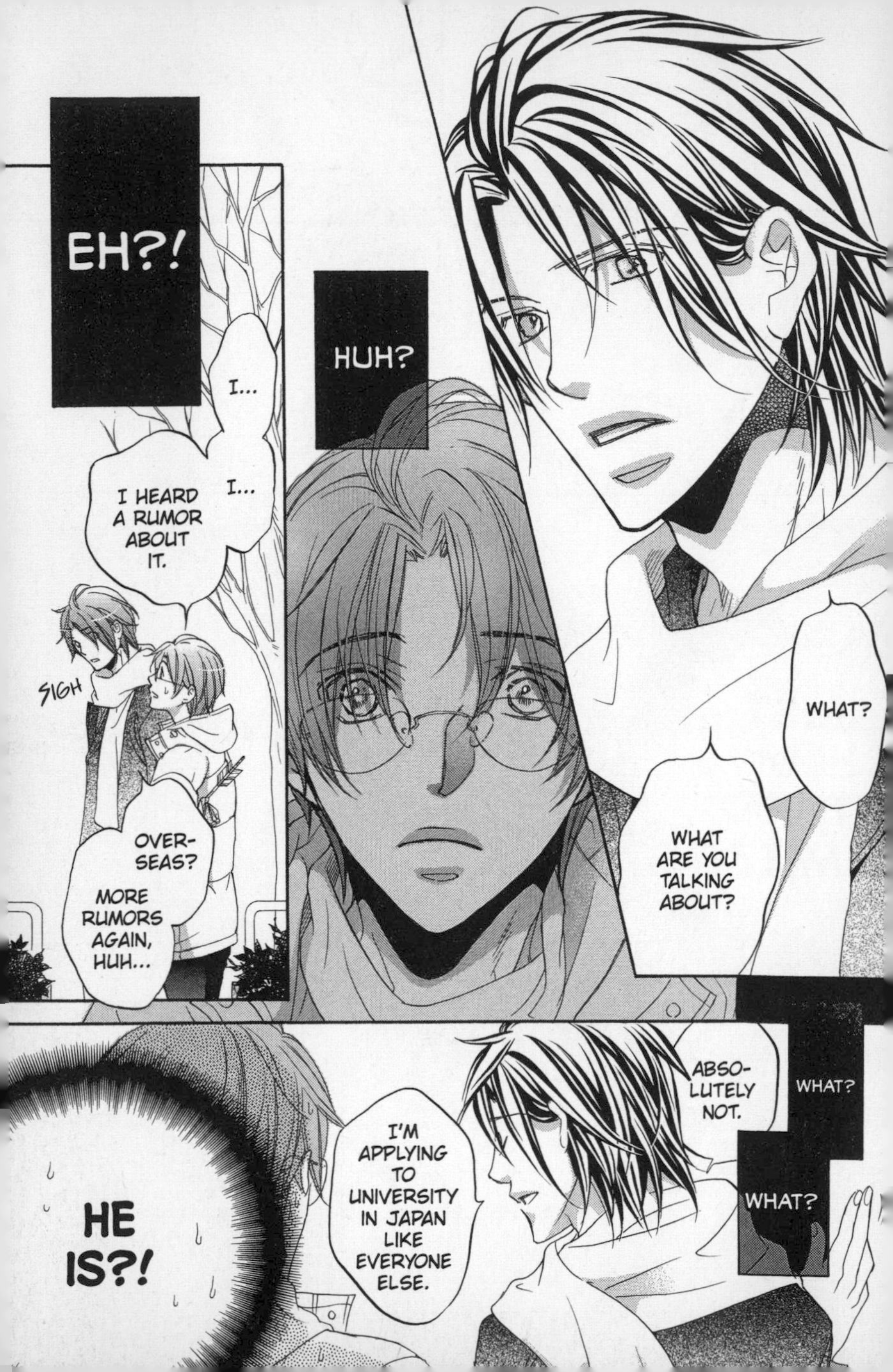
WHAT?
WHAT ARE YOU TALKING ABOUT?
HUH?
EH?!
I...
I...
I HEARD A RUMOR ABOUT IT.
SIGH
OVER-SEAS? MORE RUMORS AGAIN, HUH...
WHAT?
WHAT?
ABSO-LUTELY NOT.
I'M APPLYING TO UNIVERSITY IN JAPAN LIKE EVERYONE ELSE.
HE IS?!

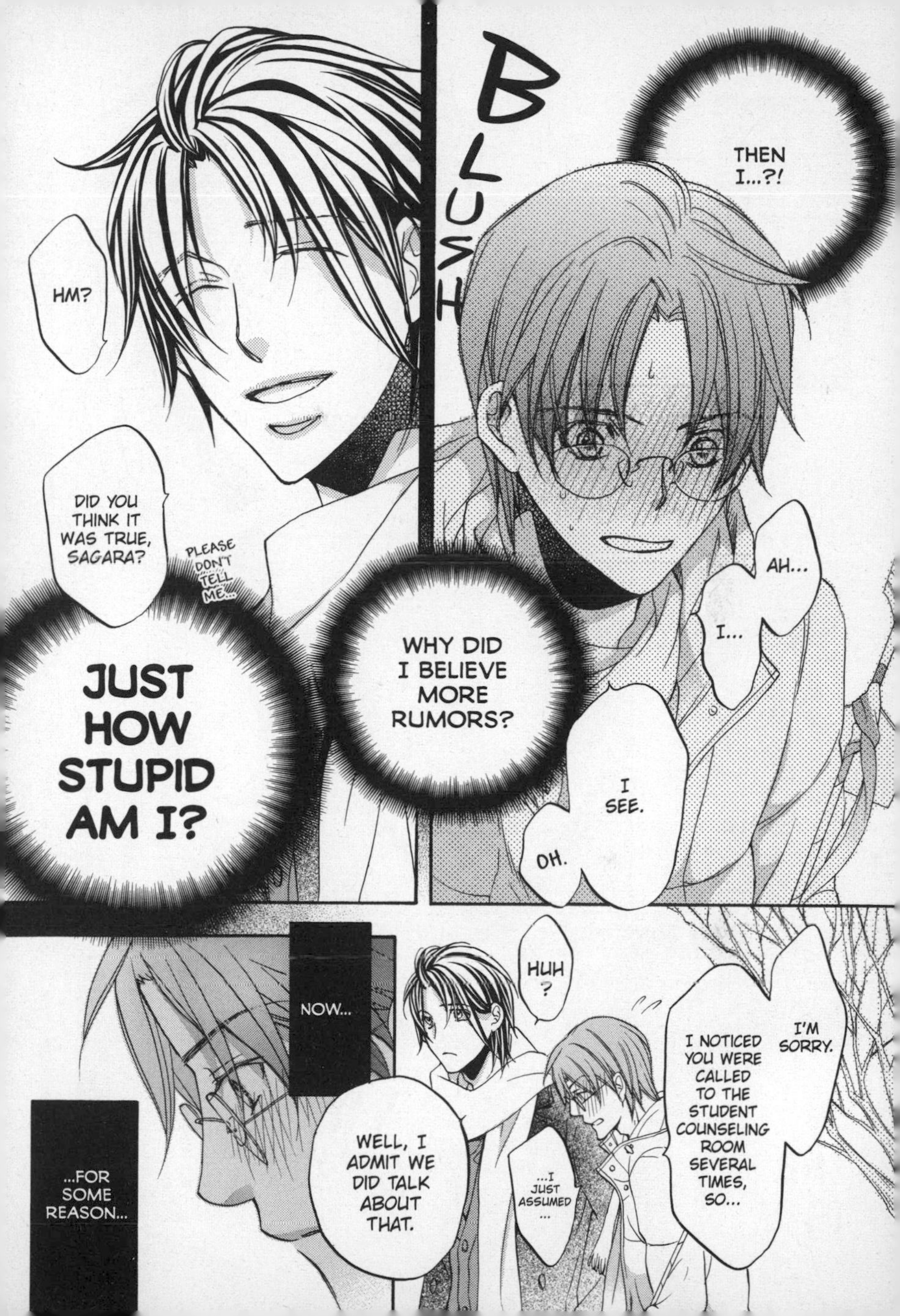
THEN I...?!
BLUSH
AH...
I...
I SEE.
OH.
WHY DID I BELIEVE MORE RUMORS?
HM?
DID YOU THINK IT WAS TRUE, SAGARA?
PLEASE DON'T TELL ME...
JUST HOW STUPID AM I?
I'M SORRY.
I NOTICED YOU WERE CALLED TO THE STUDENT COUNSELING ROOM SEVERAL TIMES, SO...
HUH?
...I JUST ASSUMED...
WELL, I ADMIT WE DID TALK ABOUT THAT.
NOW...
...FOR SOME REASON...

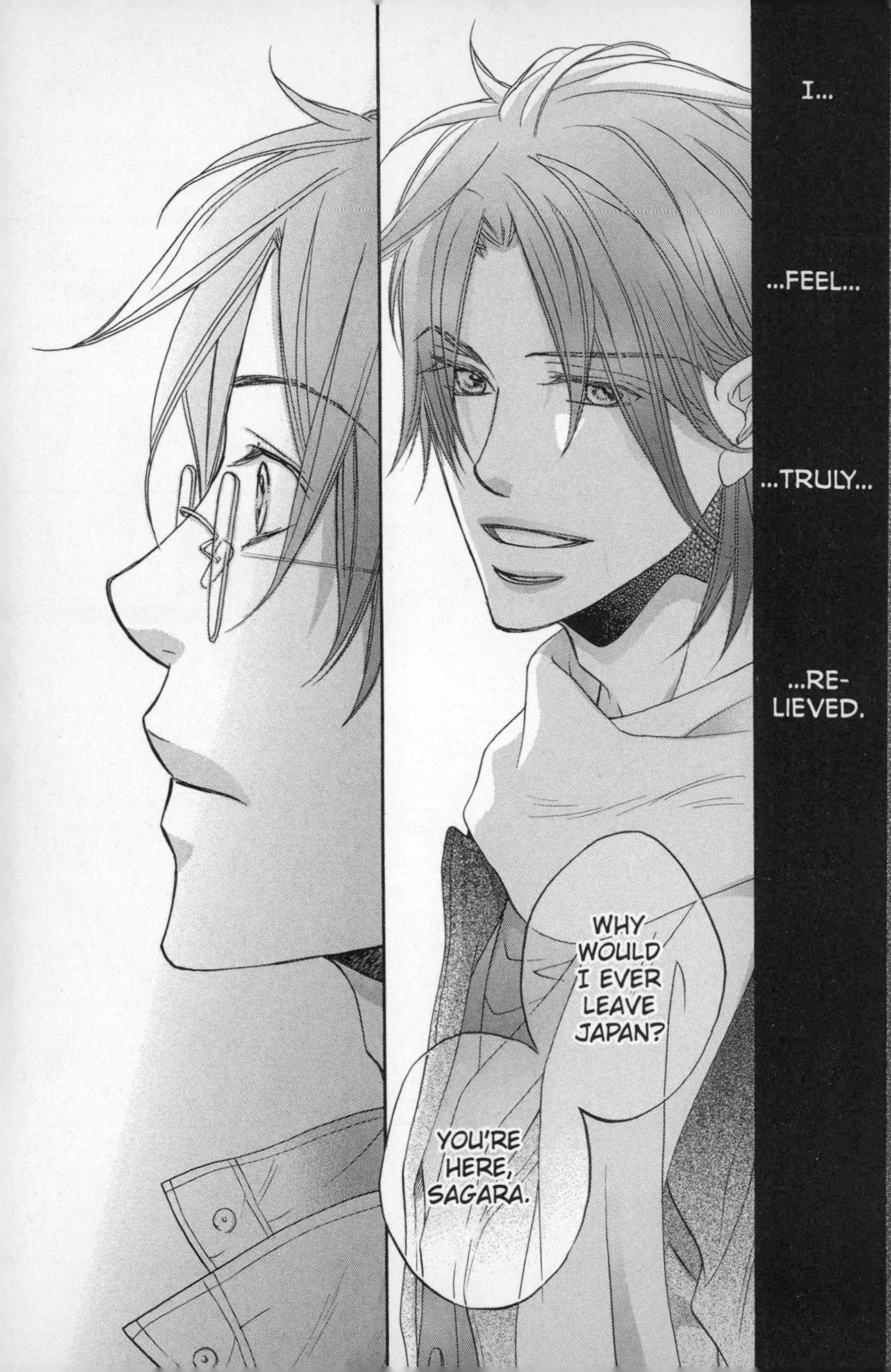
I...
...FEEL...
...TRULY...
...RE-
LIEVED.
WHY WOULD I EVER LEAVE JAPAN?
YOU'RE HERE, SAGARA.

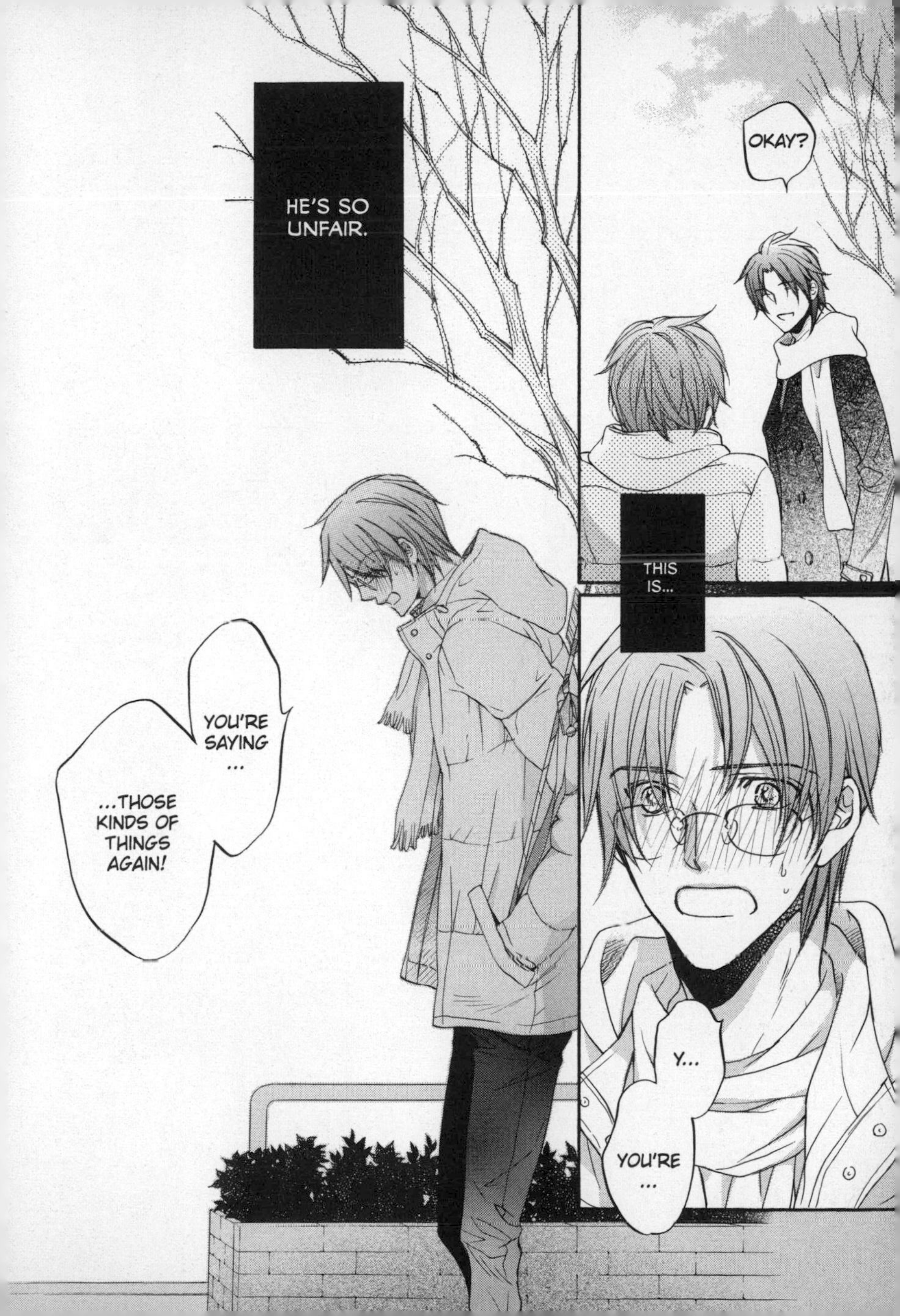
OKAY?
THIS IS...
Y...
YOU'RE ...
HE'S SO UNFAIR.
YOU'RE SAYING ...
...THOSE KINDS OF THINGS AGAIN!

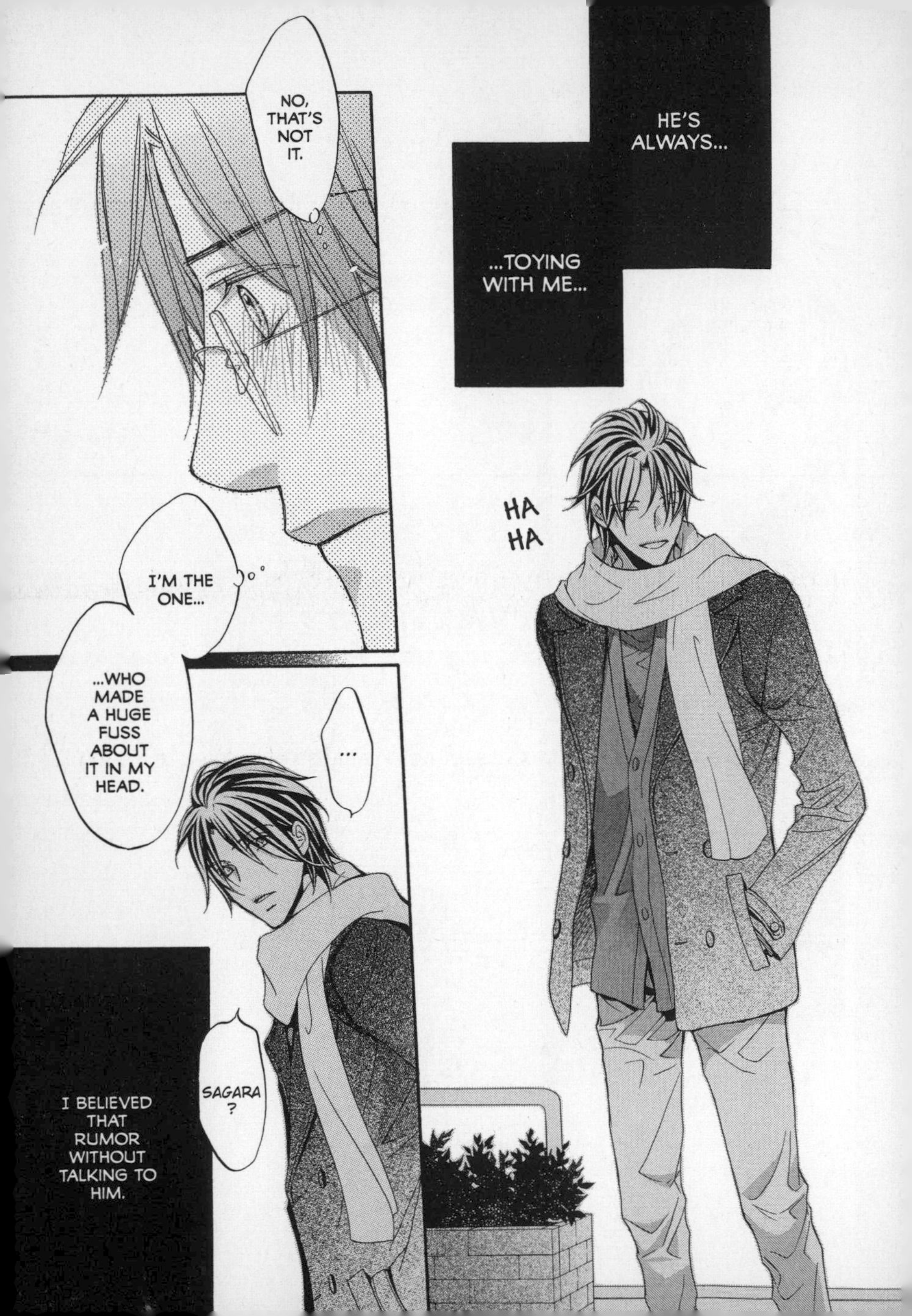
HE'S ALWAYS...
...TOYING WITH ME...
HA HA
NO, THAT'S NOT IT.
I'M THE ONE...
...WHO MADE A HUGE FUSS ABOUT IT IN MY HEAD.
...
SAGARA?
I BELIEVED THAT RUMOR WITHOUT TALKING TO HIM.

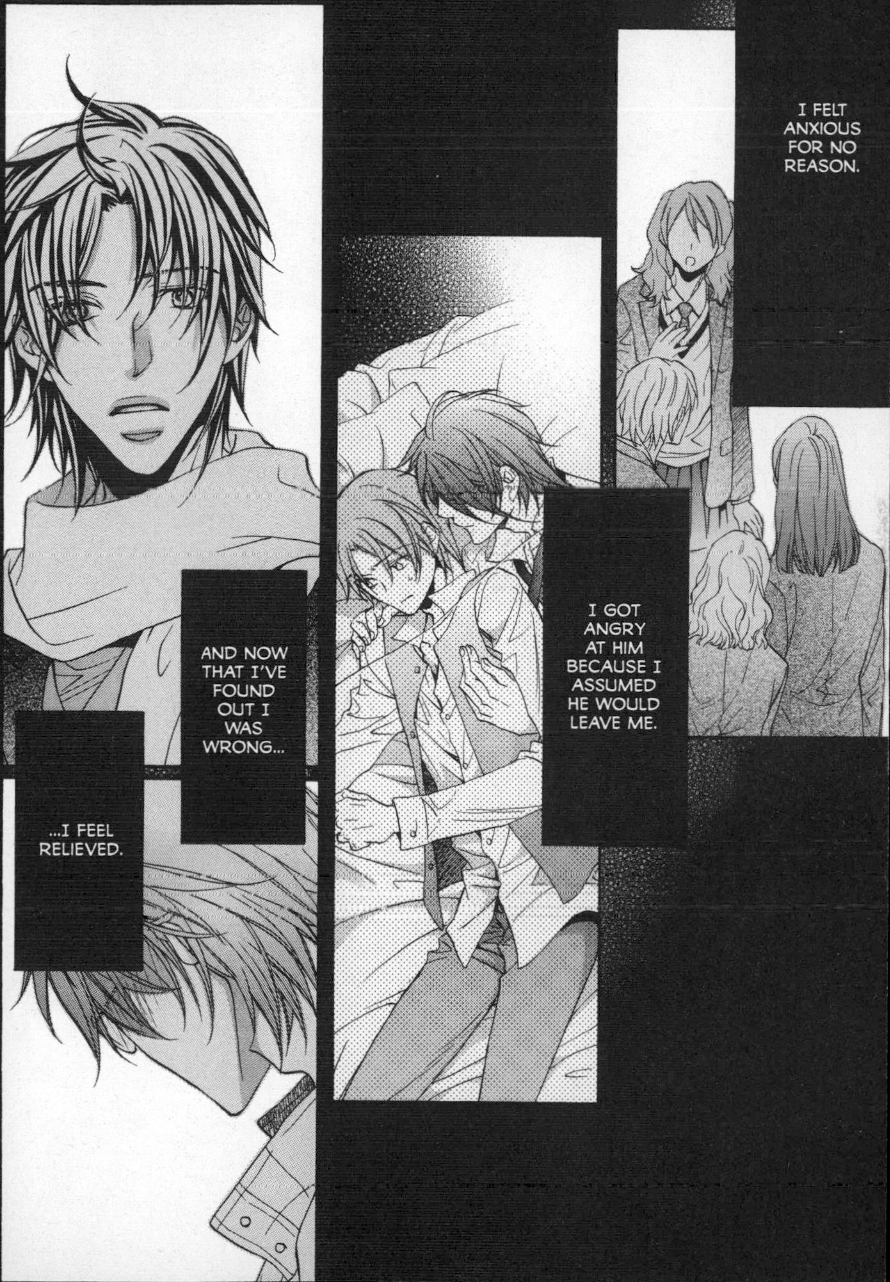
I FELT ANXIOUS FOR NO REASON.
I GOT ANGRY AT HIM BECAUSE I ASSUMED HE WOULD LEAVE ME.
AND NOW THAT I'VE FOUND OUT I WAS WRONG...
...I FEEL RELIEVED.

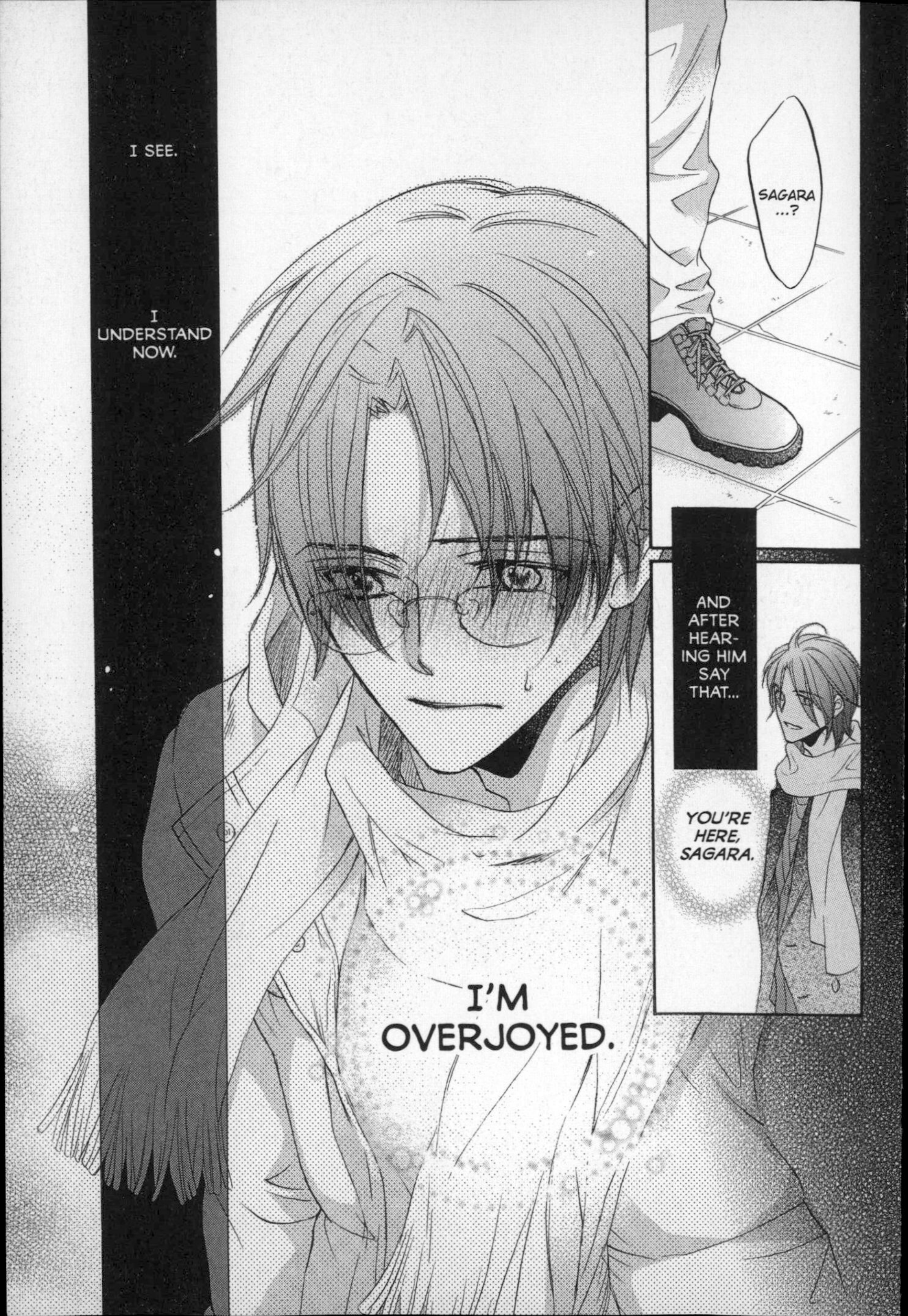
SAGARA ...?
AND AFTER HEARING HIM SAY THAT...
YOU'RE HERE, SAGARA.
I SEE.
I UNDERSTAND NOW.
I'M OVERJOYED.

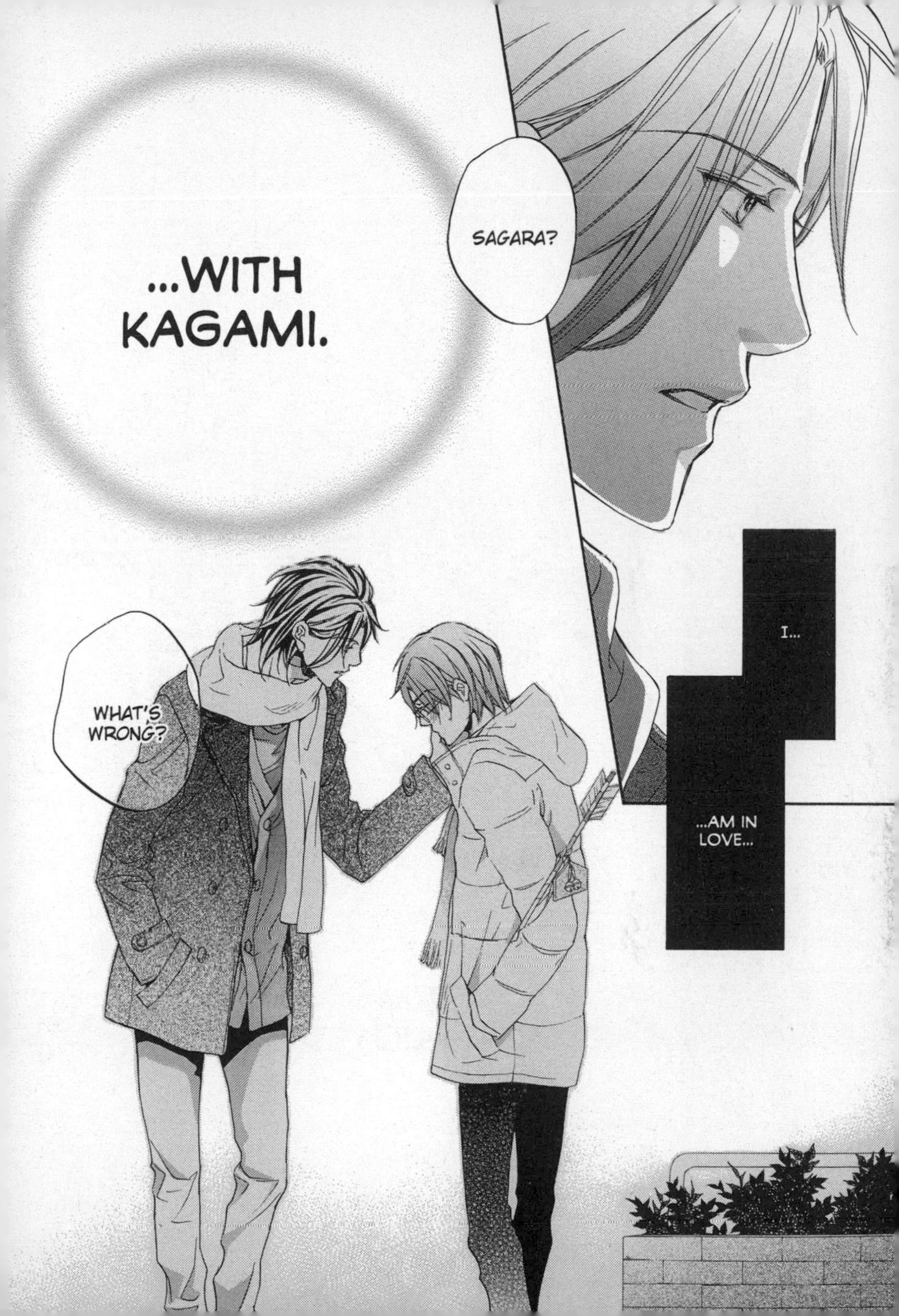
SAGARA?
I...
...AM IN LOVE...
...WITH KAGAMI.
WHAT'S WRONG?

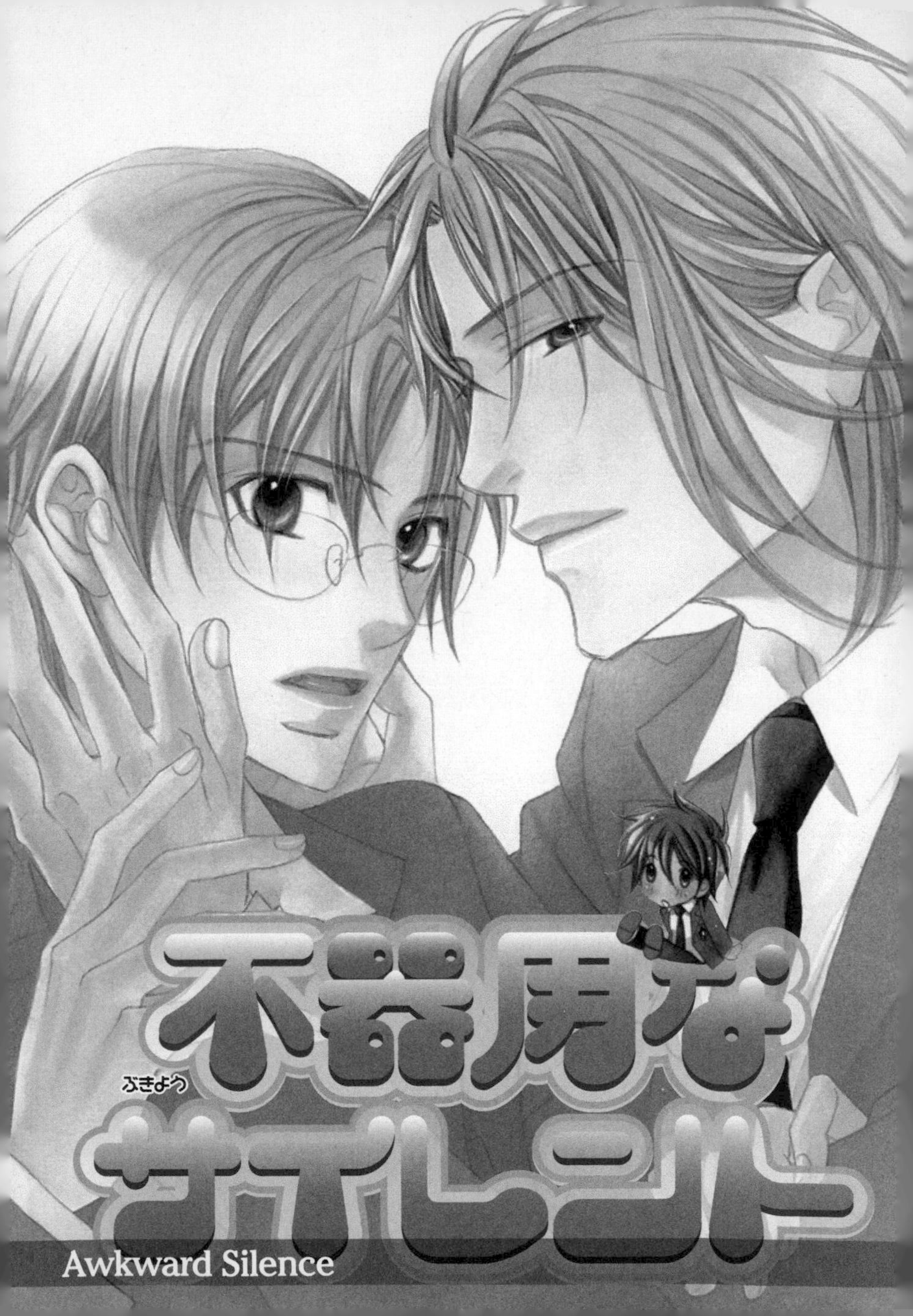
ぶきよう
不器用なサイレント
Awkward Silence

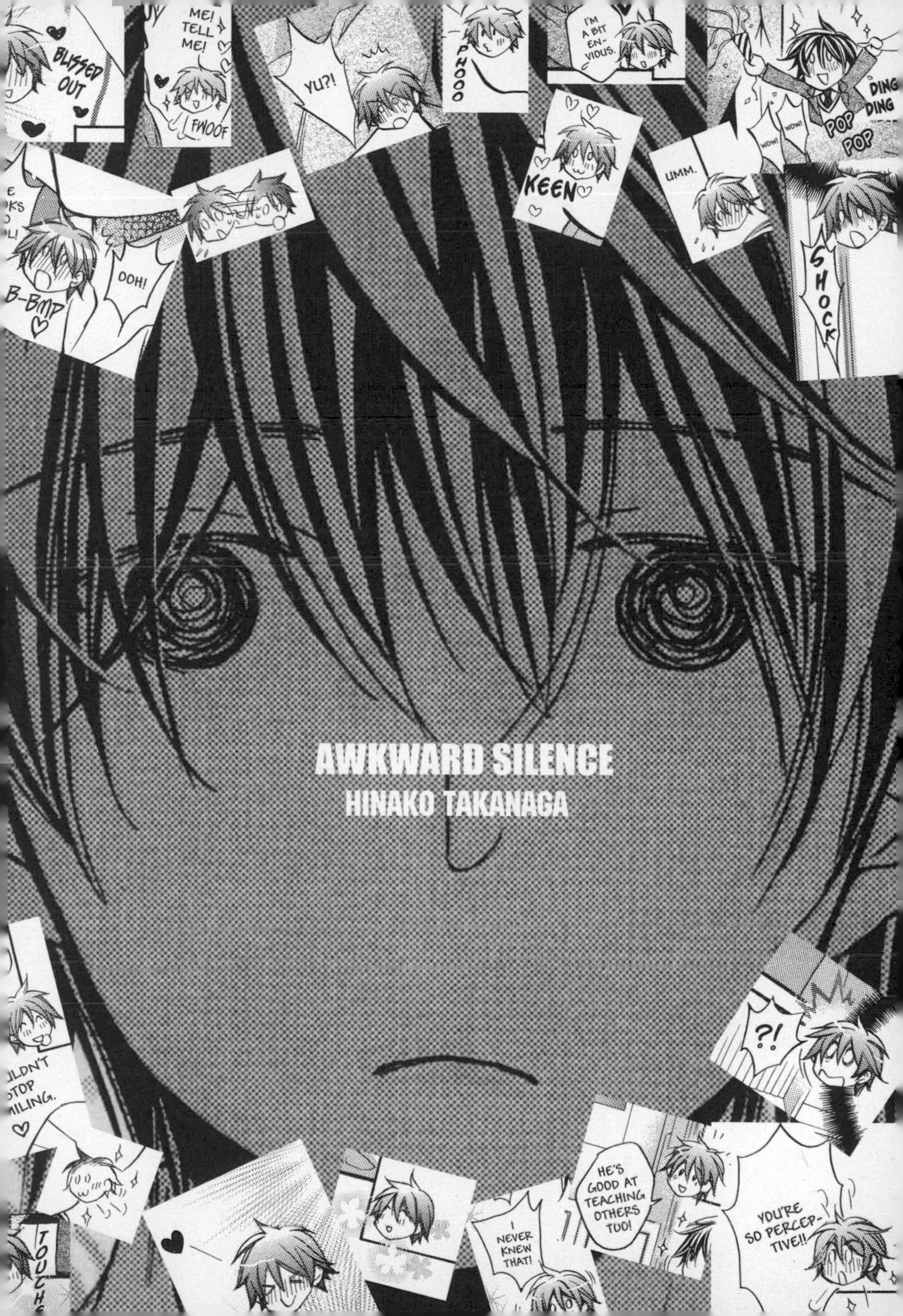
DING DING
POP POP
WOW!
WOW!
I'M A BIT EN-VIOUS.
PHOOOO
YU?!
ME! TELL ME!
FWOOF
BLISSED OUT
UMM.
SHOCK
KEEN
OOH!
B-BMP
AWKWARD SILENCE
HINAKO TAKANAGA
?!
YOU'RE SO PERCEP-TIVE!!
HE'S GOOD AT TEACHING OTHERS TOO!
I NEVER KNEW THAT!

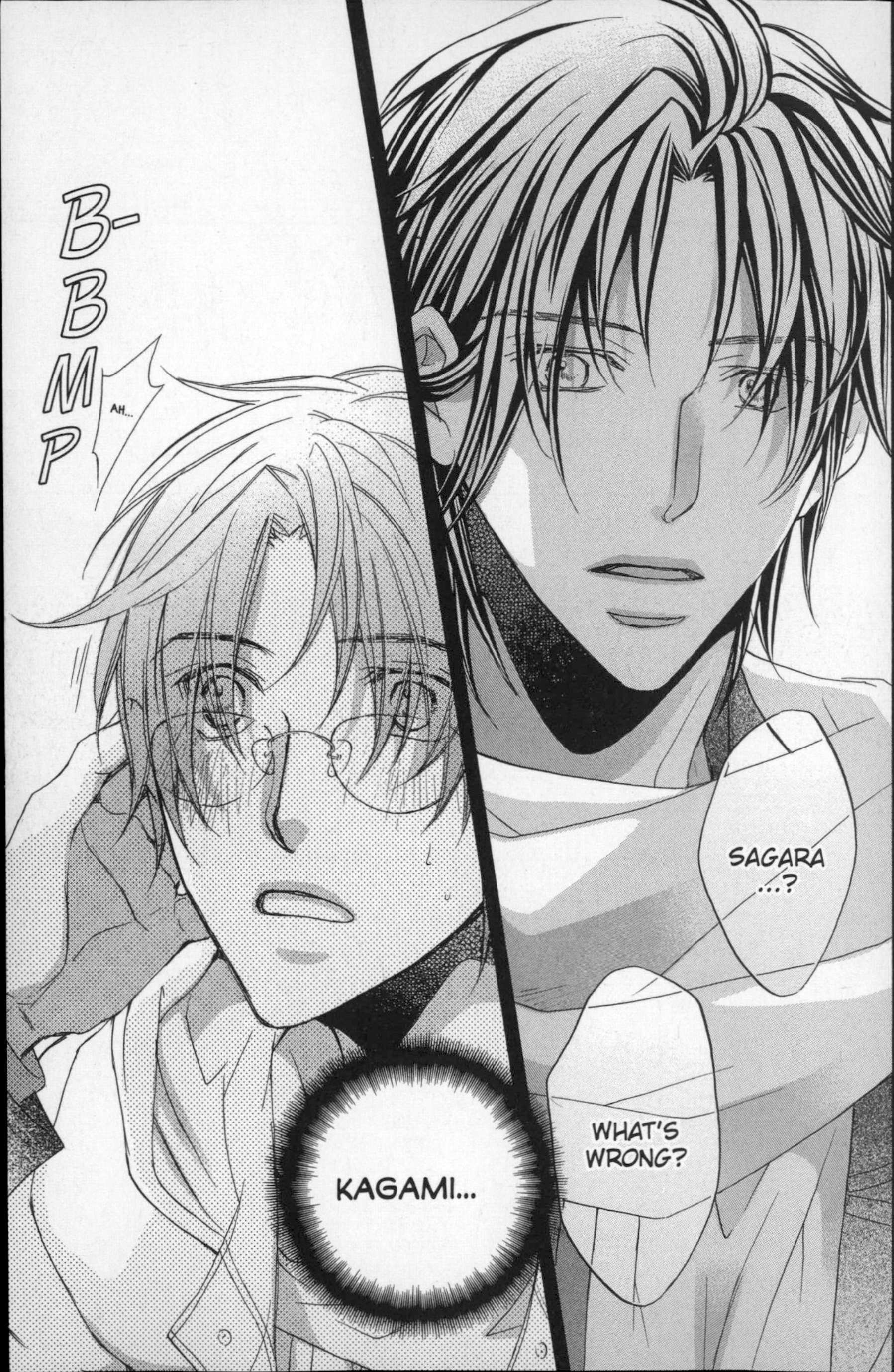
SAGARA ...?
WHAT'S WRONG?
B-BMP
AH...
KAGAMI...

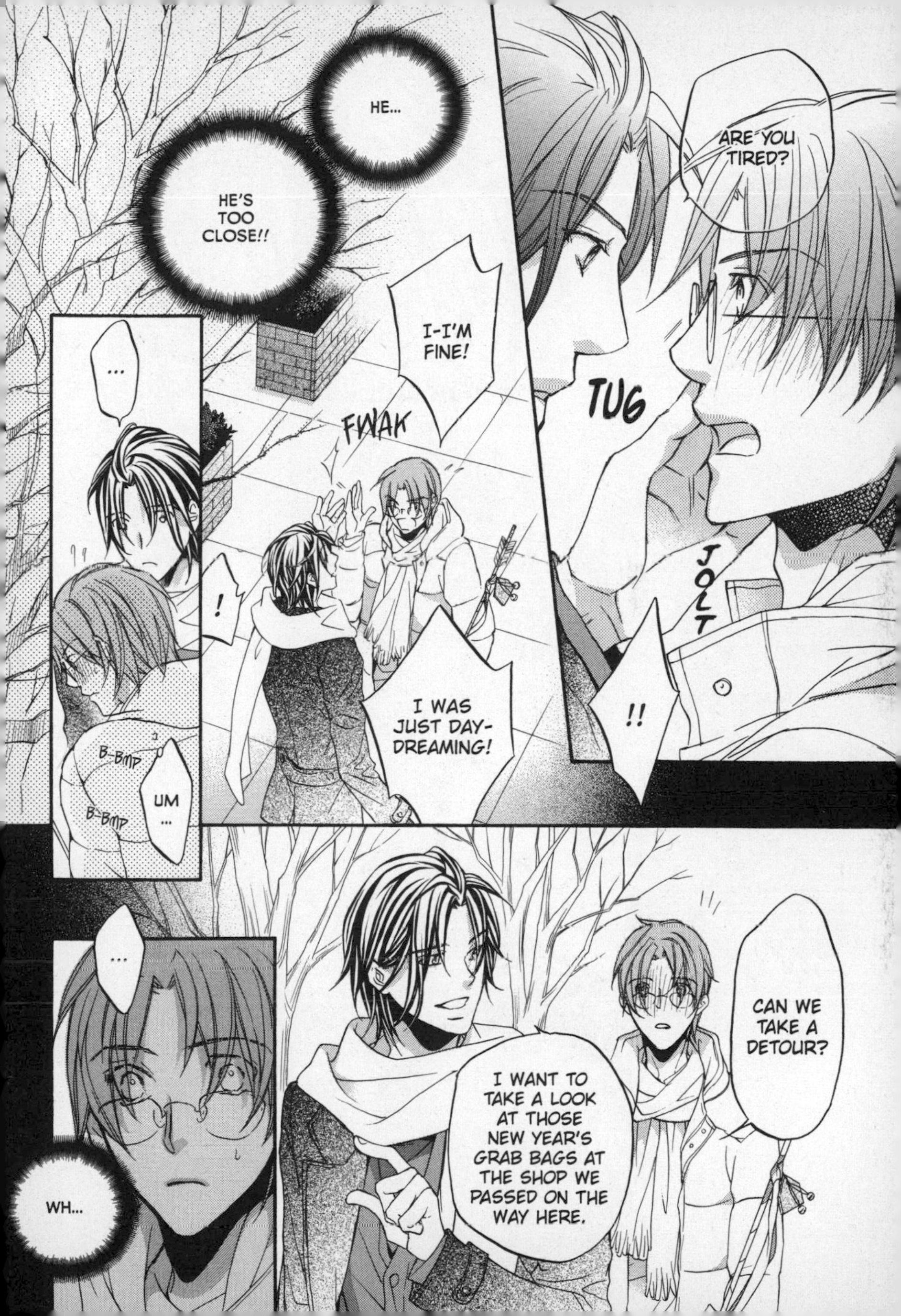

ARE YOU TIRED?
TUG
JOLT
!!
HE...
HE'S TOO CLOSE!!
I-I'M FINE!
FWAK
!
I WAS JUST DAY-DREAMING!
...
B-BMP
B-BMP
UM...
CAN WE TAKE A DETOUR?
I WANT TO TAKE A LOOK AT THOSE NEW YEAR'S GRAB BAGS AT THE SHOP WE PASSED ON THE WAY HERE.
...
WH...

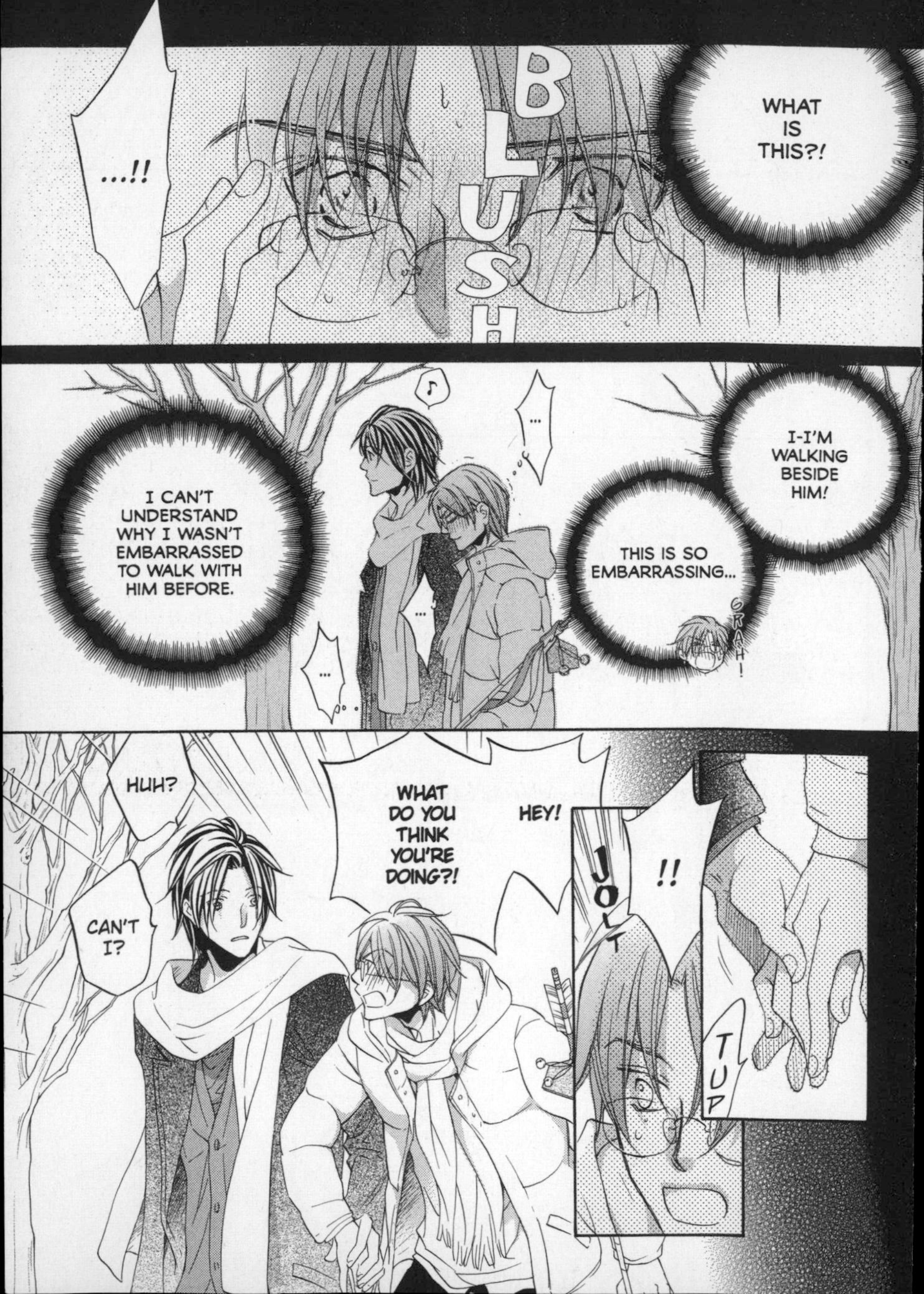
WHAT IS THIS?!
BLUSH
...!!
I-I'M WALKING BESIDE HIM!
THIS IS SO EMBARRASSING...
GRAAH!
♪
...
...
...
I CAN'T UNDERSTAND WHY I WASN'T EMBARRASSED TO WALK WITH HIM BEFORE.
!!
JOLT
TUP
HEY!
WHAT DO YOU THINK YOU'RE DOING?!
HUH?
CAN'T I?

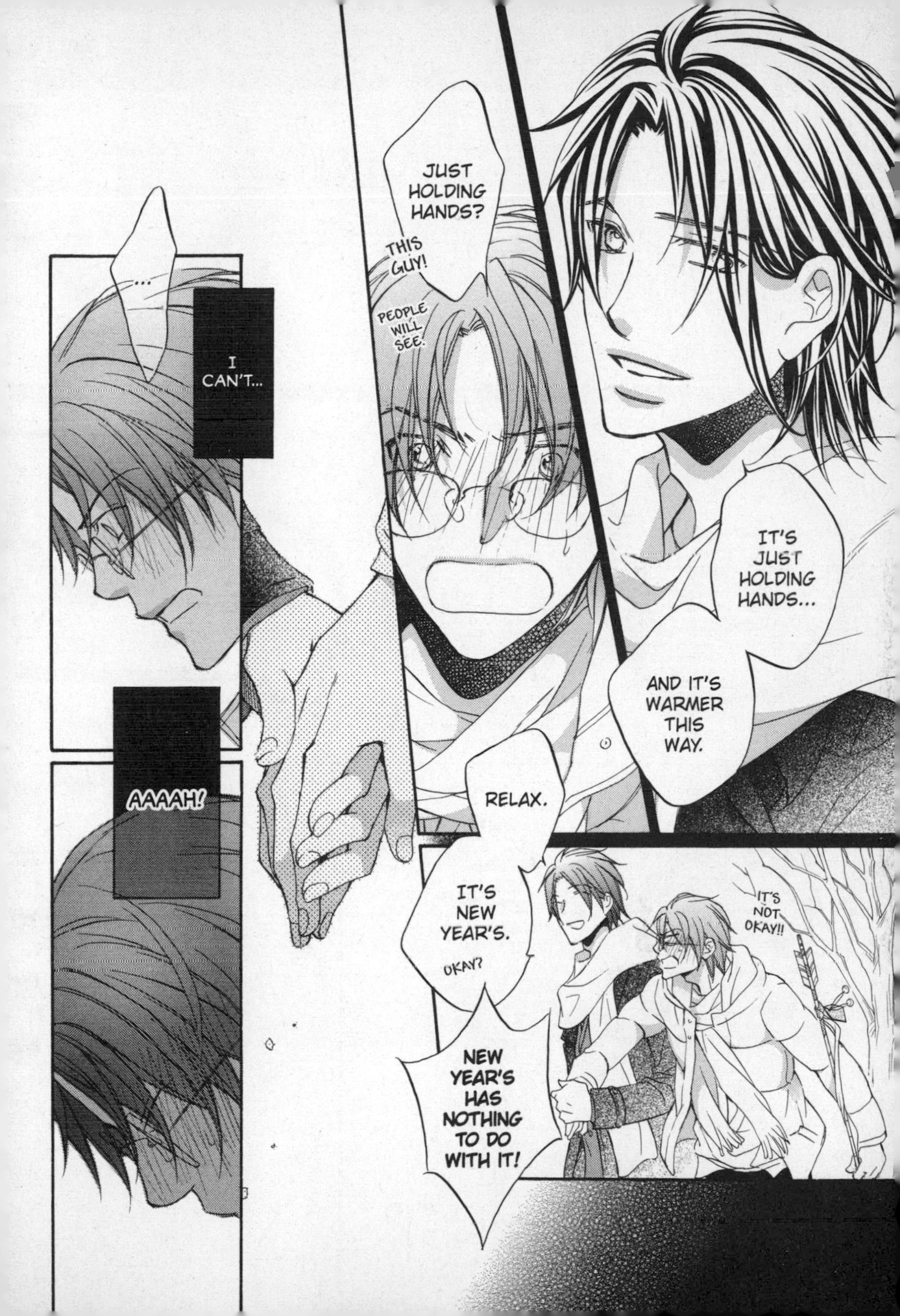
IT'S JUST HOLDING HANDS...
AND IT'S WARMER THIS WAY.
JUST HOLDING HANDS?
THIS GUY!
PEOPLE WILL SEE.
RELAX.
IT'S NEW YEAR'S.
OKAY?
IT'S NOT OKAY!!
NEW YEAR'S HAS NOTHING TO DO WITH IT!
...
I CAN'T...
AAAAH!

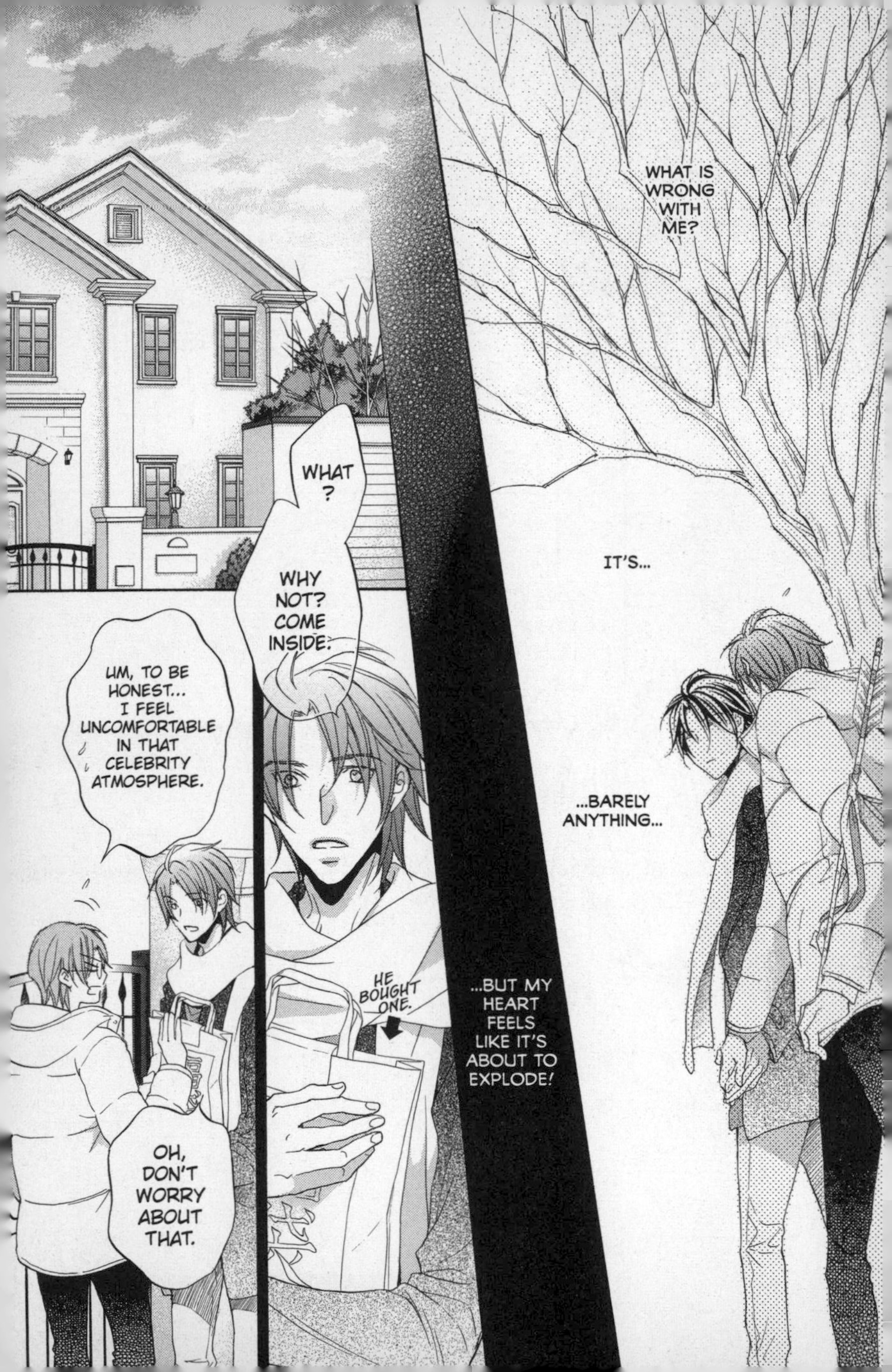
WHAT IS WRONG WITH ME?
IT'S...
...BARELY ANYTHING...
...BUT MY HEART FEELS LIKE IT'S ABOUT TO EXPLODE!
WHAT?
WHY NOT? COME INSIDE.
HE BOUGHT ONE.
UM, TO BE HONEST... I FEEL UNCOMFORTABLE IN THAT CELEBRITY ATMOSPHERE.
OH, DON'T WORRY ABOUT THAT.

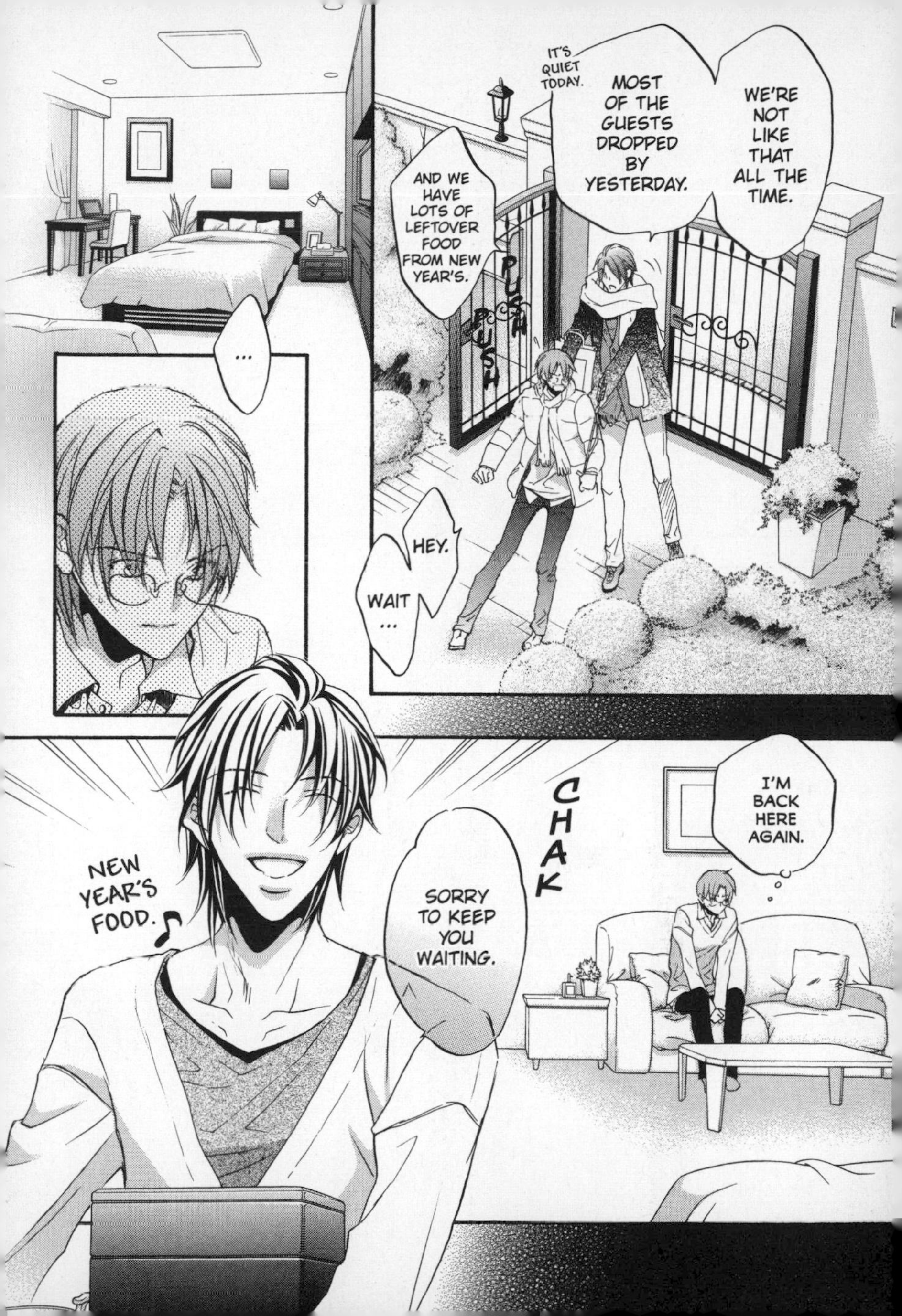
WE'RE NOT LIKE THAT ALL THE TIME.
MOST OF THE GUESTS DROPPED BY YESTERDAY.
IT'S QUIET TODAY.
AND WE HAVE LOTS OF LEFTOVER FOOD FROM NEW YEAR'S.
PUSH
PUSH
HEY.
WAIT ...
...
I'M BACK HERE AGAIN.
CHAK
SORRY TO KEEP YOU WAITING.
NEW YEAR'S FOOD. ♪

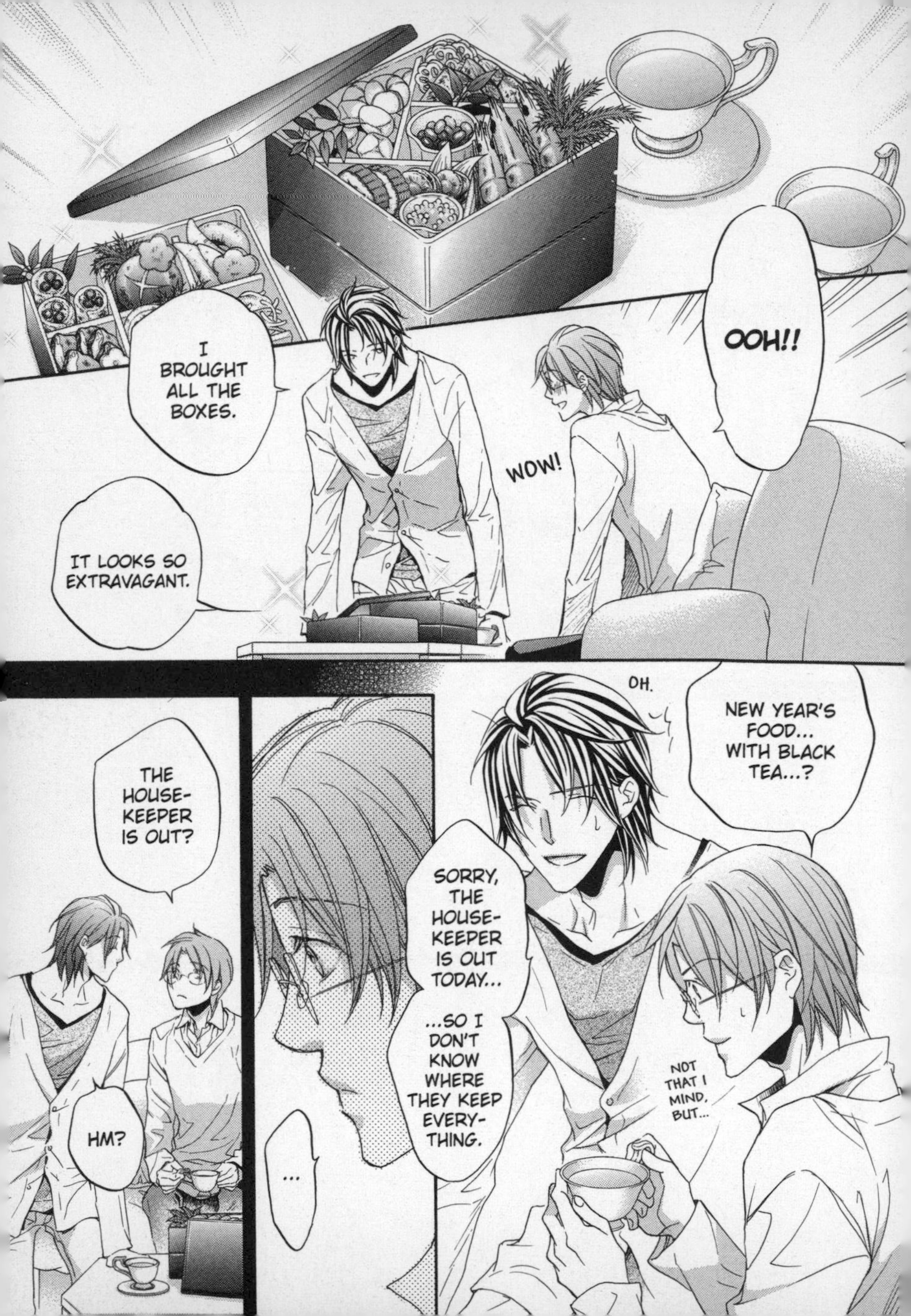
OOH!!
WOW!
I BROUGHT ALL THE BOXES.
IT LOOKS SO EXTRAVAGANT.
OH.
NEW YEAR'S FOOD... WITH BLACK TEA...?
NOT THAT I MIND, BUT...
SORRY, THE HOUSE-KEEPER IS OUT TODAY...
...SO I DON'T KNOW WHERE THEY KEEP EVERY-THING.
...
THE HOUSE-KEEPER IS OUT?
HM?

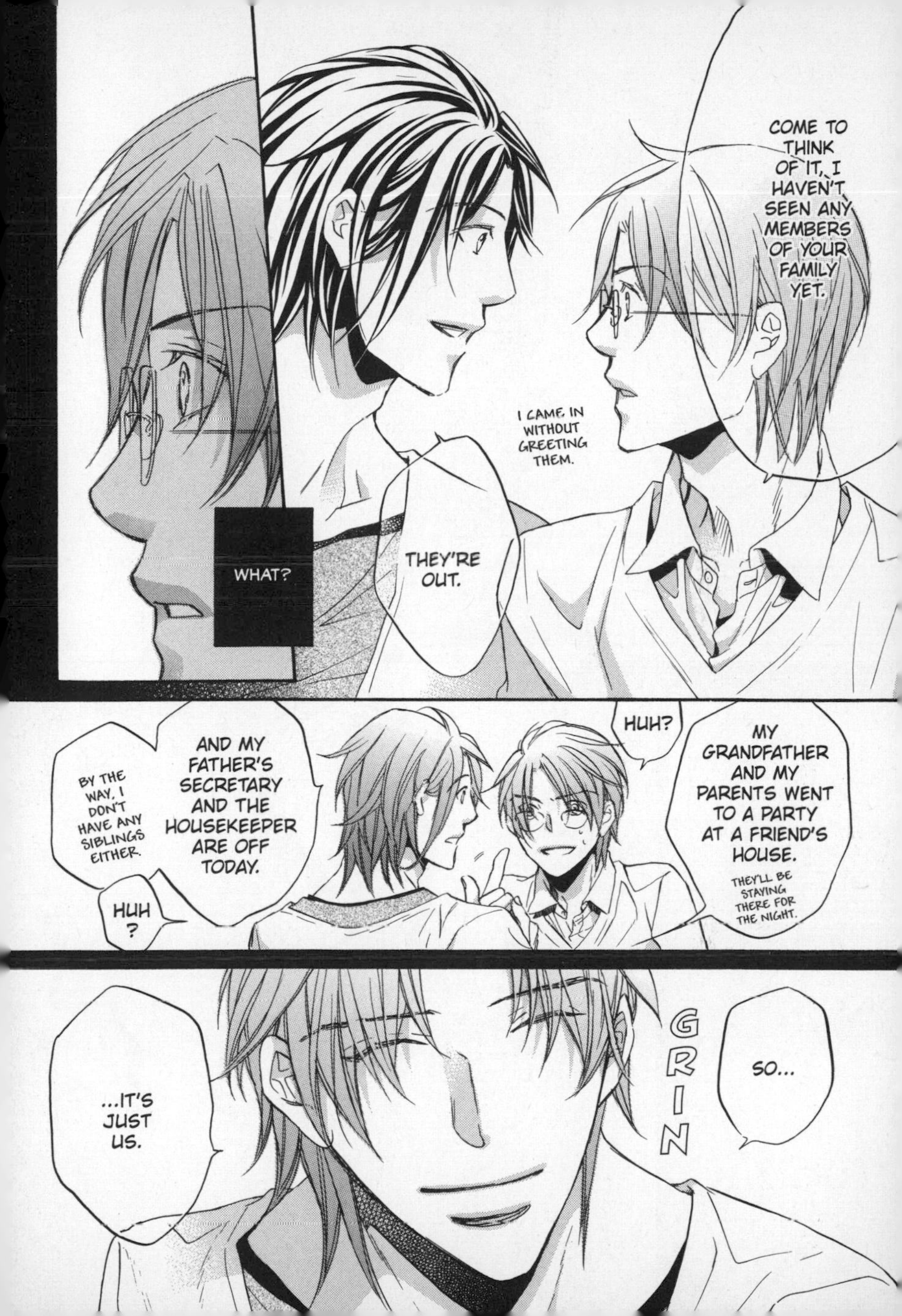
COME TO THINK OF IT, I HAVEN'T SEEN ANY MEMBERS OF YOUR FAMILY YET.
I CAME IN WITHOUT GREETING THEM.
THEY'RE OUT.
WHAT?
HUH?
MY GRANDFATHER AND MY PARENTS WENT TO A PARTY AT A FRIEND'S HOUSE.
THEY'LL BE STAYING THERE FOR THE NIGHT.
AND MY FATHER'S SECRETARY AND THE HOUSEKEEPER ARE OFF TODAY.
BY THE WAY, I DON'T HAVE ANY SIBLINGS EITHER.
HUH?
SO...
GRIN
...IT'S JUST US.

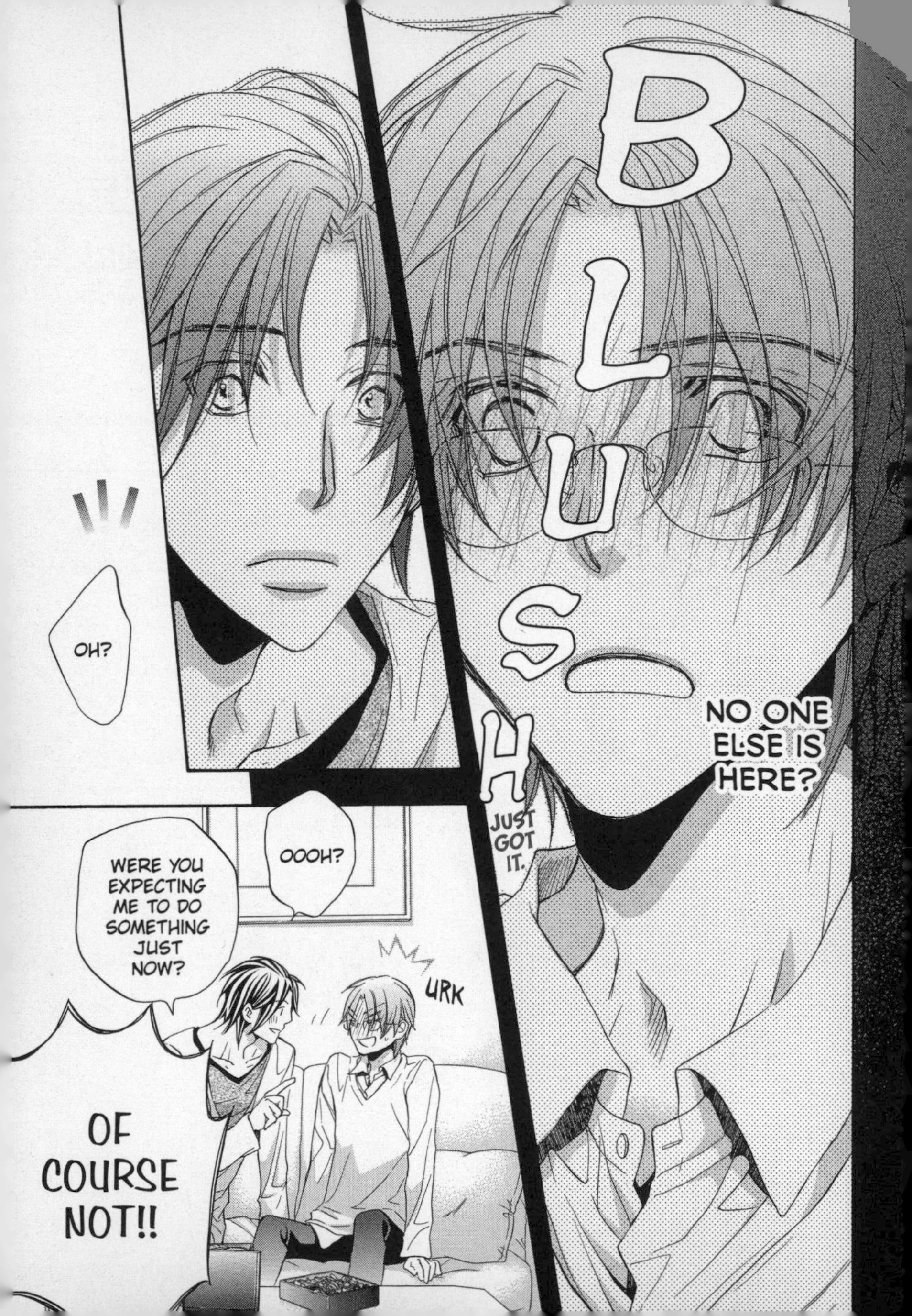

NO ONE ELSE IS HERE?
BLUSH
JUST GOT IT.
OH?
OOOH?
WERE YOU EXPECTING ME TO DO SOMETHING JUST NOW?
URK
OF COURSE NOT!!

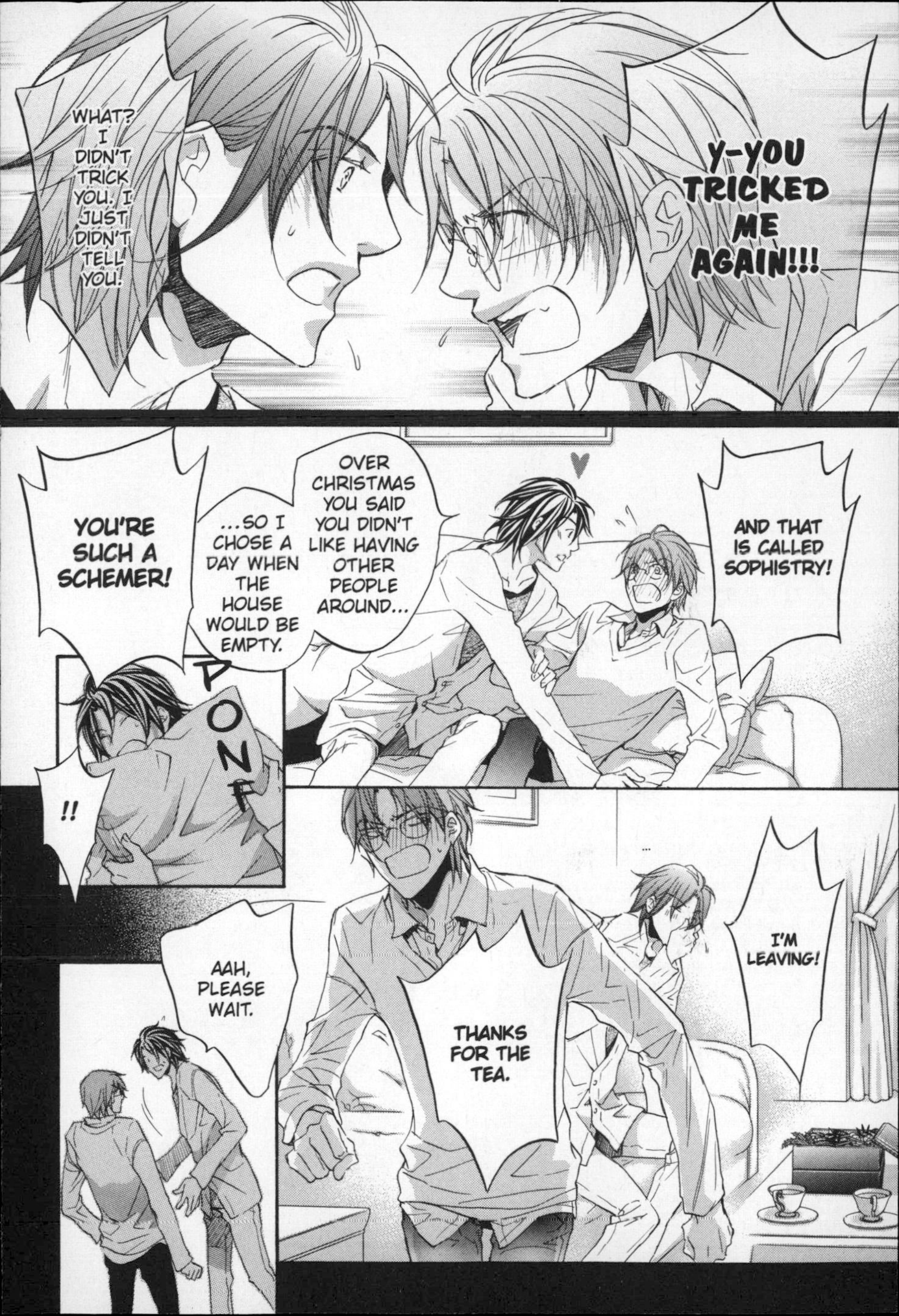
Y-YOU TRICKED ME AGAIN!!!
WHAT? I DIDN'T TRICK YOU. I JUST DIDN'T TELL YOU.
AND THAT IS CALLED SOPHISTRY!
OVER CHRISTMAS YOU SAID YOU DIDN'T LIKE HAVING OTHER PEOPLE AROUND...
...SO I CHOSE A DAY WHEN THE HOUSE WOULD BE EMPTY.
YOU'RE SUCH A SCHEMER!
PONF
!!
I'M LEAVING!
THANKS FOR THE TEA.
AAH, PLEASE WAIT.

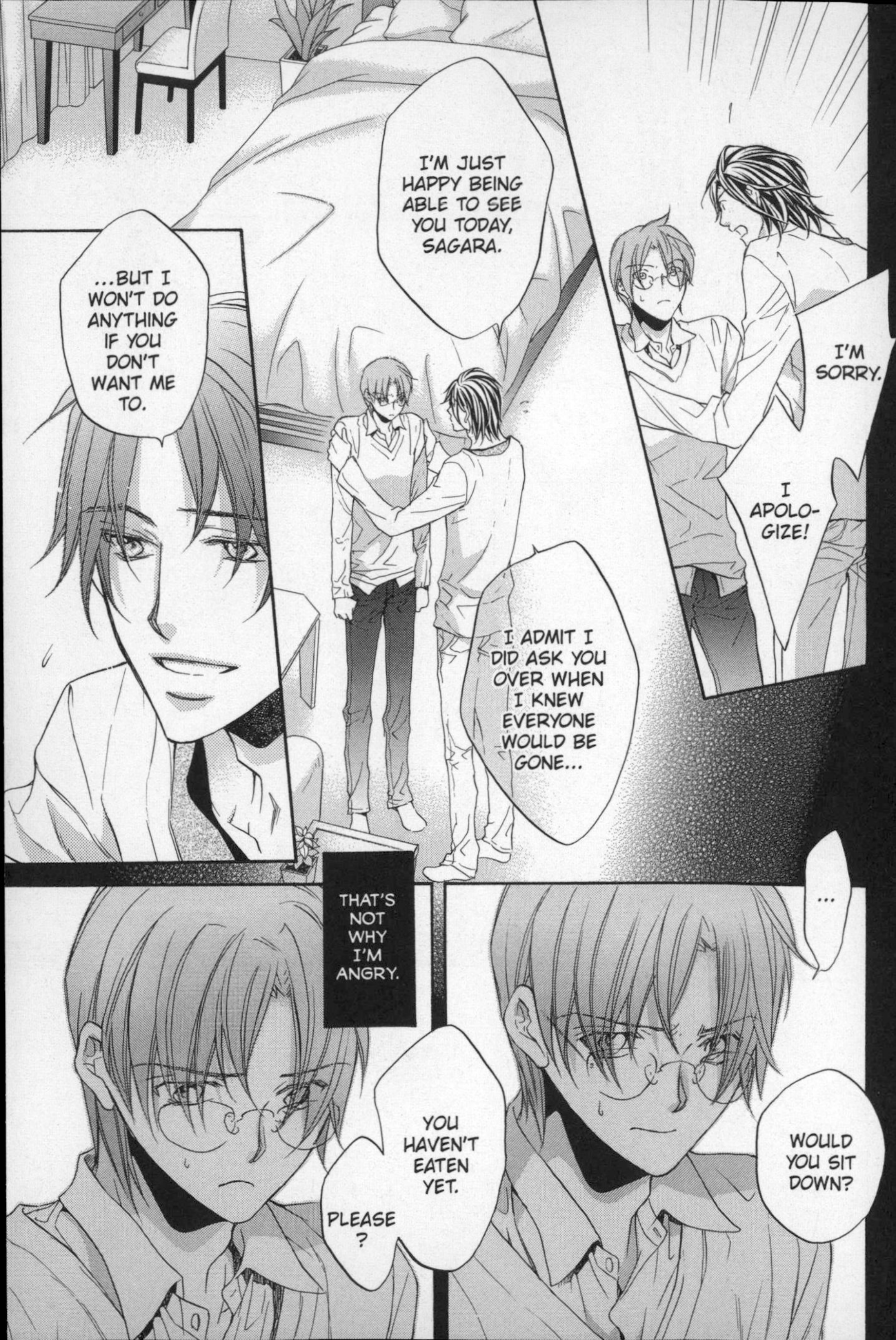
I'M SORRY.
I APOLOGIZE!
I ADMIT I DID ASK YOU OVER WHEN I KNEW EVERYONE WOULD BE GONE...
...BUT I WON'T DO ANYTHING IF YOU DON'T WANT ME TO.
I'M JUST HAPPY BEING ABLE TO SEE YOU TODAY, SAGARA.
...
THAT'S NOT WHY I'M ANGRY.
WOULD YOU SIT DOWN?
YOU HAVEN'T EATEN YET.
PLEASE?

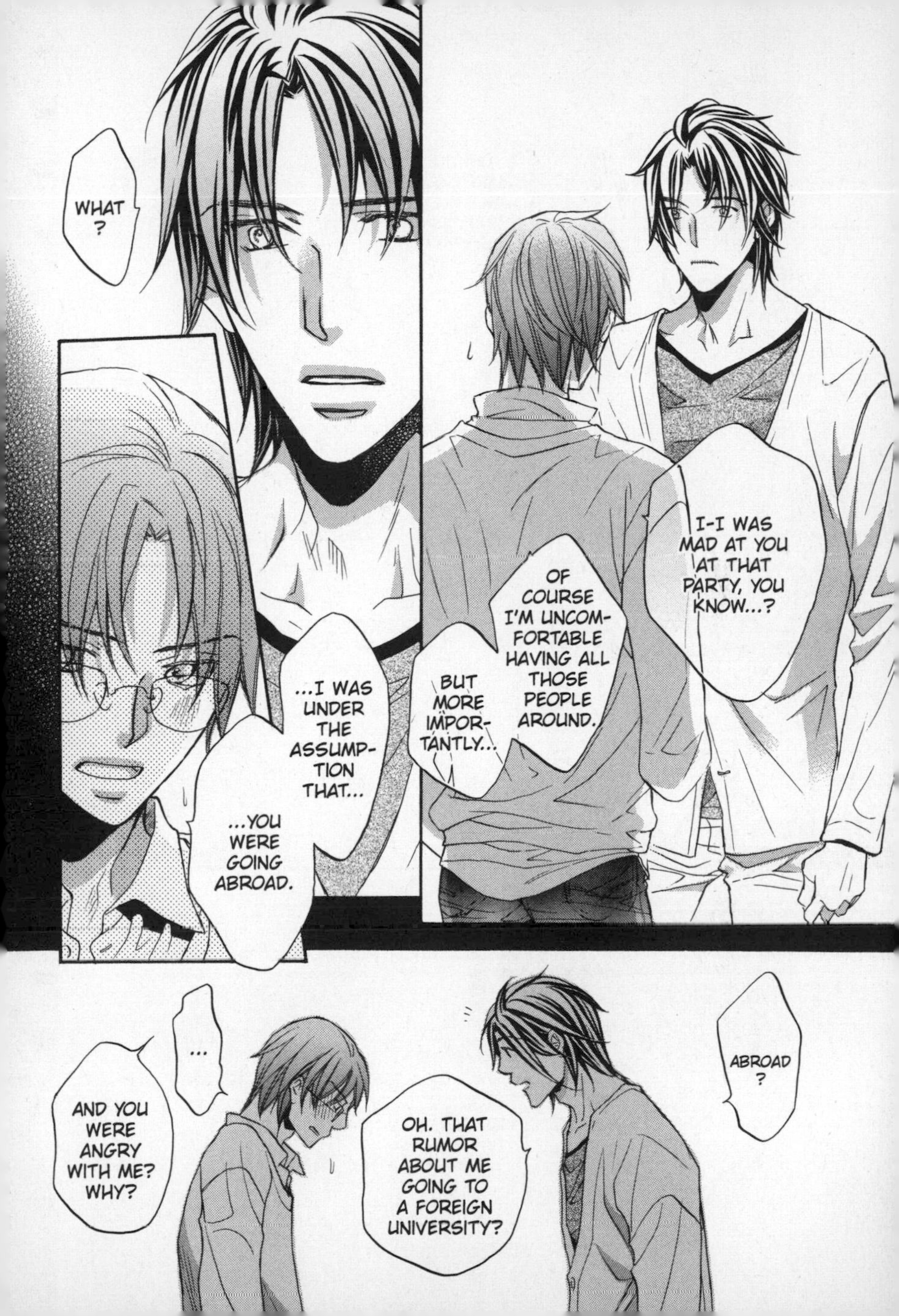
I-I WAS MAD AT YOU AT THAT PARTY, YOU KNOW...?
OF COURSE I'M UNCOMFORTABLE HAVING ALL THOSE PEOPLE AROUND.
BUT MORE IMPORTANTLY...
WHAT?
...I WAS UNDER THE ASSUMPTION THAT...
...YOU WERE GOING ABROAD.
ABROAD?
OH. THAT RUMOR ABOUT ME GOING TO A FOREIGN UNIVERSITY?
...
AND YOU WERE ANGRY WITH ME? WHY?

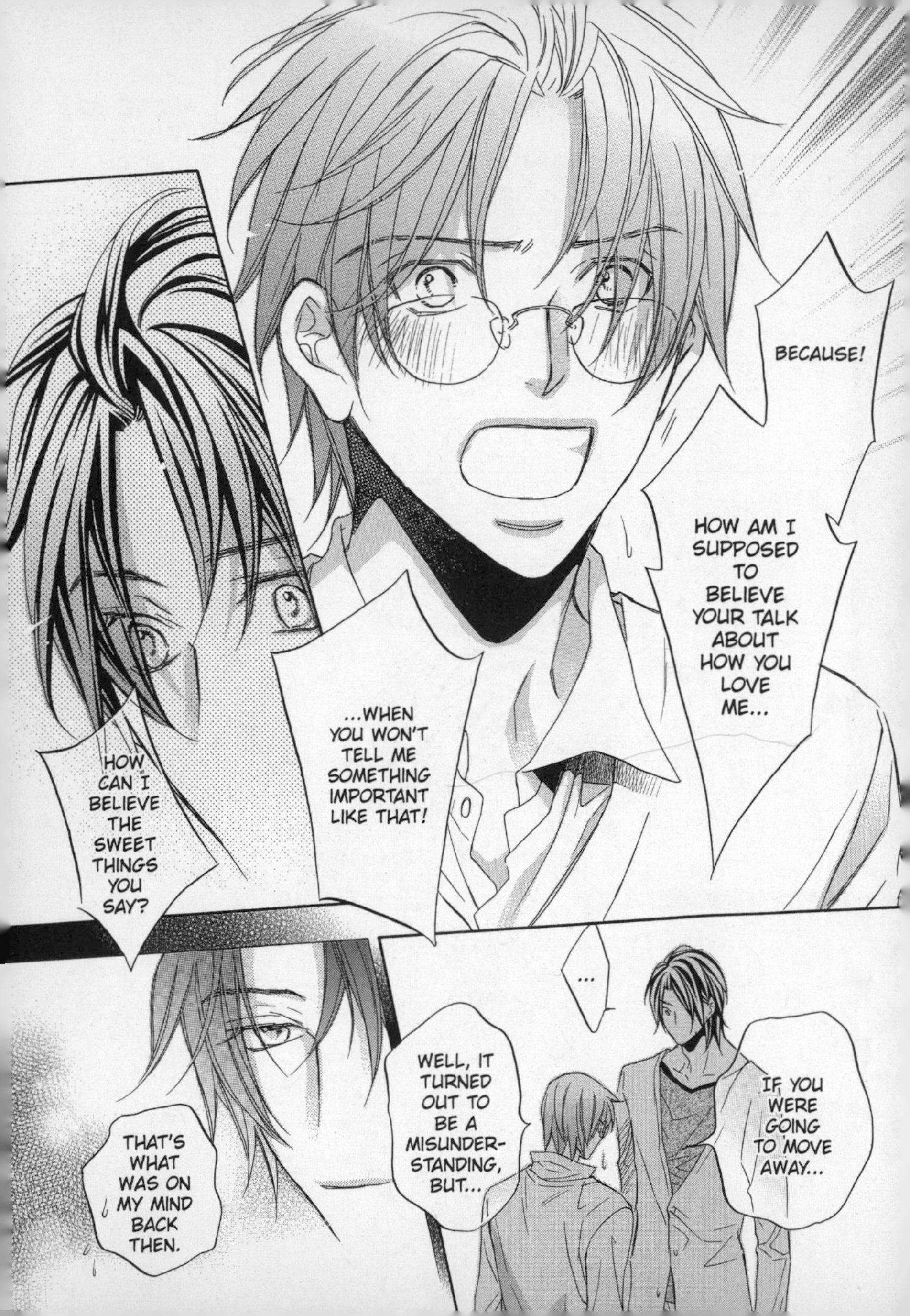
BECAUSE!
HOW AM I SUPPOSED TO BELIEVE YOUR TALK ABOUT HOW YOU LOVE ME...
...WHEN YOU WON'T TELL ME SOMETHING IMPORTANT LIKE THAT!
HOW CAN I BELIEVE THE SWEET THINGS YOU SAY?
...
IF YOU WERE GOING TO MOVE AWAY...
WELL, IT TURNED OUT TO BE A MISUNDER-STANDING, BUT...
THAT'S WHAT WAS ON MY MIND BACK THEN.

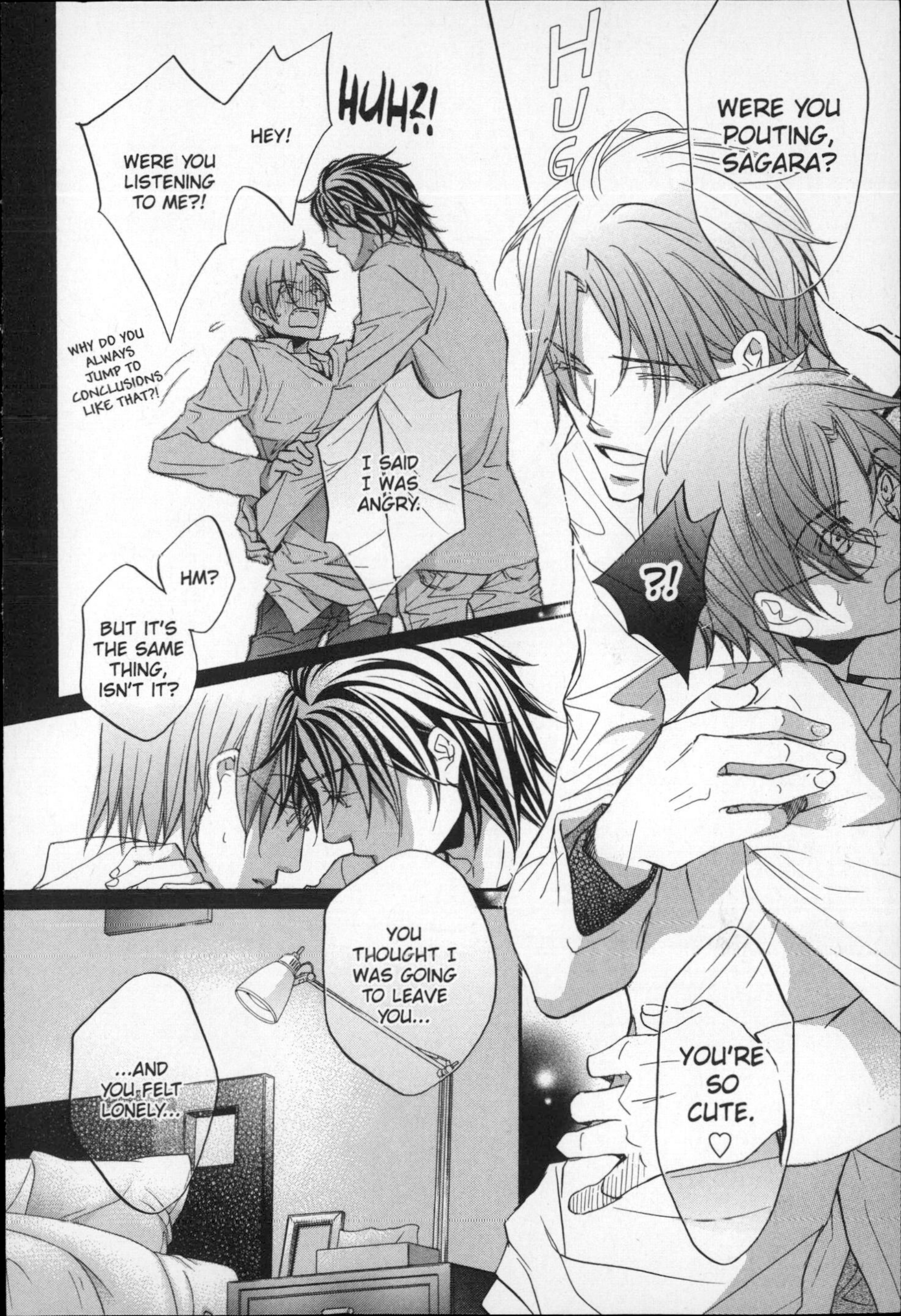
HUH?!
HEY!
WERE YOU LISTENING TO ME?!
WHY DO YOU ALWAYS JUMP TO CONCLUSIONS LIKE THAT?!
I SAID I WAS ANGRY.
HM?
BUT IT'S THE SAME THING, ISN'T IT?
YOU THOUGHT I WAS GOING TO LEAVE YOU...
...AND YOU FELT LONELY...
HUG
WERE YOU POUTING, SAGARA?
?!
YOU'RE SO CUTE. ♡

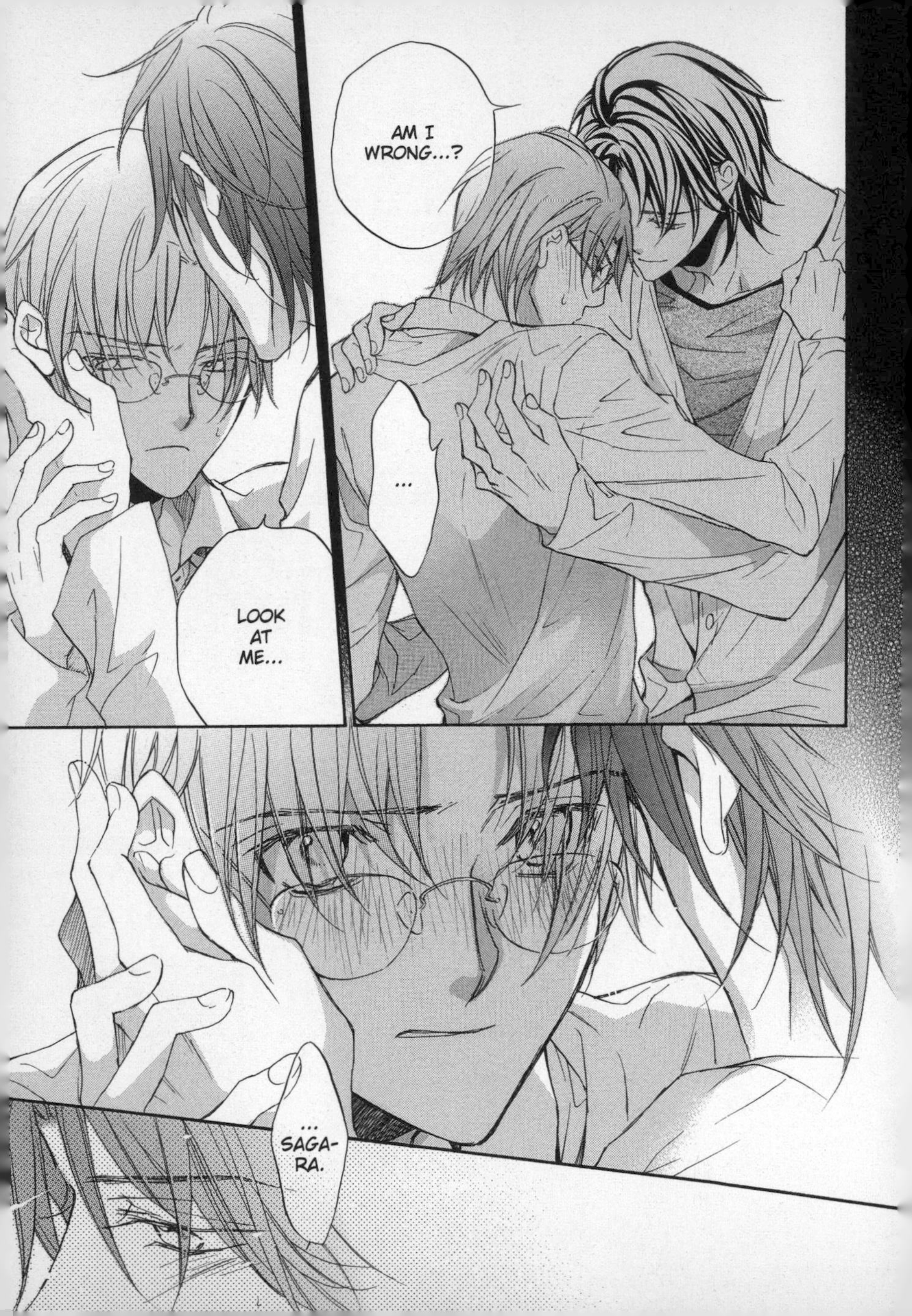

AM I WRONG...?
...
LOOK AT ME...
...SAGARA.

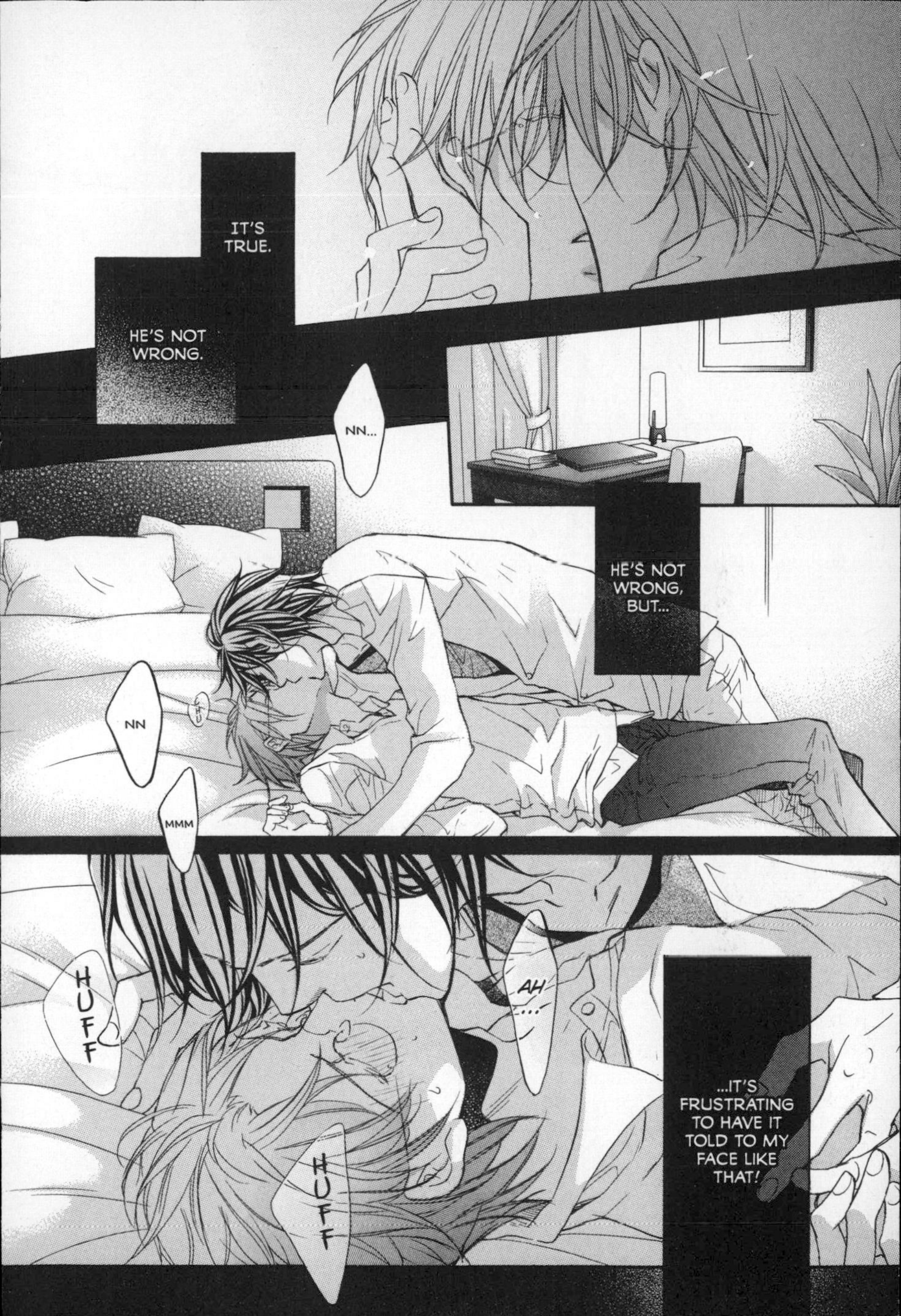
IT'S TRUE.
HE'S NOT WRONG.
NN...
HE'S NOT WRONG, BUT...
NN
MMM
...IT'S FRUSTRATING TO HAVE IT TOLD TO MY FACE LIKE THAT!
AH...
HUFF
HUFF

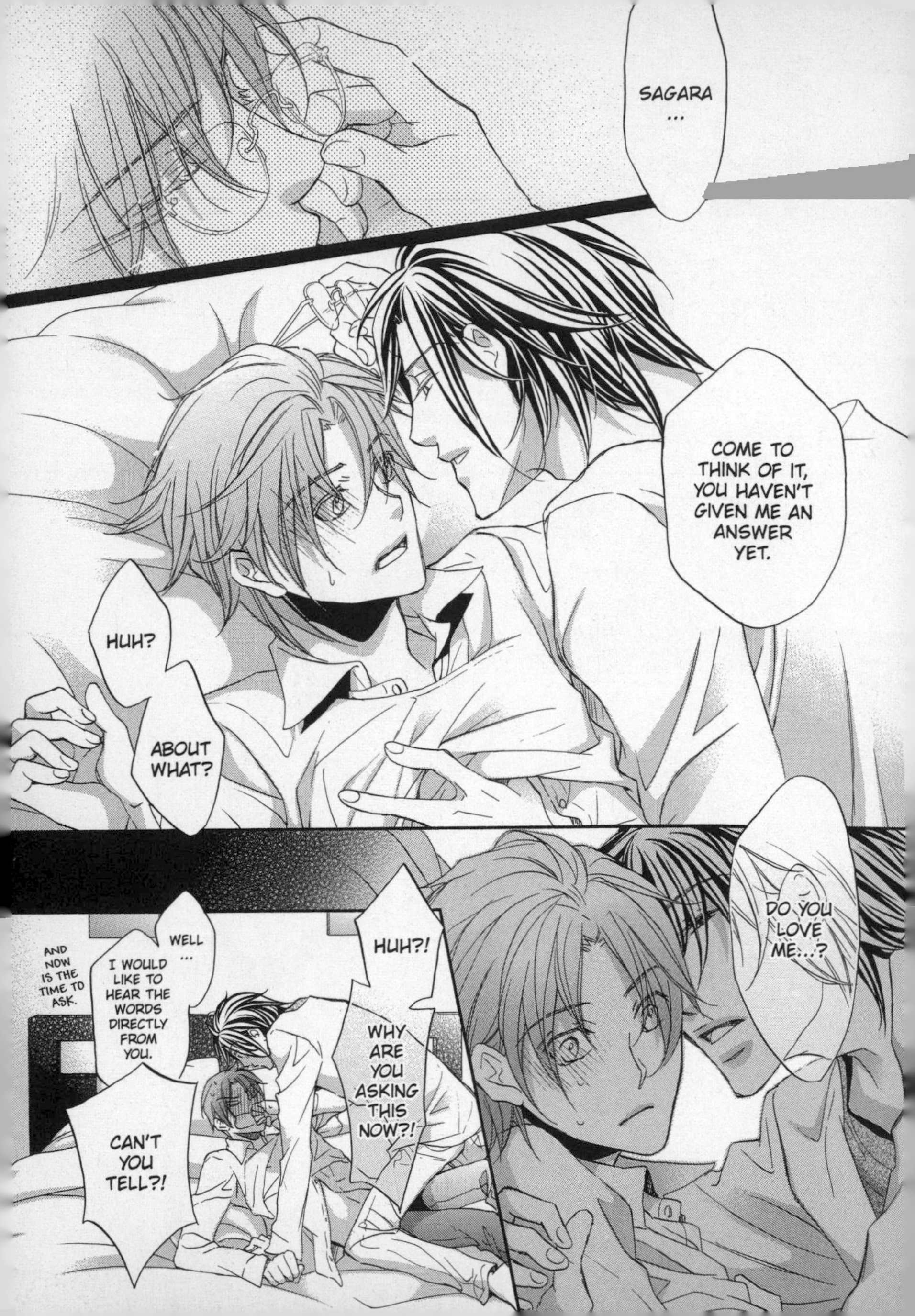
SAGARA ...
COME TO THINK OF IT, YOU HAVEN'T GIVEN ME AN ANSWER YET.
HUH?
ABOUT WHAT?
DO YOU LOVE ME...?
HUH?!
WHY ARE YOU ASKING THIS NOW?!
WELL ... I WOULD LIKE TO HEAR THE WORDS DIRECTLY FROM YOU.
AND NOW IS THE TIME TO ASK.
CAN'T YOU TELL?!

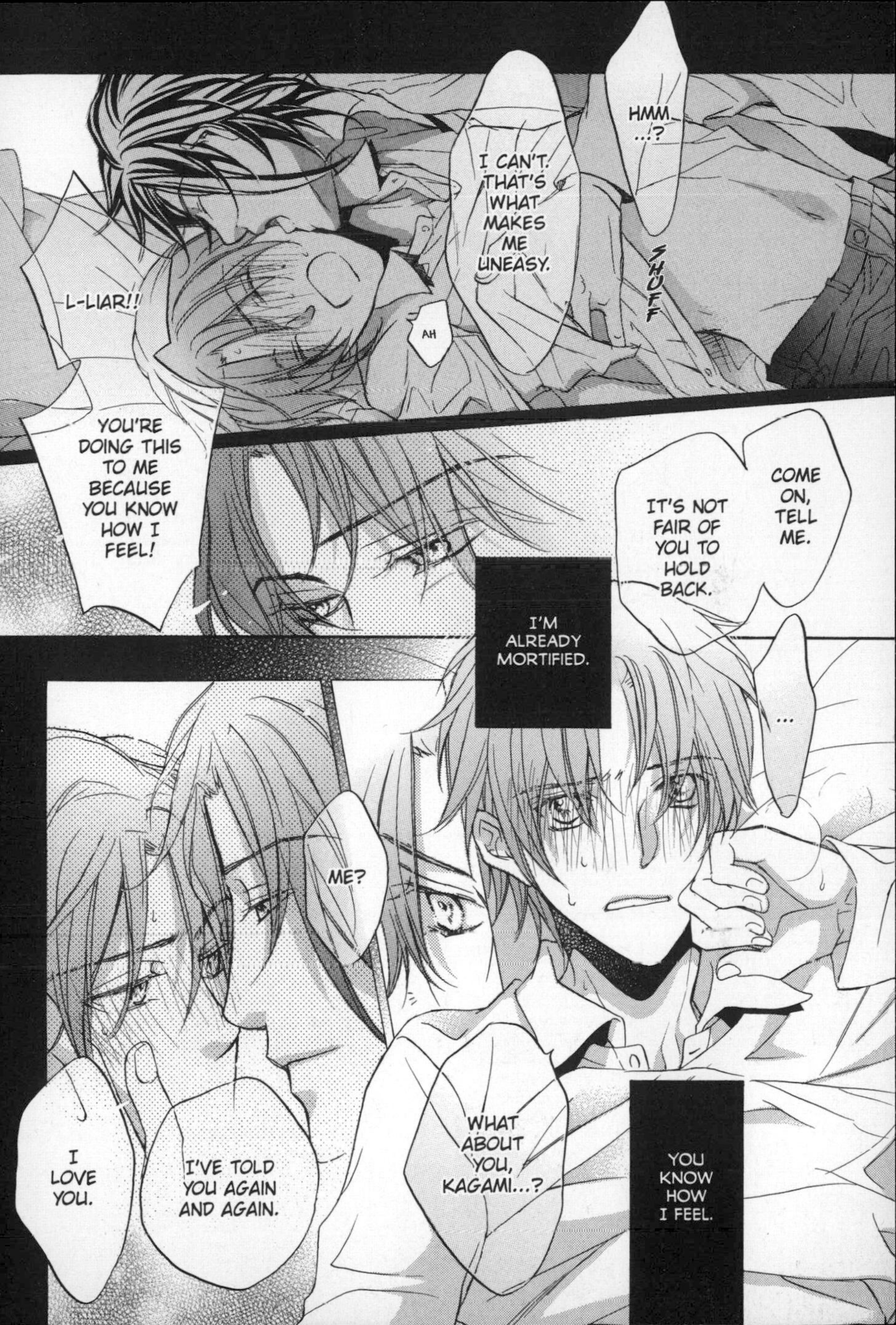
HMM...?
I CAN'T. THAT'S WHAT MAKES ME UNEASY.
SHUFF
AH
L-LIAR!!
COME ON, TELL ME.
IT'S NOT FAIR OF YOU TO HOLD BACK.
YOU'RE DOING THIS TO ME BECAUSE YOU KNOW HOW I FEEL!
I'M ALREADY MORTIFIED.
...
ME?
YOU KNOW HOW I FEEL.
WHAT ABOUT YOU, KAGAMI...?
I'VE TOLD YOU AGAIN AND AGAIN.
I LOVE YOU.

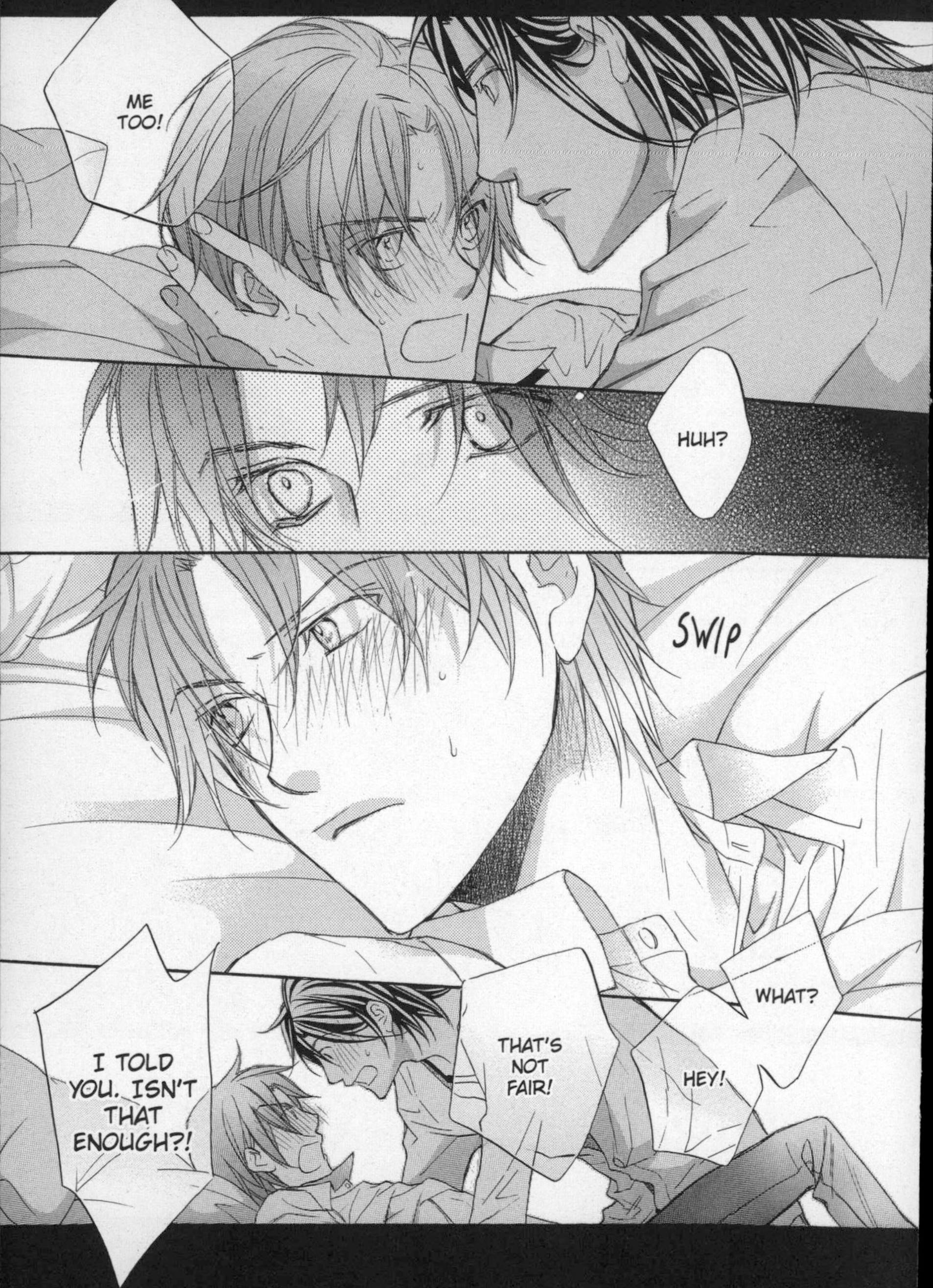
ME TOO!
HUH?
SWIP
WHAT?
HEY!
THAT'S NOT FAIR!
I TOLD YOU. ISN'T THAT ENOUGH?!

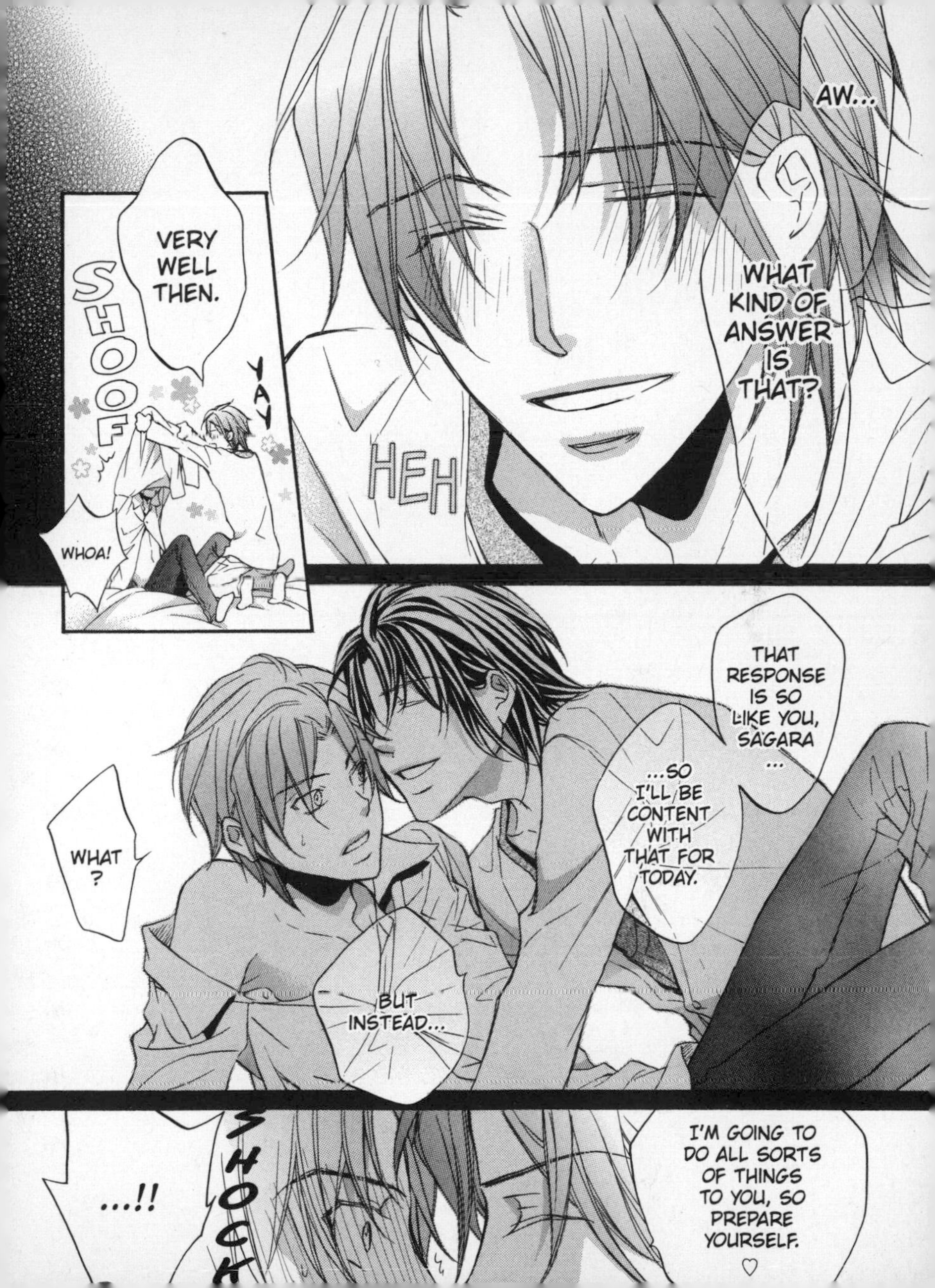
AW...
WHAT KIND OF ANSWER IS THAT?
HEH
VERY WELL THEN.
SHOOF
YAY
WHOA!
THAT RESPONSE IS SO LIKE YOU, SAGARA...
...SO I'LL BE CONTENT WITH THAT FOR TODAY.
BUT INSTEAD...
WHAT?
I'M GOING TO DO ALL SORTS OF THINGS TO YOU, SO PREPARE YOURSELF. ♡
SHOCK
...!!

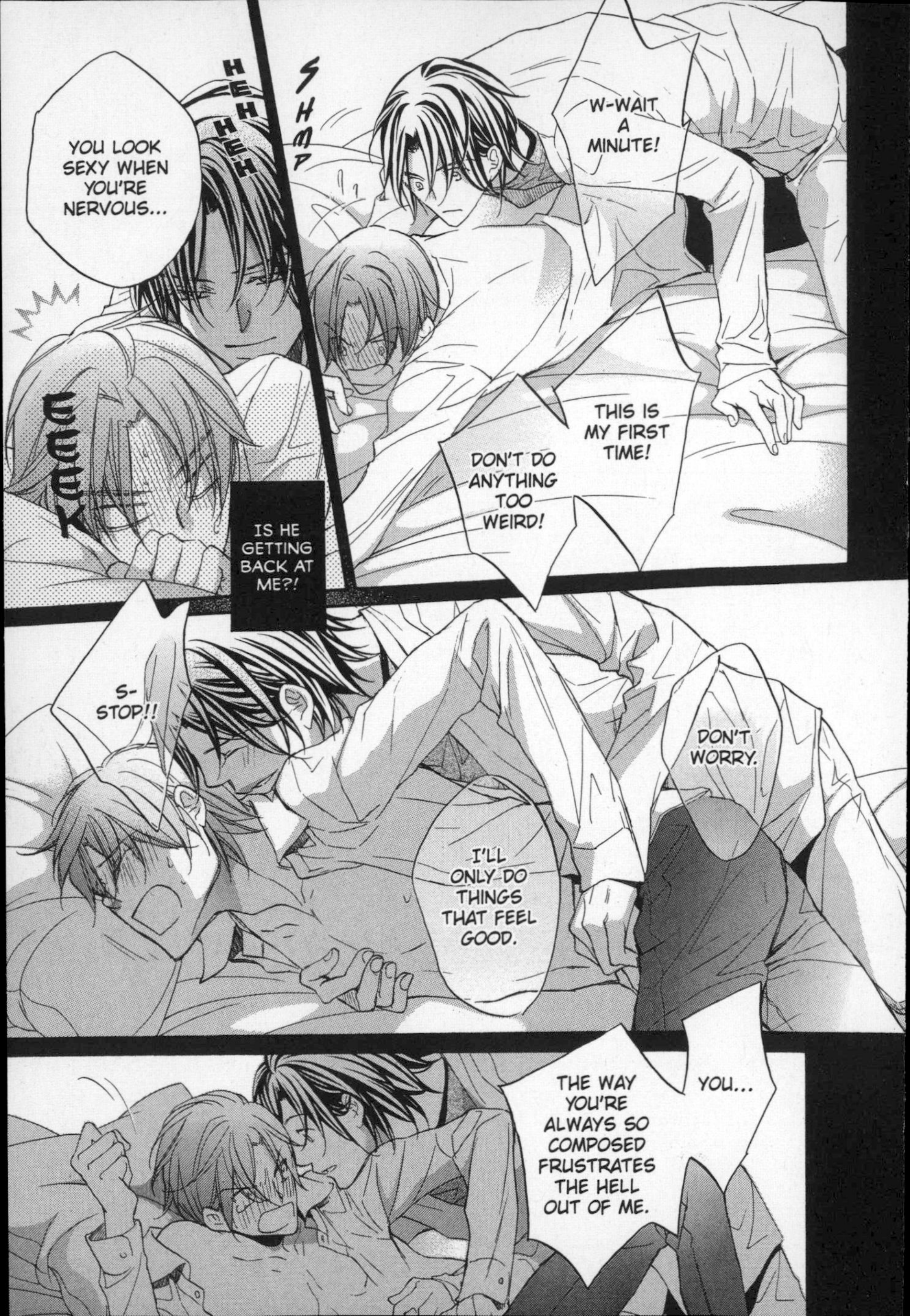
W-WAIT A MINUTE!
THIS IS MY FIRST TIME!
DON'T DO ANYTHING TOO WEIRD!
SHMP
HEH HEH HEH
YOU LOOK SEXY WHEN YOU'RE NERVOUS...
EEEK
IS HE GETTING BACK AT ME?!
DON'T WORRY.
I'LL ONLY DO THINGS THAT FEEL GOOD.
S-STOP!!
YOU...
THE WAY YOU'RE ALWAYS SO COMPOSED FRUSTRATES THE HELL OUT OF ME.

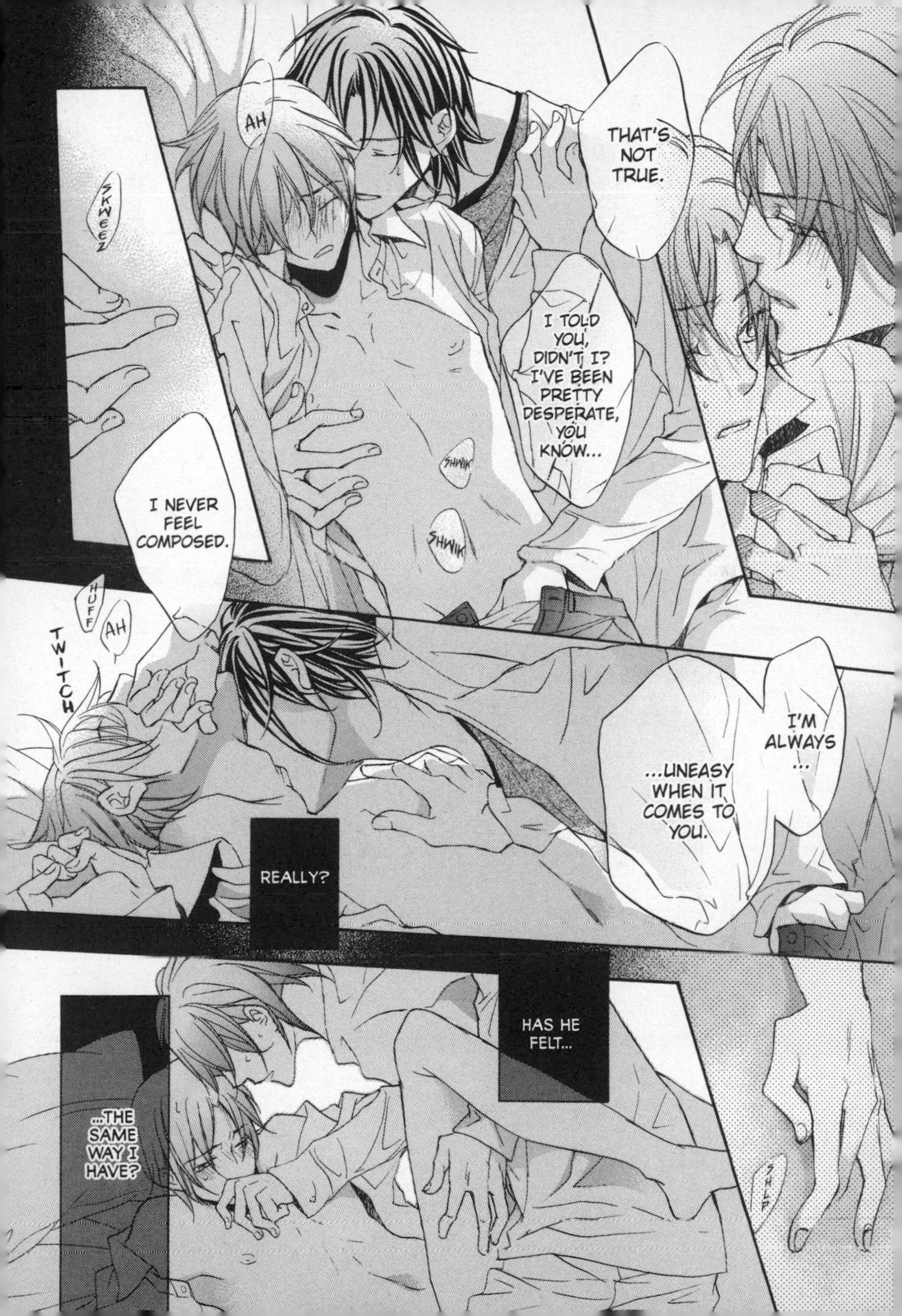
THAT'S NOT TRUE.
AH
I TOLD YOU, DIDN'T I? I'VE BEEN PRETTY DESPERATE, YOU KNOW...
SKWEEZ
SHWIK
SHWIK
I NEVER FEEL COMPOSED.
I'M ALWAYS...
...UNEASY WHEN IT COMES TO YOU.
REALLY?
AH
HUFF
TWITCH
SHLP
HAS HE FELT...
...THE SAME WAY I HAVE?

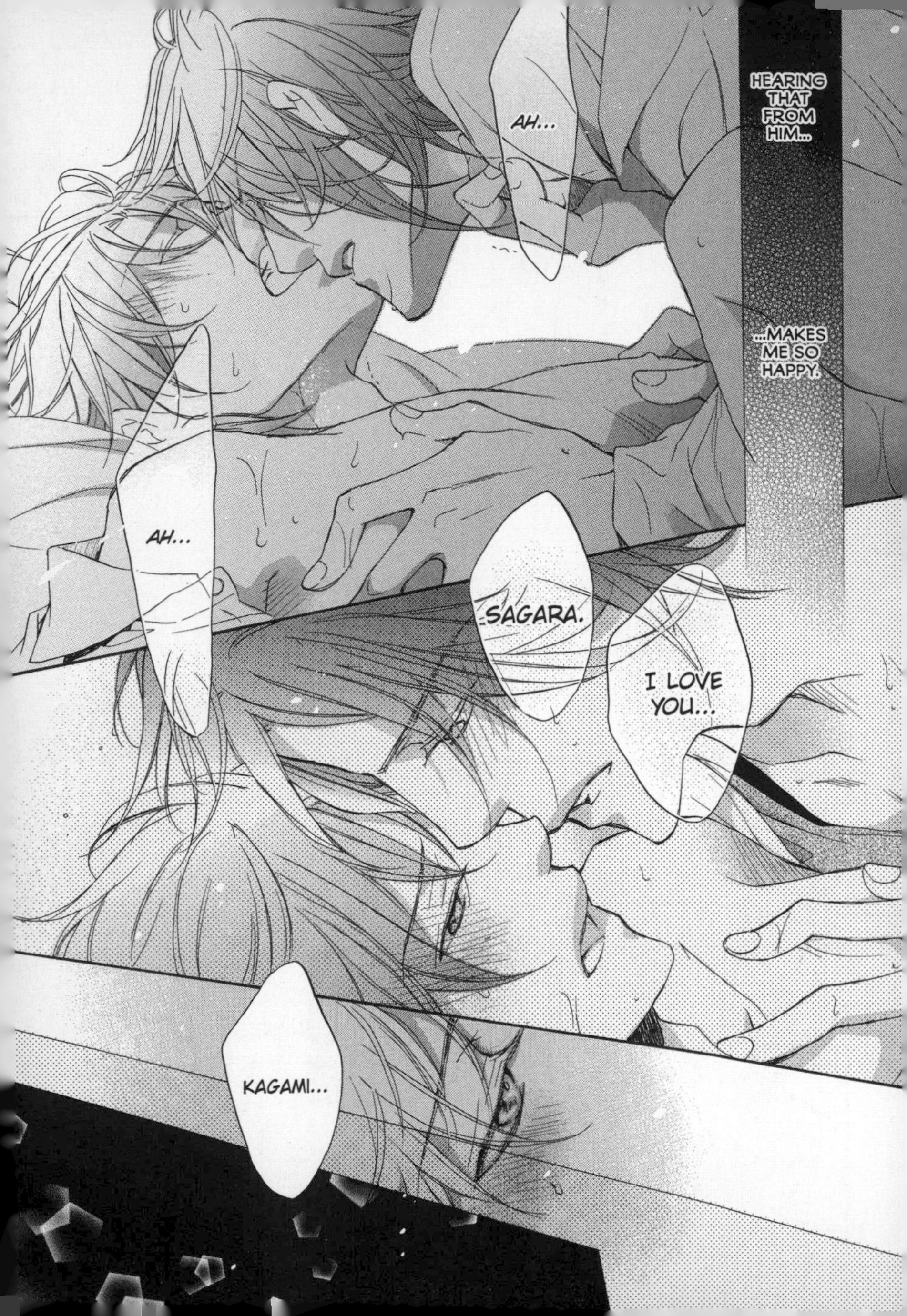
HEARING THAT FROM HIM...
AH...
...MAKES ME SO HAPPY.
AH...
SAGARA.
I LOVE YOU...
KAGAMI...

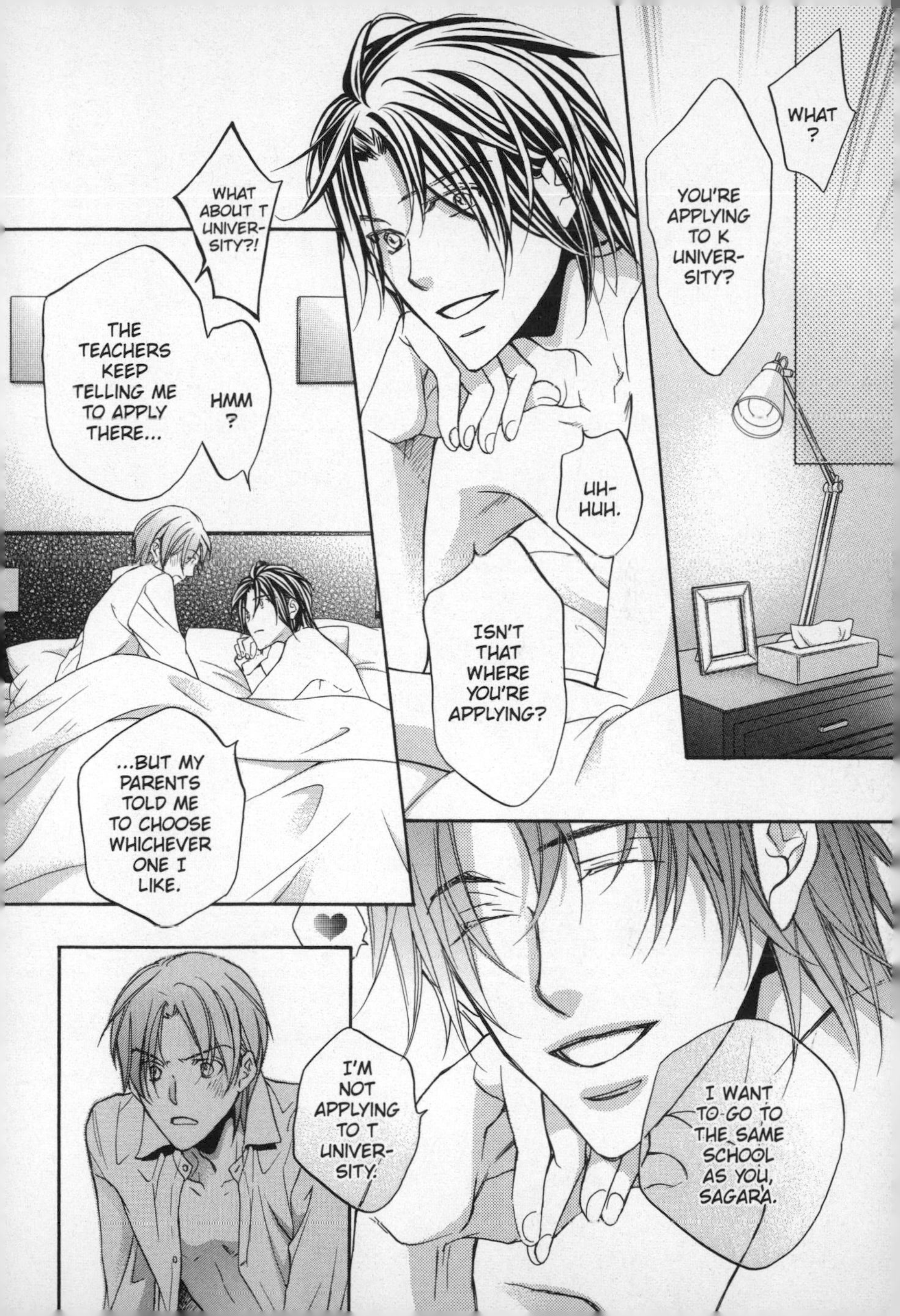
WHAT ?
YOU'RE APPLYING TO K UNIVER-SITY?
UH-HUH.
ISN'T THAT WHERE YOU'RE APPLYING?
WHAT ABOUT T UNIVER-SITY?!
HMM ?
THE TEACHERS KEEP TELLING ME TO APPLY THERE...
...BUT MY PARENTS TOLD ME TO CHOOSE WHICHEVER ONE I LIKE.
I WANT TO GO TO THE SAME SCHOOL AS YOU, SAGARA.
I'M NOT APPLYING TO T UNIVER-SITY.

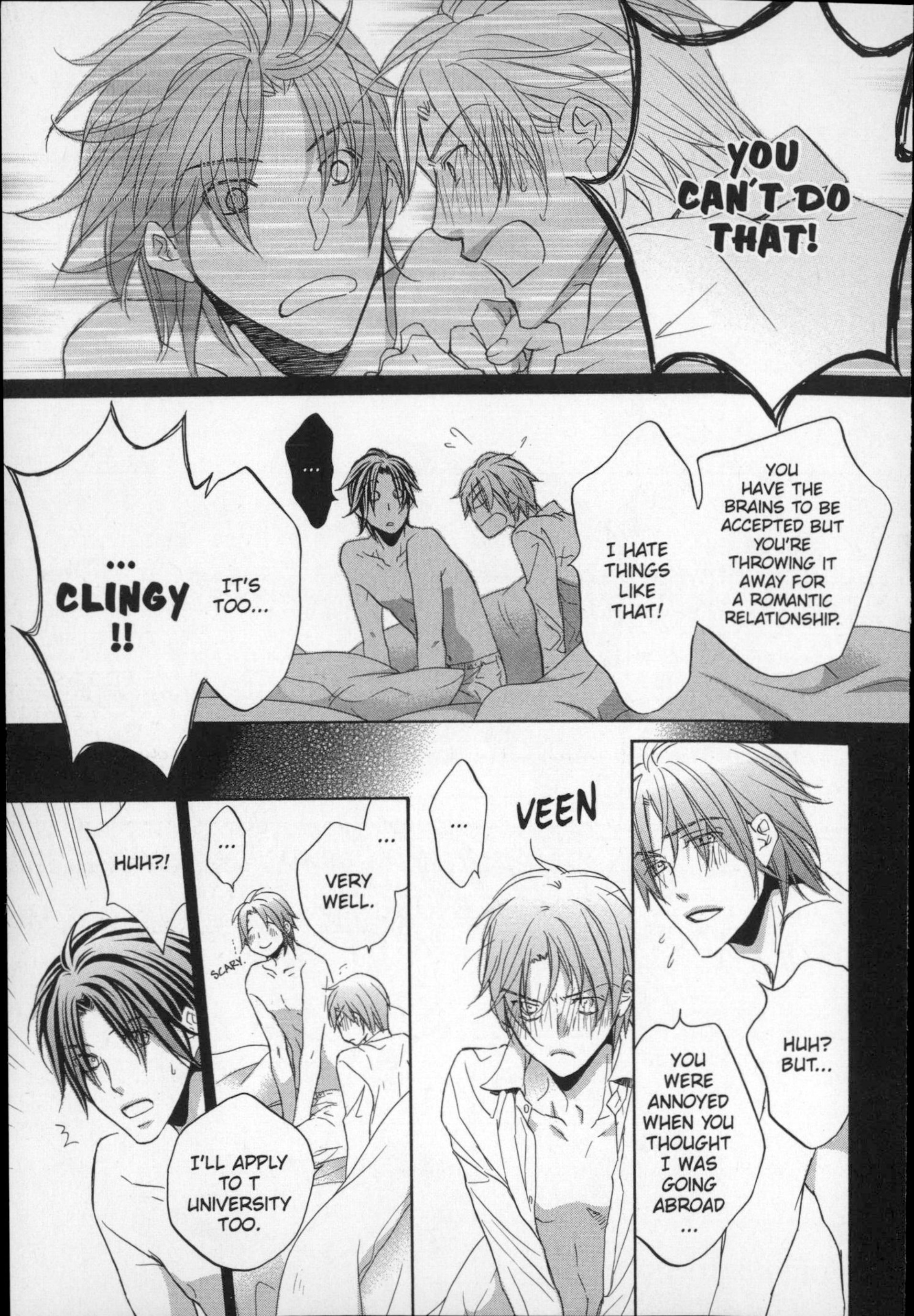
YOU CAN'T DO THAT!
YOU HAVE THE BRAINS TO BE ACCEPTED BUT YOU'RE THROWING IT AWAY FOR A ROMANTIC RELATIONSHIP.
I HATE THINGS LIKE THAT!
...
IT'S TOO...
...CLINGY!!
HUH? BUT...
YOU WERE ANNOYED WHEN YOU THOUGHT I WAS GOING ABROAD ...
VEEN
...
... VERY WELL.
...
SCARY.
I'LL APPLY TO T UNIVERSITY TOO.
HUH?!

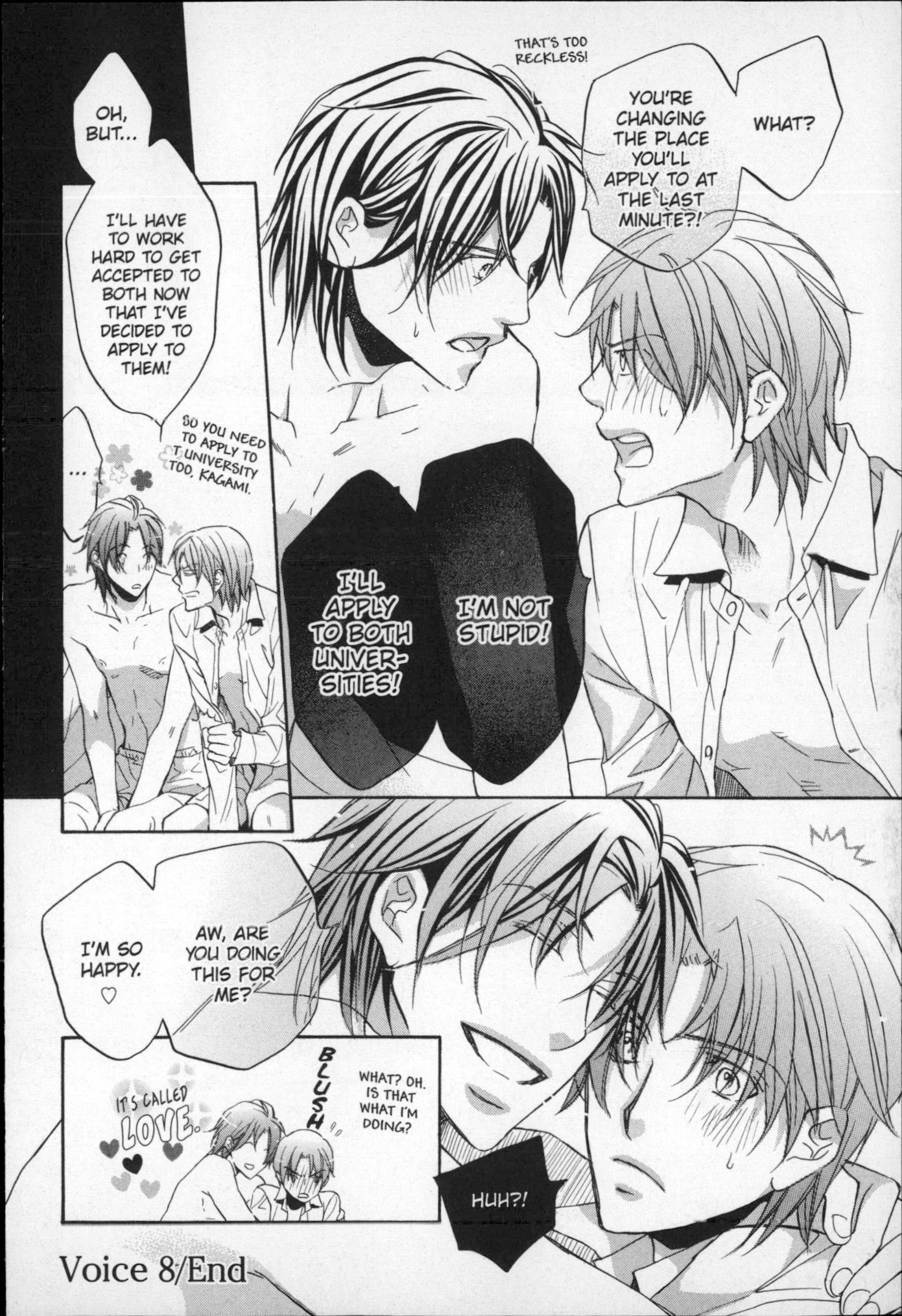
WHAT?
YOU'RE CHANGING THE PLACE YOU'LL APPLY TO AT THE LAST MINUTE?!
THAT'S TOO RECKLESS!
I'M NOT STUPID!
I'LL APPLY TO BOTH UNIVER-SITIES!
OH, BUT...
I'LL HAVE TO WORK HARD TO GET ACCEPTED TO BOTH NOW THAT I'VE DECIDED TO APPLY TO THEM!
SO YOU NEED TO APPLY TO T UNIVERSITY TOO, KAGAMI.
...
AW, ARE YOU DOING THIS FOR ME?
I'M SO HAPPY. ♡
HUH?!
WHAT? OH. IS THAT WHAT I'M DOING?
BLUSH
IT'S CALLED LOVE.

Voice 8/End

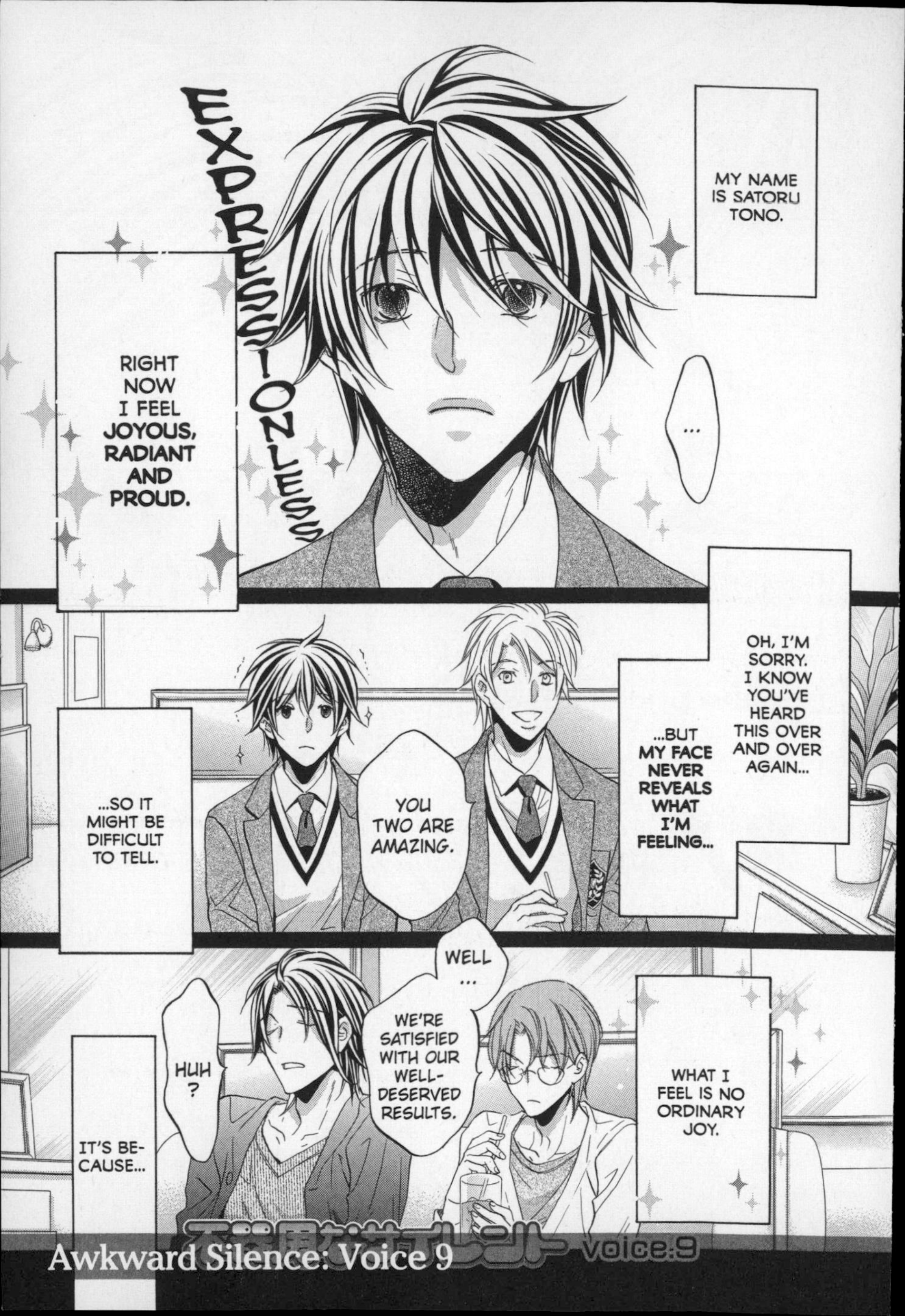
MY NAME IS SATORU TONO.
...
EXPRESSIONLESS
RIGHT NOW I FEEL JOYOUS, RADIANT AND PROUD.
OH, I'M SORRY. I KNOW YOU'VE HEARD THIS OVER AND OVER AGAIN...
...BUT MY FACE NEVER REVEALS WHAT I'M FEELING...
YOU TWO ARE AMAZING.
...SO IT MIGHT BE DIFFICULT TO TELL.
WHAT I FEEL IS NO ORDINARY JOY.
WELL ...
WE'RE SATISFIED WITH OUR WELL-DESERVED RESULTS.
HUH ?
IT'S BE-CAUSE...
voice:9

Awkward Silence: Voice 9

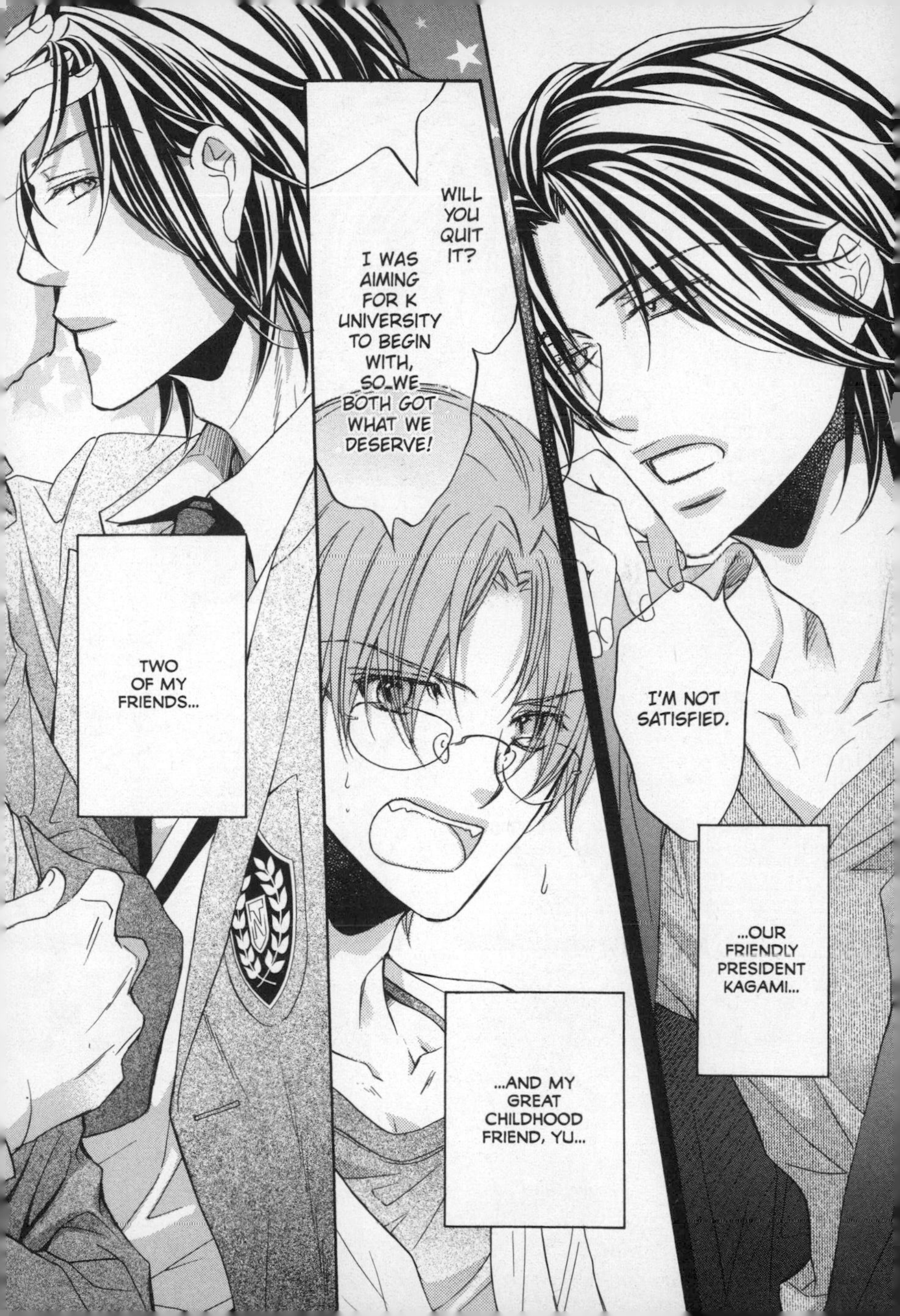
I'M NOT SATISFIED.
...OUR FRIENDLY PRESIDENT KAGAMI...
WILL YOU QUIT IT?
I WAS AIMING FOR K UNIVERSITY TO BEGIN WITH, SO WE BOTH GOT WHAT WE DESERVE!
...AND MY GREAT CHILDHOOD FRIEND, YU...
TWO OF MY FRIENDS...

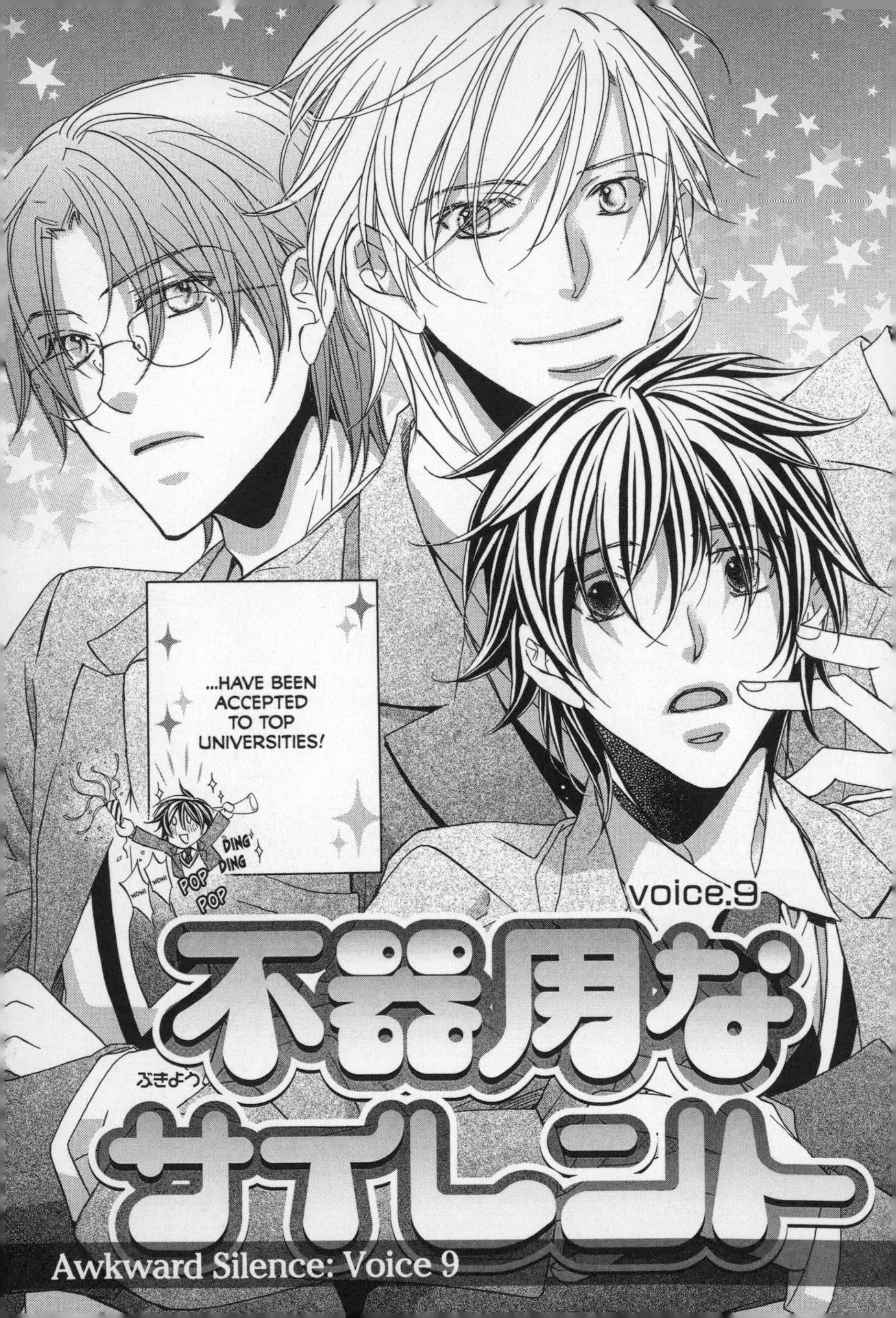
...HAVE BEEN ACCEPTED TO TOP UNIVERSITIES!
DING DING
POP POP
WOW! WOW!
voice.9
不器用なサイレント
ぶきよう
Awkward Silence: Voice 9

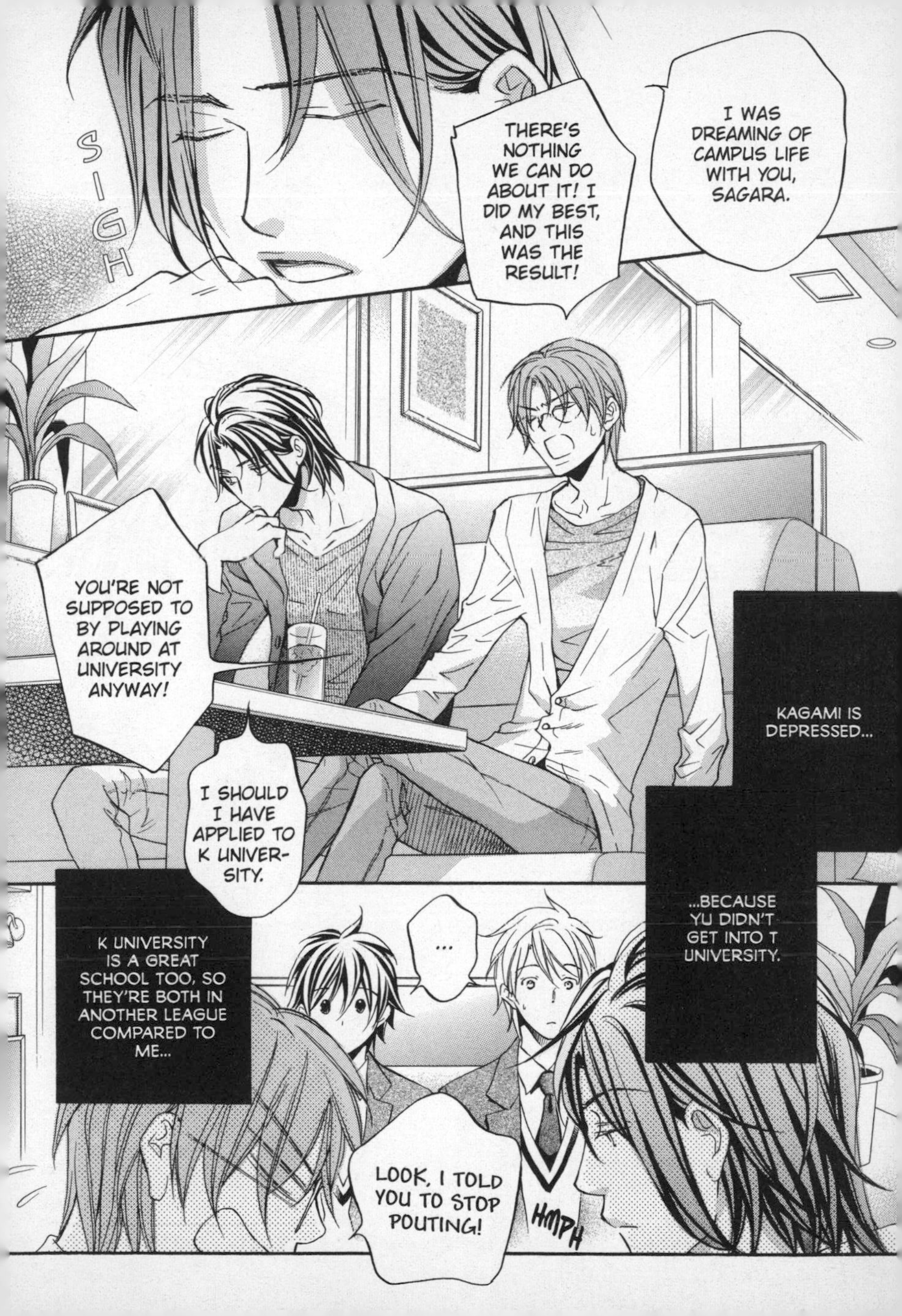
I WAS DREAMING OF CAMPUS LIFE WITH YOU, SAGARA.
THERE'S NOTHING WE CAN DO ABOUT IT! I DID MY BEST, AND THIS WAS THE RESULT!
SIGH
KAGAMI IS DEPRESSED...
YOU'RE NOT SUPPOSED TO BY PLAYING AROUND AT UNIVERSITY ANYWAY!
I SHOULD I HAVE APPLIED TO K UNIVERSITY.
...BECAUSE YU DIDN'T GET INTO T UNIVERSITY.
...
K UNIVERSITY IS A GREAT SCHOOL TOO, SO THEY'RE BOTH IN ANOTHER LEAGUE COMPARED TO ME...
LOOK, I TOLD YOU TO STOP POUTING!
HMPH

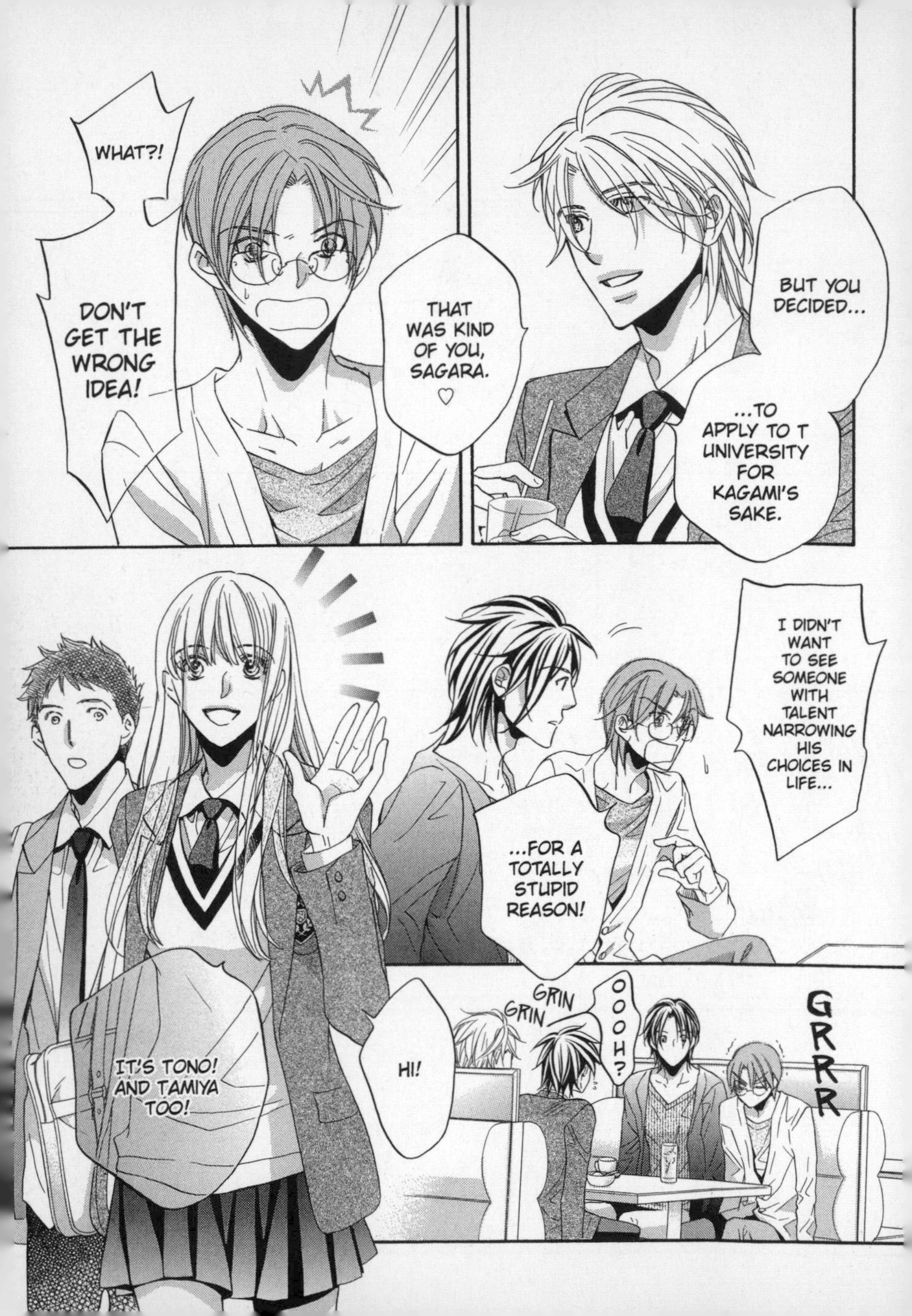
BUT YOU DECIDED...
...TO APPLY TO T UNIVERSITY FOR KAGAMI'S SAKE.
THAT WAS KIND OF YOU, SAGARA. ♡
WHAT?!
DON'T GET THE WRONG IDEA!
I DIDN'T WANT TO SEE SOMEONE WITH TALENT NARROWING HIS CHOICES IN LIFE...
...FOR A TOTALLY STUPID REASON!
GRRR
OOOOH?
GRIN GRIN
HI!
IT'S TONO! AND TAMIYA TOO!

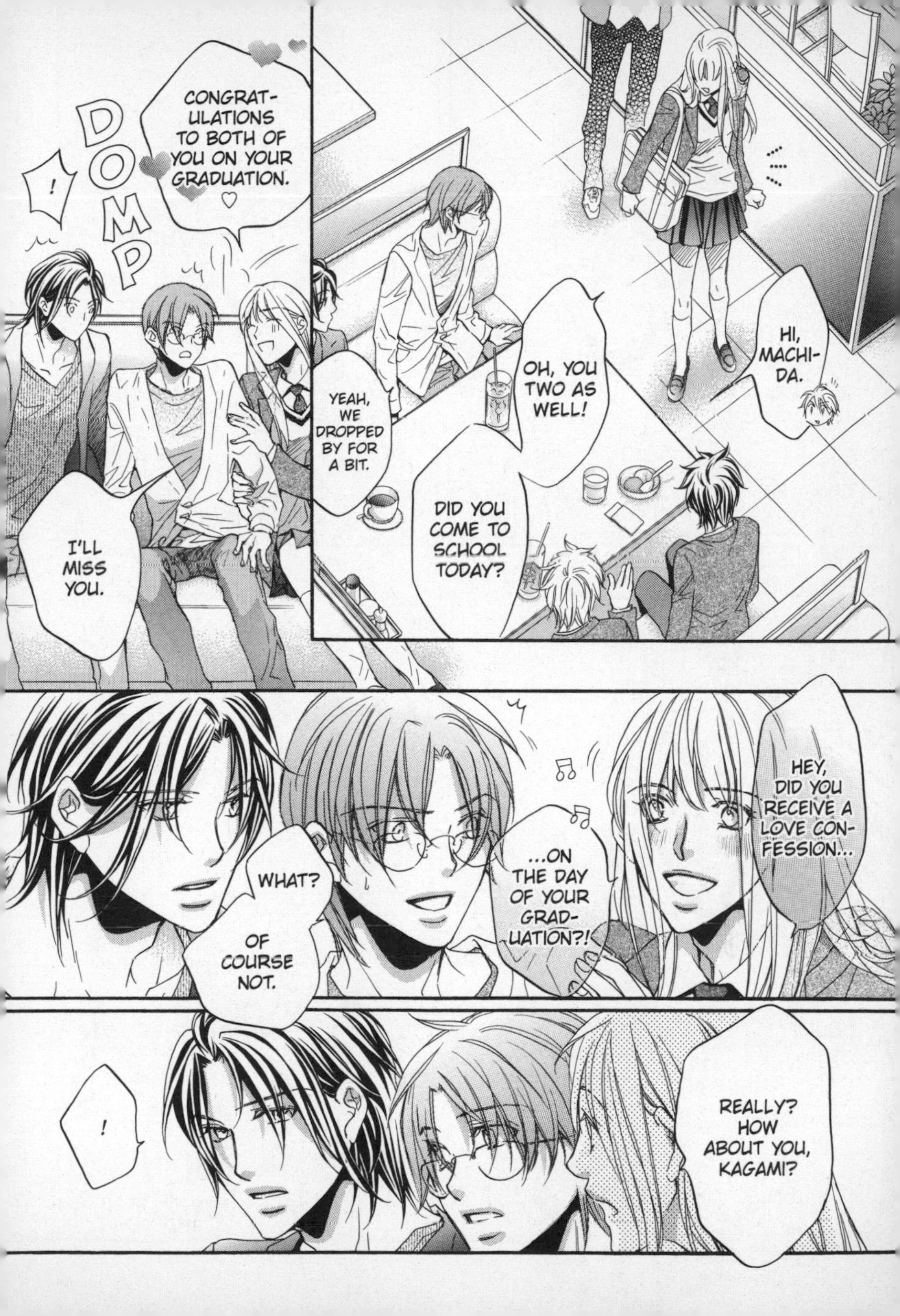
HI, MACHI-DA.
OH, YOU TWO AS WELL!
DID YOU COME TO SCHOOL TODAY?
YEAH, WE DROPPED BY FOR A BIT.
CONGRAT-ULATIONS TO BOTH OF YOU ON YOUR GRADUATION. ♡
DOMP
!
I'LL MISS YOU.
HEY, DID YOU RECEIVE A LOVE CON-FESSION...
...ON THE DAY OF YOUR GRAD-UATION?!
WHAT?
OF COURSE NOT.
REALLY? HOW ABOUT YOU, KAGAMI?
!

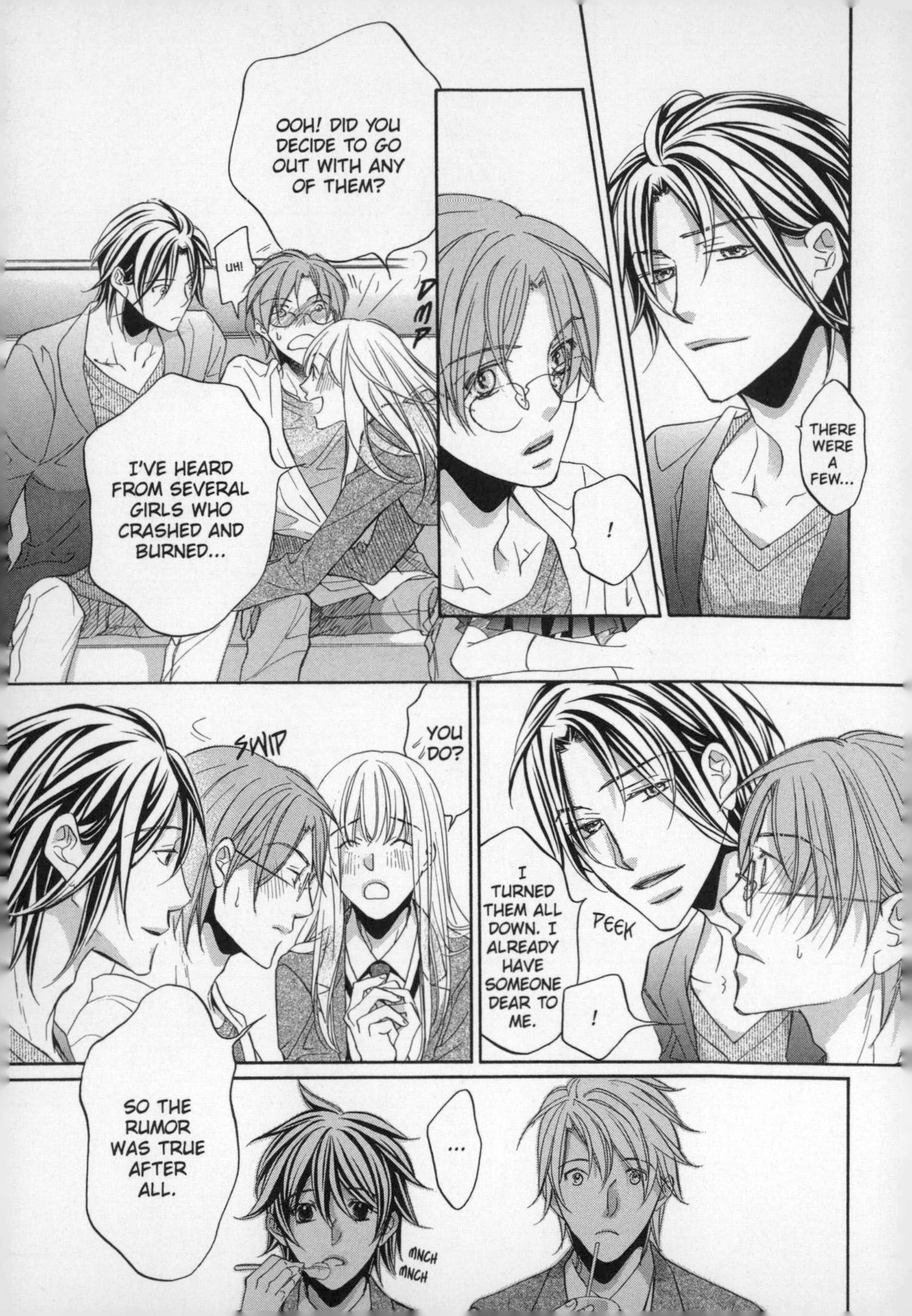
THERE WERE A FEW...
!
OOH! DID YOU DECIDE TO GO OUT WITH ANY OF THEM?
UH!
DMP
I'VE HEARD FROM SEVERAL GIRLS WHO CRASHED AND BURNED...
I TURNED THEM ALL DOWN. I ALREADY HAVE SOMEONE DEAR TO ME.
PEEK
!
YOU DO?
SWIP
...
SO THE RUMOR WAS TRUE AFTER ALL.
MNCH MNCH

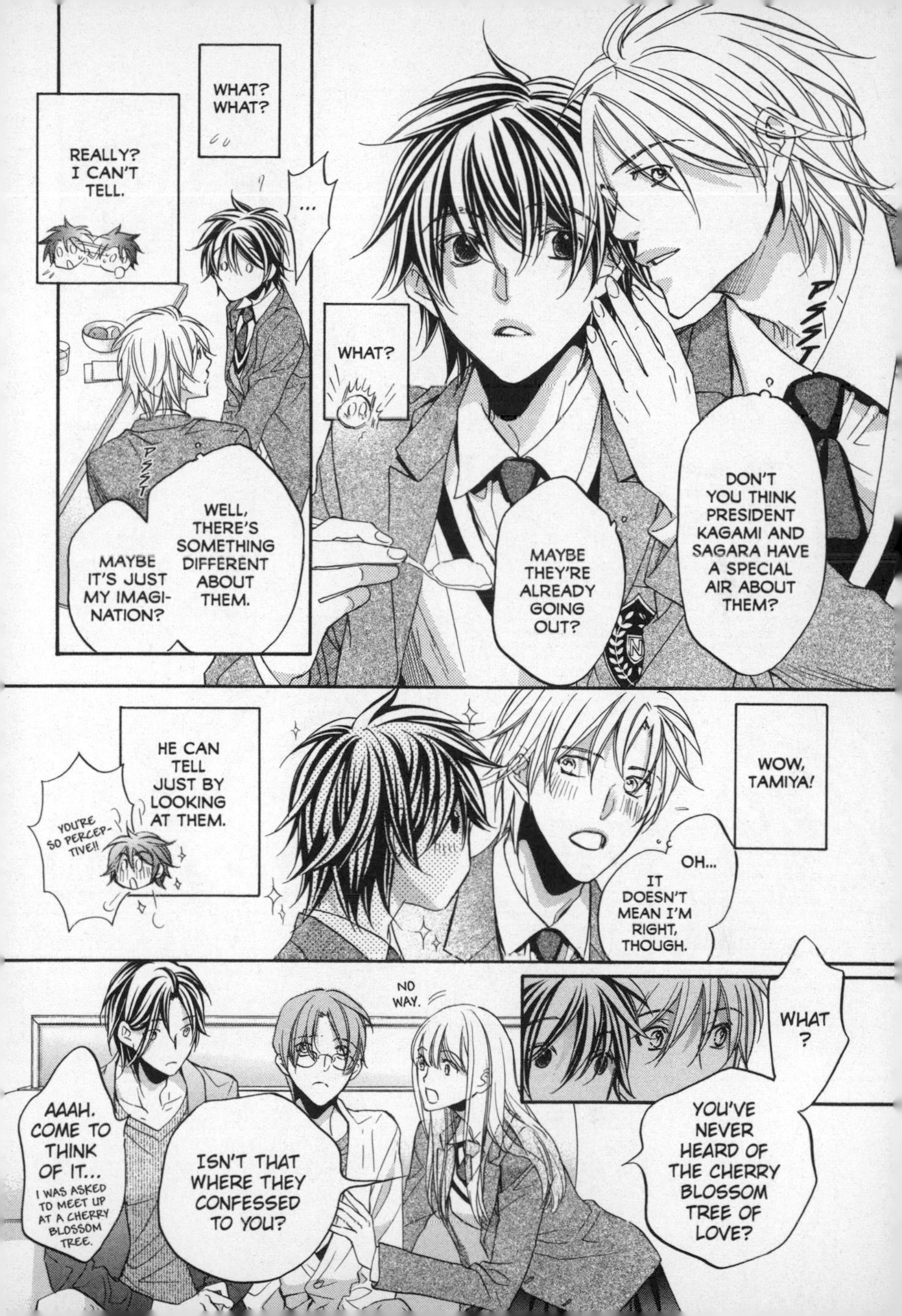
DON'T YOU THINK PRESIDENT KAGAMI AND SAGARA HAVE A SPECIAL AIR ABOUT THEM?
PSSST
MAYBE THEY'RE ALREADY GOING OUT?
WHAT?
WHAT? WHAT?
...
WELL, THERE'S SOMETHING DIFFERENT ABOUT THEM.
MAYBE IT'S JUST MY IMAGINATION?
PSST
REALLY? I CAN'T TELL.
WOW, TAMIYA!
OH...
IT DOESN'T MEAN I'M RIGHT, THOUGH.
HE CAN TELL JUST BY LOOKING AT THEM.
YOU'RE SO PERCEPTIVE!!
WHAT?
YOU'VE NEVER HEARD OF THE CHERRY BLOSSOM TREE OF LOVE?
NO WAY.
ISN'T THAT WHERE THEY CONFESSED TO YOU?
AAAH. COME TO THINK OF IT...
I WAS ASKED TO MEET UP AT A CHERRY BLOSSOM TREE.

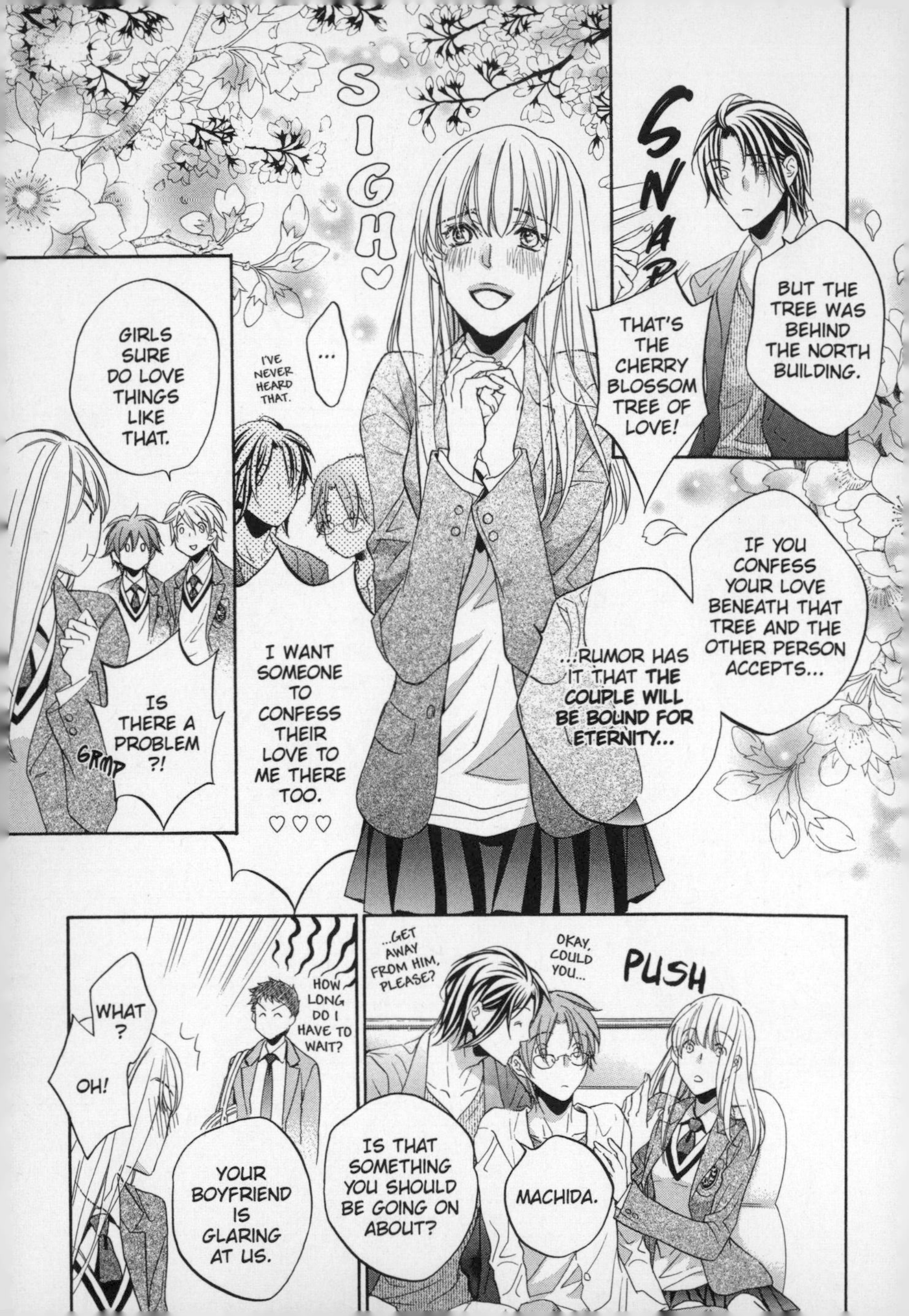
SNAP
BUT THE TREE WAS BEHIND THE NORTH BUILDING.
SIGH♡
THAT'S THE CHERRY BLOSSOM TREE OF LOVE!
IF YOU CONFESS YOUR LOVE BENEATH THAT TREE AND THE OTHER PERSON ACCEPTS...
...RUMOR HAS IT THAT THE COUPLE WILL BE BOUND FOR ETERNITY...
I WANT SOMEONE TO CONFESS THEIR LOVE TO ME THERE TOO. ♡♡♡
...
I'VE NEVER HEARD THAT.
GIRLS SURE DO LOVE THINGS LIKE THAT.
IS THERE A PROBLEM ?!
GRMP
PUSH
OKAY, COULD YOU...
...GET AWAY FROM HIM, PLEASE?
MACHIDA.
IS THAT SOMETHING YOU SHOULD BE GOING ON ABOUT?
HOW LONG DO I HAVE TO WAIT?
WHAT ?
OH!
YOUR BOYFRIEND IS GLARING AT US.

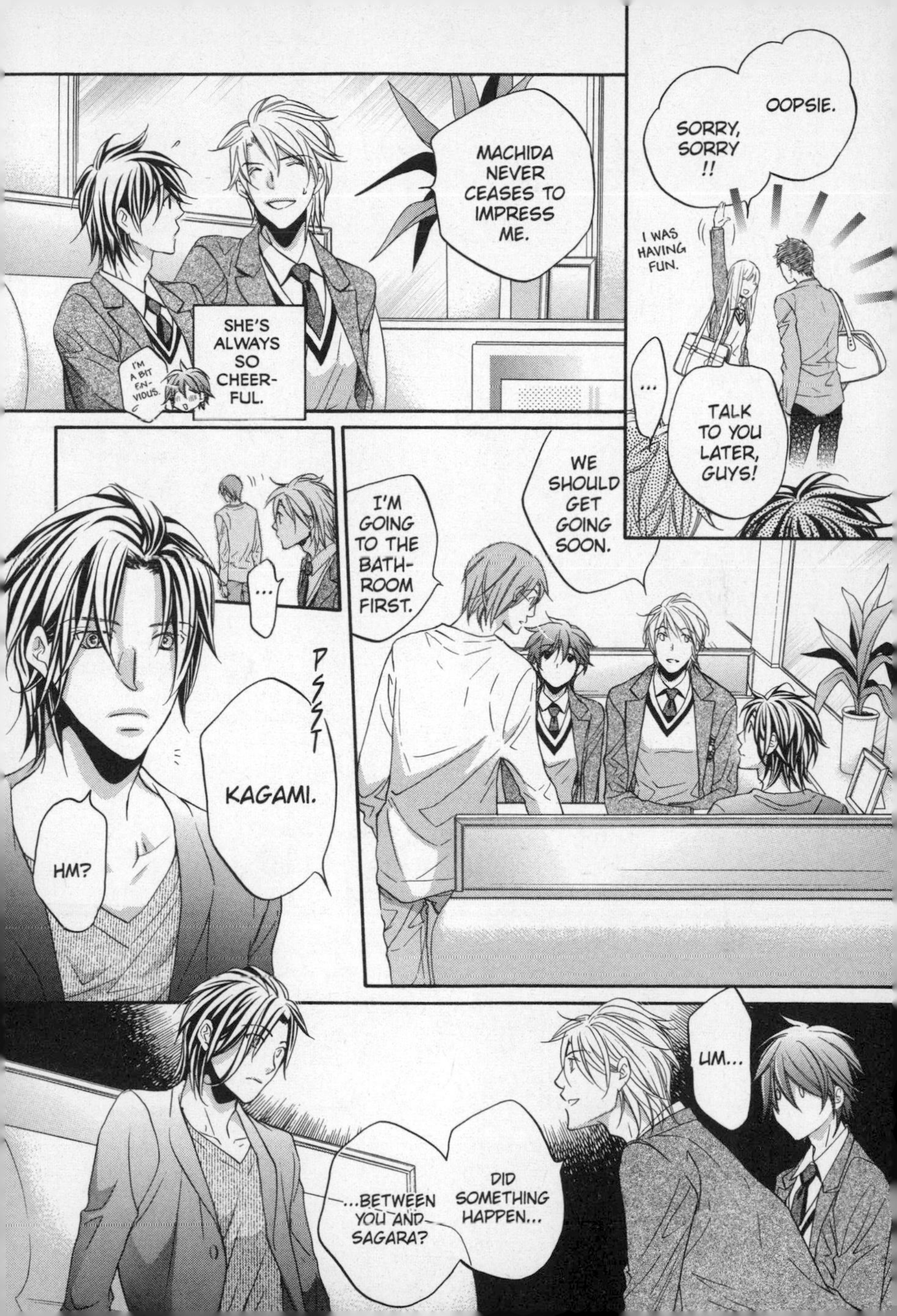
OOPSIE.
SORRY, SORRY !!
I WAS HAVING FUN.
TALK TO YOU LATER, GUYS!
...
MACHIDA NEVER CEASES TO IMPRESS ME.
SHE'S ALWAYS SO CHEERFUL.
I'M A BIT ENVIOUS.
WE SHOULD GET GOING SOON.
I'M GOING TO THE BATHROOM FIRST.
...
PSST
KAGAMI.
HM?
UM...
DID SOMETHING HAPPEN...
...BETWEEN YOU AND SAGARA?

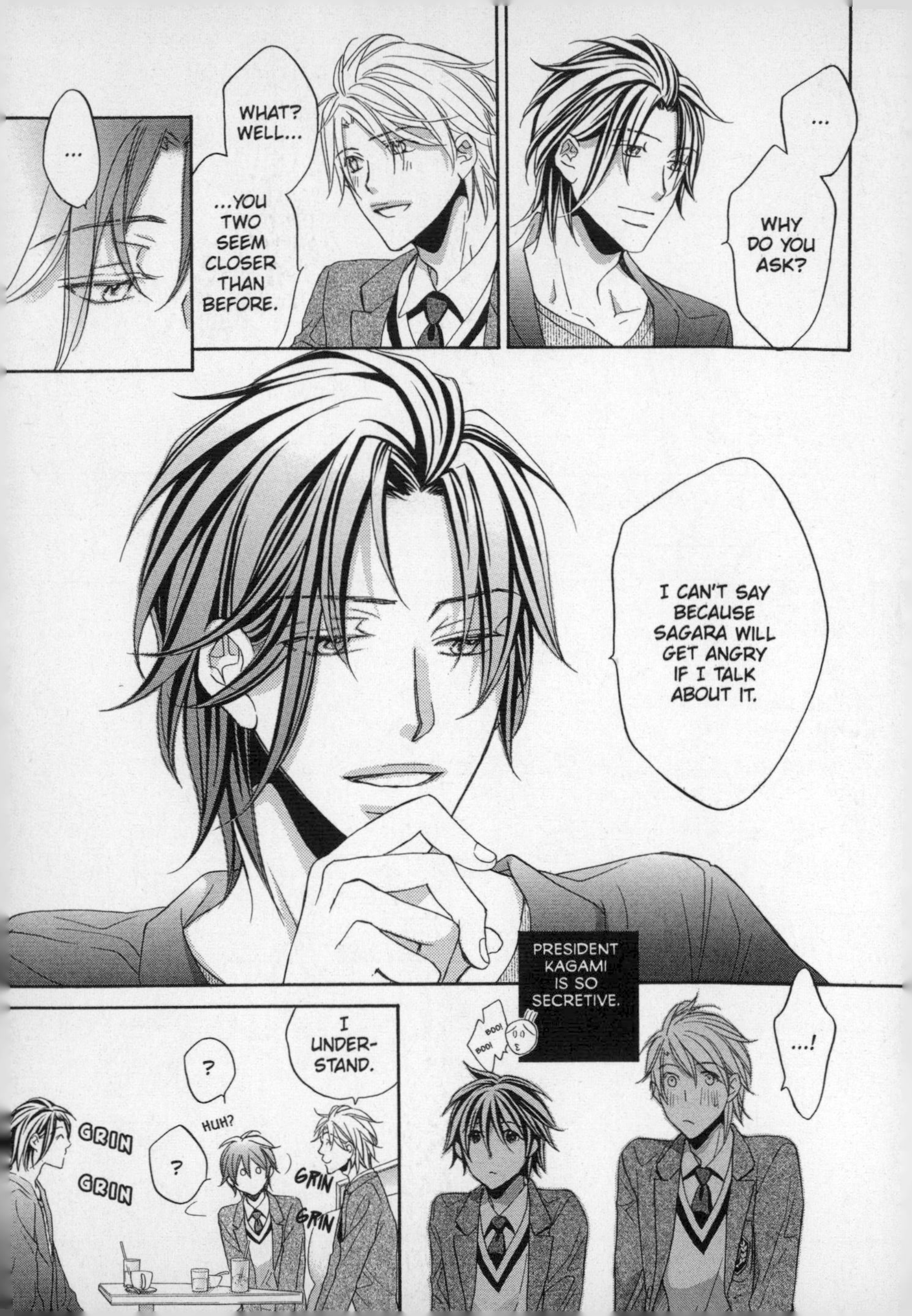
...
WHY DO YOU ASK?
WHAT? WELL...
...YOU TWO SEEM CLOSER THAN BEFORE.
...
I CAN'T SAY BECAUSE SAGARA WILL GET ANGRY IF I TALK ABOUT IT.
...!
PRESIDENT KAGAMI IS SO SECRETIVE.
BOO! BOO!
I UNDER-STAND.
GRIN GRIN
?
HUH?
?
GRIN GRIN

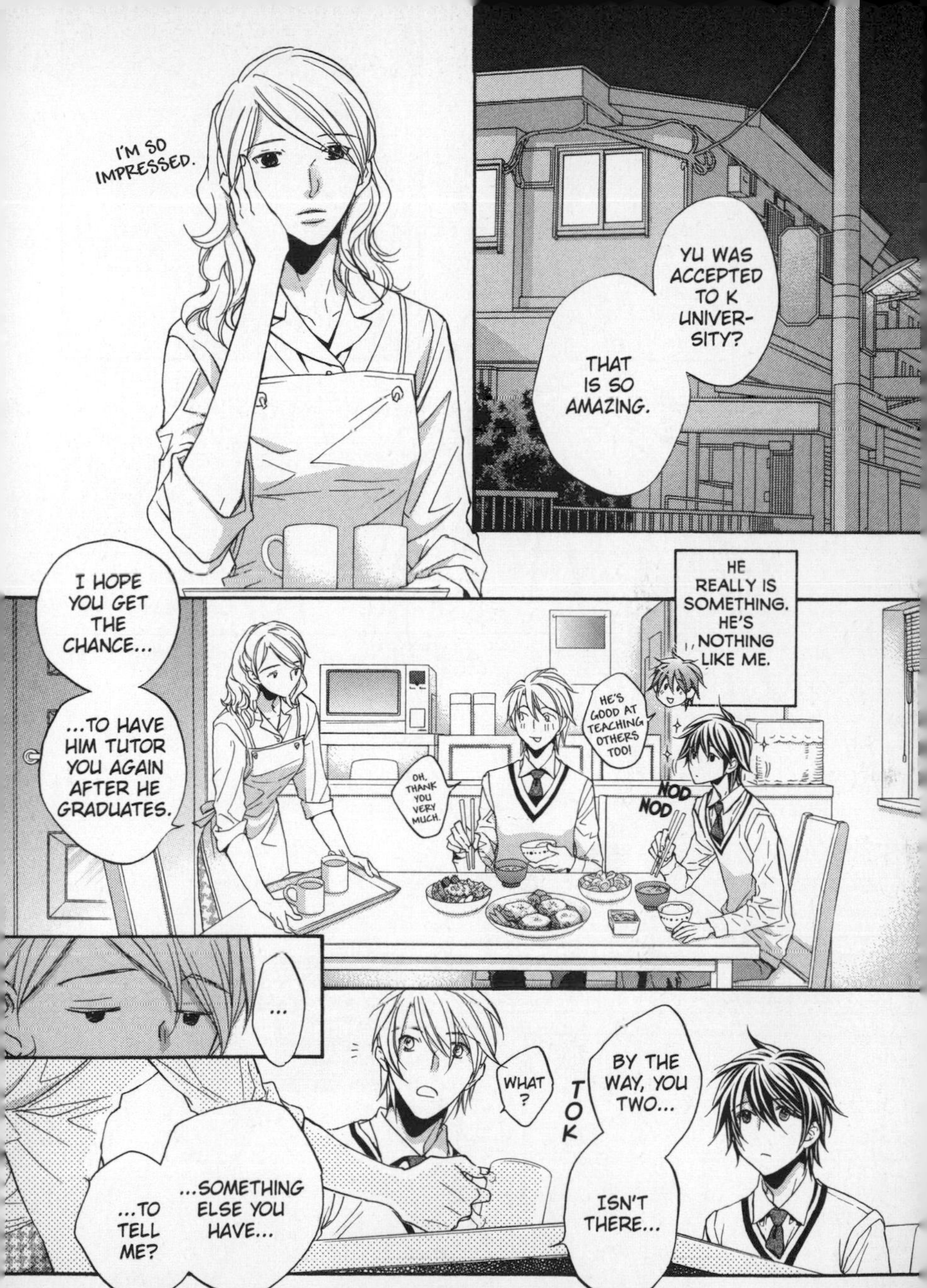

YU WAS ACCEPTED TO K UNIVERSITY?
THAT IS SO AMAZING.
I'M SO IMPRESSED.
HE REALLY IS SOMETHING. HE'S NOTHING LIKE ME.
HE'S GOOD AT TEACHING OTHERS TOO!
NOD NOD
OH, THANK YOU VERY MUCH.
I HOPE YOU GET THE CHANCE...
...TO HAVE HIM TUTOR YOU AGAIN AFTER HE GRADUATES.
BY THE WAY, YOU TWO...
TOK
WHAT?
...
ISN'T THERE...
...SOMETHING ELSE YOU HAVE...
...TO TELL ME?

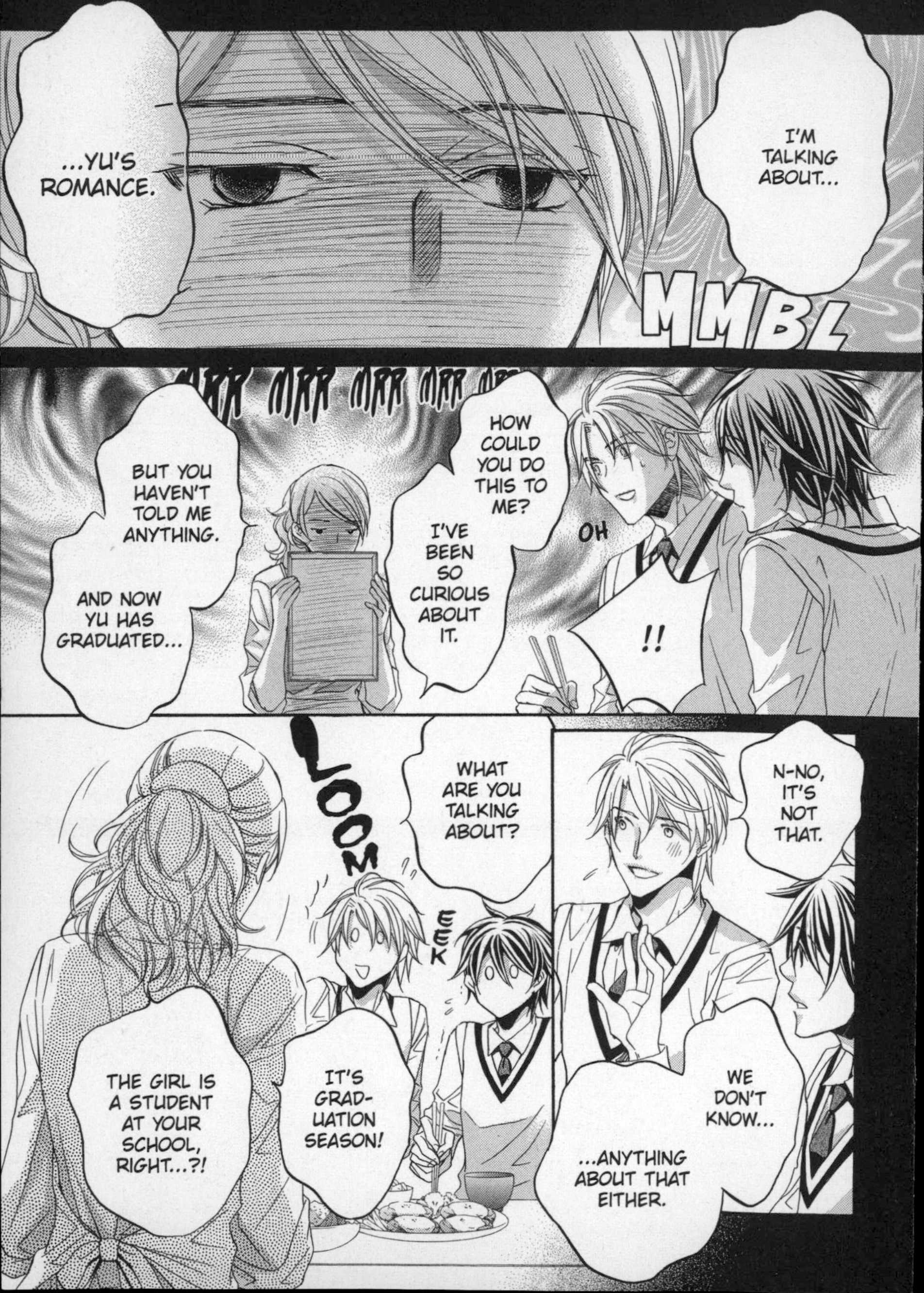
I'M TALKING ABOUT...
MMBL
...YU'S ROMANCE.
MRR MRR MRR MRR
!!
OH
HOW COULD YOU DO THIS TO ME?
I'VE BEEN SO CURIOUS ABOUT IT.
BUT YOU HAVEN'T TOLD ME ANYTHING.
AND NOW YU HAS GRADUATED...
N-NO, IT'S NOT THAT.
WHAT ARE YOU TALKING ABOUT?
LOOM
EEK
WE DON'T KNOW...
...ANYTHING ABOUT THAT EITHER.
IT'S GRAD-UATION SEASON!
THE GIRL IS A STUDENT AT YOUR SCHOOL, RIGHT...?!

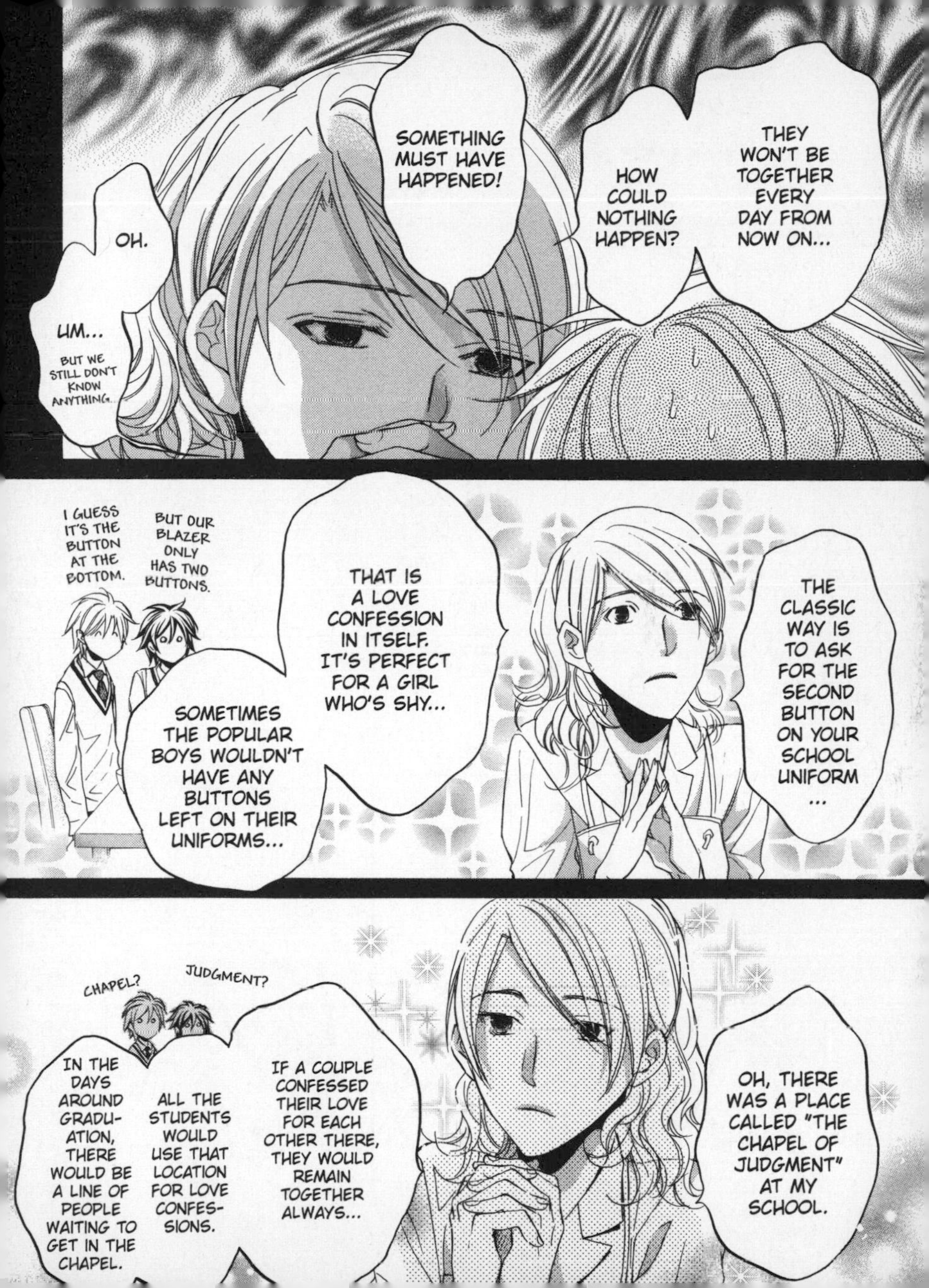
THEY WON'T BE TOGETHER EVERY DAY FROM NOW ON...
HOW COULD NOTHING HAPPEN?
SOMETHING MUST HAVE HAPPENED!
OH.
UM...
BUT WE STILL DON'T KNOW ANYTHING...
THE CLASSIC WAY IS TO ASK FOR THE SECOND BUTTON ON YOUR SCHOOL UNIFORM ...
THAT IS A LOVE CONFESSION IN ITSELF. IT'S PERFECT FOR A GIRL WHO'S SHY...
SOMETIMES THE POPULAR BOYS WOULDN'T HAVE ANY BUTTONS LEFT ON THEIR UNIFORMS...
BUT OUR BLAZER ONLY HAS TWO BUTTONS.
I GUESS IT'S THE BUTTON AT THE BOTTOM.
OH, THERE WAS A PLACE CALLED "THE CHAPEL OF JUDGMENT" AT MY SCHOOL.
IF A COUPLE CONFESSED THEIR LOVE FOR EACH OTHER THERE, THEY WOULD REMAIN TOGETHER ALWAYS...
ALL THE STUDENTS WOULD USE THAT LOCATION FOR LOVE CONFESSIONS.
IN THE DAYS AROUND GRADUATION, THERE WOULD BE A LINE OF PEOPLE WAITING TO GET IN THE CHAPEL.
JUDGMENT?
CHAPEL?

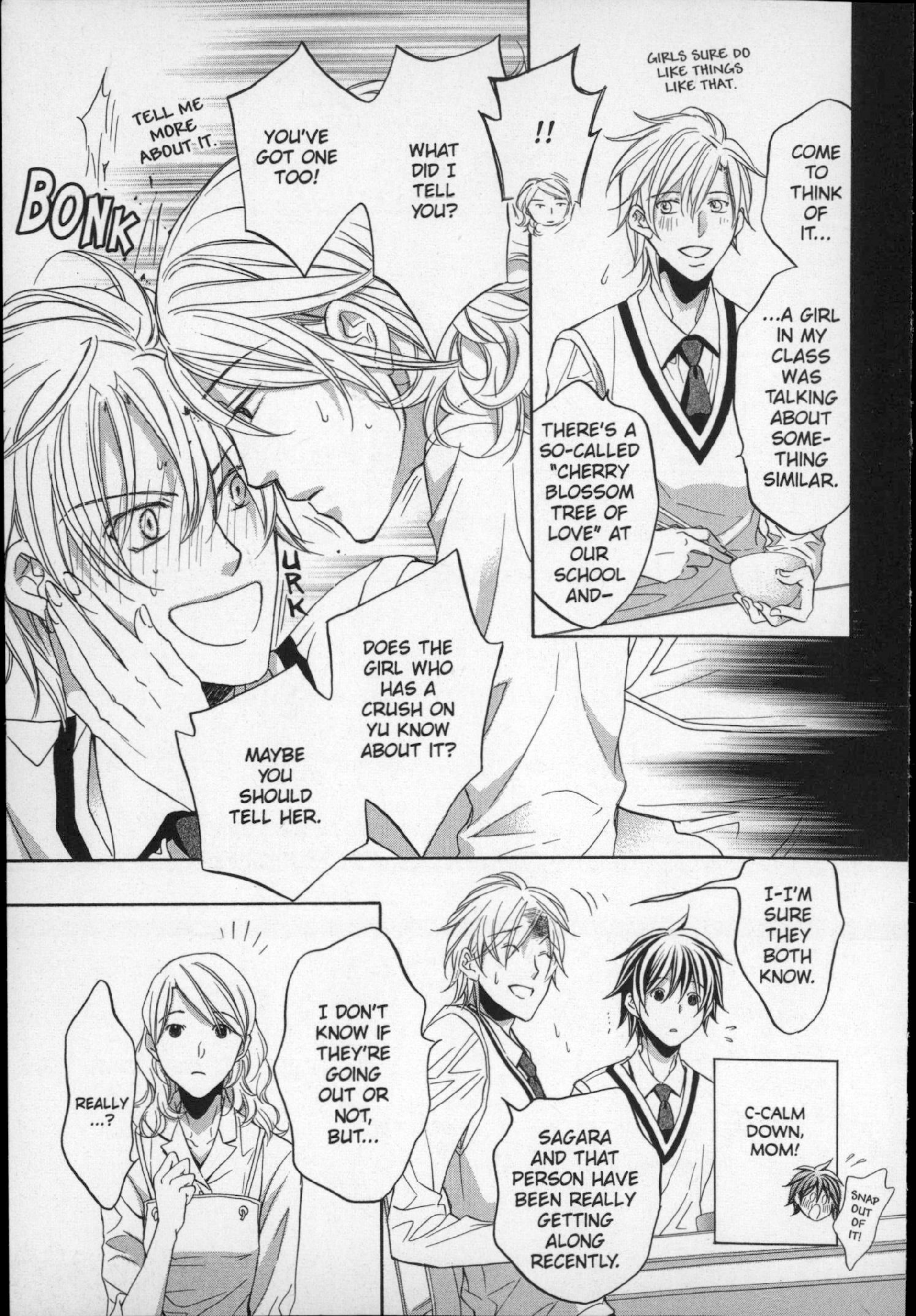

GIRLS SURE DO LIKE THINGS LIKE THAT.
COME TO THINK OF IT...
...A GIRL IN MY CLASS WAS TALKING ABOUT SOME-THING SIMILAR.
THERE'S A SO-CALLED "CHERRY BLOSSOM TREE OF LOVE" AT OUR SCHOOL AND–
!!
WHAT DID I TELL YOU?
YOU'VE GOT ONE TOO!
TELL ME MORE ABOUT IT.
BONK
URK
DOES THE GIRL WHO HAS A CRUSH ON YU KNOW ABOUT IT?
MAYBE YOU SHOULD TELL HER.
I-I'M SURE THEY BOTH KNOW.
C-CALM DOWN, MOM!
SNAP OUT OF IT!
I DON'T KNOW IF THEY'RE GOING OUT OR NOT, BUT...
SAGARA AND THAT PERSON HAVE BEEN REALLY GETTING ALONG RECENTLY.
REALLY ...?

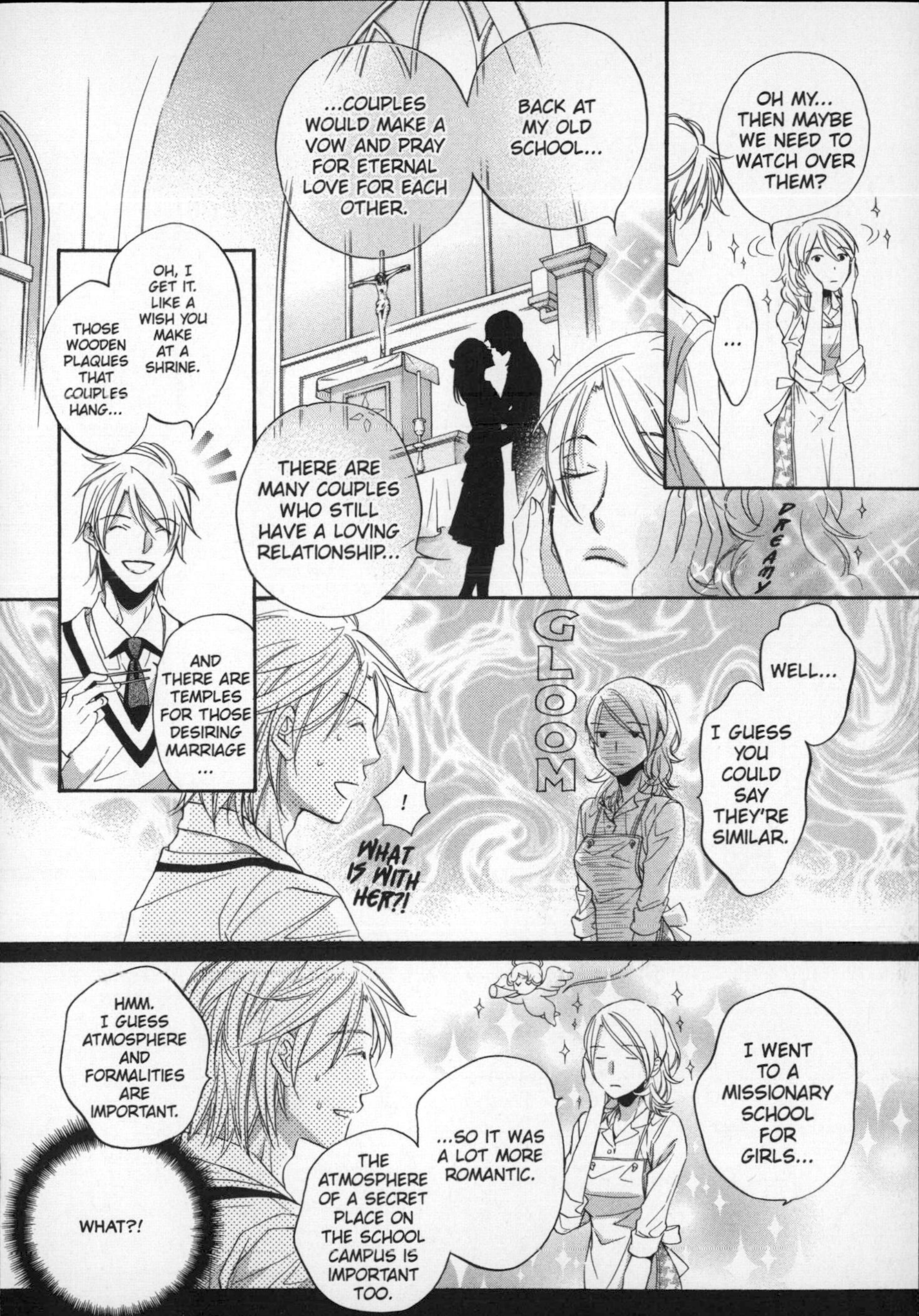
OH MY... THEN MAYBE WE NEED TO WATCH OVER THEM?
...
BACK AT MY OLD SCHOOL...
...COUPLES WOULD MAKE A VOW AND PRAY FOR ETERNAL LOVE FOR EACH OTHER.
THERE ARE MANY COUPLES WHO STILL HAVE A LOVING RELATIONSHIP...
DREAMY
OH, I GET IT. LIKE A WISH YOU MAKE AT A SHRINE.
THOSE WOODEN PLAQUES THAT COUPLES HANG...
AND THERE ARE TEMPLES FOR THOSE DESIRING MARRIAGE ...
WELL...
I GUESS YOU COULD SAY THEY'RE SIMILAR.
GLOOM
!
WHAT IS WITH HER?!
I WENT TO A MISSIONARY SCHOOL FOR GIRLS...
...SO IT WAS A LOT MORE ROMANTIC.
THE ATMOSPHERE OF A SECRET PLACE ON THE SCHOOL CAMPUS IS IMPORTANT TOO.
HMM. I GUESS ATMOSPHERE AND FORMALITIES ARE IMPORTANT.
WHAT?!

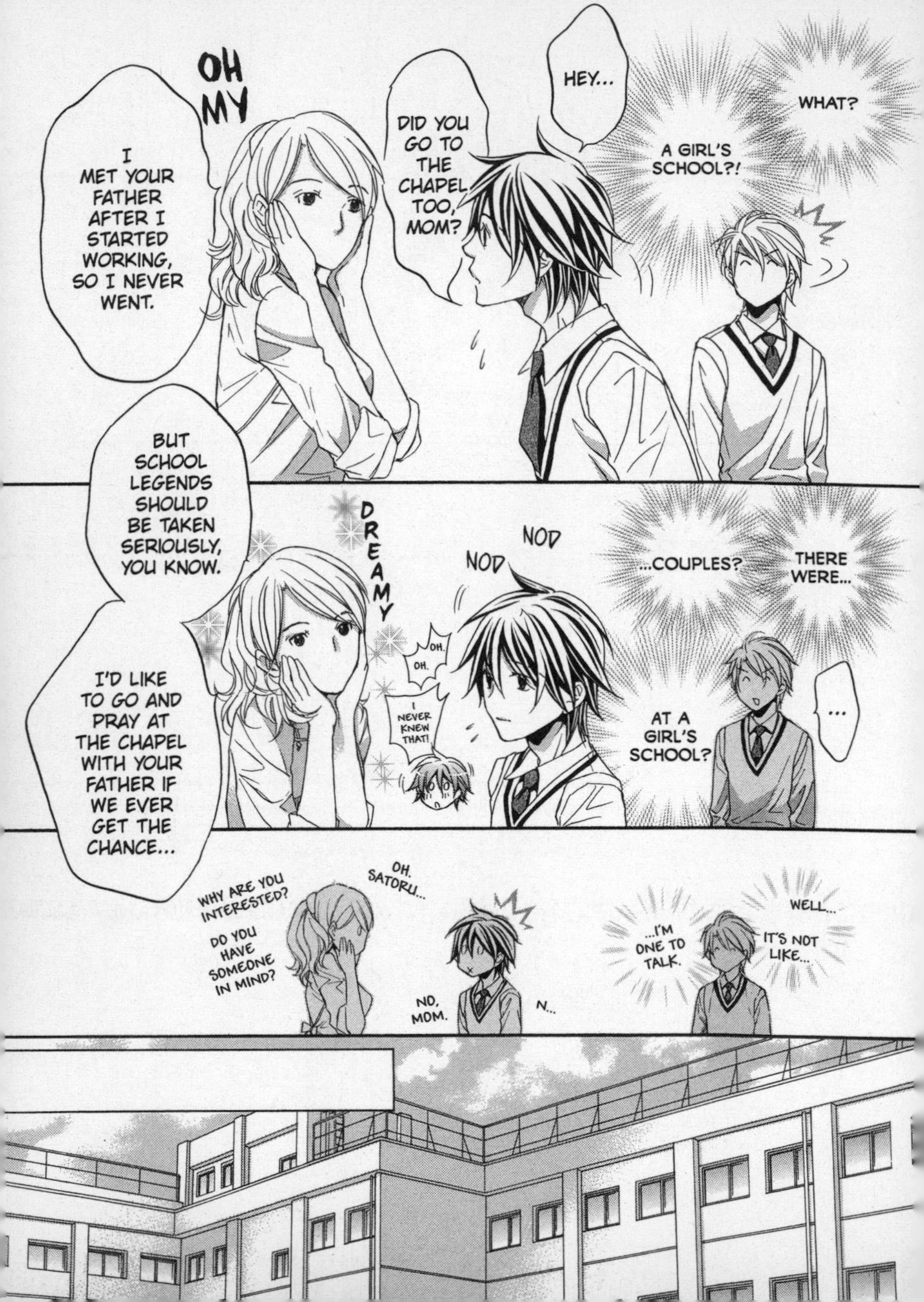
WHAT?
A GIRL'S SCHOOL?!
HEY...
DID YOU GO TO THE CHAPEL TOO, MOM?
OH MY
I MET YOUR FATHER AFTER I STARTED WORKING, SO I NEVER WENT.
THERE WERE...
...COUPLES?
AT A GIRL'S SCHOOL?
...
NOD
NOD
OH.
OH.
I NEVER KNEW THAT!
DREAMY
BUT SCHOOL LEGENDS SHOULD BE TAKEN SERIOUSLY, YOU KNOW.
I'D LIKE TO GO AND PRAY AT THE CHAPEL WITH YOUR FATHER IF WE EVER GET THE CHANCE...
WELL...
IT'S NOT LIKE...
...I'M ONE TO TALK.
N...
NO, MOM.
OH. SATORU...
WHY ARE YOU INTERESTED?
DO YOU HAVE SOMEONE IN MIND?

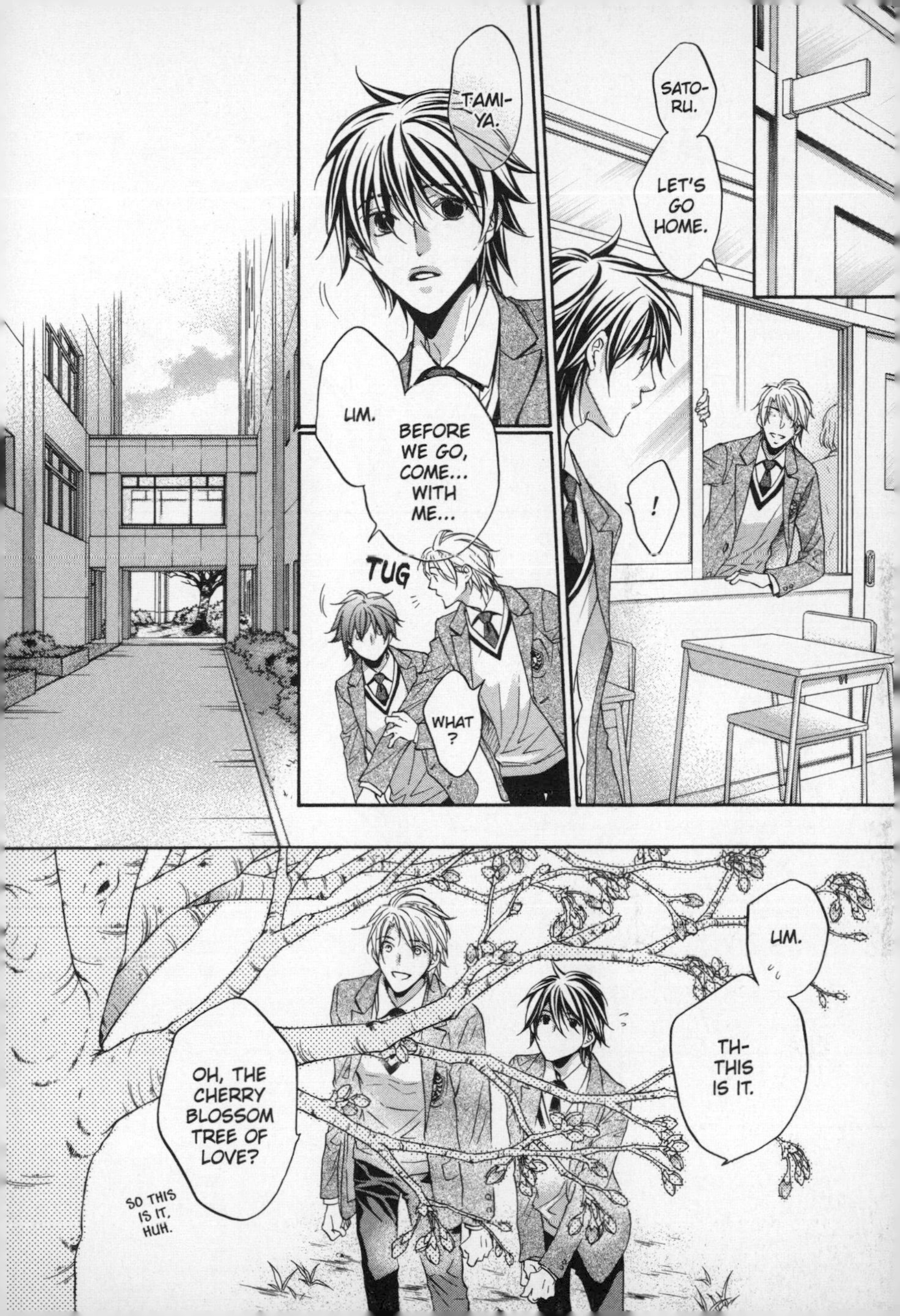
SATO-RU.
LET'S GO HOME.
!
TAMI-YA.
UM.
BEFORE WE GO, COME... WITH ME...
TUG
WHAT?
UM.
TH- THIS IS IT.
OH, THE CHERRY BLOSSOM TREE OF LOVE?
SO THIS IS IT, HUH.

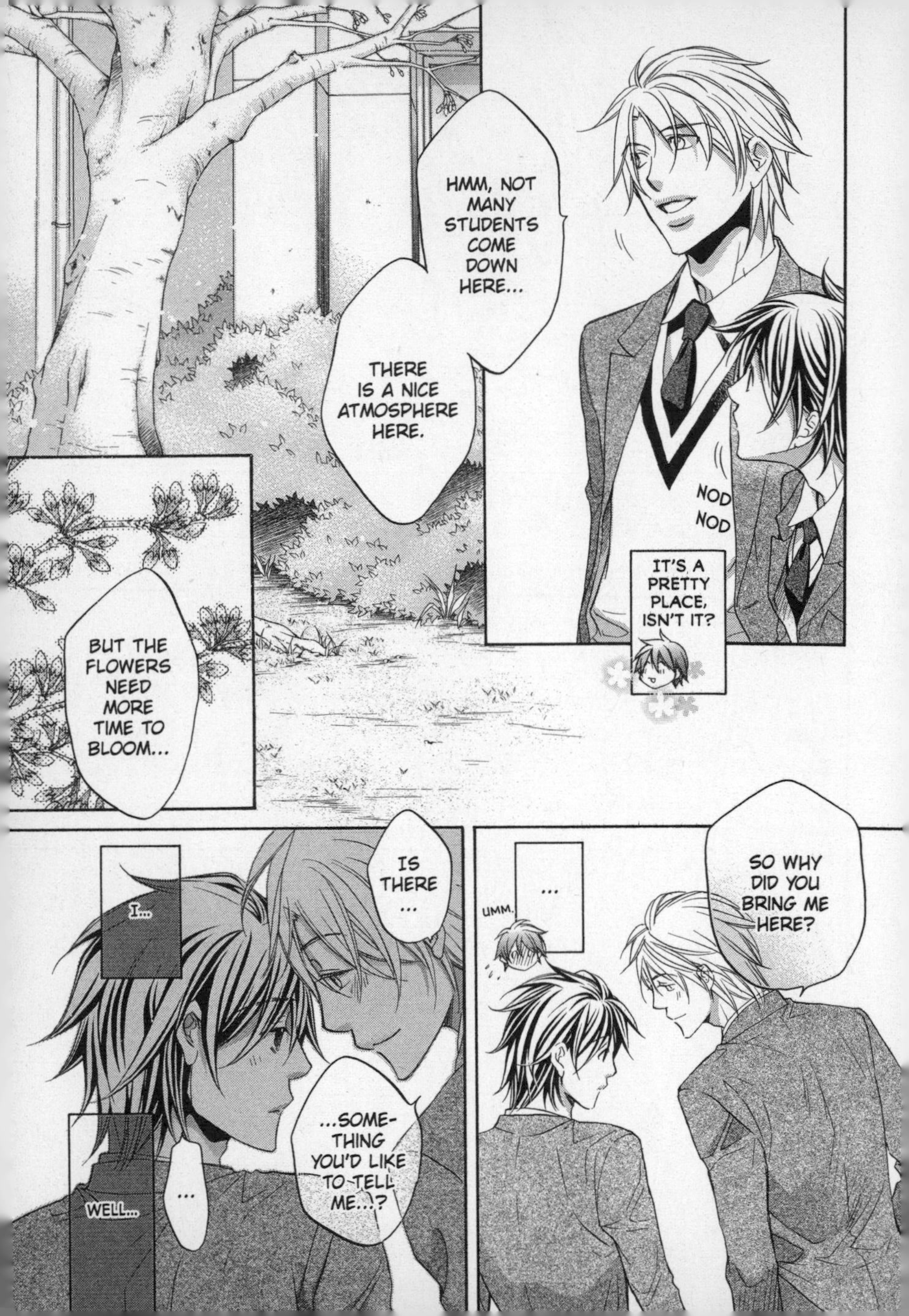

HMM, NOT MANY STUDENTS COME DOWN HERE...
THERE IS A NICE ATMOSPHERE HERE.
NOD NOD
IT'S A PRETTY PLACE, ISN'T IT?
BUT THE FLOWERS NEED MORE TIME TO BLOOM...
SO WHY DID YOU BRING ME HERE?
...
UMM.
IS THERE ...
I...
...SOME-THING YOU'D LIKE TO TELL ME...?
...
WELL...

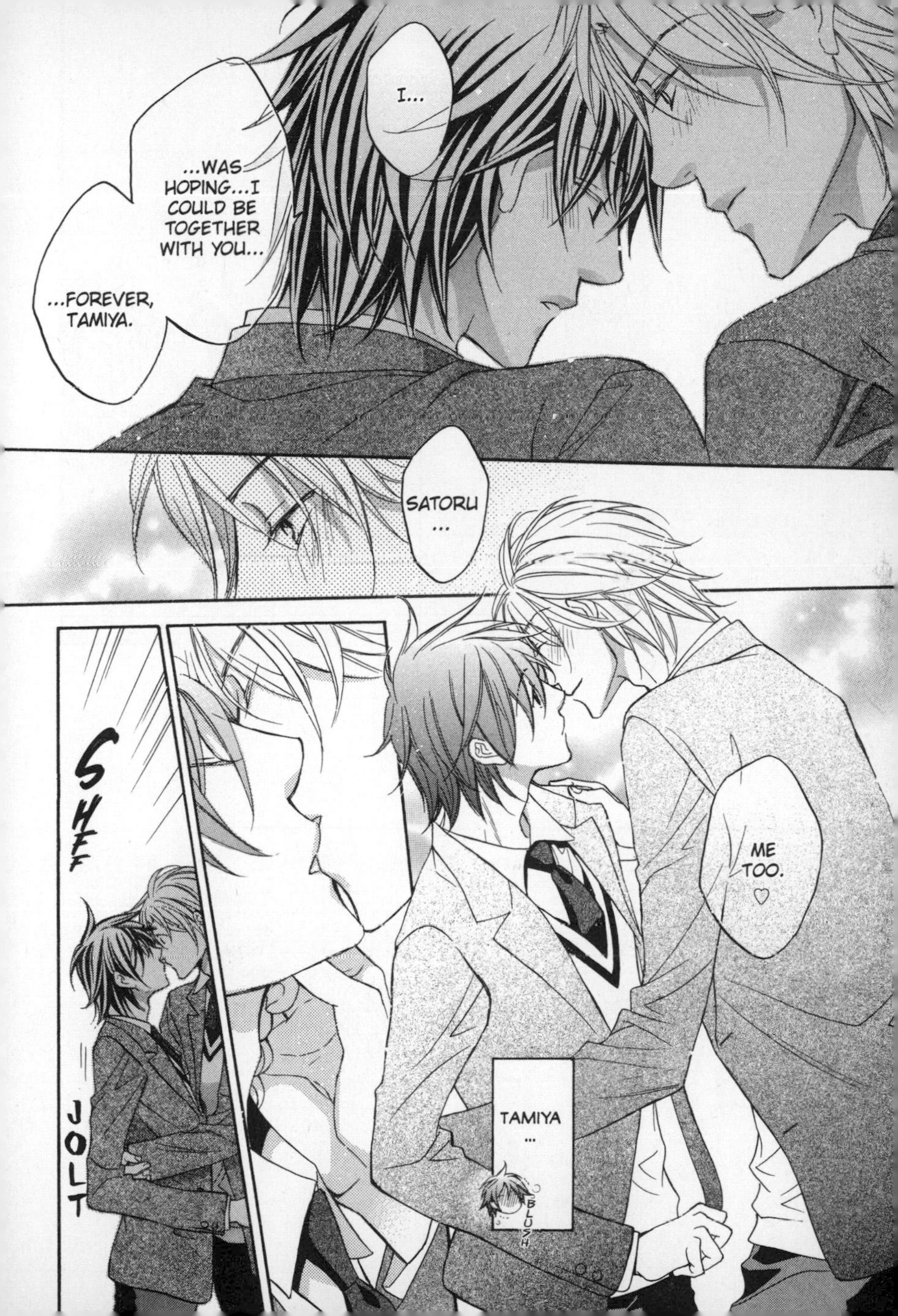
I...
...WAS HOPING...I COULD BE TOGETHER WITH YOU...
...FOREVER, TAMIYA.
SATORU ...
ME TOO. ♡
TAMIYA ...
BLUSH
SHFF
JOLT

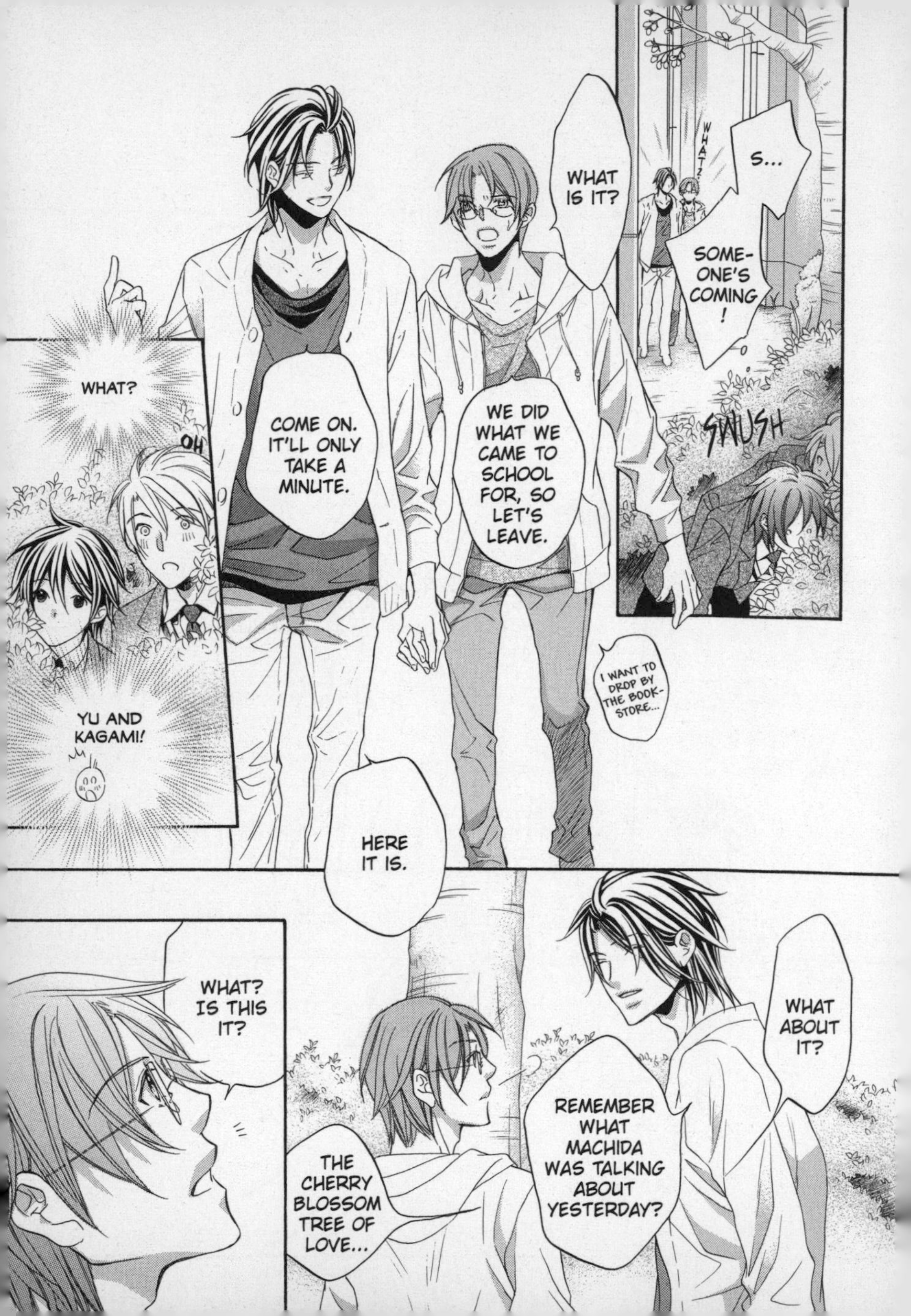
S...
WHAT IS IT?
WHAT?!
SOME-ONE'S COMING!
SWUSH
WE DID WHAT WE CAME TO SCHOOL FOR, SO LET'S LEAVE.
I WANT TO DROP BY THE BOOK-STORE...
COME ON. IT'LL ONLY TAKE A MINUTE.
WHAT?
OH
YU AND KAGAMI!
HERE IT IS.
WHAT? IS THIS IT?
REMEMBER WHAT MACHIDA WAS TALKING ABOUT YESTERDAY?
WHAT ABOUT IT?
THE CHERRY BLOSSOM TREE OF LOVE...

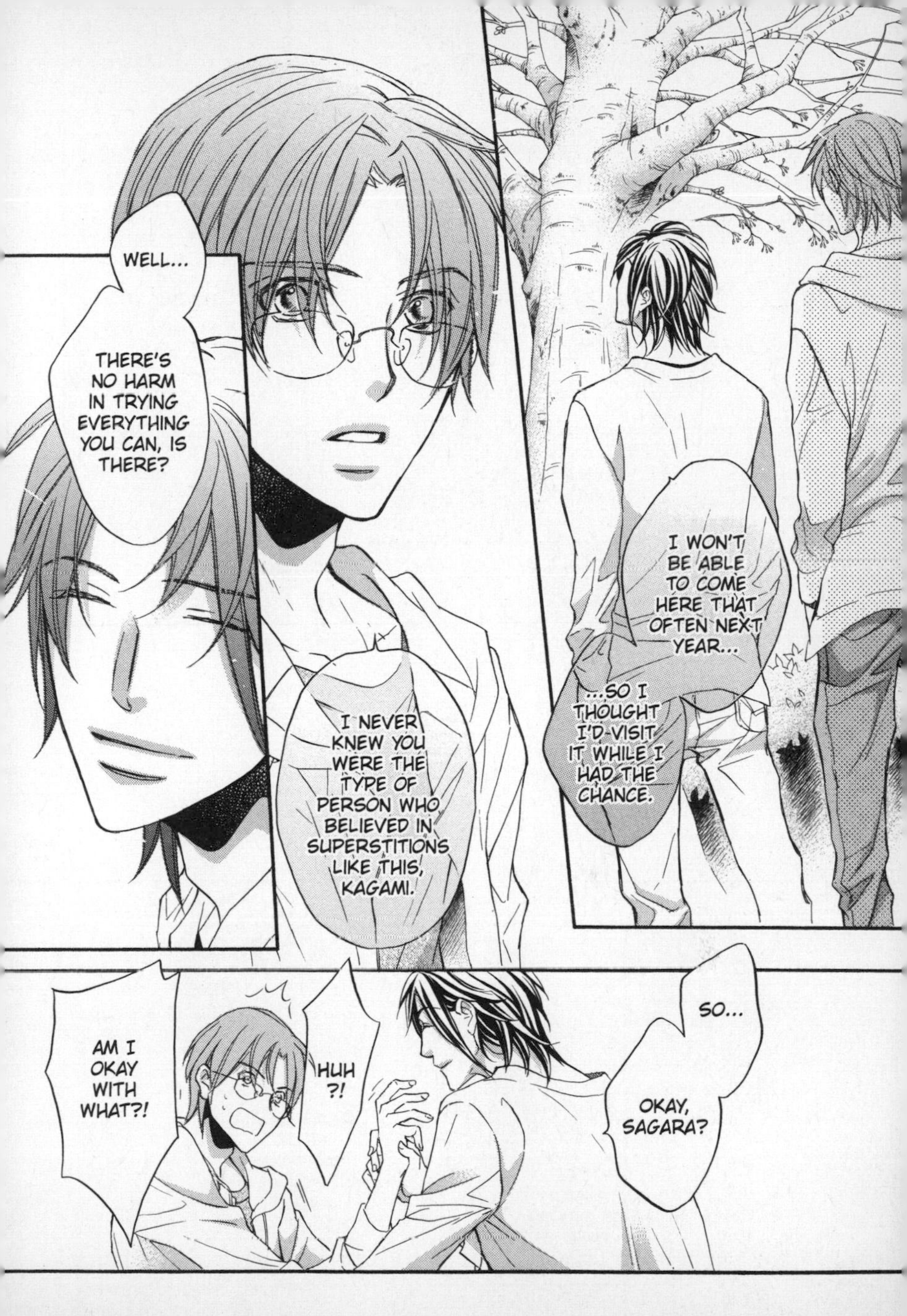
I WON'T BE ABLE TO COME HERE THAT OFTEN NEXT YEAR...
...SO I THOUGHT I'D VISIT IT WHILE I HAD THE CHANCE.
I NEVER KNEW YOU WERE THE TYPE OF PERSON WHO BELIEVED IN SUPERSTITIONS LIKE THIS, KAGAMI.
WELL...
THERE'S NO HARM IN TRYING EVERYTHING YOU CAN, IS THERE?
SO...
OKAY, SAGARA?
HUH?!
AM I OKAY WITH WHAT?!

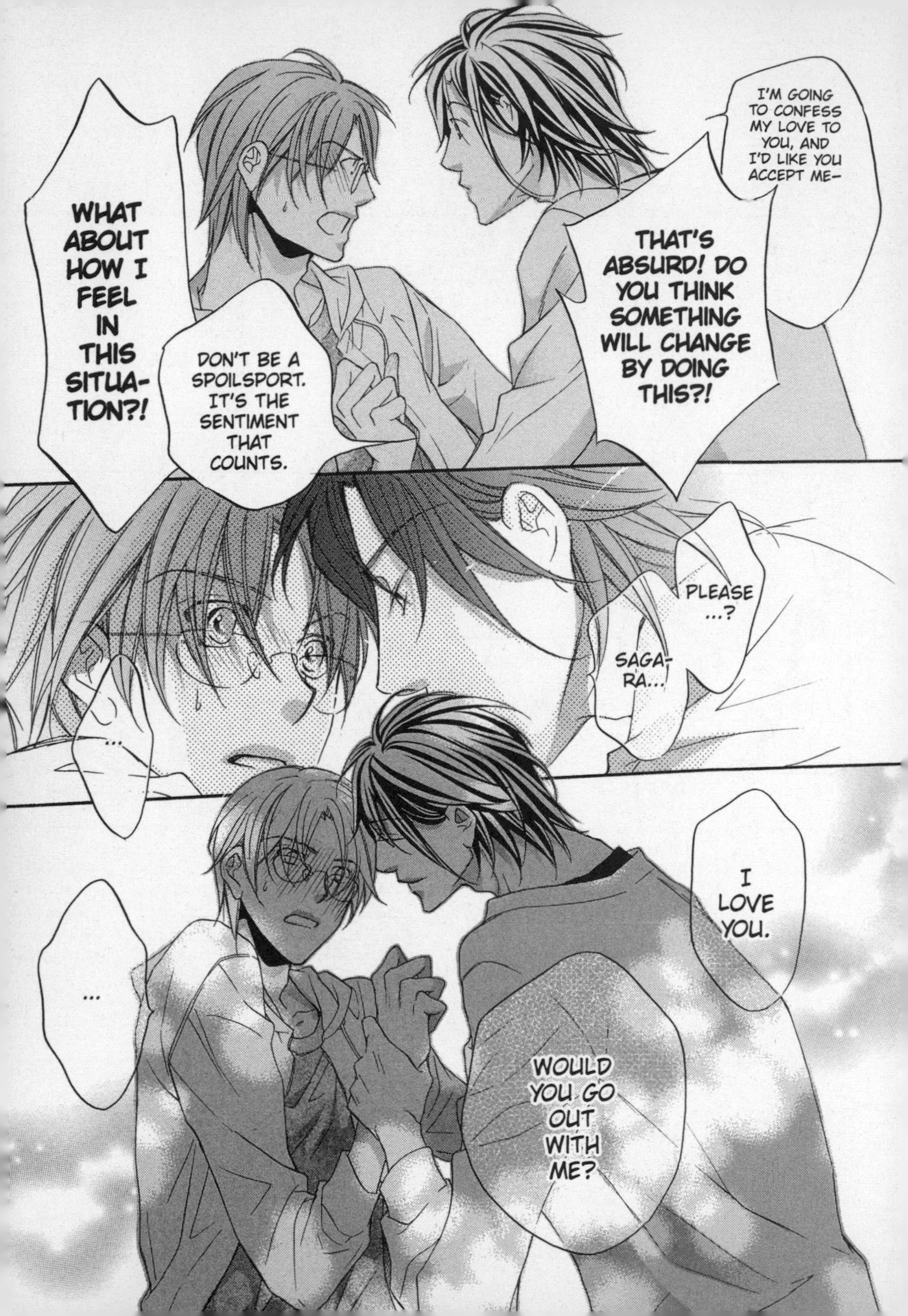
I'M GOING TO CONFESS MY LOVE TO YOU, AND I'D LIKE YOU ACCEPT ME-
THAT'S ABSURD! DO YOU THINK SOMETHING WILL CHANGE BY DOING THIS?!
DON'T BE A SPOILSPORT. IT'S THE SENTIMENT THAT COUNTS.
WHAT ABOUT HOW I FEEL IN THIS SITUATION?!
PLEASE ...?
SAGA-RA...
...
I LOVE YOU.
WOULD YOU GO OUT WITH ME?
...

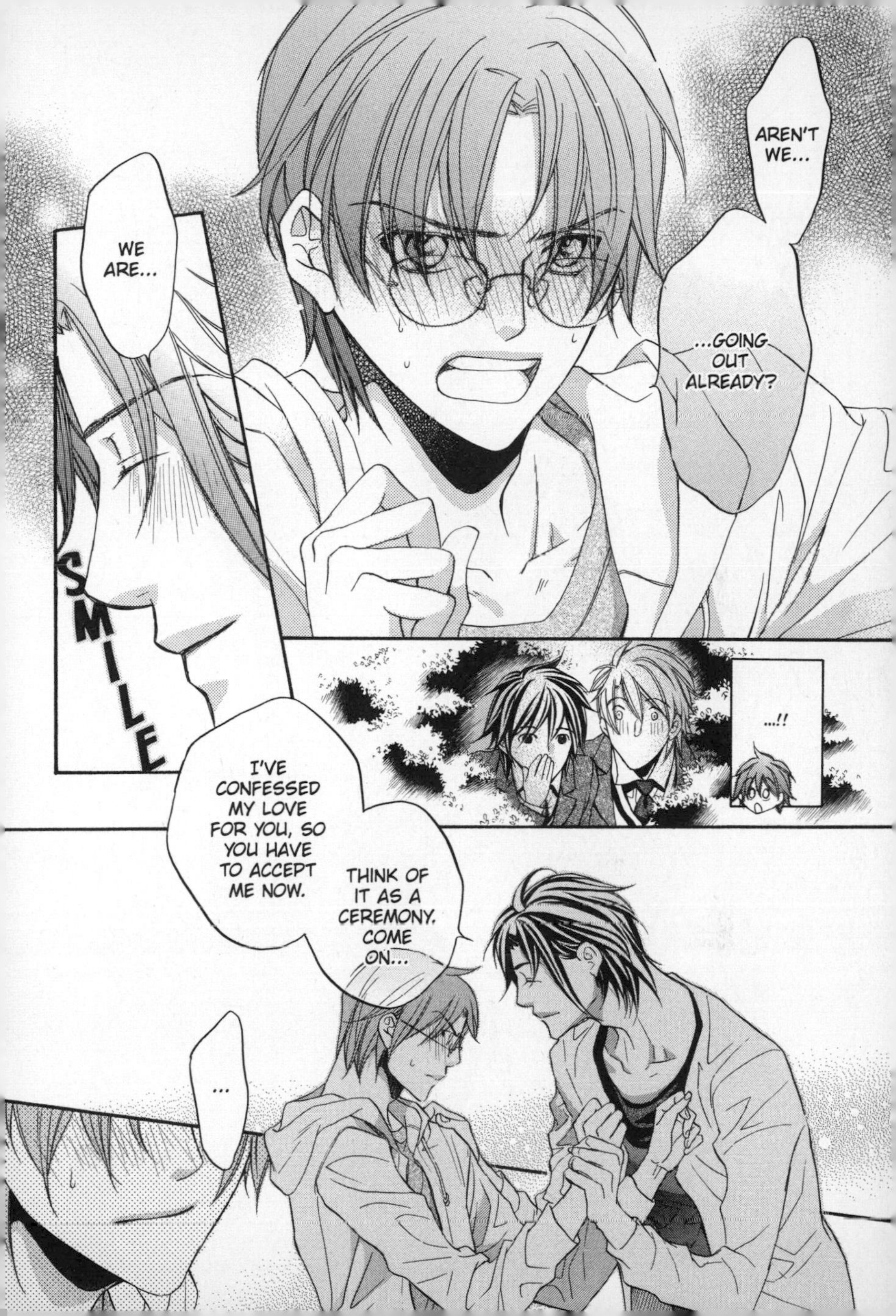
AREN'T WE...
...GOING OUT ALREADY?
WE ARE...
SMILE
...!!
I'VE CONFESSED MY LOVE FOR YOU, SO YOU HAVE TO ACCEPT ME NOW.
THINK OF IT AS A CEREMONY. COME ON...
...

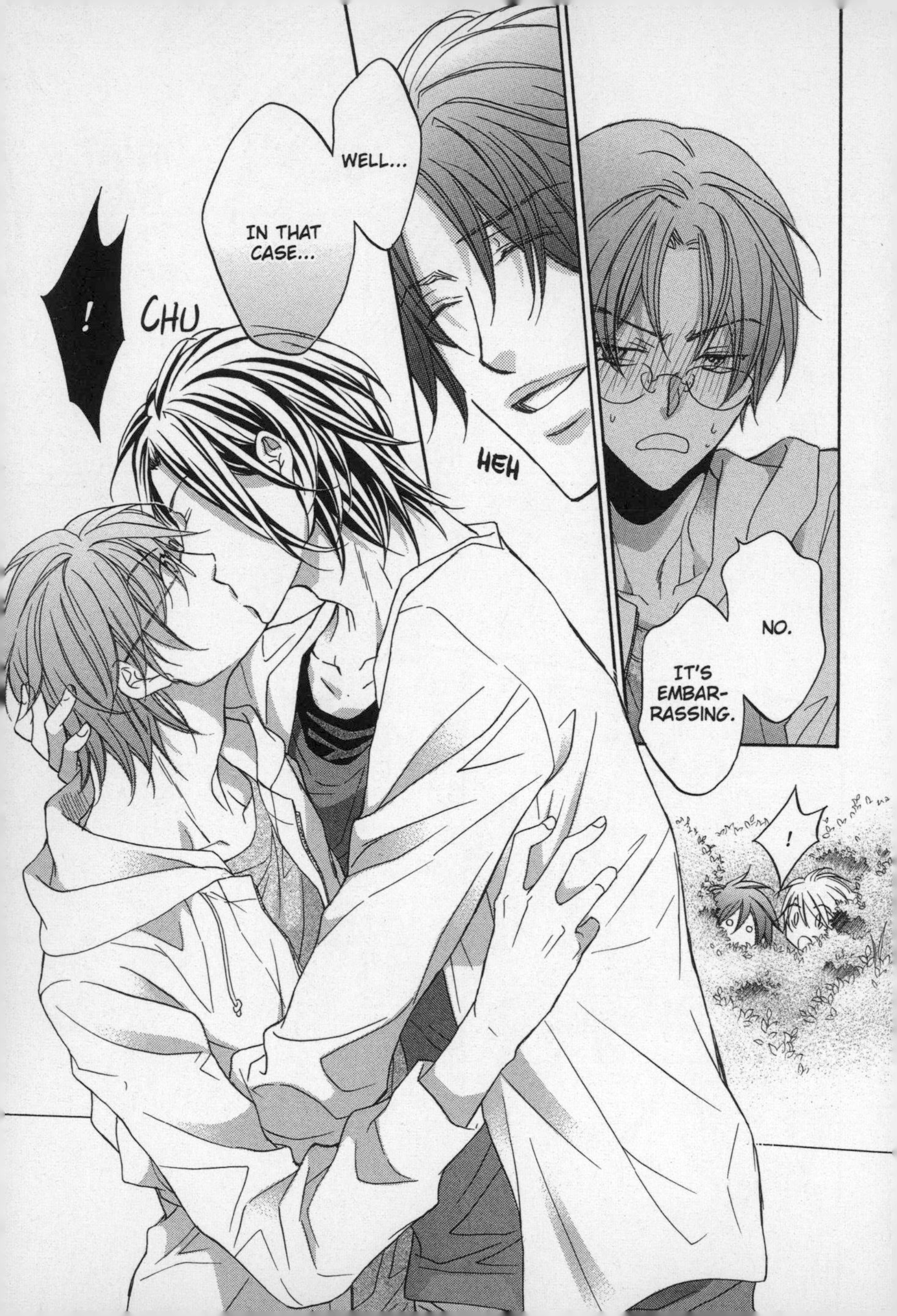
NO.
IT'S EMBARRASSING.
HEH
WELL...
IN THAT CASE...
CHU
!
!

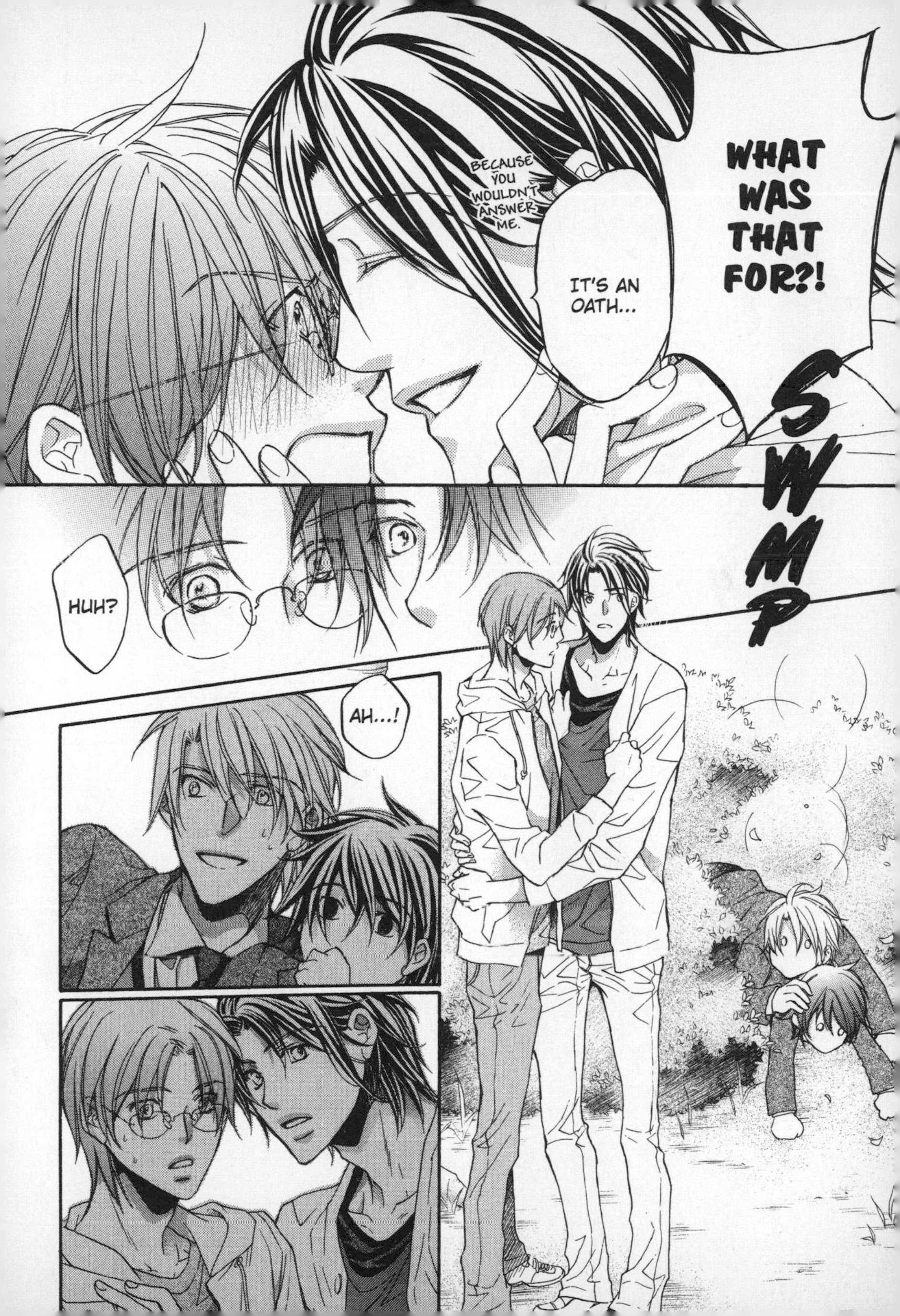

WHAT WAS THAT FOR?!
IT'S AN OATH...
BECAUSE YOU WOULDN'T ANSWER ME.
SWMP
HUH?
AH...!

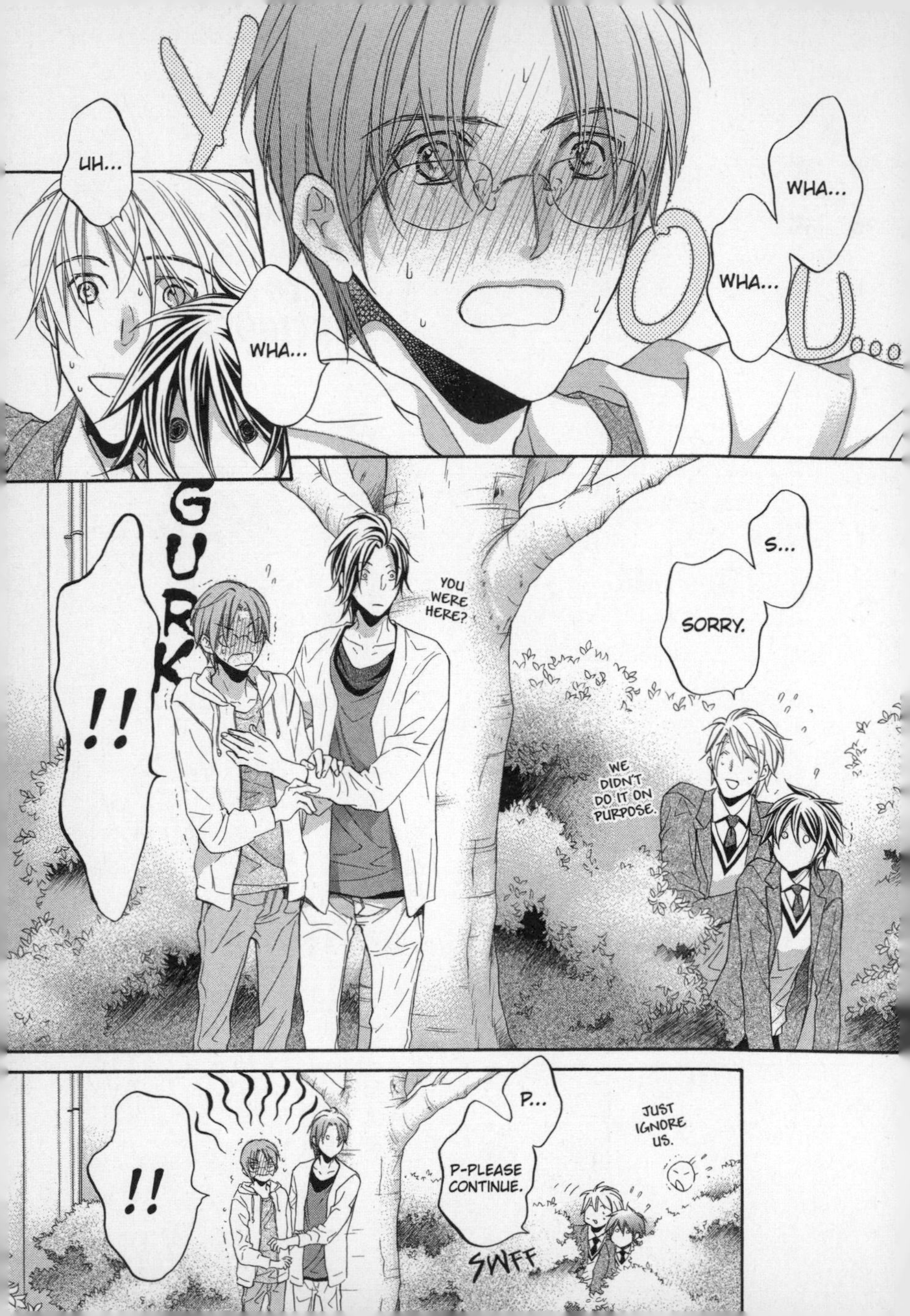
WHA...
WHA...
YOU...
WHA...
UH...
S...
SORRY.
WE DIDN'T DO IT ON PURPOSE.
YOU WERE HERE?
GURK
!!
JUST IGNORE US.
P...
P-PLEASE CONTINUE.
SWFF
!!

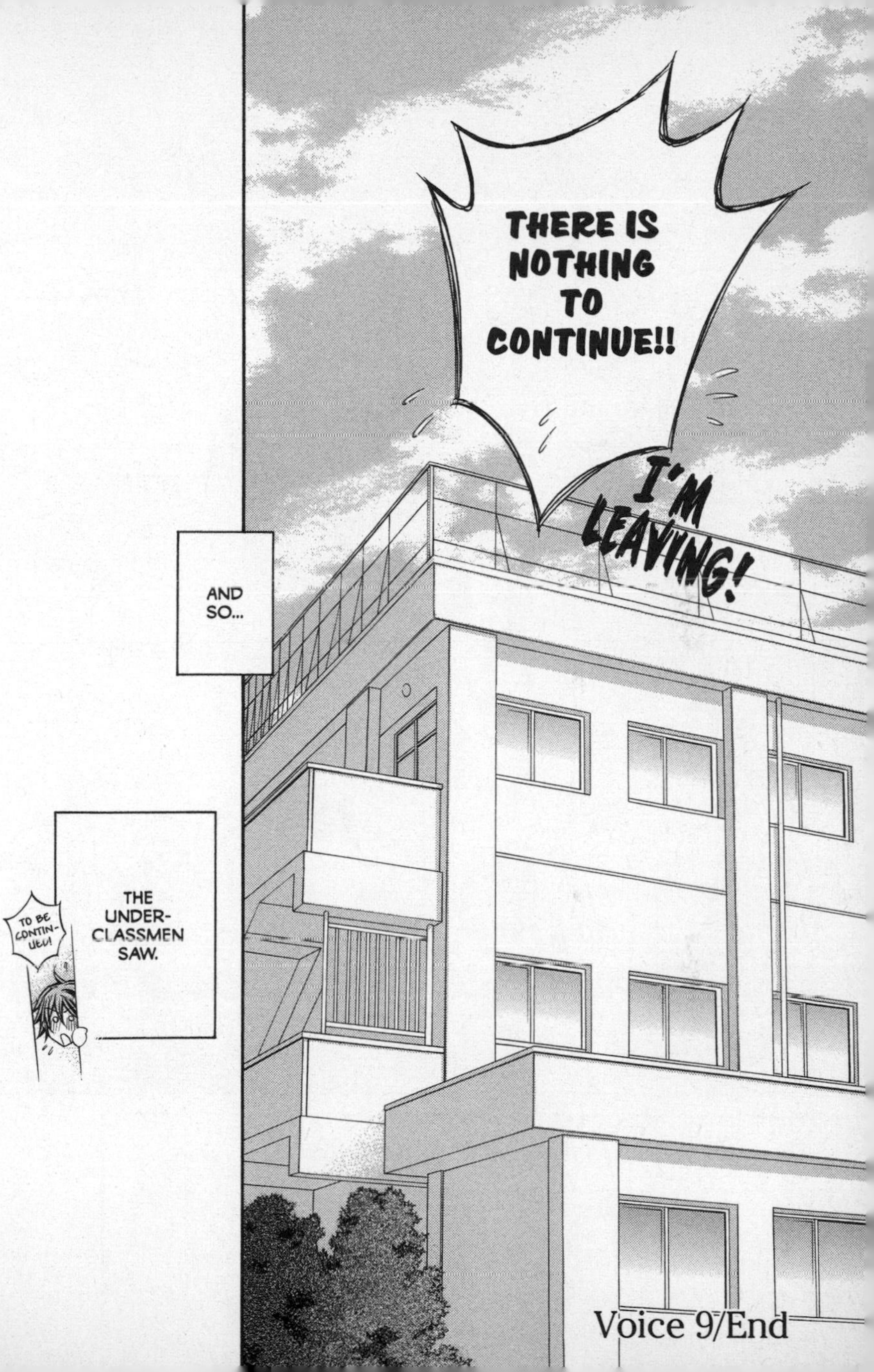
THERE IS NOTHING TO CONTINUE!!
I'M LEAVING!
Voice 9/End
AND SO...
THE UNDER-CLASSMEN SAW.
TO BE CONTIN-UED!

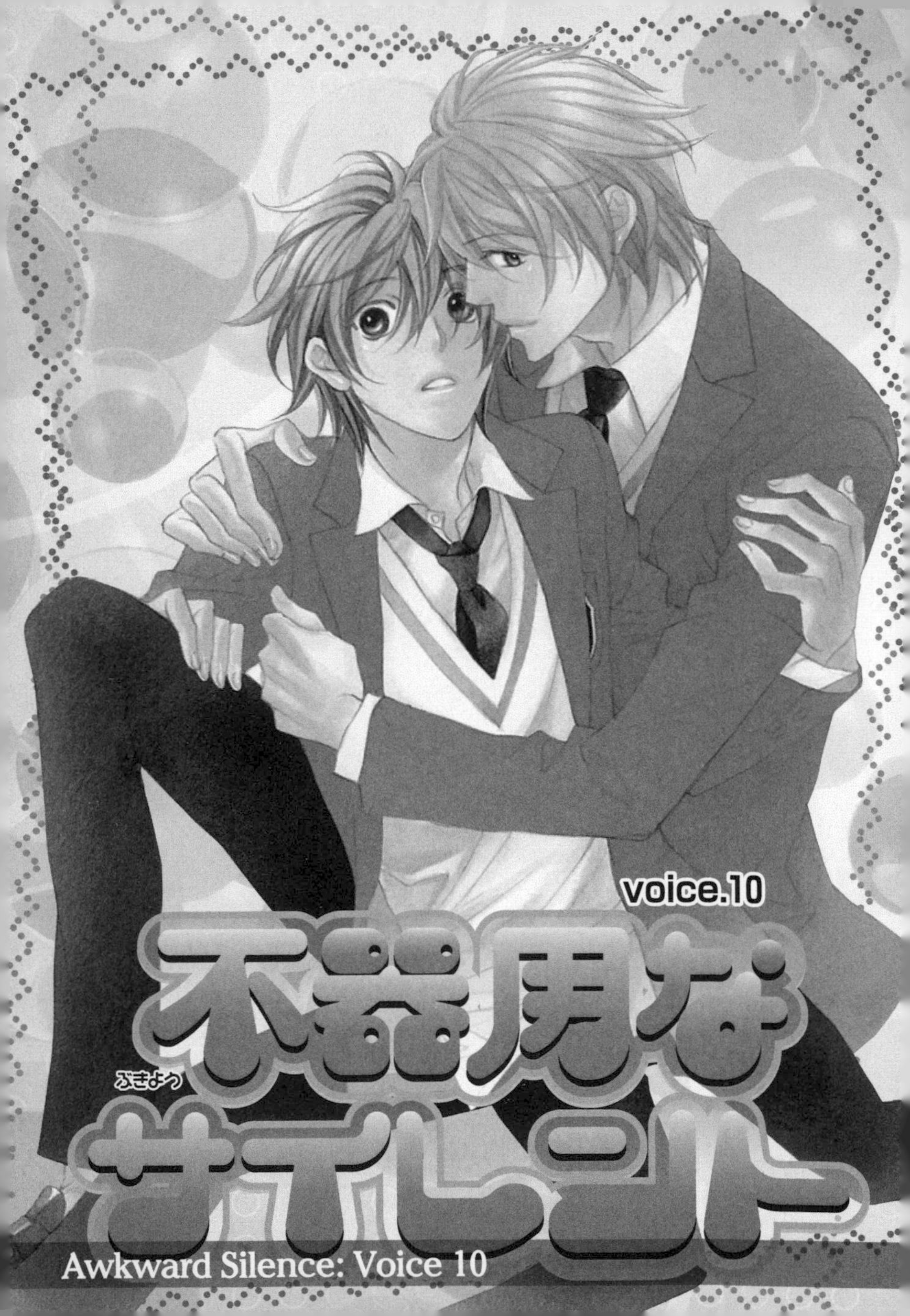
voice.10
不器用な
ぶきよう
サイレント
Awkward Silence: Voice 10

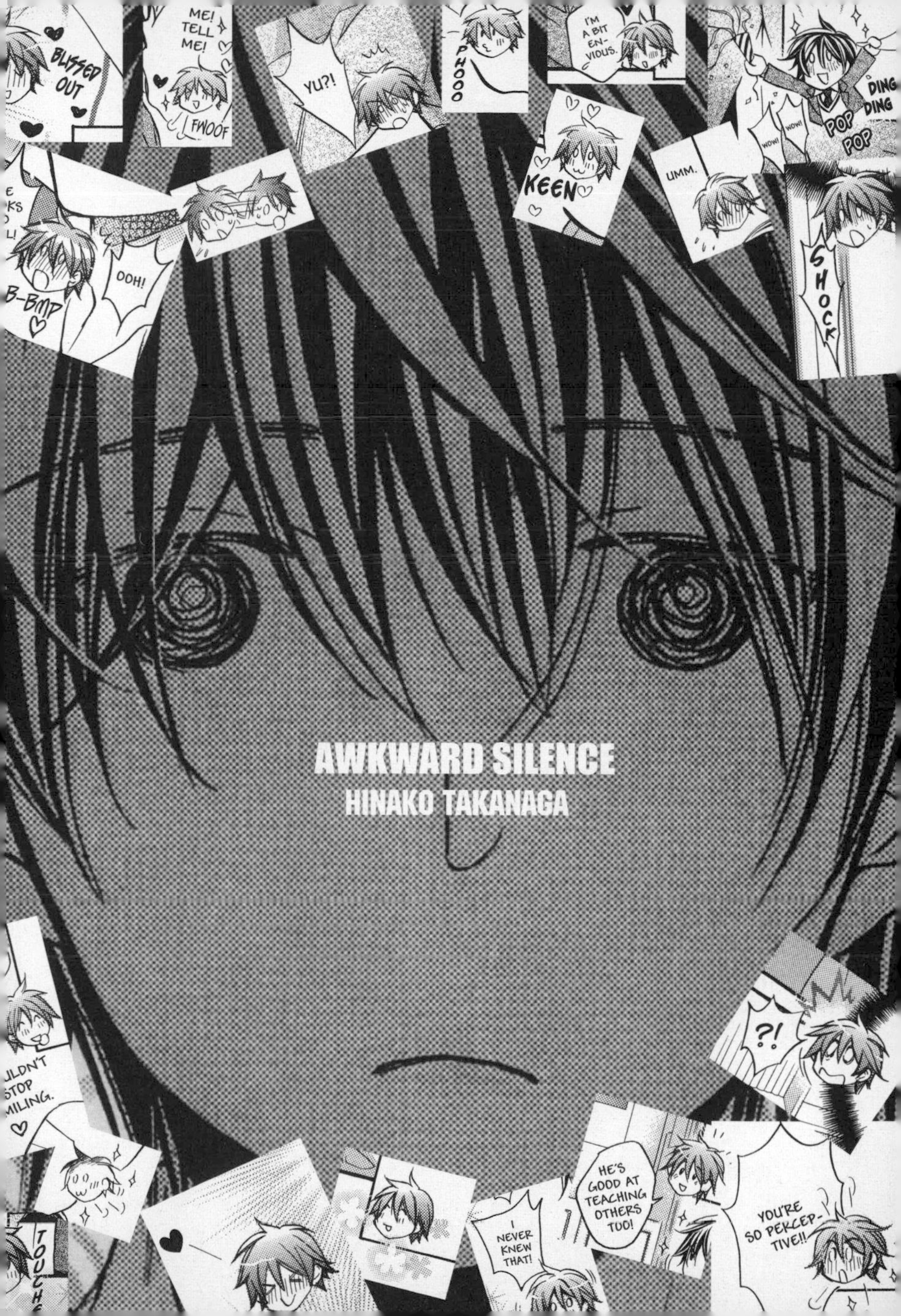
DING DING
POP POP
WOW!
WOW!
I'M A BIT EN-VIOUS.
PHOOOO
YU?!
ME! TELL ME!
FWOOF
BLISSED OUT
SHOCK
UMM.
KEEN
OOH!
AWKWARD SILENCE
HINAKO TAKANAGA
?!
YOU'RE SO PERCEP-TIVE!!
HE'S GOOD AT TEACHING OTHERS TOO!
I NEVER KNEW THAT!

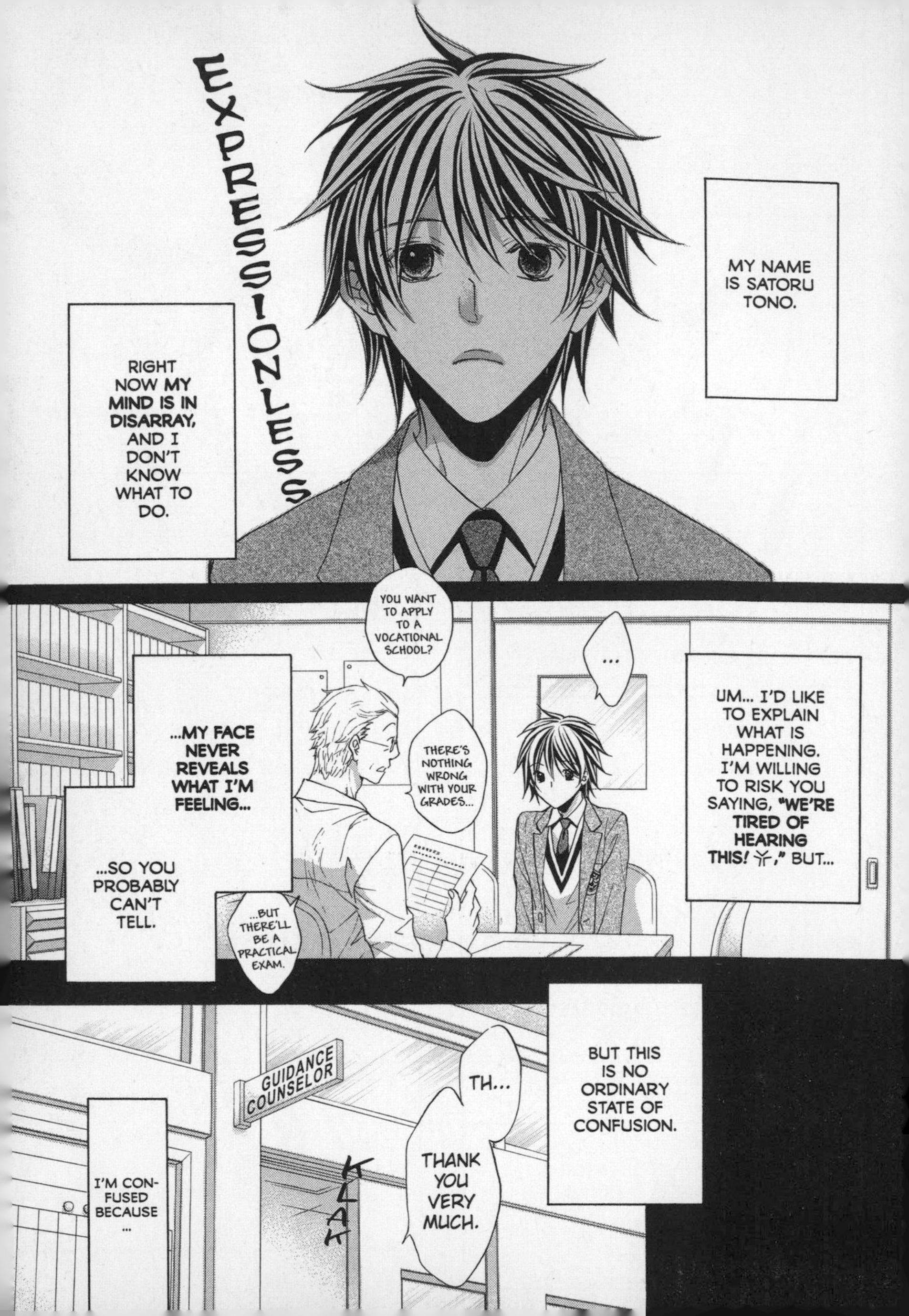

MY NAME IS SATORU TONO.
EXPRESSIONLESS
RIGHT NOW MY MIND IS IN DISARRAY, AND I DON'T KNOW WHAT TO DO.
UM... I'D LIKE TO EXPLAIN WHAT IS HAPPENING. I'M WILLING TO RISK YOU SAYING, "WE'RE TIRED OF HEARING THIS!," BUT...
...
YOU WANT TO APPLY TO A VOCATIONAL SCHOOL?
THERE'S NOTHING WRONG WITH YOUR GRADES...
...MY FACE NEVER REVEALS WHAT I'M FEELING...
...SO YOU PROBABLY CAN'T TELL.
...BUT THERE'LL BE A PRACTICAL EXAM.
BUT THIS IS NO ORDINARY STATE OF CONFUSION.
TH...
THANK YOU VERY MUCH.
GUIDANCE COUNSELOR
KLAK
I'M CON-FUSED BECAUSE ...

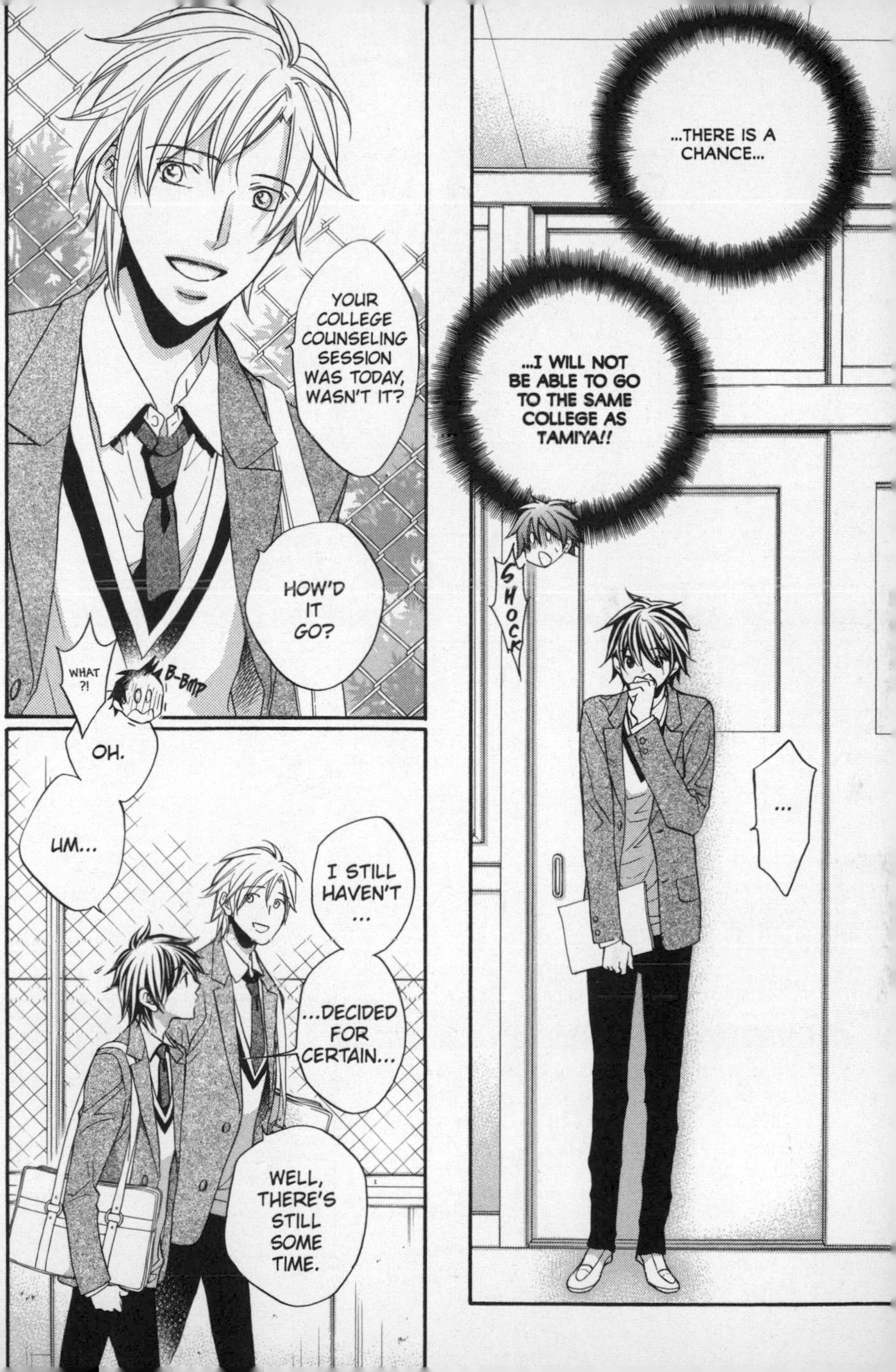
...THERE IS A CHANCE...
...I WILL NOT BE ABLE TO GO TO THE SAME COLLEGE AS TAMIYA!!
SHOCK
...
YOUR COLLEGE COUNSELING SESSION WAS TODAY, WASN'T IT?
HOW'D IT GO?
B-BMP
WHAT ?!
OH.
UM...
I STILL HAVEN'T ...
...DECIDED FOR CERTAIN...
WELL, THERE'S STILL SOME TIME.

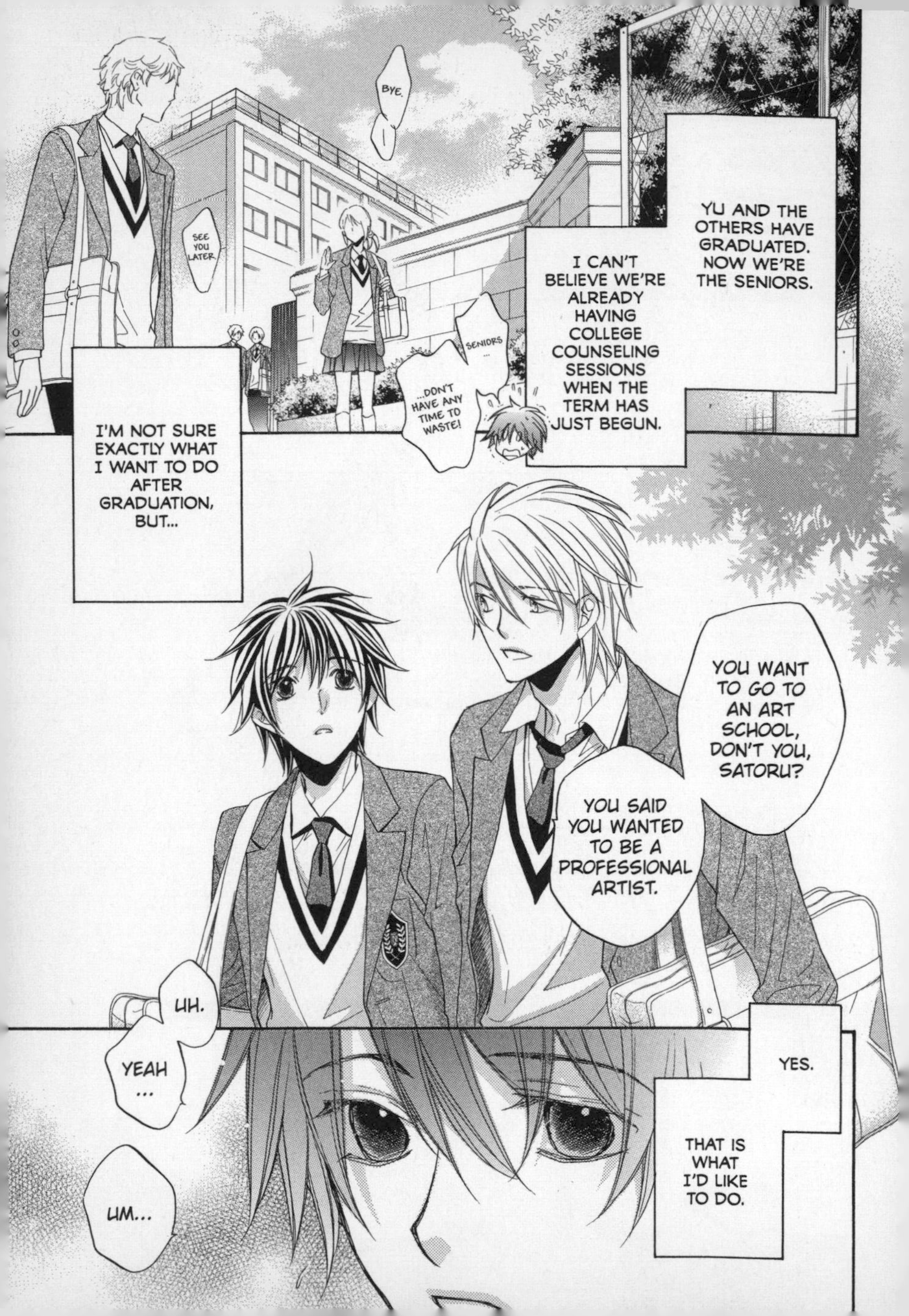
YU AND THE OTHERS HAVE GRADUATED. NOW WE'RE THE SENIORS.
I CAN'T BELIEVE WE'RE ALREADY HAVING COLLEGE COUNSELING SESSIONS WHEN THE TERM HAS JUST BEGUN.
SENIORS...
...DON'T HAVE ANY TIME TO WASTE!
BYE.
SEE YOU LATER.
I'M NOT SURE EXACTLY WHAT I WANT TO DO AFTER GRADUATION, BUT...
YOU WANT TO GO TO AN ART SCHOOL, DON'T YOU, SATORU?
YOU SAID YOU WANTED TO BE A PROFESSIONAL ARTIST.
UH.
YES.
THAT IS WHAT I'D LIKE TO DO.
YEAH...
UM...

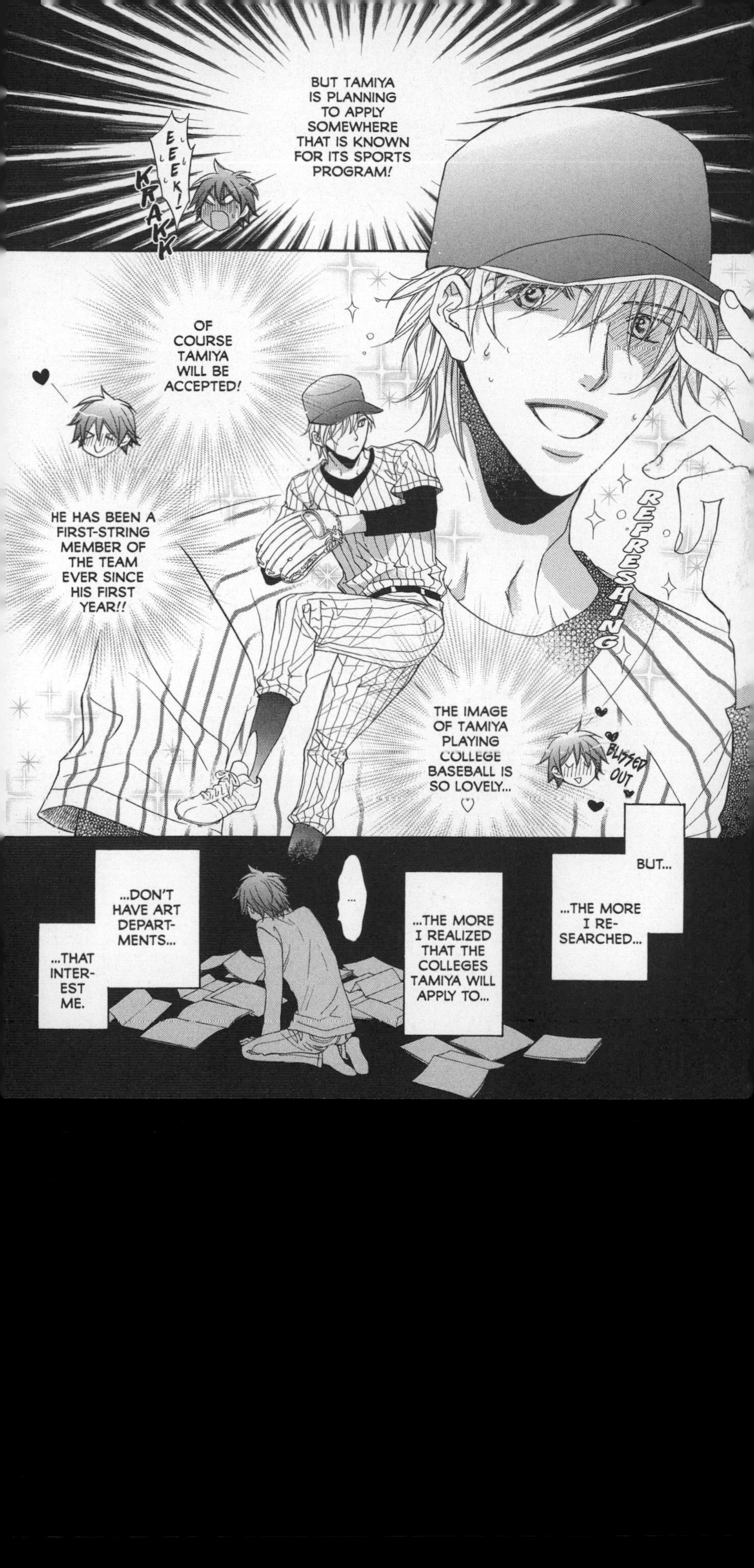
BUT TAMIYA IS PLANNING TO APPLY SOMEWHERE THAT IS KNOWN FOR ITS SPORTS PROGRAM!
EEEK!
KRAKK
OF COURSE TAMIYA WILL BE ACCEPTED!
HE HAS BEEN A FIRST-STRING MEMBER OF THE TEAM EVER SINCE HIS FIRST YEAR!!
REFRESHING
THE IMAGE OF TAMIYA PLAYING COLLEGE BASEBALL IS SO LOVELY... ♡
BLISSED OUT
BUT...
...THE MORE I RE-SEARCHED...
...THE MORE I REALIZED THAT THE COLLEGES TAMIYA WILL APPLY TO...
...
...DON'T HAVE ART DEPART-MENTS...
...THAT INTER-EST ME.

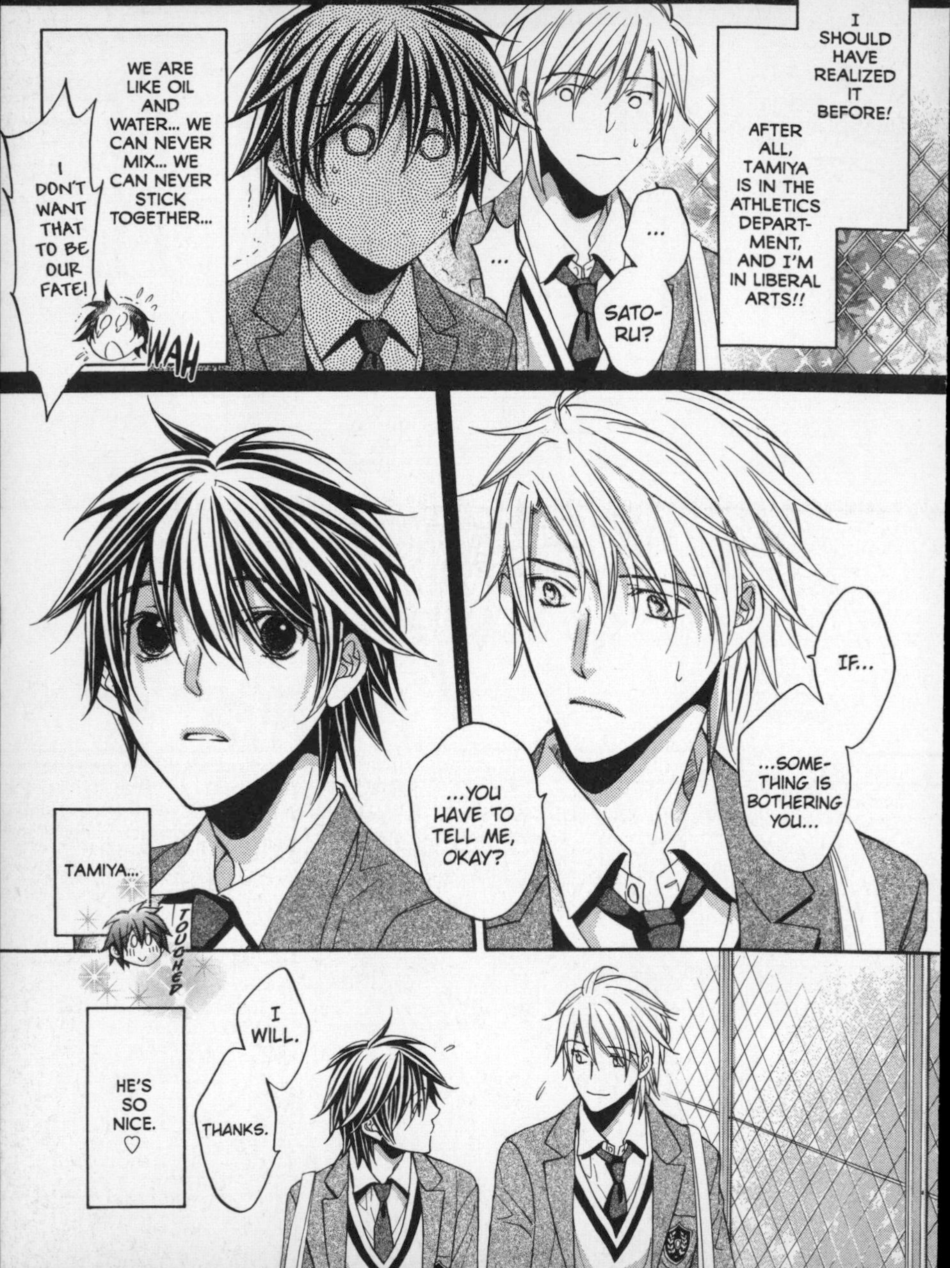
I SHOULD HAVE REALIZED IT BEFORE!
AFTER ALL, TAMIYA IS IN THE ATHLETICS DEPARTMENT, AND I'M IN LIBERAL ARTS!!
...
SATO-RU?
...
WE ARE LIKE OIL AND WATER... WE CAN NEVER MIX... WE CAN NEVER STICK TOGETHER...
I DON'T WANT THAT TO BE OUR FATE!
WAH
IF...
...SOME-THING IS BOTHERING YOU...
...YOU HAVE TO TELL ME, OKAY?
TAMIYA...
TOUCHED
I WILL.
THANKS.
HE'S SO NICE. ♡

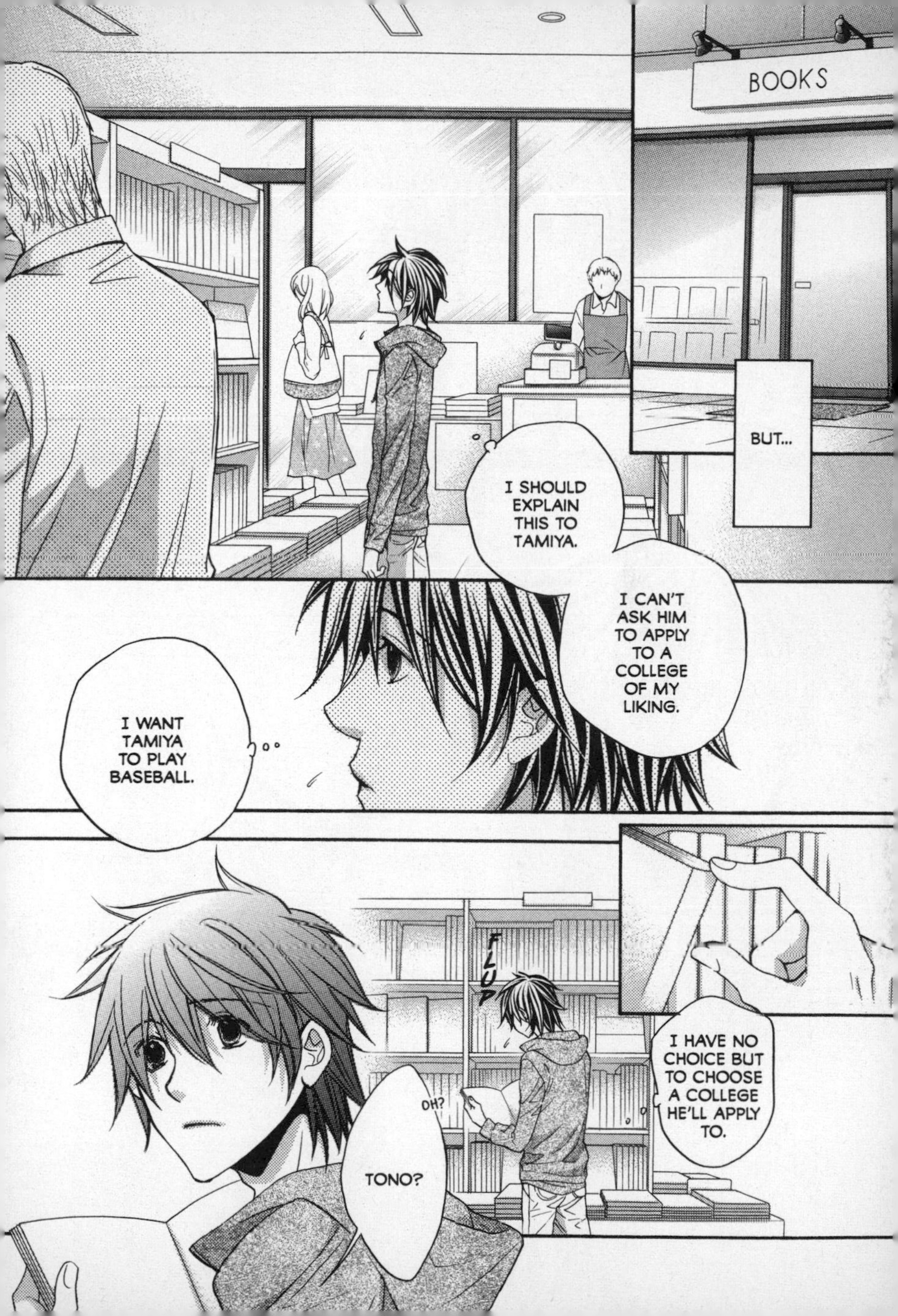
BOOKS
BUT...
I SHOULD EXPLAIN THIS TO TAMIYA.
I CAN'T ASK HIM TO APPLY TO A COLLEGE OF MY LIKING.
I WANT TAMIYA TO PLAY BASEBALL.
FLUP
I HAVE NO CHOICE BUT TO CHOOSE A COLLEGE HE'LL APPLY TO.
OH?
TONO?

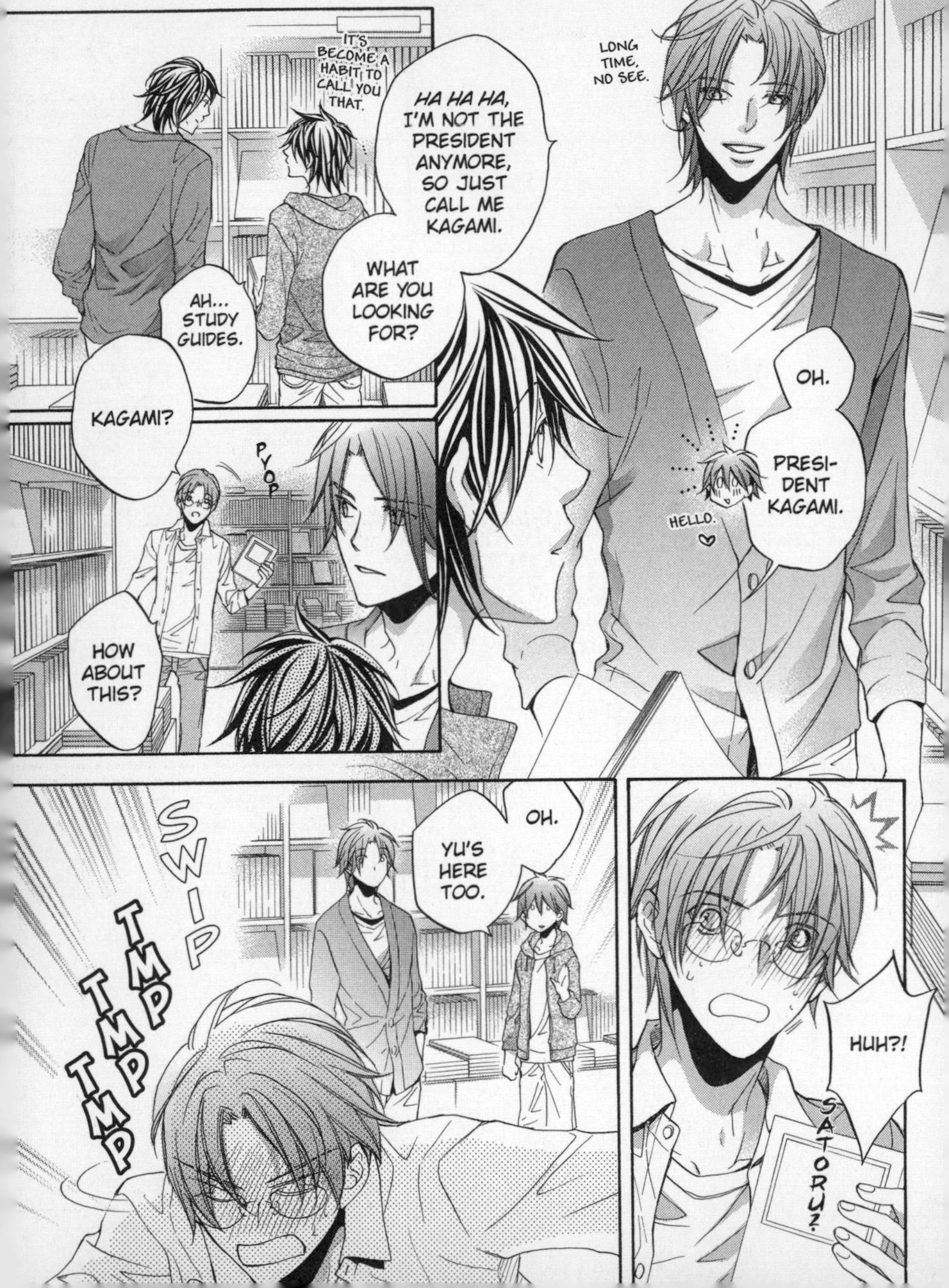
LONG TIME, NO SEE.
OH.
PRESIDENT KAGAMI.
HELLO.
HA HA HA, I'M NOT THE PRESIDENT ANYMORE, SO JUST CALL ME KAGAMI.
IT'S BECOME A HABIT TO CALL YOU THAT.
WHAT ARE YOU LOOKING FOR?
AH... STUDY GUIDES.
KAGAMI?
PYOP
HOW ABOUT THIS?
HUH?!
SATORU?
OH.
YU'S HERE TOO.
SWIP
TMP TMP TMP

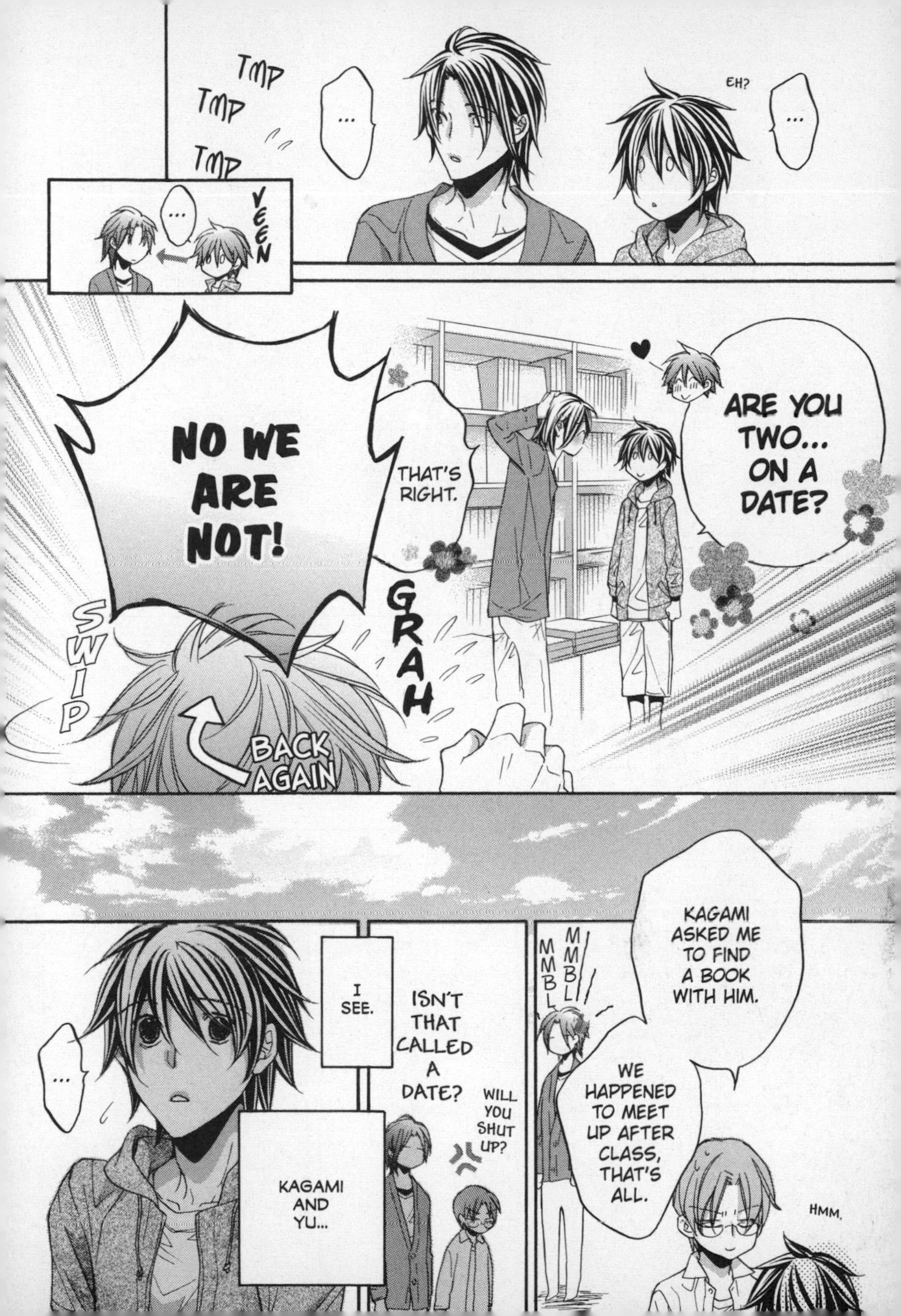
EH?
...
...
TMP
TMP
TMP
...
VEEN
ARE YOU TWO... ON A DATE?
THAT'S RIGHT.
NO WE ARE NOT!
GRAH
SWIP
BACK AGAIN
KAGAMI ASKED ME TO FIND A BOOK WITH HIM.
MMBL
MMBL
WE HAPPENED TO MEET UP AFTER CLASS, THAT'S ALL.
HMM.
ISN'T THAT CALLED A DATE?
WILL YOU SHUT UP?
I SEE.
...
KAGAMI AND YU...

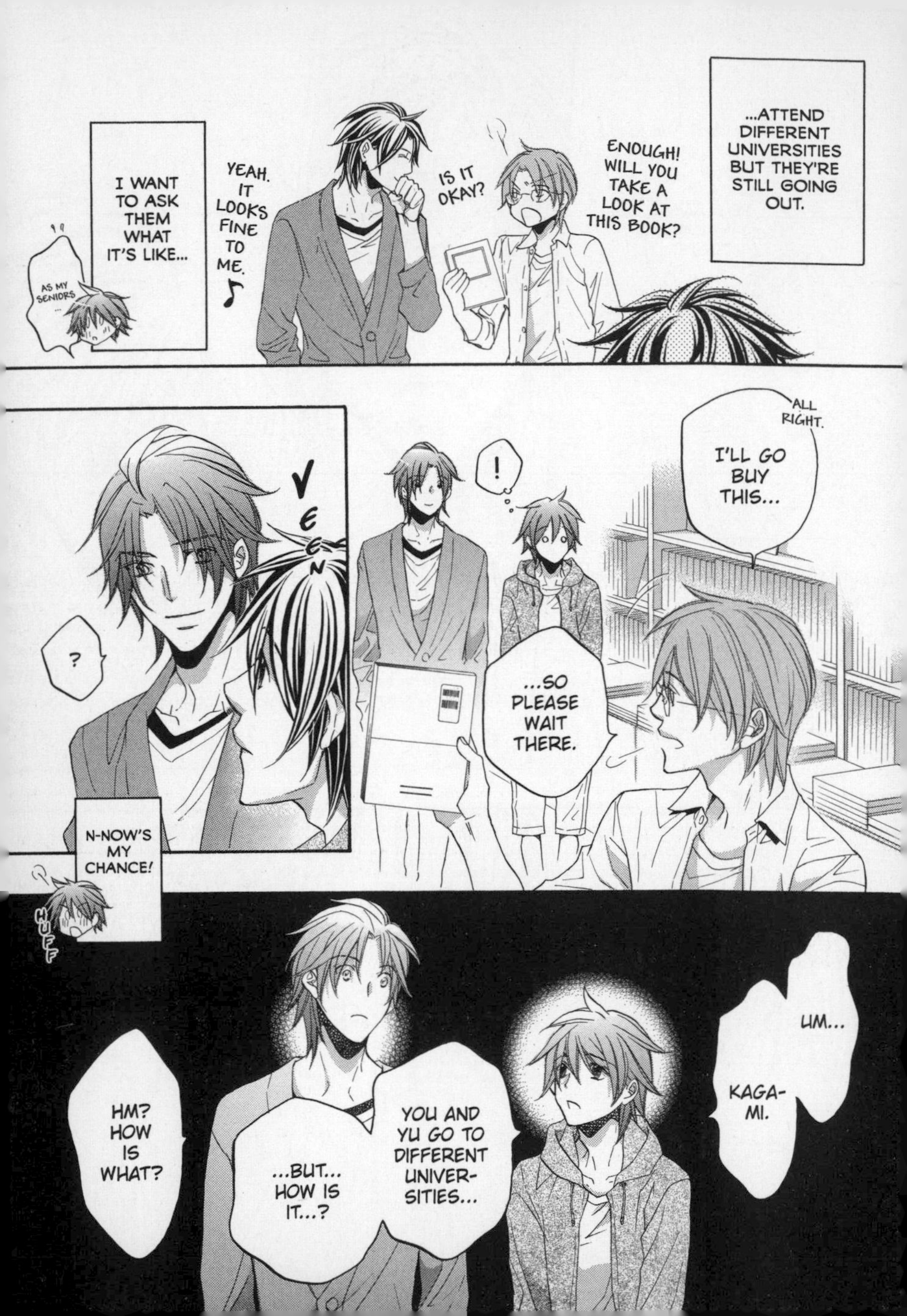
...ATTEND DIFFERENT UNIVERSITIES BUT THEY'RE STILL GOING OUT.
ENOUGH! WILL YOU TAKE A LOOK AT THIS BOOK?
IS IT OKAY?
YEAH. IT LOOKS FINE TO ME. ♪
I WANT TO ASK THEM WHAT IT'S LIKE...
AS MY SENIORS...
ALL RIGHT.
I'LL GO BUY THIS...
...SO PLEASE WAIT THERE.
!
VEEEN
?
N-NOW'S MY CHANCE!
HUFF
UM...
KAGAMI.
YOU AND YU GO TO DIFFERENT UNIVERSITIES...
...BUT... HOW IS IT...?
HM? HOW IS WHAT?

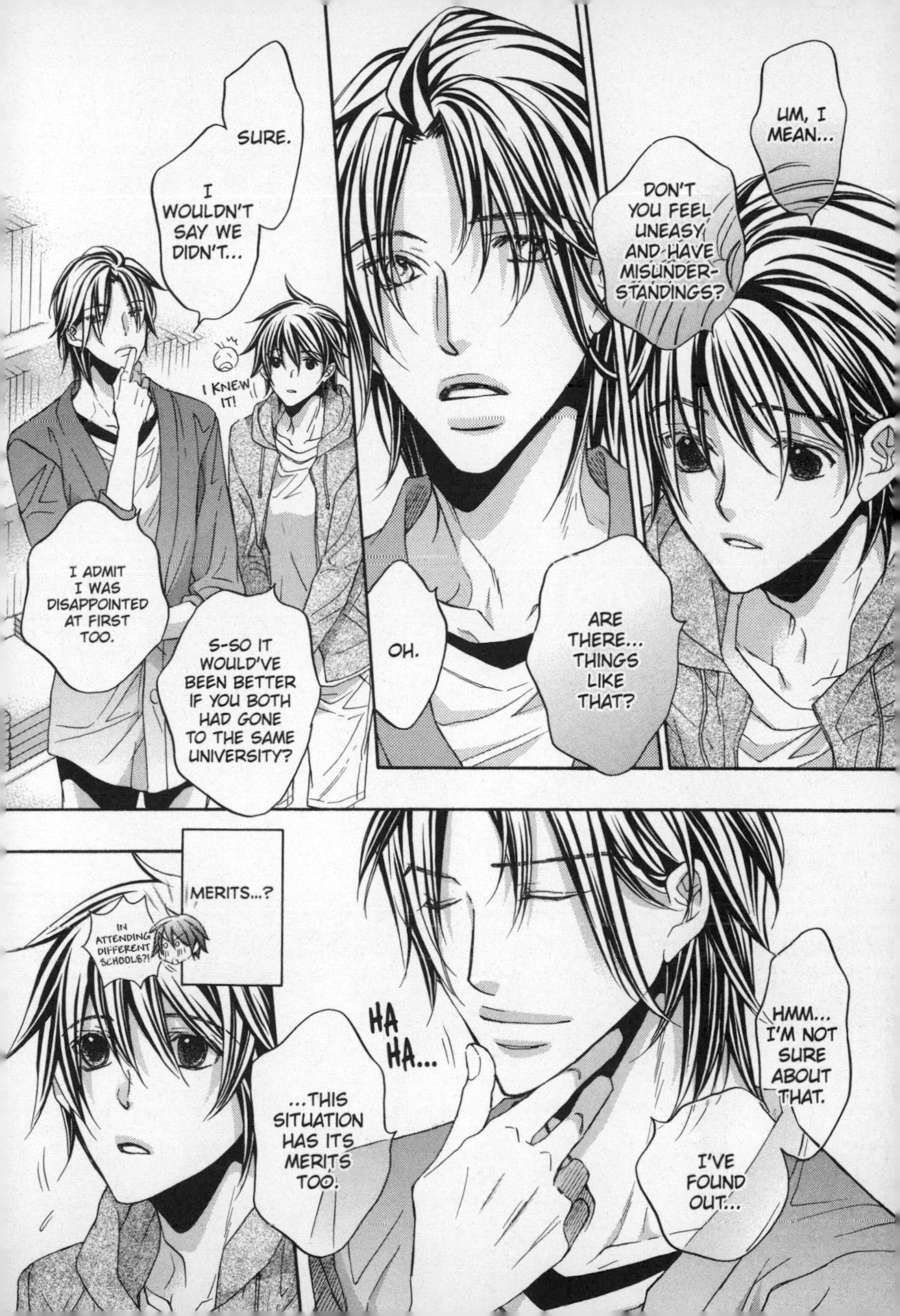
UM, I MEAN...
DON'T YOU FEEL UNEASY AND HAVE MISUNDERSTANDINGS?
ARE THERE... THINGS LIKE THAT?
OH.
SURE.
I WOULDN'T SAY WE DIDN'T...
I KNEW IT!
I ADMIT I WAS DISAPPOINTED AT FIRST TOO.
S-SO IT WOULD'VE BEEN BETTER IF YOU BOTH HAD GONE TO THE SAME UNIVERSITY?
HMM... I'M NOT SURE ABOUT THAT.
I'VE FOUND OUT...
HA HA...
...THIS SITUATION HAS ITS MERITS TOO.
MERITS...?
IN ATTENDING DIFFERENT SCHOOLS?!

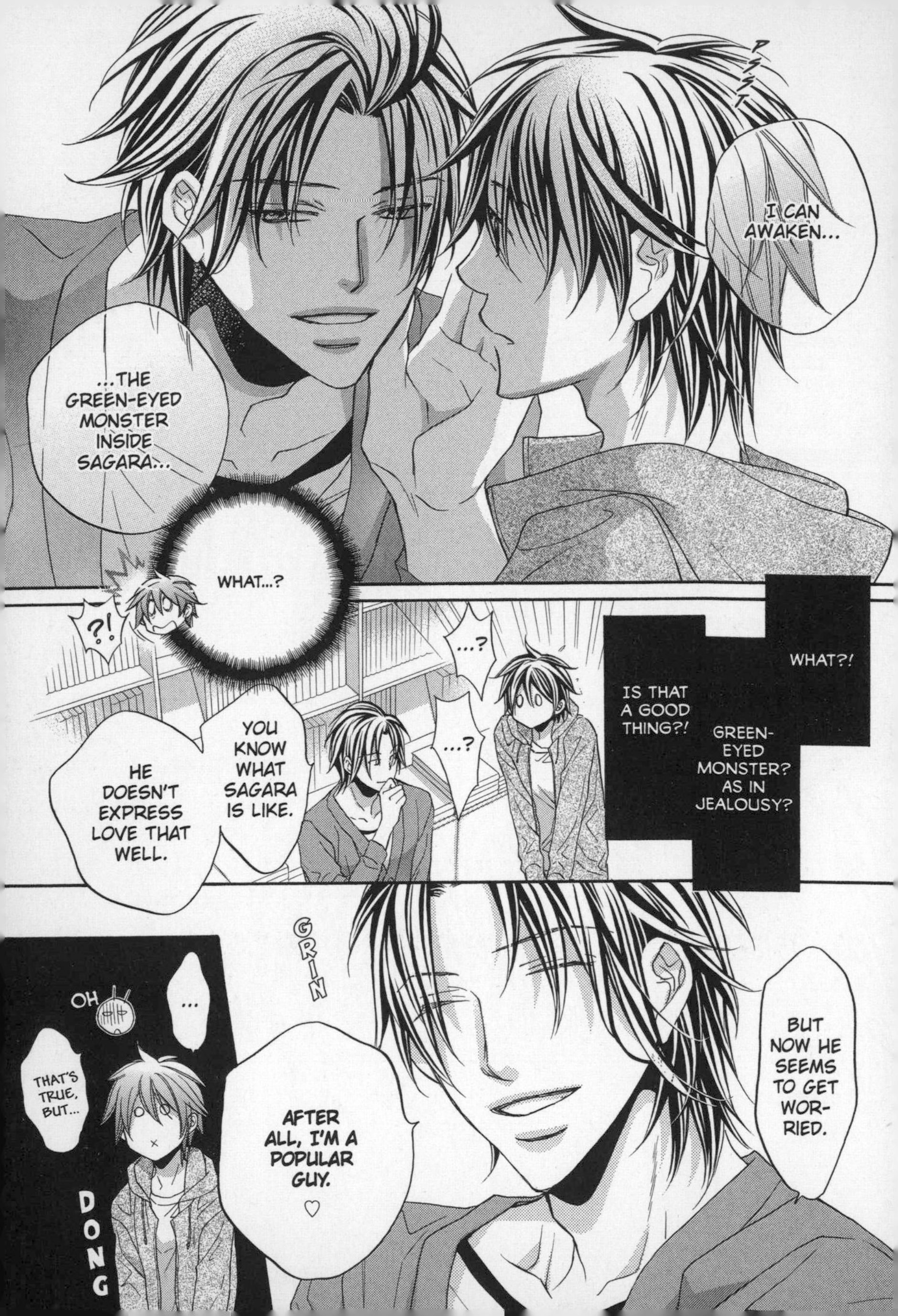
PSSST
I CAN AWAKEN...
...THE GREEN-EYED MONSTER INSIDE SAGARA...
WHAT...?
?!
WHAT?!
GREEN-EYED MONSTER? AS IN JEALOUSY?
IS THAT A GOOD THING?!
...?
...?
YOU KNOW WHAT SAGARA IS LIKE.
HE DOESN'T EXPRESS LOVE THAT WELL.
BUT NOW HE SEEMS TO GET WOR-RIED.
GRIN
AFTER ALL, I'M A POPULAR GUY. ♡
...
OH
THAT'S TRUE, BUT...
DONG

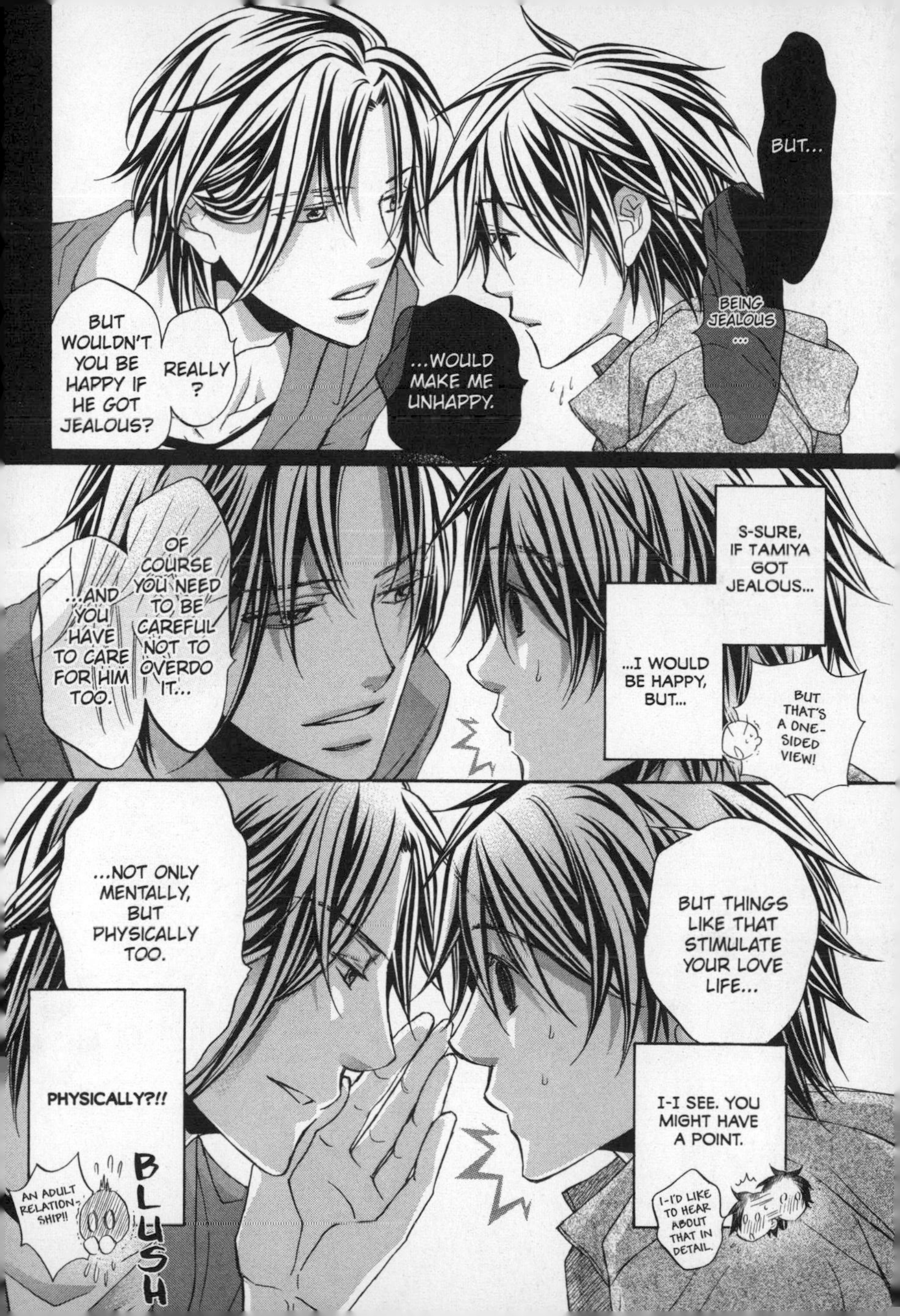
BUT...
BEING JEALOUS ...
...WOULD MAKE ME UNHAPPY.
REALLY ?
BUT WOULDN'T YOU BE HAPPY IF HE GOT JEALOUS?
S-SURE, IF TAMIYA GOT JEALOUS...
...I WOULD BE HAPPY, BUT...
BUT THAT'S A ONE-SIDED VIEW!
OF COURSE YOU NEED TO BE CAREFUL NOT TO OVERDO IT...
...AND YOU HAVE TO CARE FOR HIM TOO.
BUT THINGS LIKE THAT STIMULATE YOUR LOVE LIFE...
I-I SEE. YOU MIGHT HAVE A POINT.
I-I'D LIKE TO HEAR ABOUT THAT IN DETAIL.
...NOT ONLY MENTALLY, BUT PHYSICALLY TOO.
PHYSICALLY?!!
BLUSH
AN ADULT RELATION-SHIP!!

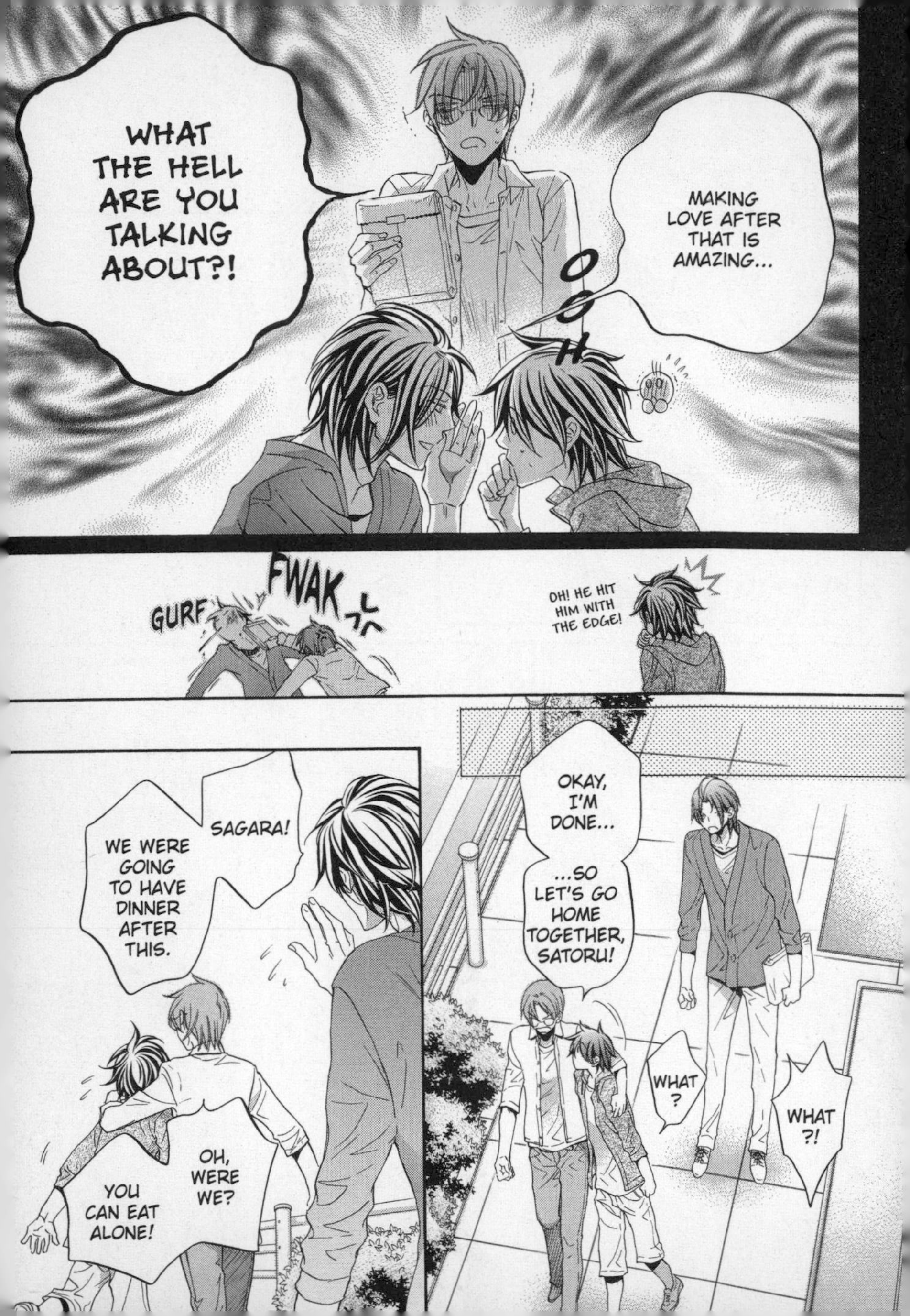
MAKING LOVE AFTER THAT IS AMAZING...
OOH
WHAT THE HELL ARE YOU TALKING ABOUT?!
OH! HE HIT HIM WITH THE EDGE!
FWAK
GURF
OKAY, I'M DONE...
...SO LET'S GO HOME TOGETHER, SATORU!
WHAT?!
WHAT?
SAGARA!
WE WERE GOING TO HAVE DINNER AFTER THIS.
OH, WERE WE?
YOU CAN EAT ALONE!

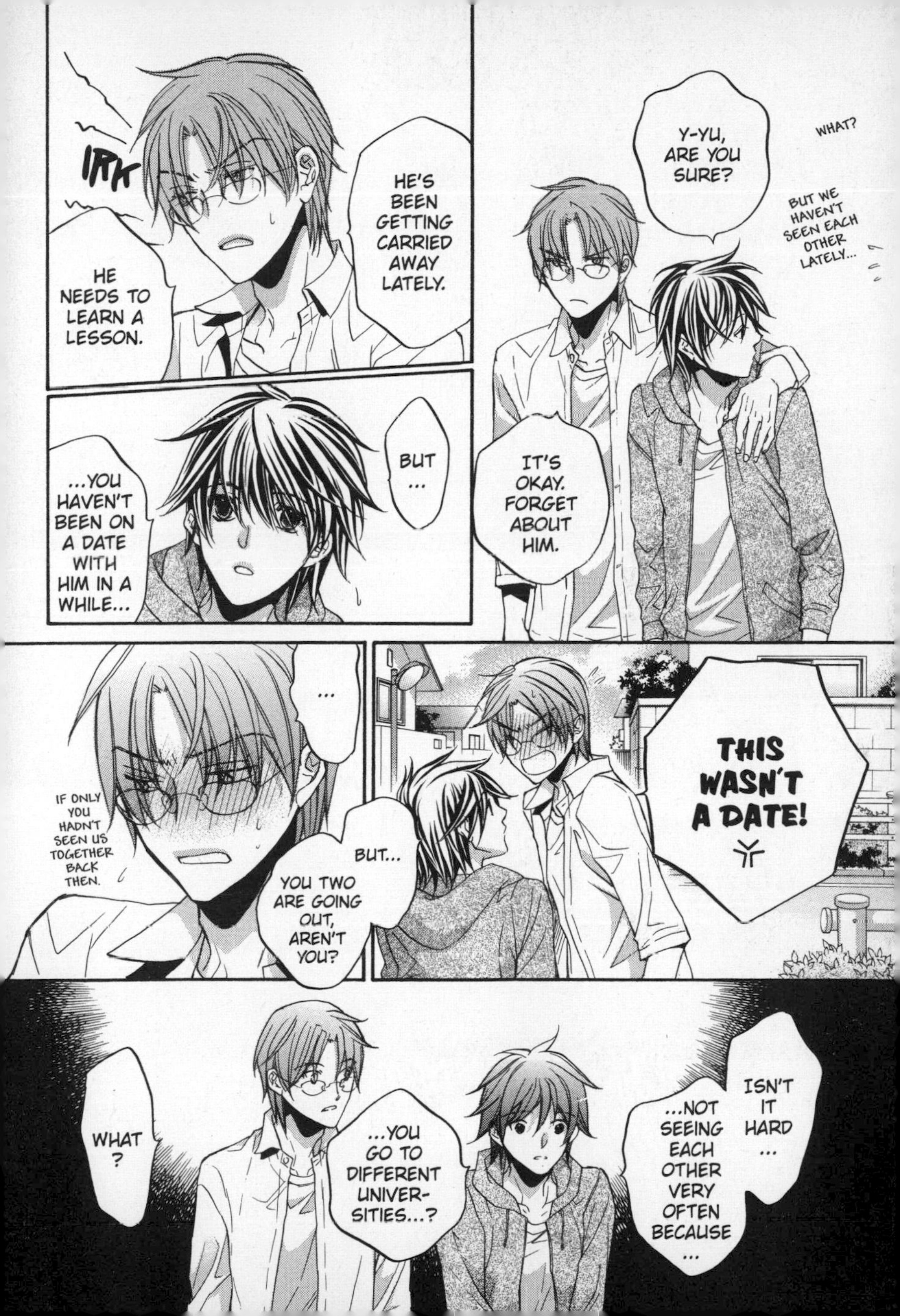
Y-YU, ARE YOU SURE?
WHAT?
BUT WE HAVEN'T SEEN EACH OTHER LATELY...
IT'S OKAY. FORGET ABOUT HIM.
HE'S BEEN GETTING CARRIED AWAY LATELY.
IRK
HE NEEDS TO LEARN A LESSON.
BUT ...
...YOU HAVEN'T BEEN ON A DATE WITH HIM IN A WHILE...
THIS WASN'T A DATE!
BUT...
YOU TWO ARE GOING OUT, AREN'T YOU?
...
IF ONLY YOU HADN'T SEEN US TOGETHER BACK THEN.
ISN'T IT HARD ...
...NOT SEEING EACH OTHER VERY OFTEN BECAUSE ...
...YOU GO TO DIFFERENT UNIVER-SITIES...?
WHAT ?

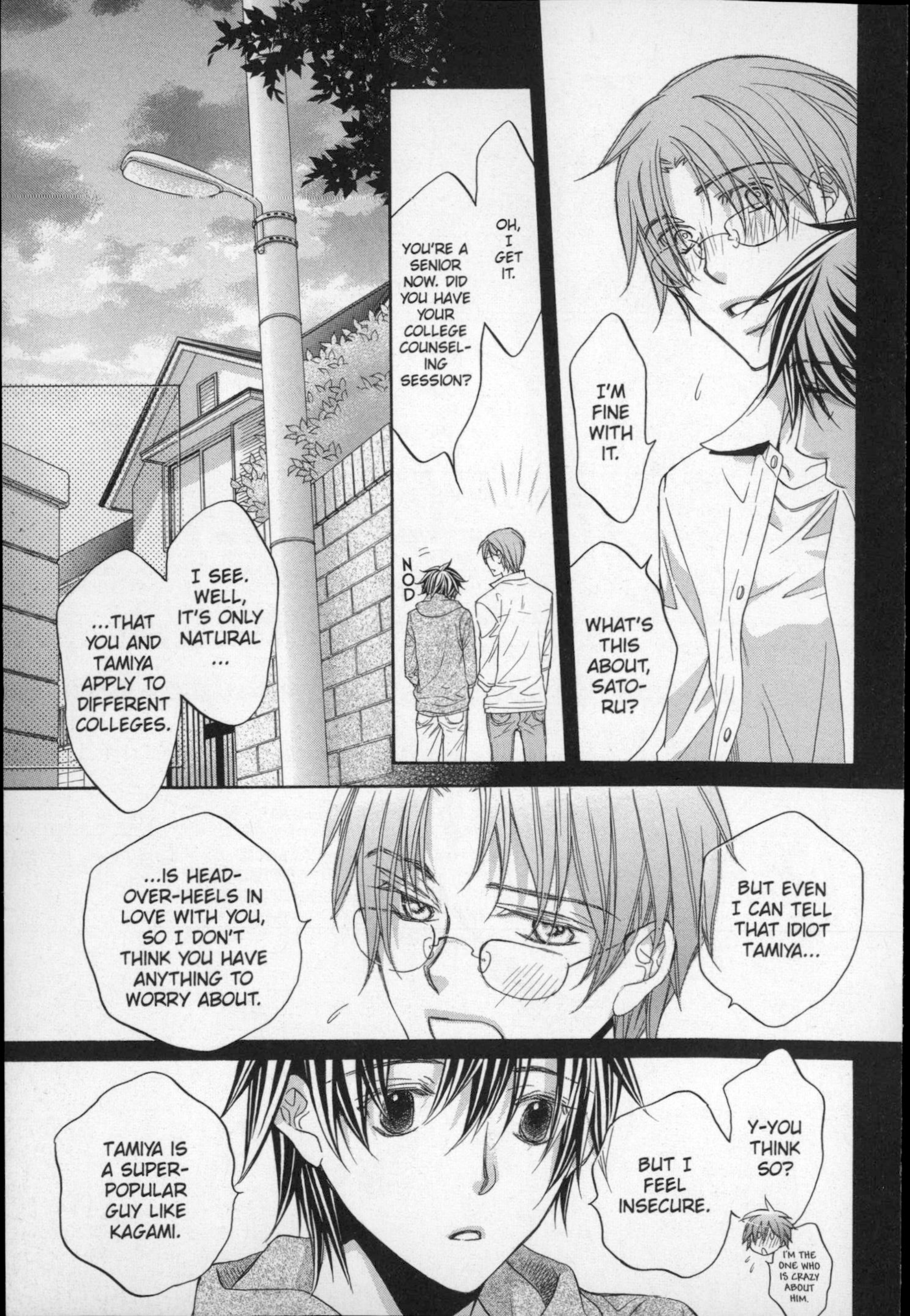
I'M FINE WITH IT.
WHAT'S THIS ABOUT, SATORU?
OH, I GET IT.
YOU'RE A SENIOR NOW. DID YOU HAVE YOUR COLLEGE COUNSEL-ING SESSION?
NOD
I SEE. WELL, IT'S ONLY NATURAL...
...THAT YOU AND TAMIYA APPLY TO DIFFERENT COLLEGES.
BUT EVEN I CAN TELL THAT IDIOT TAMIYA...
...IS HEAD-OVER-HEELS IN LOVE WITH YOU, SO I DON'T THINK YOU HAVE ANYTHING TO WORRY ABOUT.
Y-YOU THINK SO?
BUT I FEEL INSECURE.
I'M THE ONE WHO IS CRAZY ABOUT HIM.
TAMIYA IS A SUPER-POPULAR GUY LIKE KAGAMI.

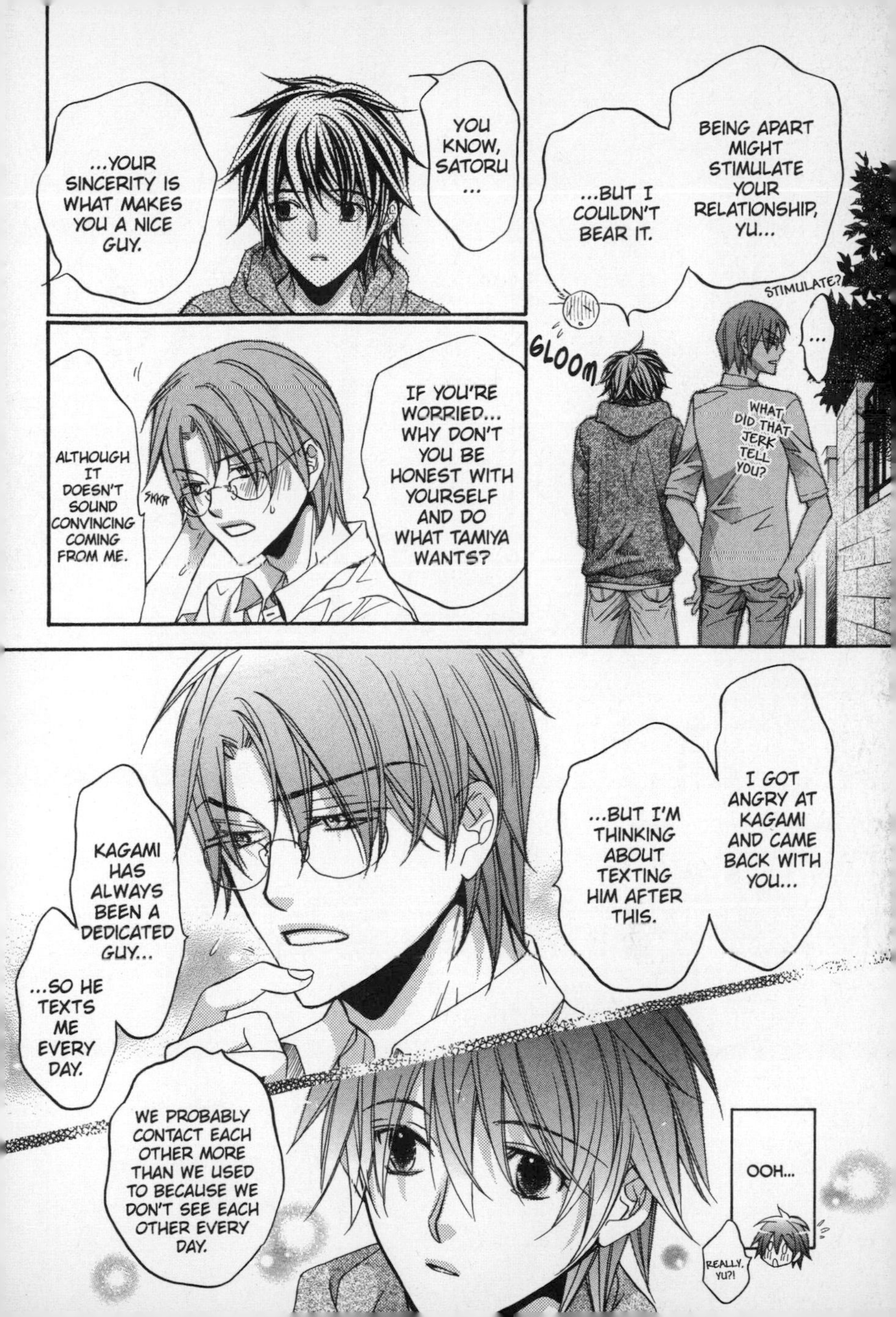
BEING APART MIGHT STIMULATE YOUR RELATIONSHIP, YU...
...BUT I COULDN'T BEAR IT.
STIMULATE?
...
GLOOM
WHAT DID THAT JERK TELL YOU?
YOU KNOW, SATORU...
...YOUR SINCERITY IS WHAT MAKES YOU A NICE GUY.
IF YOU'RE WORRIED... WHY DON'T YOU BE HONEST WITH YOURSELF AND DO WHAT TAMIYA WANTS?
SKKR
ALTHOUGH IT DOESN'T SOUND CONVINCING COMING FROM ME.
I GOT ANGRY AT KAGAMI AND CAME BACK WITH YOU...
...BUT I'M THINKING ABOUT TEXTING HIM AFTER THIS.
KAGAMI HAS ALWAYS BEEN A DEDICATED GUY...
...SO HE TEXTS ME EVERY DAY.
OOH...
REALLY, YU?!
WE PROBABLY CONTACT EACH OTHER MORE THAN WE USED TO BECAUSE WE DON'T SEE EACH OTHER EVERY DAY.

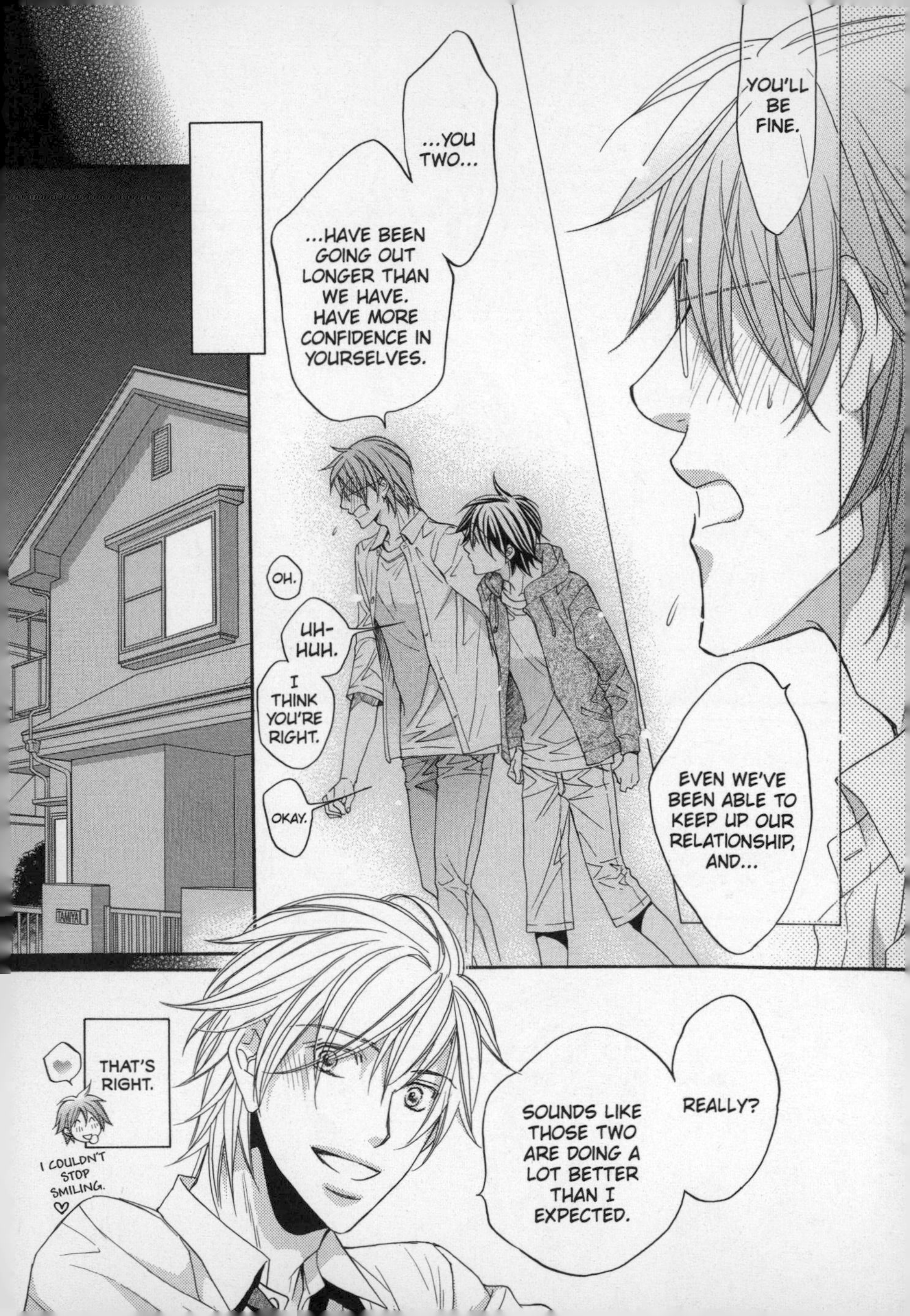
YOU'LL BE FINE.
EVEN WE'VE BEEN ABLE TO KEEP UP OUR RELATIONSHIP, AND...
...YOU TWO...
...HAVE BEEN GOING OUT LONGER THAN WE HAVE. HAVE MORE CONFIDENCE IN YOURSELVES.
OH.
UH-HUH.
I THINK YOU'RE RIGHT.
OKAY.
TAMIYA
REALLY?
SOUNDS LIKE THOSE TWO ARE DOING A LOT BETTER THAN I EXPECTED.
THAT'S RIGHT.
I COULDN'T STOP SMILING.

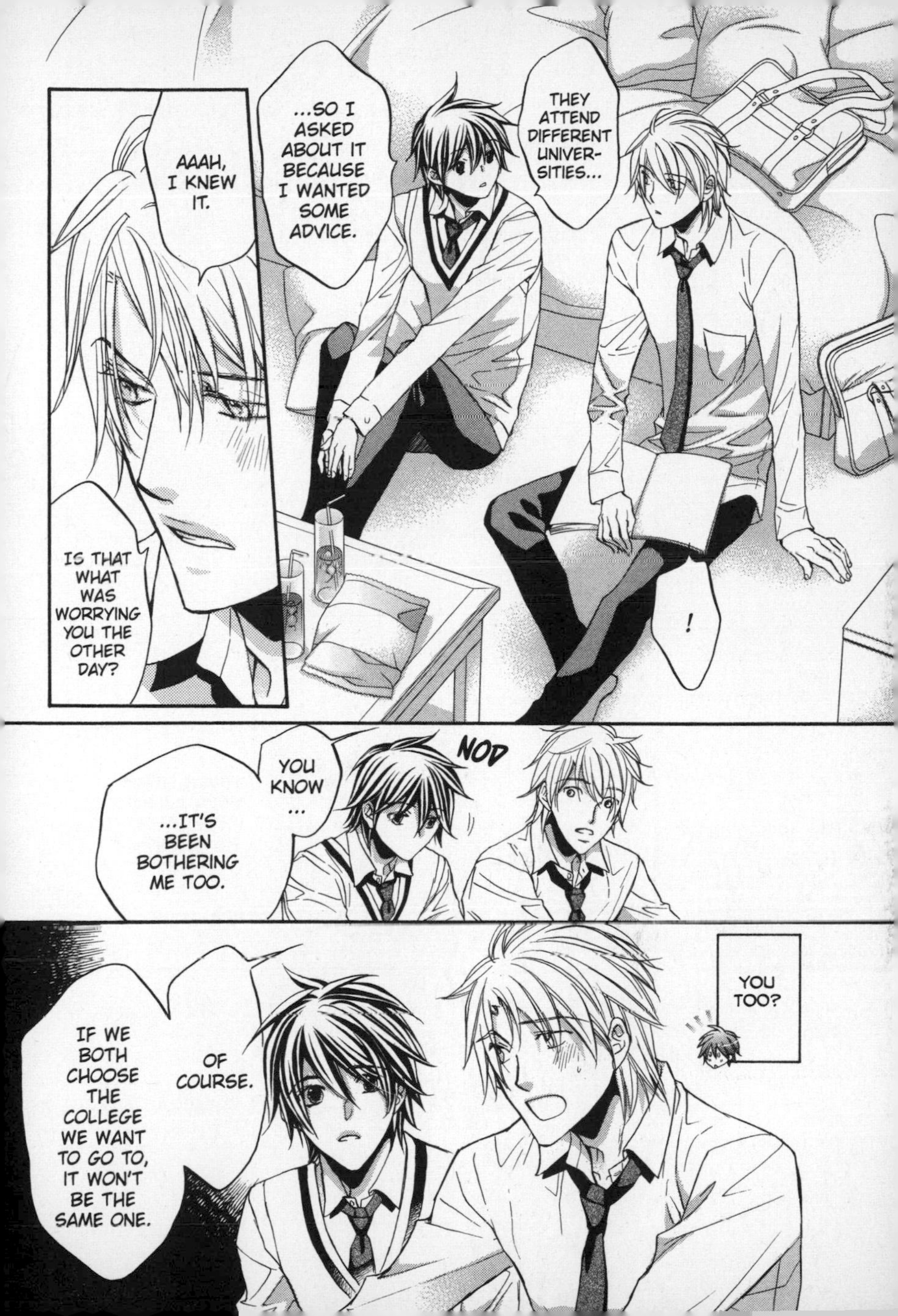
THEY ATTEND DIFFERENT UNIVER-SITIES...
...SO I ASKED ABOUT IT BECAUSE I WANTED SOME ADVICE.
!
AAAH, I KNEW IT.
IS THAT WHAT WAS WORRYING YOU THE OTHER DAY?
NOD
YOU KNOW ...
...IT'S BEEN BOTHERING ME TOO.
YOU TOO?
OF COURSE.
IF WE BOTH CHOOSE THE COLLEGE WE WANT TO GO TO, IT WON'T BE THE SAME ONE.

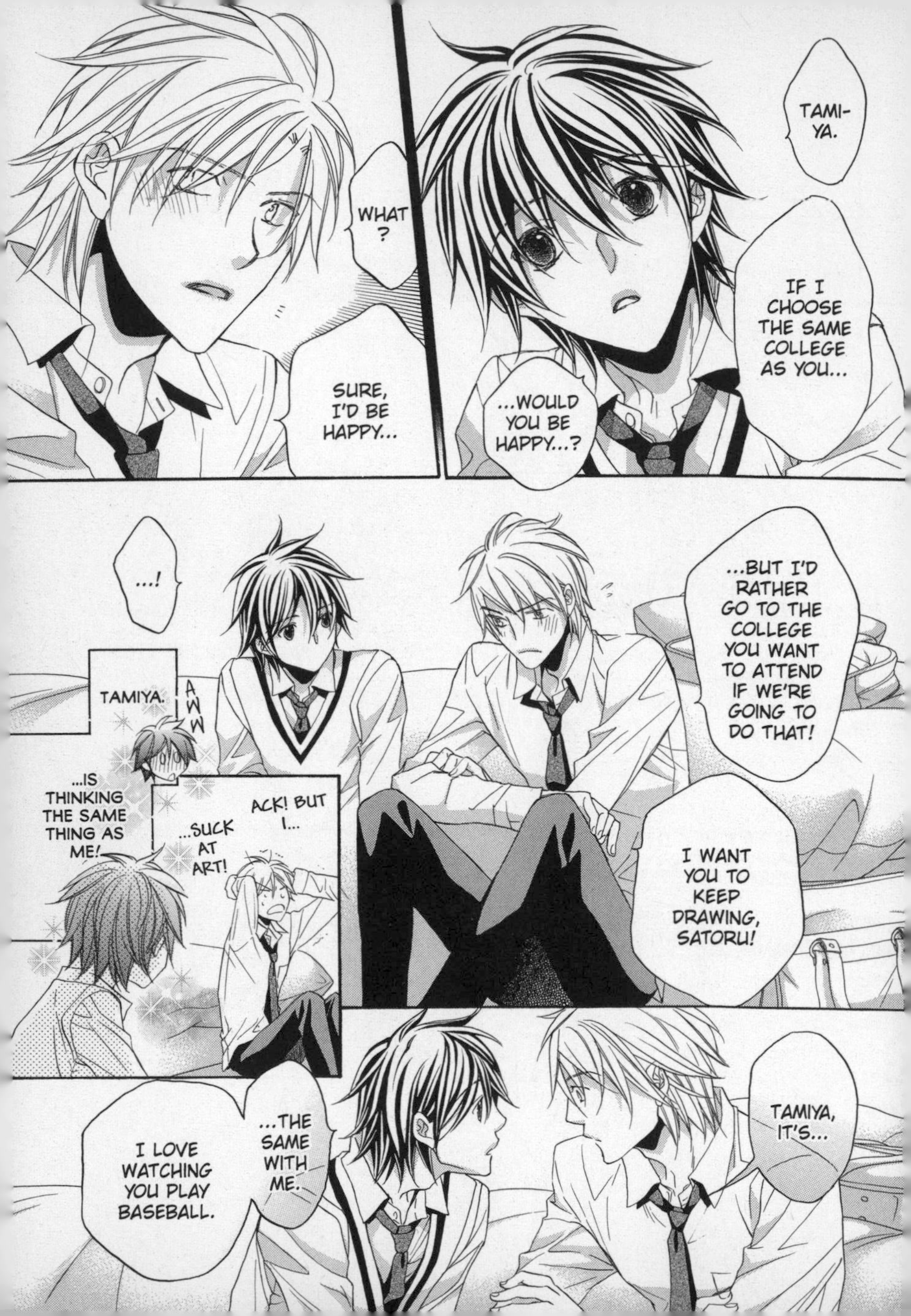
TAMI-YA.
IF I CHOOSE THE SAME COLLEGE AS YOU...
...WOULD YOU BE HAPPY...?
WHAT?
SURE, I'D BE HAPPY...
...BUT I'D RATHER GO TO THE COLLEGE YOU WANT TO ATTEND IF WE'RE GOING TO DO THAT!
I WANT YOU TO KEEP DRAWING, SATORU!
...!
TAMIYA.
AWW
...IS THINKING THE SAME THING AS ME!
ACK! BUT I...
...SUCK AT ART!
TAMIYA, IT'S...
...THE SAME WITH ME.
I LOVE WATCHING YOU PLAY BASEBALL.

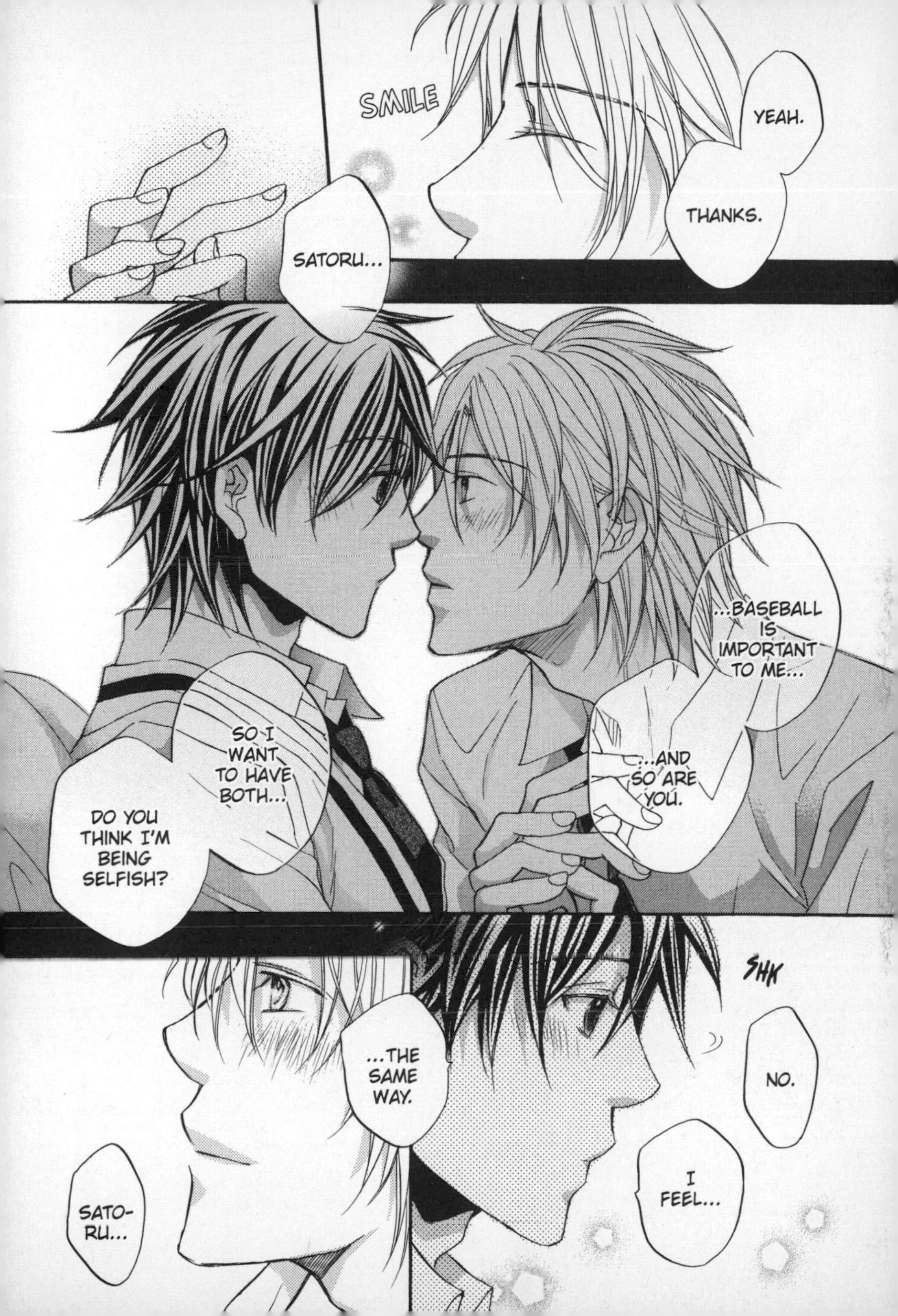
YEAH.
SMILE
THANKS.
SATORU...
...BASEBALL IS IMPORTANT TO ME...
...AND SO ARE YOU.
SO I WANT TO HAVE BOTH...
DO YOU THINK I'M BEING SELFISH?
SHK
NO.
I FEEL...
...THE SAME WAY.
SATO-RU...

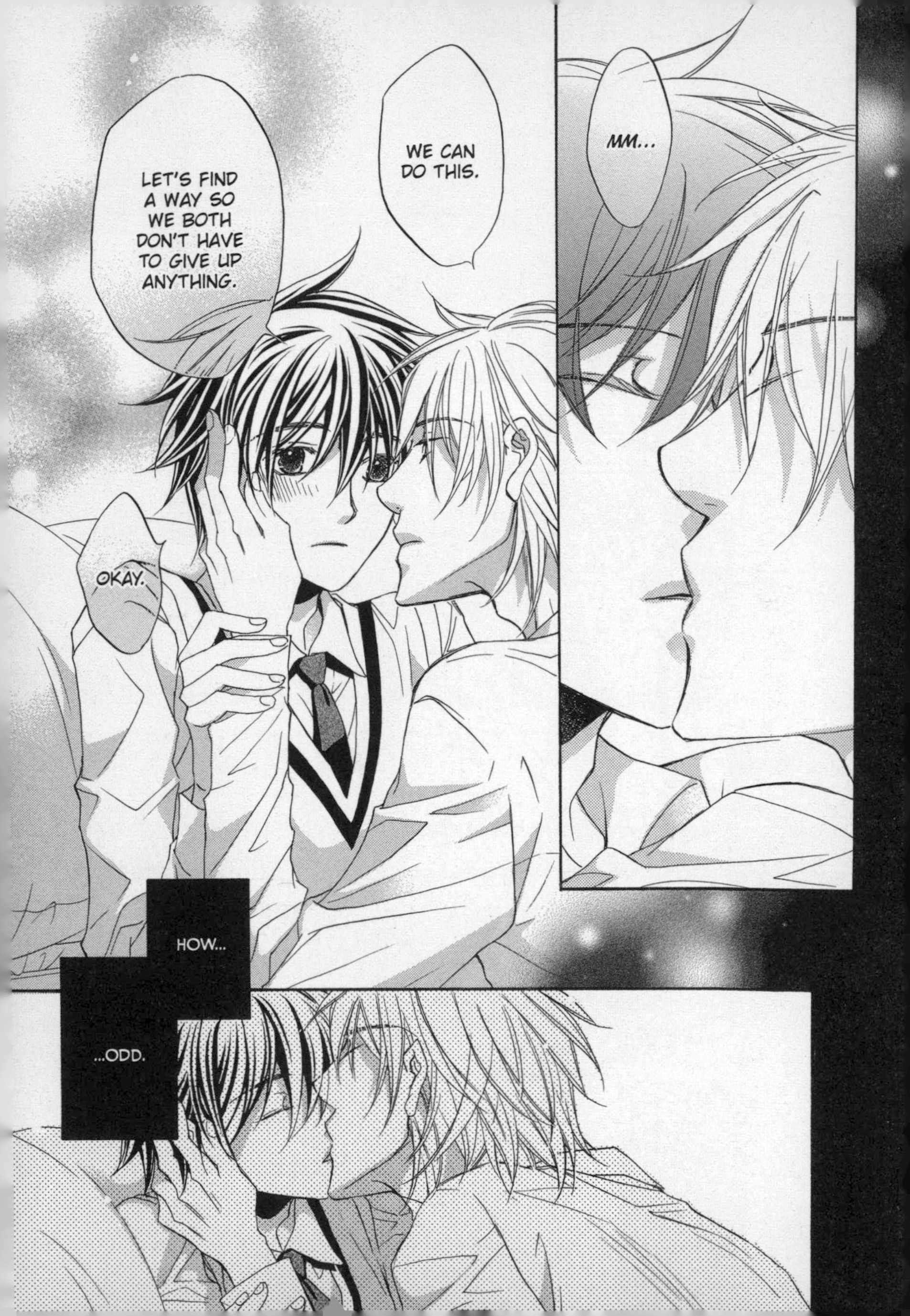
MM...
WE CAN DO THIS.
LET'S FIND A WAY SO WE BOTH DON'T HAVE TO GIVE UP ANYTHING.
OKAY.
HOW...
...ODD.

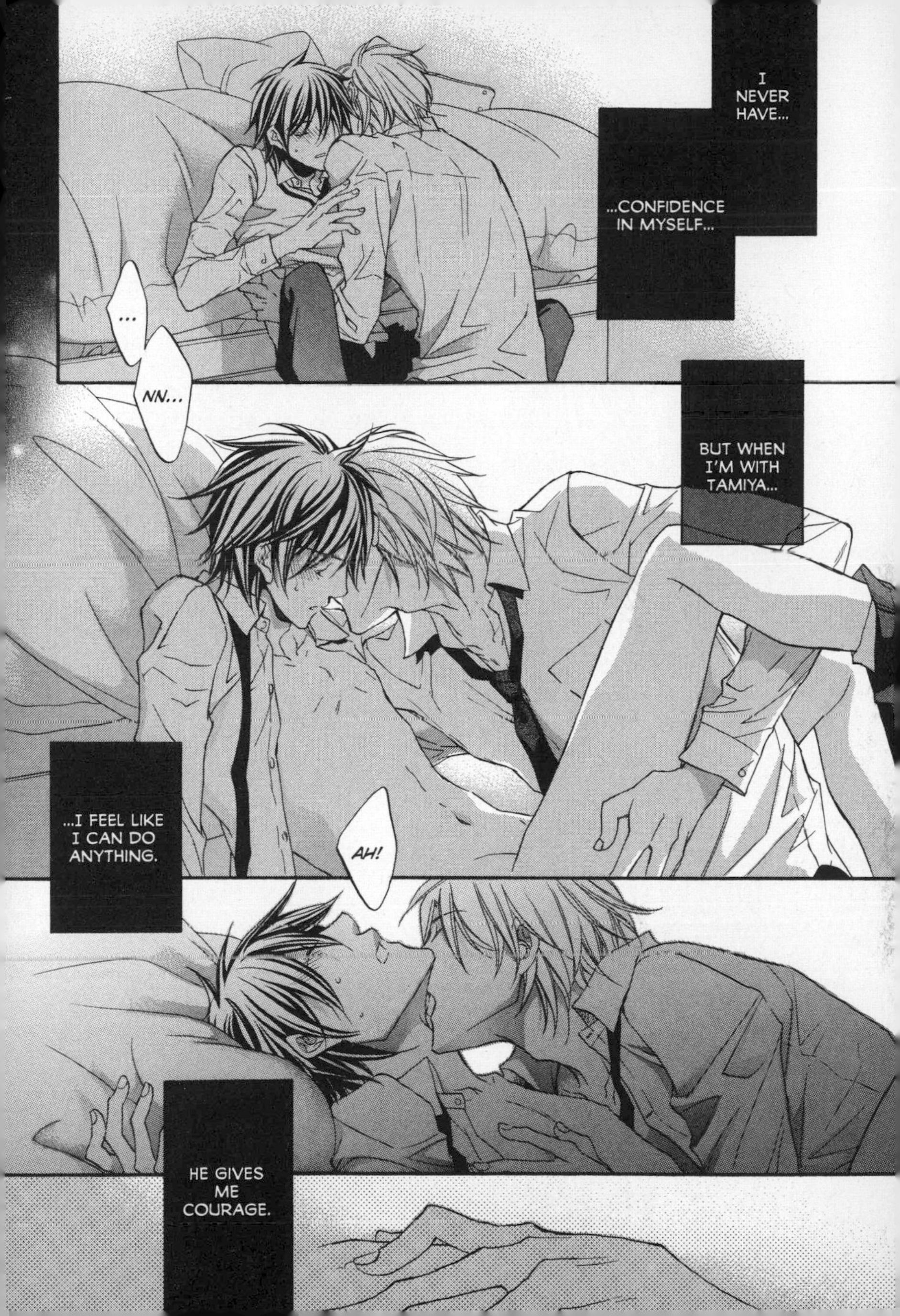
I NEVER HAVE...
...CONFIDENCE IN MYSELF...
...
BUT WHEN I'M WITH TAMIYA...
NN...
...I FEEL LIKE I CAN DO ANYTHING.
AH!
HE GIVES ME COURAGE.

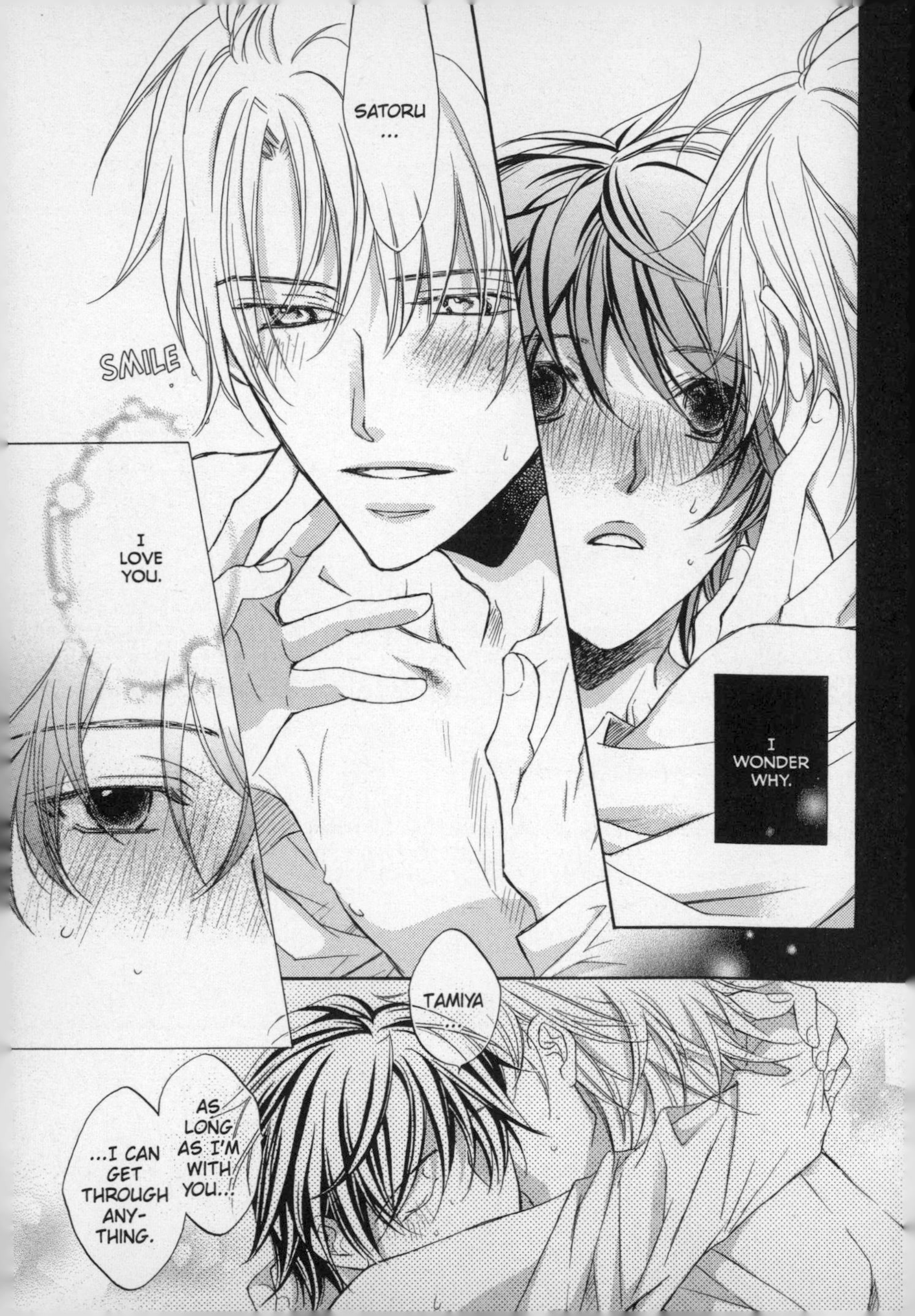
I WONDER WHY.
SATORU ...
SMILE
I LOVE YOU.
TAMIYA ...
AS LONG AS I'M WITH YOU...!
...I CAN GET THROUGH ANY-THING.

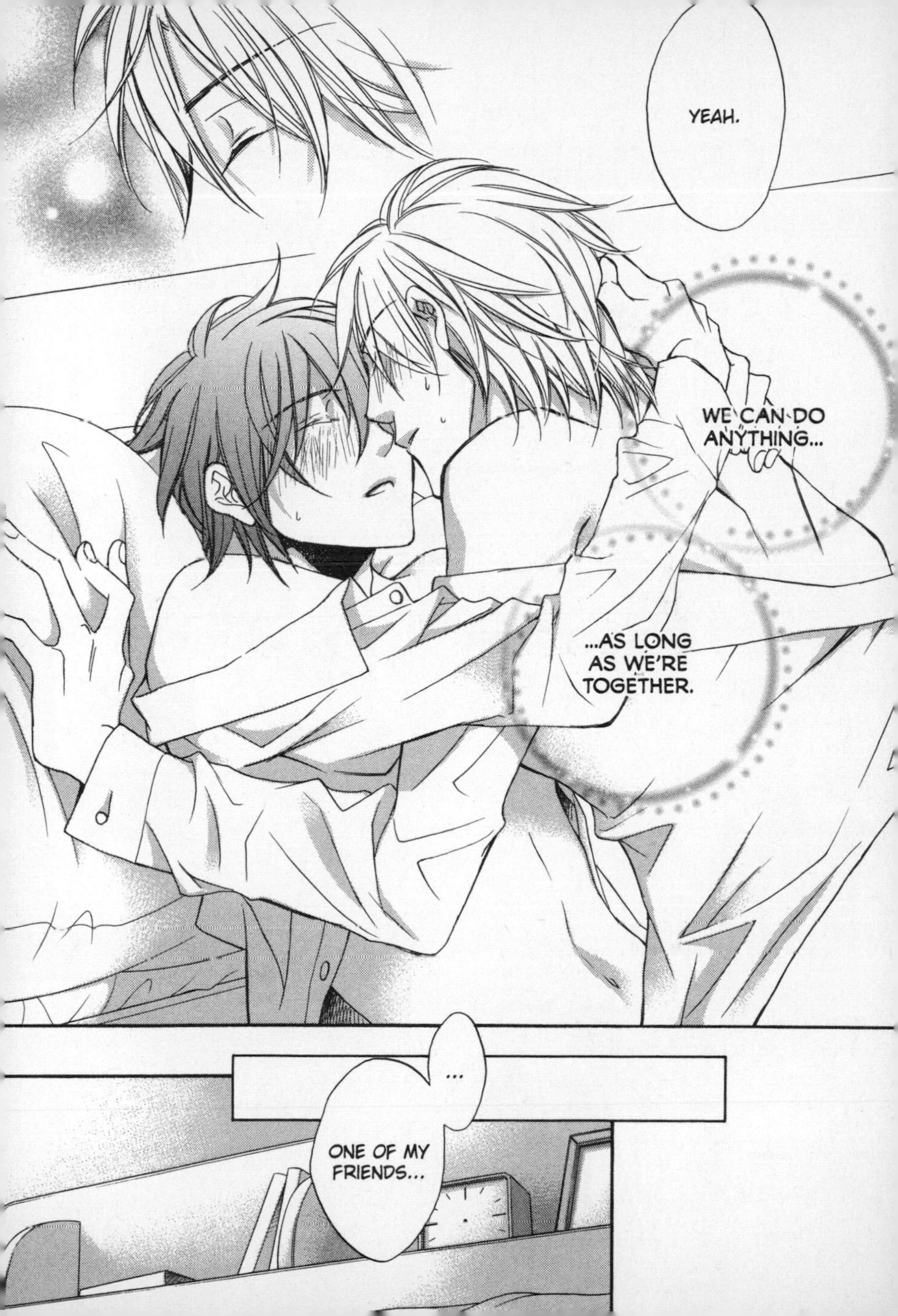
YEAH.
WE CAN DO ANYTHING...
...AS LONG AS WE'RE TOGETHER.
...
ONE OF MY FRIENDS...

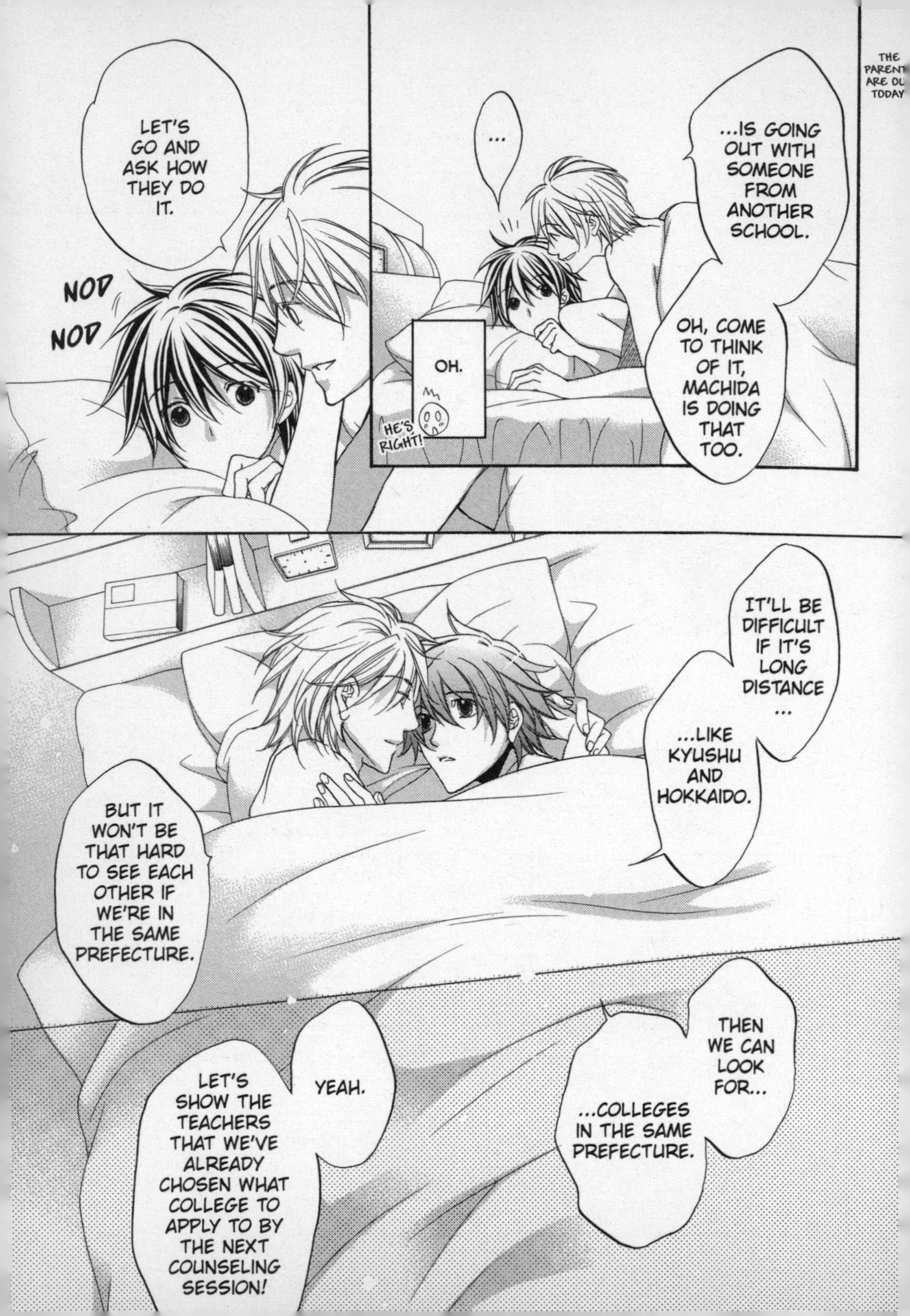

THE PARENT ARE OU TODAY
OH, COME TO THINK OF IT, MACHIDA IS DOING THAT TOO.
...IS GOING OUT WITH SOMEONE FROM ANOTHER SCHOOL.
...
OH.
HE'S RIGHT!
LET'S GO AND ASK HOW THEY DO IT.
NOD
NOD
IT'LL BE DIFFICULT IF IT'S LONG DISTANCE...
...LIKE KYUSHU AND HOKKAIDO.
BUT IT WON'T BE THAT HARD TO SEE EACH OTHER IF WE'RE IN THE SAME PREFECTURE.
THEN WE CAN LOOK FOR...
...COLLEGES IN THE SAME PREFECTURE.
YEAH.
LET'S SHOW THE TEACHERS THAT WE'VE ALREADY CHOSEN WHAT COLLEGE TO APPLY TO BY THE NEXT COUNSELING SESSION!

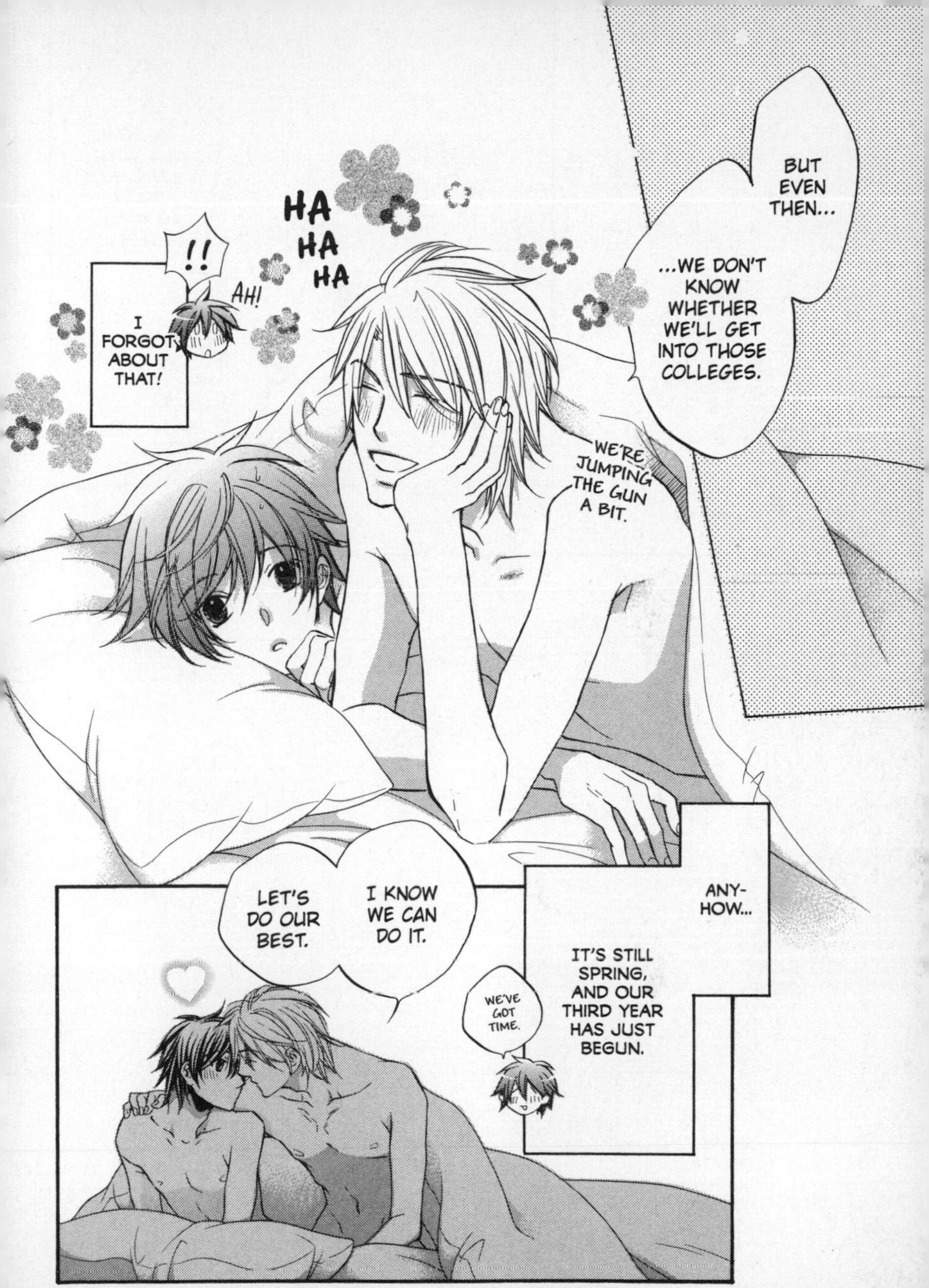
BUT EVEN THEN...
...WE DON'T KNOW WHETHER WE'LL GET INTO THOSE COLLEGES.
WE'RE JUMPING THE GUN A BIT.
HA HA HA
!!
AH!
I FORGOT ABOUT THAT!
ANY-HOW...
IT'S STILL SPRING, AND OUR THIRD YEAR HAS JUST BEGUN.
WE'VE GOT TIME.
I KNOW WE CAN DO IT.
LET'S DO OUR BEST.

Voice 10/End

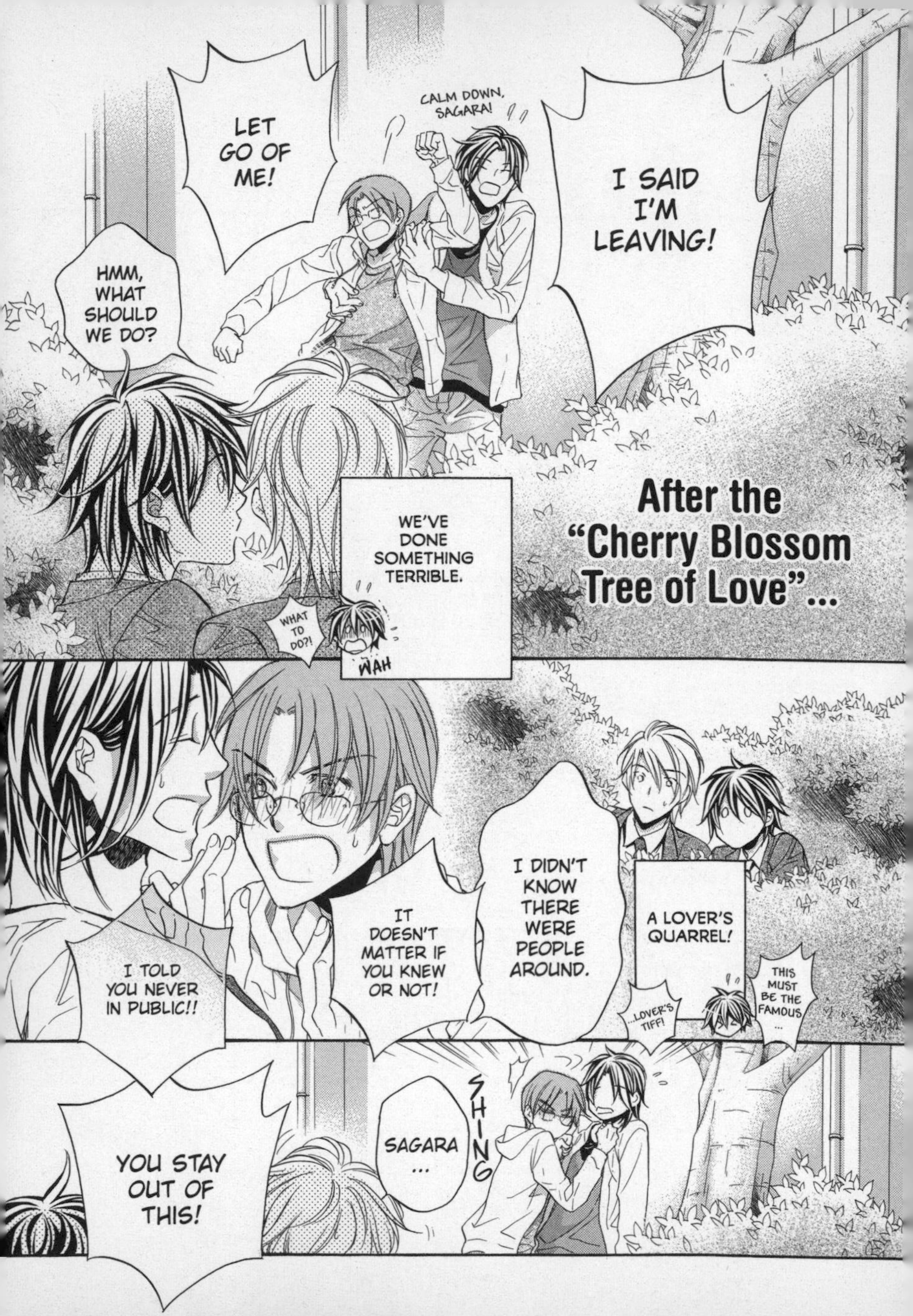
After the "Cherry Blossom Tree of Love"...
I SAID I'M LEAVING!
CALM DOWN, SAGARA!
LET GO OF ME!
HMM, WHAT SHOULD WE DO?
WE'VE DONE SOMETHING TERRIBLE.
WHAT TO DO?!
WAH
THIS MUST BE THE FAMOUS...
...LOVER'S TIFF!
A LOVER'S QUARREL!
I DIDN'T KNOW THERE WERE PEOPLE AROUND.
IT DOESN'T MATTER IF YOU KNEW OR NOT!
I TOLD YOU NEVER IN PUBLIC!!
SHING
SAGARA ...
YOU STAY OUT OF THIS!

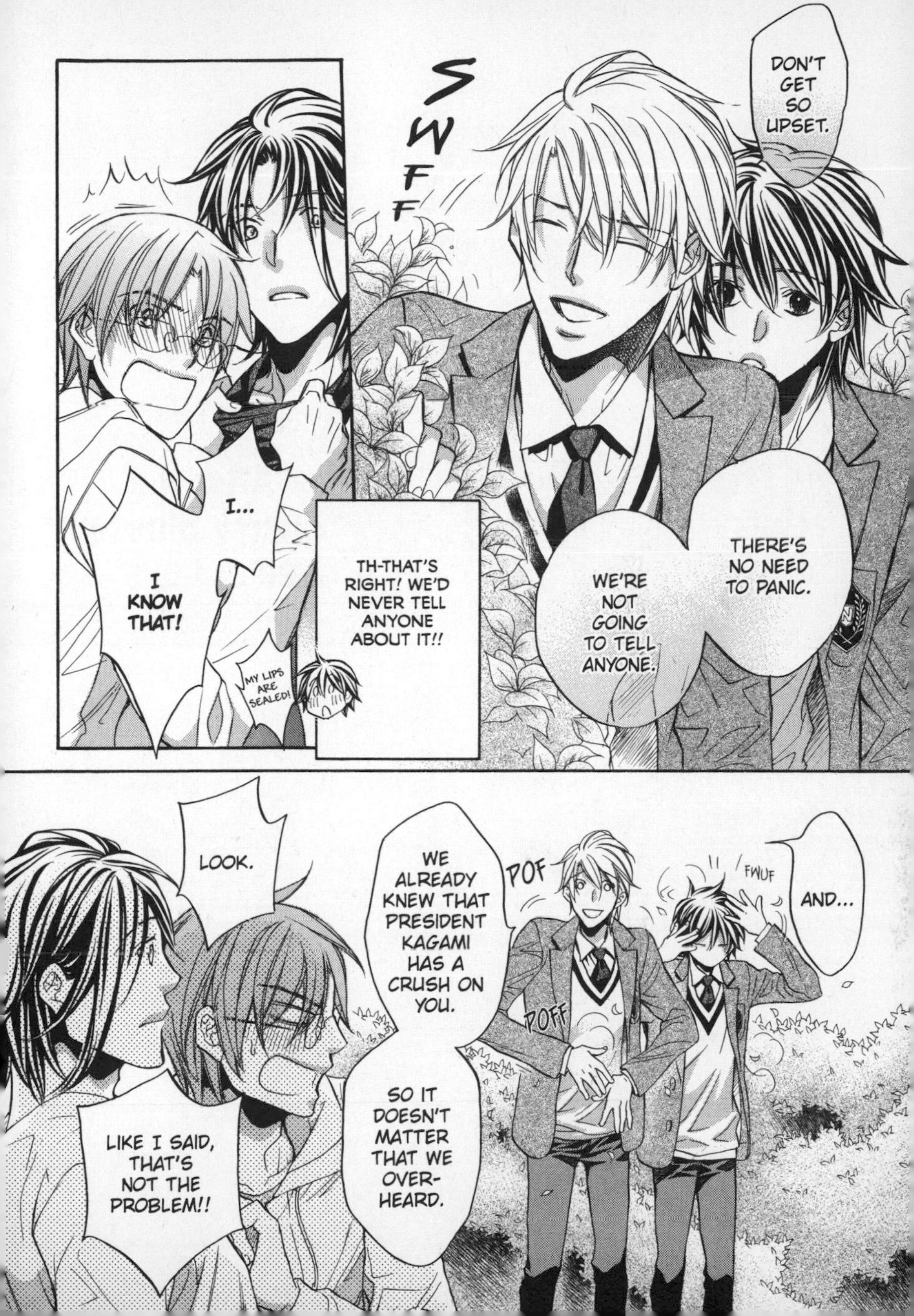
DON'T GET SO UPSET.
SWFF
THERE'S NO NEED TO PANIC.
WE'RE NOT GOING TO TELL ANYONE.
TH-THAT'S RIGHT! WE'D NEVER TELL ANYONE ABOUT IT!!
MY LIPS ARE SEALED!
I...
I KNOW THAT!
AND...
FWUF
POF
POFF
WE ALREADY KNEW THAT PRESIDENT KAGAMI HAS A CRUSH ON YOU.
SO IT DOESN'T MATTER THAT WE OVER-HEARD.
LOOK.
LIKE I SAID, THAT'S NOT THE PROBLEM!!

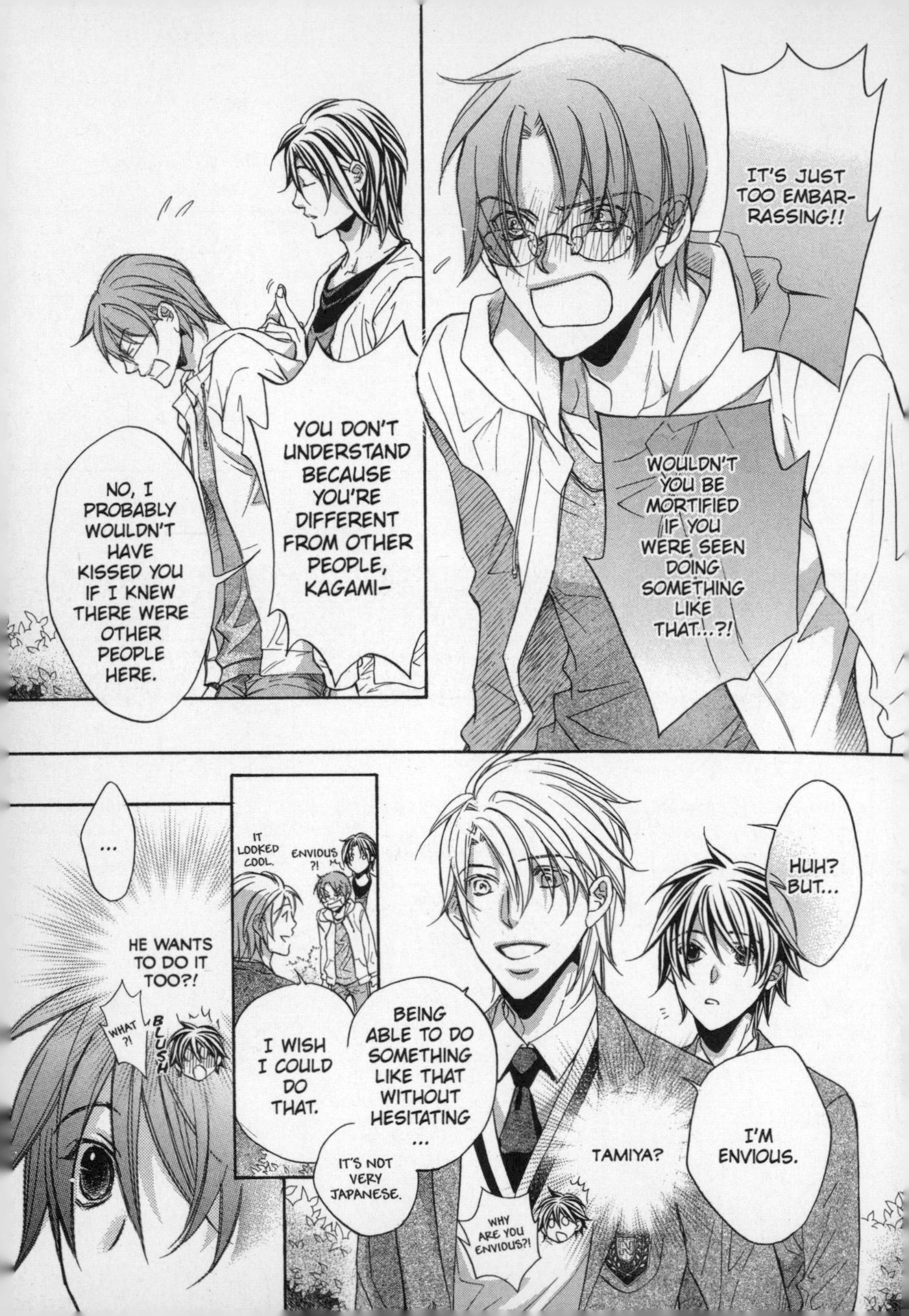
IT'S JUST TOO EMBARRASSING!!
WOULDN'T YOU BE MORTIFIED IF YOU WERE SEEN DOING SOMETHING LIKE THAT...?!
YOU DON'T UNDERSTAND BECAUSE YOU'RE DIFFERENT FROM OTHER PEOPLE, KAGAMI–
NO, I PROBABLY WOULDN'T HAVE KISSED YOU IF I KNEW THERE WERE OTHER PEOPLE HERE.
HUH? BUT...
I'M ENVIOUS.
TAMIYA?
WHY ARE YOU ENVIOUS?!
BEING ABLE TO DO SOMETHING LIKE THAT WITHOUT HESITATING...
IT'S NOT VERY JAPANESE.
I WISH I COULD DO THAT.
ENVIOUS?!
IT LOOKED COOL.
...
HE WANTS TO DO IT TOO?!
WHAT?!
BLUSH

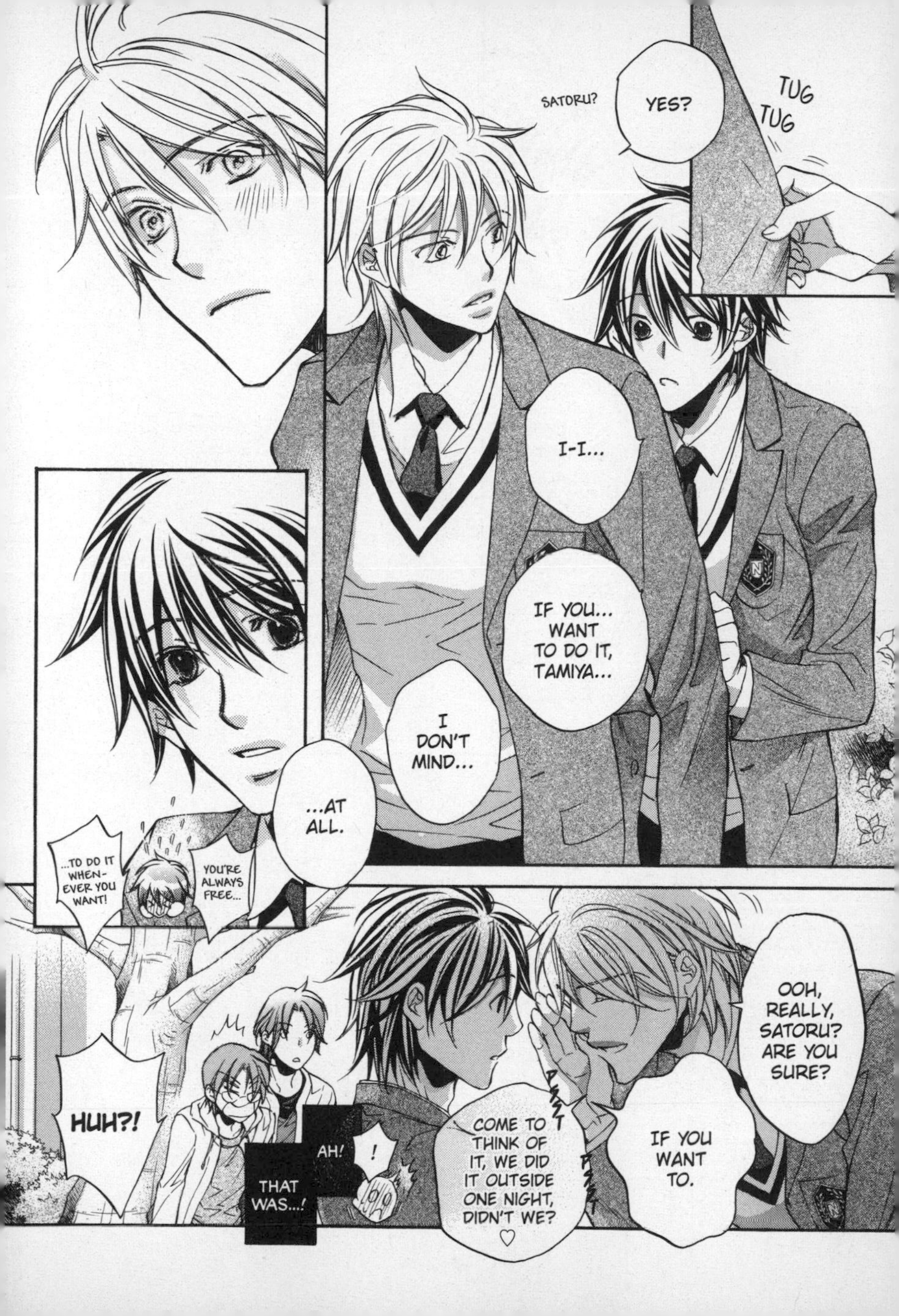

TUG
TUG
SATORU?
YES?
I-I...
IF YOU... WANT TO DO IT, TAMIYA...
I DON'T MIND...
...AT ALL.
YOU'RE ALWAYS FREE...
...TO DO IT WHEN-EVER YOU WANT!
OOH, REALLY, SATORU? ARE YOU SURE?
IF YOU WANT TO.
COME TO THINK OF IT, WE DID IT OUTSIDE ONE NIGHT, DIDN'T WE? ♡
!
AH!
THAT WAS...!
HUH?!

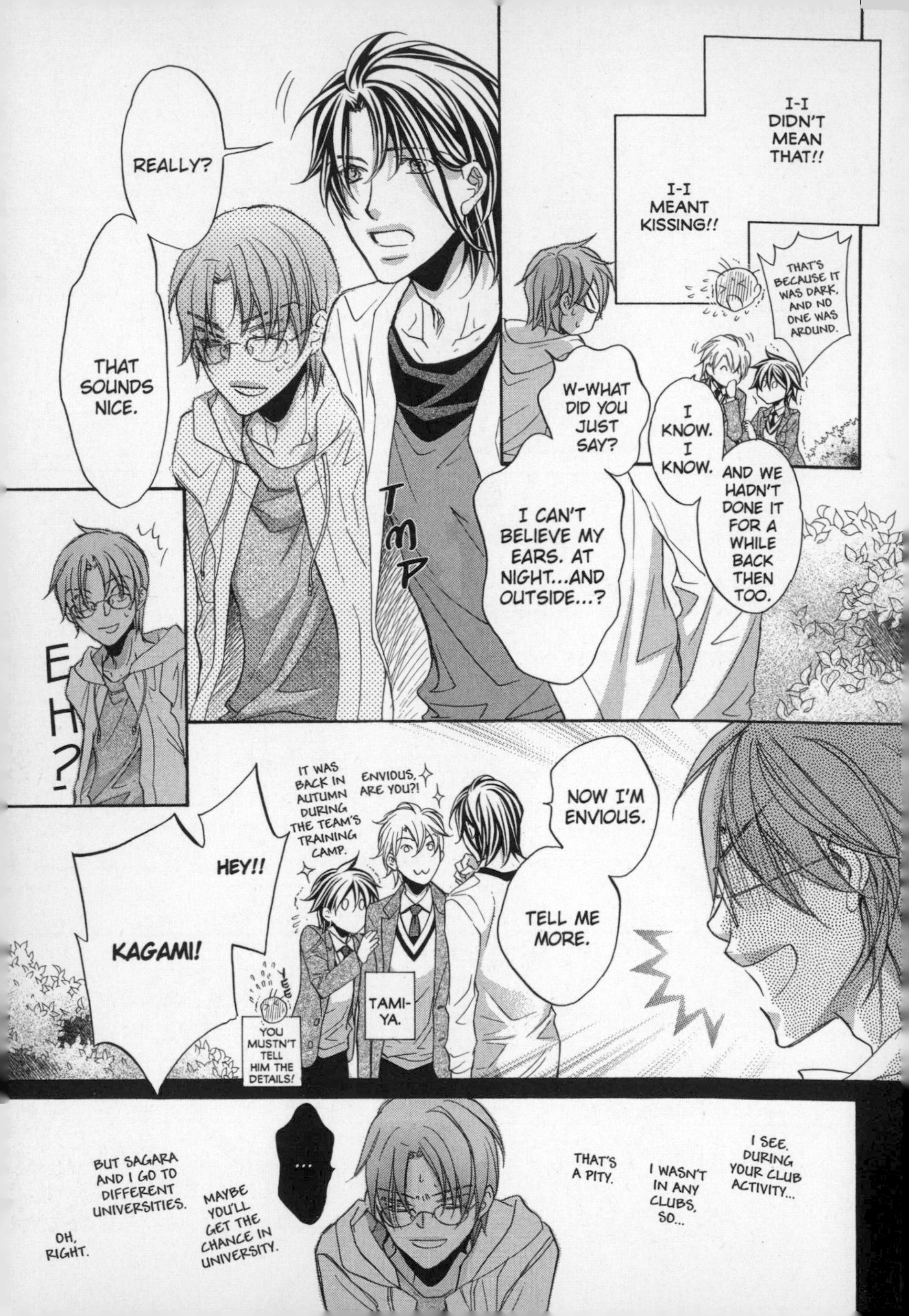
I-I DIDN'T MEAN THAT!!
I-I MEANT KISSING!!
THAT'S BECAUSE IT WAS DARK, AND NO ONE WAS AROUND.
W-WHAT DID YOU JUST SAY?
I KNOW. I KNOW.
AND WE HADN'T DONE IT FOR A WHILE BACK THEN TOO.
I CAN'T BELIEVE MY EARS. AT NIGHT...AND OUTSIDE...?
REALLY?
THAT SOUNDS NICE.
TMP
EH?
NOW I'M ENVIOUS.
TELL ME MORE.
ENVIOUS, ARE YOU?!
IT WAS BACK IN AUTUMN DURING THE TEAM'S TRAINING CAMP.
TAMI-YA.
YEE
YOU MUSTN'T TELL HIM THE DETAILS!
HEY!!
KAGAMI!
I SEE. DURING YOUR CLUB ACTIVITY...
I WASN'T IN ANY CLUBS, SO...
THAT'S A PITY.
...
MAYBE YOU'LL GET THE CHANCE IN UNIVERSITY.
BUT SAGARA AND I GO TO DIFFERENT UNIVERSITIES.
OH, RIGHT.

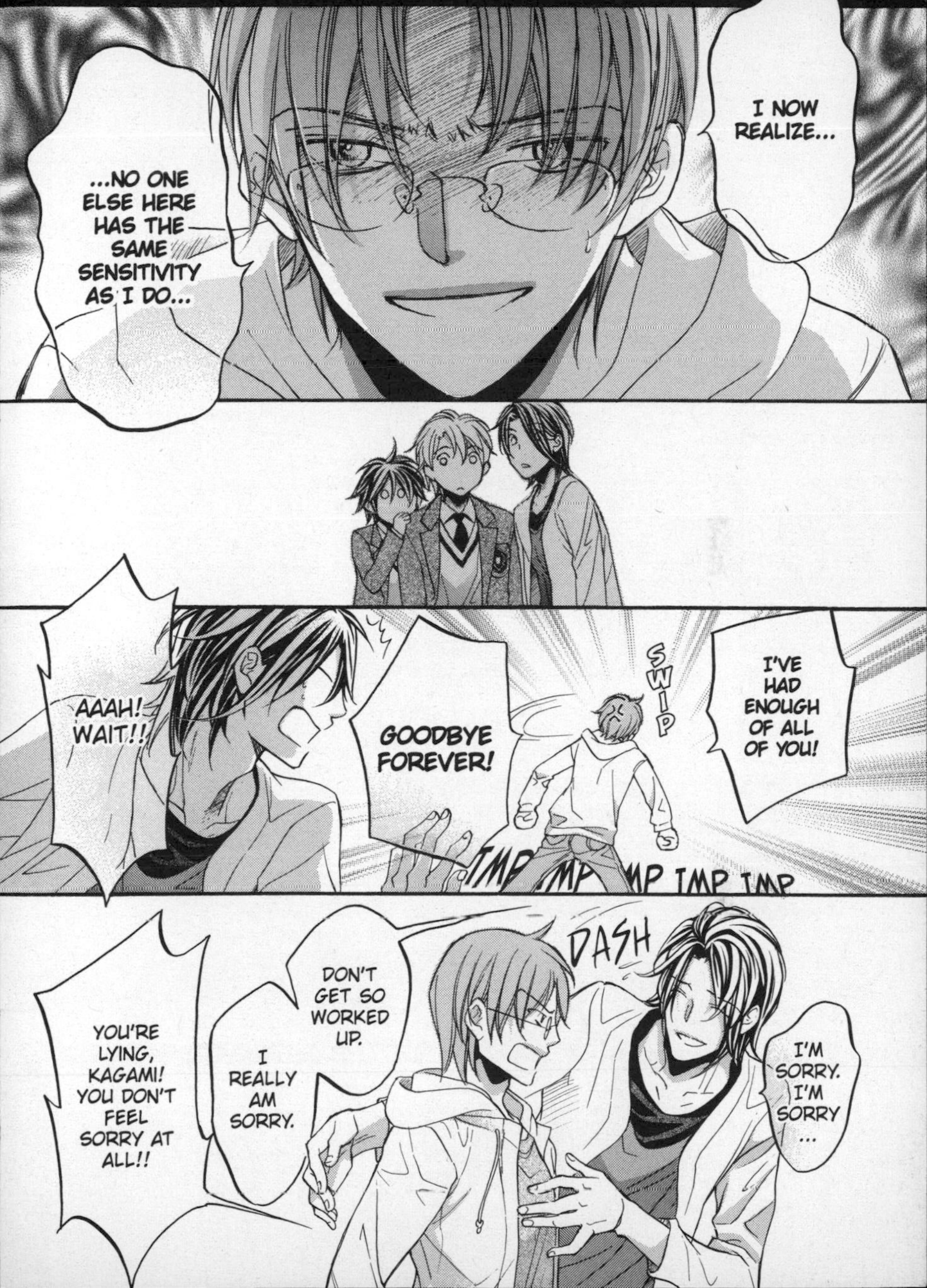
I NOW REALIZE...
...NO ONE ELSE HERE HAS THE SAME SENSITIVITY AS I DO...
I'VE HAD ENOUGH OF ALL OF YOU!
SWIP
GOODBYE FOREVER!
AAAH! WAIT!!
TMP MP MP TMP TMP
I'M SORRY. I'M SORRY ...
DASH
DON'T GET SO WORKED UP.
I REALLY AM SORRY.
YOU'RE LYING, KAGAMI! YOU DON'T FEEL SORRY AT ALL!!

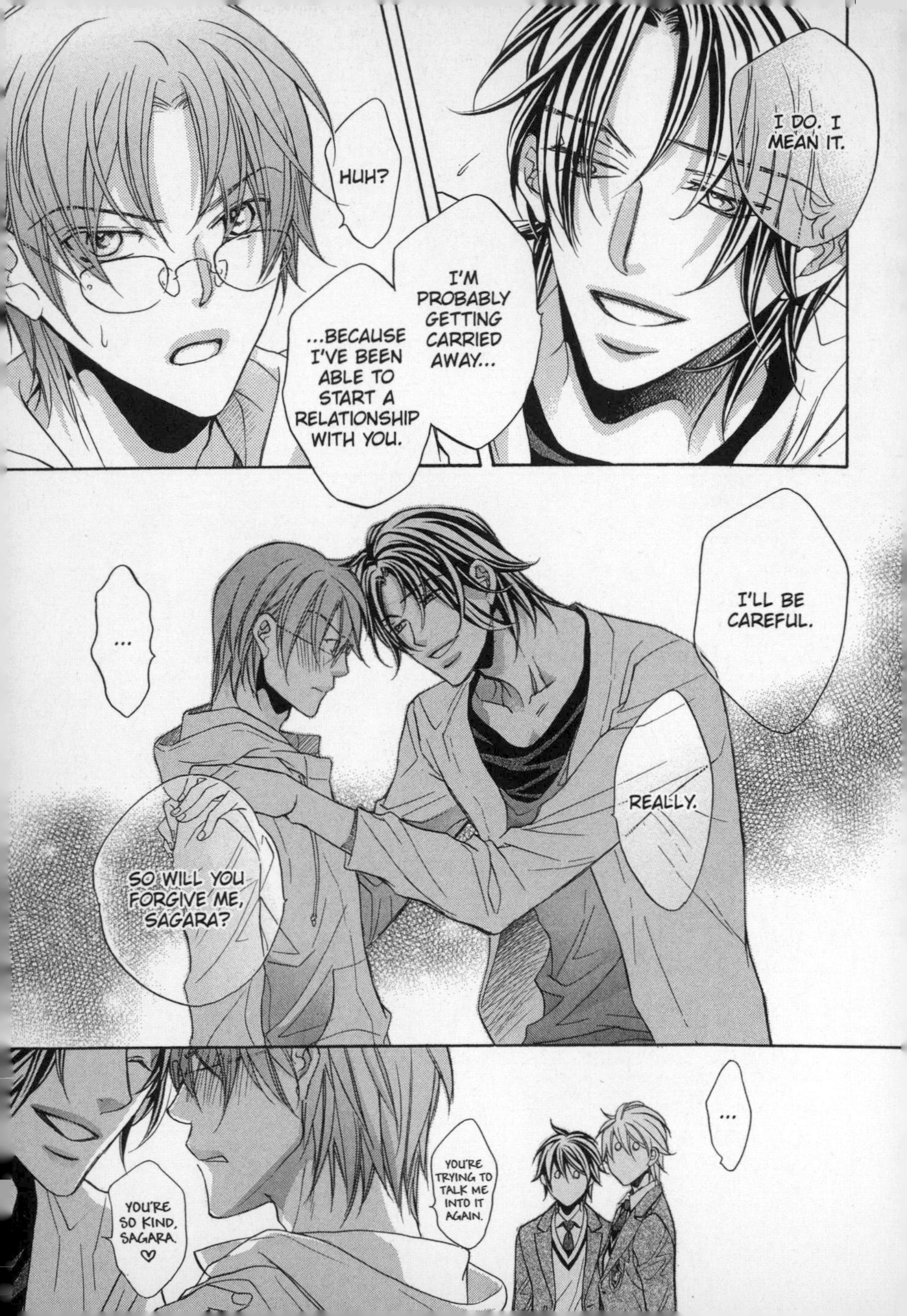
I DO. I MEAN IT.
HUH?
I'M PROBABLY GETTING CARRIED AWAY...
...BECAUSE I'VE BEEN ABLE TO START A RELATIONSHIP WITH YOU.
I'LL BE CAREFUL.
REALLY.
...
SO WILL YOU FORGIVE ME, SAGARA?
...
YOU'RE TRYING TO TALK ME INTO IT AGAIN.
YOU'RE SO KIND, SAGARA. ♡

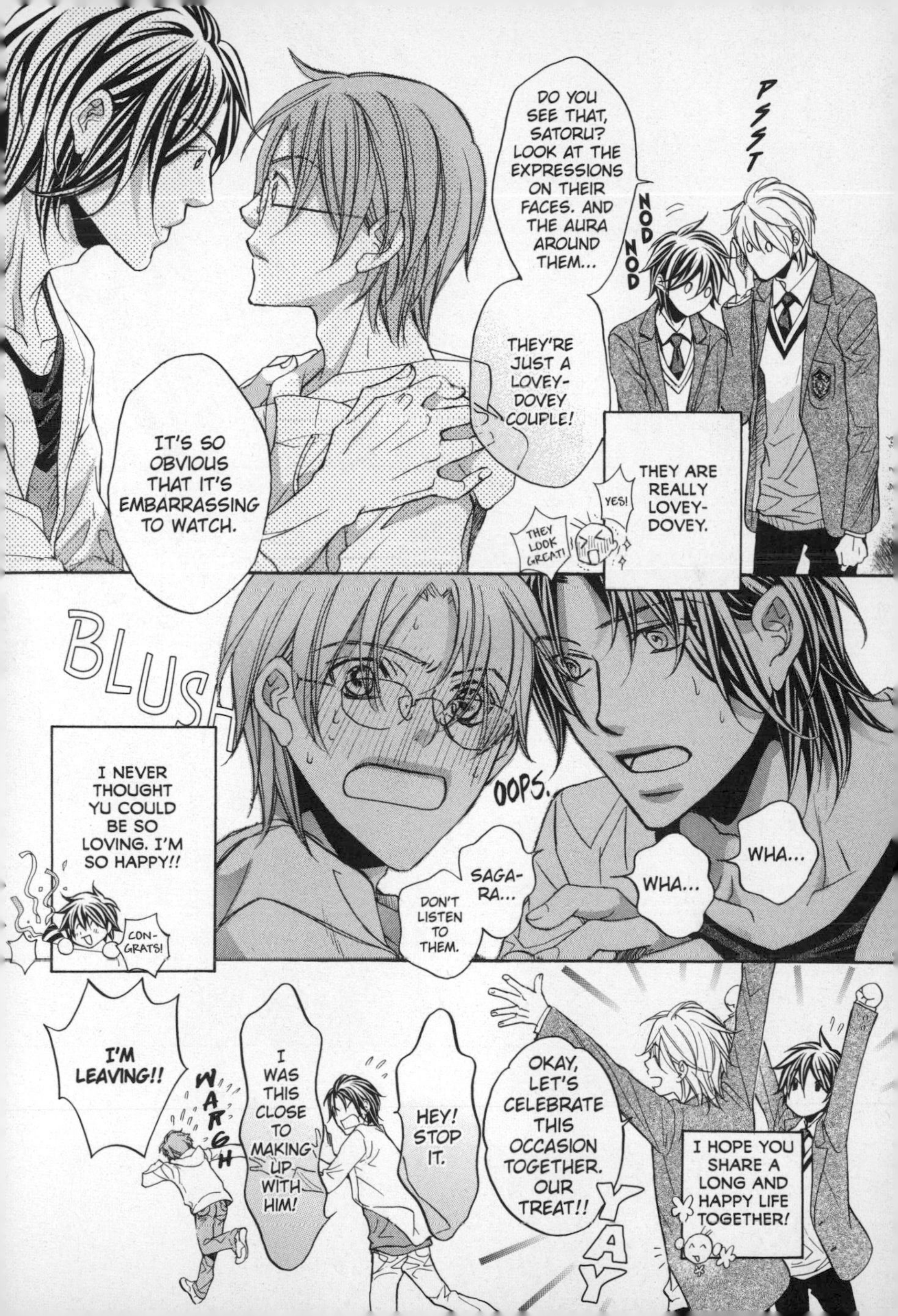
PSST
DO YOU SEE THAT, SATORU? LOOK AT THE EXPRESSIONS ON THEIR FACES. AND THE AURA AROUND THEM...
NOD NOD
THEY'RE JUST A LOVEY-DOVEY COUPLE!
THEY ARE REALLY LOVEY-DOVEY.
YES!
THEY LOOK GREAT!
IT'S SO OBVIOUS THAT IT'S EMBARRASSING TO WATCH.
WHA...
WHA...
OOPS.
SAGARA...
DON'T LISTEN TO THEM.
BLUSH
I NEVER THOUGHT YU COULD BE SO LOVING. I'M SO HAPPY!!
CONGRATS!
I HOPE YOU SHARE A LONG AND HAPPY LIFE TOGETHER!
OKAY, LET'S CELEBRATE THIS OCCASION TOGETHER. OUR TREAT!!
YAY
HEY! STOP IT.
I WAS THIS CLOSE TO MAKING UP WITH HIM!
WARGH
I'M LEAVING!!

✿ Hello! I'm Hinako Takanaga. Thank you very much for reading *Awkward Silence* Volume 4! Did you enjoy it? ✿ The series has already reached Volume 4. Yu and Kagami have graduated, and Satoru and Keigo have become seniors. Even though this is a school comedy, the clock is ticking... I have no time to waste...!

✿ By the way, there is a special full-color booklet for Volume 4! [The booklet is available digitally at http://www.sublimemanga.com. -Ed.] How gorgeous!! I'd like to thank the editorial office for coming up with such a lovely idea...♢ The booklet is a collection of the "Animal Ears Awkward Silence" mini manga series, which I had created for the magazines *Be × Boy* and *Junk! Boy*. The colorist colored it very nicely, so it ended up as a very cute booklet. ♡♡ It would be great if you could take a look at the cute booklet♡ You get to see a Tamiya dog, a Satoru cat, a Yu cat, and a President Kagami dog all barking and meowing at each other in a friendly manner.♡ Please check it out. ♡ If you already have it, thank you very much! Please tell me your thoughts.✿✿

✿ Well then, in this volume the main characters have become seniors and only have a short time left together at school. I never imagined this series to go on for such a long time when I started it, so I am very grateful that it has. The series will go on for a little more, so I hope you will continue to support it!

✿ I'd like to apologize to my editor for causing so much trouble all the time. And thank you to my assistants for helping me all the time. ♡♡ And of course, I would like to thank all the readers for reading and supporting my manga! Thank you very much! I hope we will meet again someday. ♡ Thank you very much for reading this long comment.✿

Hinako Takanaga ✿

OFFICIAL BLOG ♦ HTTP://ANAGURANZ.BLOG95.FC2.COM/
TWITTER ID ♦ TKHINA
*(AS OF MARCH 2013)

About the Author

Hinako Takanaga was born on September 16th in Nagoya, Japan. She is the creator of many popular series, including *The Tyrant Falls in Love*, which was also adapted into an anime series. She is a Virgo, blood type O, and a self-proclaimed coffee addict who can get violent if she doesn't get her daily dose. A fortune-teller once told her she wasn't suited to be a manga artist, but she doesn't believe in fortune-telling anyway. She currently lives with her lovely cats Choro and Mame.